INTERACTIONAL ETHNOGRAPHY

Focusing specifically on Interactional Ethnography (IE) as a distinct, discourse-based form of ethnography, this book introduces readers to the logic and practice behind IE and exemplifies the logic of ethnographic inquiry through a range of example-based chapters.

Edited by two of the foremost scholars in the field of IE, this book brings together a body of work that has until now been largely dispersed. Illustrating how IE intersects with ethnographic methods – including observation, interviews, and fieldwork – the book highlights considerations relating to data analysis, researcher positionality, and the ethics of engaging participants in research. Offering examples of IE in international contexts and across a range of social science and educational settings, the book provides foundational principles and key examples of IE to guide readers' work.

This book offers researchers, scholars, and teacher educators a definitive, novel contribution to current methodological literature on IE broadly, and will be of particular use to ethnographers starting out in their career. Due to the interdisciplinary nature of the volume in illustrating the use of IE in a range of educational sub-disciplines, the book's relevance extends to the fields of medical education, teacher education, arts and literacy research, as well as providing situated examples of IE in settings with relevance to the social sciences, anthropology, and cultural studies.

Audra Skukauskaitė is Professor in the College of Community Innovation and Education at the University of Central Florida, USA.

Judith L. Green is Distinguished Emerita Professor in the Gevirtz Graduate School of Education at the University of California, Santa Barbara, USA.

INTERACTIONAL ETHNOGRAPHY

Designing and Conducting
Discourse-Based
Ethnographic Research

*Edited by Audra Skukauskaitė
and Judith L. Green*

Routledge
Taylor & Francis Group

NEW YORK AND LONDON

Cover image: © Audra Skukauskaitė

First published 2023
by Routledge
605 Third Avenue, New York, NY 10158

and by Routledge
4 Park Square, Milton Park, Abingdon, Oxon, OX14 4RN

Routledge is an imprint of the Taylor & Francis Group, an informa business

Library of Congress Cataloging-in-Publication Data
A catalog record for this title has been requested

ISBN: 9781032104690 (hbk)
ISBN: 9781032104683 (pbk)
ISBN: 9781003215479 (ebk)

DOI: 10.4324/9781003215479

Typeset in Bembo
by KnowledgeWorks Global Ltd.

This volume is funded, in part, by the
European Social Fund according to the activity
"Improvement of Researchers' Qualification
by Implementing World-Class R&D Projects"
of Measure No. 09.3.3-LMT-K-712.

CONTENTS

FIGURES

TABLES

CONTRIBUTORS

W. Douglas Baker is a Professor of English Education in the Department of English Language and Literature at Eastern Michigan University. His research focuses on applying an ethnographic perspective to interactions in educational settings and how relationships and local knowledge are constructed for particular purposes over time. He has chaired the National Council Teachers of English Assembly for Research and the Language and Social Processes SIG for the American Research Educational Association. In 2014, the Michigan Council of Teachers of English presented him with the Charles Carpenter Fries Award in "Recognition of a distinguished career in the teaching of English and dedication to the advancement of the profession".

David Bloome is an Emeritus Professor at The Ohio State University. His research focuses on how people use spoken and written languaging for learning in classroom and non-classroom settings, and how people use languaging to create and maintain social relationships, to construct knowledge, and to create communities, social institutions, and shared histories and futures. Recent coauthored books include *Discourse Analysis of Languaging and Literacy Events in Educational Settings* (2022), *Teaching Literature Using Dialogic Literary Argumentation* (2020), and *Teaching and Learning Argumentative Writing in High School English Language Arts Classrooms* (2015). Recent co-edited volumes include *Re-Theorizing Literacy Practices* (2019) and *Languaging Relations for Transforming the Literacy and Language Arts Classroom* (2019). His current scholarship includes the use of Jewish children's literature in the P-6 classroom and the role of literacy practices as affordances and obstacles to healthcare and related services.

Susan M. Bridges is the Director of the Centre for the Enhancement of Teaching and Learning and an Associate Professor at the Faculty of Education, The University of Hong Kong, where she developed a doctoral course on Interactional Ethnography. She is an Adjunct Professor at Australian Catholic University and a Senior Reviewer for the *International Society of the Learning Sciences* (ISLS) and several health professions education journals. She is also an Associate Editor for the *Interdisciplinary Journal of Problem-Based Learning* and the chair of the AERA *Problem-Based and Journal-Based Learning* SIG. An award-winning higher education teacher, researcher, and curriculum designer, her interactional research explores the "how" of inquiry-based pedagogies and integrated curriculum designs. Her latest edited volume, *Interactional Research into Problem-Based Learning*, is with Purdue University Press (Bridges & Imafuku, 2020). The invited chapter on *Interactional Ethnography* for the *Routledge Handbook of the Learning Sciences* (Green & Bridges, 2018) was a key milestone for the field.

Maria Lucia Castanheira is a professor in the School of Education, Federal University of Minas Gerais, Brazil. She is also a researcher in a literacy research center in the same institution – *Centro de Alfabetização, Leitura e Escrita* (CEALE). Her research interests focus on the examination of literacy practices in and out of school and university. She is particularly interested in examining the social construction of opportunities for learning through exploring, ethnography, discourse analysis, and microethnographic approaches. She has recently co-edited the book on *Re-theorizing Literacy Practices* (2019) and a Special Issue of the Brazilian journal *Trabalhos em Linguística Aplicada* (2020) in English and Spanish on Studying Literacies across Languages and Social Domains with international scholars.

Monaliza Maximo Chian is a Post-doctoral Fellow and part-time Lecturer of various qualitative research methods in the Faculty of Education at The University of Hong Kong (HKU). Monaliza's experiences as an immigrant student, English Language Learner, former educator in a K-8 public district, instructor in higher education, researcher, and mother shape her research studies in education across national and international contexts. Her research interests center on investigating the inter-relationship of sociocultural and cognitive theories and how they influence learning across various contexts through qualitative research methodologies. Monaliza aims to contribute to growing understanding of the complexities of learning to inform theories, practices, and policies related to professional preparation and development, program and curriculum design, teaching, and learning processes that promote socially just and equitable education for all students.

Stephanie Couch is the Executive Director of the Lemelson-MIT Program administered by the School of Engineering at the Massachusetts Institute of

Technology. Her research explores ways prolific inventors find and develop technological solutions to problems. She also examines factors that support or constrain the development of creative and inventive problem-solving capabilities among people at different age ranges and stages of development, with an emphasis on discovering ways of remedying historic inequities in the US with respect to who develops and protects their intellectual property. Insights into these subjects are informed by her Interactional Ethnographic approach to examining opportunities for learning and knowledge construction in invention education programs in secondary and higher education contexts. She co-edited a special issue of the *Journal Technology & Education* (2019) on Technology & Innovation: Invention Education.

Maria Dantas-Whitney is a Professor of ESOL and Bilingual Education at Western Oregon University, where she coordinates the Bilingual Teacher Scholars Program. She has been a Fulbright scholar in Mexico and Panama, and has held consultancies for educators in Brazil, Costa Rica, Peru, the Dominican Republic, and Cyprus. She has directed several federal- and state-funded grant projects focusing on teachers' development of critical pedagogical practices. Maria's research utilizes ethnographic methodologies and focuses on the intersection of language, culture, and education, with a particular emphasis on issues of identity and agency related to multilingualism and schooling. She is a recipient of the AERA Outstanding Dissertation Award in Second Language Research, and is a member of the Academic Committee of the International Network of Ethnography with Children in Educational Contexts (RIENN).

Rūta Girdzijauskienė is a Professor at Klaipėda University and the Lithuania Academy of Music and Theatre, and the President of the Lithuanian Music Teachers' Association. She is a board member of the *European Association for Music in Schools* (EAS) and *European Network for Music Educators and Researchers of Young Children* (EuNET MERYC). For many years, she was a secondary school teacher, a leader of a children's choir and the organizer of the Lithuanian Students' Music Olympiad. She is coauthor of Lithuanian music education programs and music textbooks. In recent years, she has participated in five national and international projects related to innovations in music education, integration of arts, and development of creativity. Her publications include two monographs, 10 teacher handbooks, more than 100 research studies and practice-based articles. Her research interests lie in the fields of arts-based research, music education, creativity, vocal pedagogy, and teacher education.

Judith L. Green is a Distinguished Professor Emerita in the Gevirtz Graduate School of Education at the University of California, Santa Barbara. As an Emerita Professor, Judith is engaged in dialogic and collaborative research with colleagues, who are engaged in Interactional Ethnographic research within and across disciplines at different levels of schooling (elementary through higher education) in national and international contexts. She was a founding co-director of the Santa Barbara Classroom Discourse Group. Her recent directions and publications focus on building deeper understandings of the ways in which IE, as a transdisciplinary logic of inquiry, provides an epistemology for (re)thinking ways of tracing developing opportunities for learning in the face of changing policies for both teachers and their students in different educational domains. She recently co-edited with Greg Kelly (2019) a book on *Theory and Methods for Sociocultural Research in Science and Engineering*.

Alba Lucy Guerrero is an Associate Professor of Education at Pontificia Universidad Javeriana in Bogotá, Colombia. She earned her Ph.D. in Education and a master's degree in Cultural Perspectives in Education at the University of California, Santa Barbara, as well as a master's degree in Social and Educational Development at CINDE-UPN in Colombia. She was a Fulbright scholar at Western Oregon University. Her research focuses on anthropology of childhood, particularly on the understanding of the relationship between childhood, education, and sociopolitical changes. Another area of interest is research methodology in collaboration with children. She coordinates the research group *Childhood, Culture and Education* at Pontificia Universidad Javeriana and is a founding member of the International Network of Ethnography with Children in Educational Contexts (RIENN), a community of researchers that work with children from a collaborative ethnographic perspective.

Huili Hong is an Associate Professor at Towson University. Her research interests focus on discourse analysis, children's literacy practices in multilingual and multicultural contexts, and teacher education. Dr. Hong's work has been published in *Journal of Early Childhood Literacy*, *Urban Education*, *International Journal of Early Childhood*, *Journal of Childhood Studies*, *Handbook of Early Childhood Literacy*, *Classroom Discourse*, etc. She currently serves on the editorial board of Urban Education and as the co-chair of Area 8 Literacy Practices Literacy Learning and Practice in Multicultural & Multilingual Contexts of Literacy Research Association (USA) and the assistant coordinator of Reading, Writing & Literacy Strand of International Association of Teachers of English to the Speakers of Other Languages.

Melinda Z. Kalainoff, Ph.D., is currently an independent education researcher and consultant who studies teaching, learning, and developmental processes in innovative STEM/STEAM learning environments using ethnographic methodologies. She works as a Research Consultant with the Lemelson-MIT Invention Education program at the Massachusetts Institute of Technology studying various invention education initiatives at K-12 and post-secondary levels. Melinda is a former Colonel in the US Army and Academy Professor in the Department of Chemistry and Life Science at the United States Military Academy and led the General Chemistry program for five years and taught chemistry and chemical engineering. She is also a former US Army Operations Research and Systems Analyst where she conducted studies to evaluate the operational capability and effectiveness of newly deployed technologies used in force protection and to counter IEDs (Improvised Explosive Devices) in Afghanistan to inform rapid acquisition decisions for the Department of Defense.

Laurie Katz is a Professor of Early Childhood Education in the Department of Teaching and Learning at the Ohio State University. Her research, teaching, and service have focused on ethnographic approaches in teacher preparation of early childhood educators, inclusion issues, relationships between families, communities and schools, and narrative styles and structures of young children. She has edited the following books: J. Scott, D. Straker, & L. Katz (Eds.) (2009). *Affirming Students' Right to Their Own Language: Bridging Educational Policies to Language/Language Arts Teaching Practices.* New York, NY: Routledge/Urbana, IL: NCTE, and L. Katz & M. Wilson (Eds.) (2021). *The Worlds of Young Children.* Information Age Publishing.

Kristiina Kumpulainen is an Associate Professor of Educational Technology and Learning Design at the Faculty of Education, Simon Fraser University, Canada, and a Professor of Education at the Faculty of Educational Sciences, University of Helsinki, Finland. She has published widely on socioculturally informed studies on the role of language and other tools in learning and education. Her ongoing research addresses how digital technologies transform communication, learning, and education across formal and informal contexts with a particular interest in learner agency and identity.

Krisanna Machtmes is an Associate Professor of Educational Research and Evaluation and the Graduate Director of the Individual Interdisciplinary Program at Ohio University. Her research explores evaluation capacity learning, evaluative thinking, and doctoral education. She is the Chair of the Special Interest Group of the American Educational Research Association for Graduate and Postdoctoral Education Across the Disciplines, and is in the Administrative leadership group for the American Evaluation Association for Organizational Learning and Evaluation Capacity Building, and Vice-President of the Ohio Program Evaluators Group. She teaches doctoral courses in program evaluation, questionnaire design, and implementation science.

Ivonne Natalia Peña is an independent researcher and consultant for the public and private sectors in Colombia on projects related to Early

Childhood, Education and Social Sciences, and is also a performing artist. She is a psychologist by training, holds a master's degree in Educational and Social Development from the National Pedagogical University (CINDE), an Interdisciplinary master's degree in Theater and Live Arts from the National University of Colombia, as well as a degree in Theater Studies from the Sorbonne University in France. As a researcher, she specializes in qualitative methodologies from different perspectives, favoring collaborative ethnography with children, as well as the systematization of processes and experiences in the educational field. She is a member of the International Network of Ethnography with Children in Educational Contexts (RIENN).

Liudmila Rupšienė is a Professor and Senior Researcher in the Department of Pedagogy at Klaipėda University, Lithuania. Dr. Rupšienė teaches research methodologies at the doctoral level. She is the author or coauthor of a number of books, three of them focusing on research methodology: *Methodology of Qualitative Research Data Collection* (2007), *Methodology of Qualitative Research* (2008), and *Educational Experiment* (2016). Dr. Rupšienė is a member or leader of international and national projects (ERASMUS+ and others) and Lithuanian principal investigator in European scientific project ESPAD. She has supervised many doctoral dissertations and has served as a chairperson, member, or opponent of around 60 doctoral dissertation defense boards. Currently, she serves as the president of Lithuanian Educational Research Association and council member of European Educational Research Association.

Kim Skinner is an Associate Professor of Curriculum and Literacy Studies at Louisiana State University. Before teaching at the university level, she was a curriculum director, reading specialist, and classroom teacher. Her current scholarship focuses on the social construction of opportunities for learning as part of reading, writing, and language processes; ethnography as a means for understanding literacy events in community and educational settings; and the impact of students' language and literacy development on their disciplinary understandings.

Audra Skukauskaitė is a Professor in the College of Community Innovation and Education at the University of Central Florida. Her research focuses on teaching and learning of research methodologies at the graduate level as well as the application of ethnographic methodologies in interdisciplinary fields. She has taught research methodologies at the graduate level in Florida, Texas, and California and has led multiple seminars on qualitative research and academic writing for faculty and graduate scholars in Lithuania and other countries. She has worked as a senior research scientist in Lithuania and an ethnographer contracting with the Lemelson-MIT Invention Education program at the Massachusetts Institute of Technology. Audra has published on ethnography, doctoral student learning of qualitative research, transparency of research, interviewing, transcribing, and invention education. In her work Audra emphasizes transparency and the need for social, cultural, epistemological, linguistic, artistic, and other forms of diverse perspectives contributing to educational practice, research, and research methodologies.

Michelle Sullivan is a doctoral candidate in the Methodology, Measurement, and Analysis track of the Ph.D. in Education program at the University of Central Florida. She completed her master's in Mental Health Counseling with a certificate in College and University Counseling at Rollins College and is currently a Registered Mental Health Counselor Intern. Her primary research interests include qualitative research methods, working with previously collected qualitative records, mental health, and social justice.

Melissa I. Wilson taught in public elementary schools for 30 years before becoming the co-director of the Columbus Area Writing Project (CAWP) while pursuing a doctorate degree. Since receiving her degree she continues to direct the CAWP and is an instructor in the early childhood teacher education program at the Ohio State University. Her research interests include language use in teacher education programs and writing with young children.

Beth V. Yeager, Ph.D., is a consultant with Rio School District in Oxnard, California, where she focuses on supporting practitioner inquiry grounded in an Interactional Ethnographic perspective and inquiry-based instructional design. She is a retired university-based researcher, from Institute for STEM Education, California State University, East Bay, and Gevirtz Graduate School of Education, University of California, Santa Barbara. She is also a retired preschool and elementary bilingual classroom teacher. Beth's research interests have been in classroom and school site research from Interactional Ethnographic and discourse perspectives, focused on culturally responsive inquiry and literacy, and development of interdisciplinary academic identities with/among linguistically diverse students. She has also led evaluation studies, grounded in Interactional Ethnography, of educational programs.

FOREWORD

Exploring the Potentials of Interactional Ethnography

Stephanie Couch

This book, assembled by two scholars (Skukauskaitė and Green) recognized internationally for their contributions to the field of ethnography in education, provides new entrants with a grand tour of the conceptual, theoretical and methodological approaches central to this research tradition. Each chapter, written with the novice ethnographer in mind as one of the intended audiences, makes visible ways those with greater experience conceptualize and enact particular aspects of their research. Studies featured within the book were conducted in different contexts across multiple continents. Each site of study offered opportunities for generating new knowledge related to teaching and learning. Variations in research contexts and topics studied illustrate the depth and breadth of studies carried out by scholars as they have adapted the common ethnographic principles to address different research questions. Collectively, the authors demonstrate the wide range of affordances, dilemmas, and complexities that are inevitable when undertaking an ethnographic research study or developing ethnographic programs of research.

I became convinced of the powerful lens interactional ethnography (IE) offers for examining teaching and learning while engaged in work to bring about technological innovations in education during the early years of the Internet. Ethnographic research studies offered empirical evidence for determining ways an innovation supported learning (or not). Information I needed to answer policymakers' questions went beyond information I could glean from standardized test results common in K–12 schools in the United States IE, for example, generated evidence for understanding how students were taking up educational opportunities, for what purposes, and with what outcomes. Complexities were revealed as we examined what individual students were able to do, under what conditions, and for what purposes. The results of our studies were so important to my work that I have included an ethnographic research layer in every major project attempted since that time. IE studies conducted with educators and students have been especially important for my work over the last seven years as the Executive Director of the Lemelson-MIT Program. In this role, I have drawn on IE to determine key elements of the program offerings I inherited, and to determine the effectiveness of new offerings being designed and tested before wider distribution. This volume shares many ideas from different scholars whose focus ranges from archiving to conversational interviewing.

Each chapter in this volume reveals ways IE has supported the work of scholars focused on the wide range of issues that need to be examined in education. The chapters illuminate a variety of factors that must be considered as the theories, principles, and practices common to IE are (re)conceptualized to create a logic-in-use for different studies. Ethnographic studies are not guided by a singular method or approach that is universally applied to different contexts. New ways of enacting the IE theories, principles, and practices must be developed for each study to be responsive to different contexts and to allow for the generation of data needed to make warranted claims that address the varied research questions. As IE researchers enter the field, engage with participants, collect artifacts, create and analyze an archive, generate data and engage in other aspects of research, the IE logic-in-use is reformulated to fit the project's unique needs. I argue, given this reality, that even the most experienced ethnographers have much to gain from reading and engaging with the ideas these authors have committed to text. New insights into one's own practice can be generated by studying the theoretical explanations and methodological decision-making processes employed by the researchers represented within this collection.

The research studies depicted in this volume demonstrate the ways in which interactional ethnography supports empirically grounded accounts of particular phenomena. The authors' accounts call attention to the evidence base being created to make warranted claims. As an education leader and researcher, I was drawn to IE because it provides systematic ways of developing and warranting claims rather than simply interpreting or sharing stories of what the researcher wants to represent from the researcher's point of view. Researchers' careful attention to grounding theories and claims in the discourse and actions of members of cultural groups is foundational to interactional ethnography. Each chapter offers insights into the different ways researchers have engaged in studying the complexities of everyday life worlds, revealing the flexible and dynamic possibilities of IE and its adaptability.

Several chapters, including the introduction written by Skukauskaitė and Green, refer to the iterative, recursive, and nonlinear nature of ethnographic research. The ability to follow new paths as needs emerge during the research process, and the ability to (re)formulate research questions in ways that could not have been known at the outset is an important element of IE. As one who depends on discourse based ethnographic studies to inform innovations in education, I have found that these processes are critical when seeking and inventing solutions to complex problems in local and global communities. The "aha" moments of discovery of new understandings are the most rewarding parts of days in the life of an ethnographer in education like myself. I invite readers new to IE to explore the accounts demonstrating the possibilities of IE presented across the volume. As you explore the chapters individually and collectively, consider ways you can adopt and adapt the theories, principles, and practices presented in this book to your own research questions and contexts.

1

ETHNOGRAPHIC SPACES OF POSSIBILITIES

Interactional Ethnography in Focus

Audra Skukauskaitė and Judith L. Green

This volume introduces readers new to ethnographic research to the logic and practice of *Interactional Ethnography (IE)*, a *discourse-based ethnographic approach* which emphasizes in time and over time engagement and learning *with* and *from* the people in dynamic social and cultural settings. As you will see when reading this book as a whole, IE offers an interdisciplinary approach to uncovering and systematically representing intricate complexities of everyday life co-constructed in and through moment-by-moment and over time interactions of people in educational and other social spaces. While the roots of IE can be traced back to the 1970s to networks of interdisciplinary scholars exploring educational opportunities and constraints on diverse students in educational settings (cf., Cazden et al., 1972), by the 1990s, IE, as a discourse-based ethnographic epistemology, was taken up across fields and national and international settings. However, to date, there has been no single book to introduce the guiding principles and epistemological processes of IE.

By bringing together an international and intergenerational network of contributors who have engaged with IE research across sites and fields of study, we address the need for a single volume that introduces the theoretical and epistemological processes of IE. As the chapters in this volume will show, IE, as a discourse-focused video-enabled approach to ethnography, supports researchers in exploring complex social and discourse processes and practices being constructed by participants in educational spaces in and across levels of schooling and other social spaces.

DOI: 10.4324/9781003215479-1

A Brief Overview of the Volume and Its Goals

In the remaining sections of this introductory chapter, we lay a foundation for readers to gain insights into conceptual perspectives guiding IE and related studies in ethnographic spaces of possibilities (Agar, 2006). We introduce underlying iterative, recursive, and abductive (IRA) logic of ethnographic inquiry, which is represented in varied ways in the work of chapter authors. We also provide a brief overview of IE and its guiding principles. Then, drawing on Mitchell's arguments about different kinds of cases in ethnographic research, we position the chapters as telling cases which make visible the theoretical and analytic ethnographic logic of inquiry and its potentials. In the last section of the introduction, we present the organization of the volume and a brief overview of the chapters.

The volume can be viewed as an invitation to what Anthropologist Michael Agar (2006) calls ethnographic spaces. Within these spaces of interrelated ethnographic possibilities, we emphasize how the researchers engage in *discourse-based* IE and *the ethnographic logic of inquiry* for studying and representing the work of the people in culturally responsive, grounded, empirical, and transparent ways. In this way, we view this network of IE scholars as laying a foundation for all of us, authors and readers, to continue a process of envisioning new ethnographic possibilities for understanding and studying complex, socially and discursively co-constructed everyday worlds of particular social groups.

Ethnography as a Space of Possibilities Through an Iterative, Recursive, and Abductive Logic of Inquiry

Anthropologist Michael Agar (2006), who has worked across disciplines in academia and as an independent researcher and whose ideas are reflected in many chapters in this book, has argued that there is no one kind of ethnography. Instead, there are many "spaces of possibilities" for ethnographic work and study of cultural processes and practices. These spaces are interconnected through *an ethnographic logic* and *underlying commitments* to understand in depth the *complexity of everyday social life*, including language use and actions, within and across particular groups, times, and spaces (Anderson-Levitt & Rockwell, 2017; Atkinson, 2017; Eisenhart, 2017; Heath & Street, 2008).

Agar and other ethnographers have (re)conceptualized ethnography not as a method, but as a way of

thinking (Atkinson, 2017),
seeing (Frank, 1999; McCarty, 2014; Wolcott, 2008),
learning (Agar, 1996; Heath & Street, 2008; Walford, 2008),

knowing (Green et al., 2012),

being and becoming (Sancho-Gil & Hernández- Hernández, 2021; Skukauskaité, 2021), and

interacting with the peoples and worlds in complex, nonlinear, and ethical ways.

In other words, *ethnography is a philosophy of research* (Anderson-Levitt, 2006), an *epistemology* (Green et al., 2012), and *a logic of inquiry* (Agar, 2006; Green, Baker et al., 2020). The perspectives on ethnography as epistemology guide the ways in which authors in this volume conceptualize phenomena we study, shape how we study and construct knowledge, how we interact and relate with sites and people studied, and how we write, represent, and translate (Agar, 2006) what we learn to new audiences.

Ethnography is guided not by particular methods or theories, but by the logic of inquiry and ways of thinking and doing through which we create the ethnographic spaces and multifaceted research projects (Atkinson, 2017; Green et al., 2015). The ethnographic logic is *abductive, iterative, and recursive* (Agar, 2006). As demonstrated across chapters in this volume, the ethnographic IRA logic enables ethnographers to engage in *multiple levels of analyses* and to *generate new concepts and understandings* of the social and discursive co-construction of everyday life at *multiple levels of scale* and in relation to *varied contexts*, actions, and interactions within and across groups. Agar wrote,

> ... more and more as time goes on, I think of ethnography as a *kind of logic* rather than any specific method or any particular unit of study. Ethnography names an *epistemology* — a way of knowing and a kind of knowledge that results — rather than a recipe or a particular focus.
>
> *(par.57)*

This ethnographic space engages researchers in an *abductive logic* for seeking and discovering new ideas, *iterative processes* that foster continuous exploration and change stemming from but transcending previous understandings, and *recursive actions* that enable the ethnographer to reach back to earlier points after exploring new pathways. Iterative, recursive, and abductive (IRA as Agar refers to it) logic is what allows ethnographers to study people's everyday activity in particular social sites in depth, from multiple perspectives, leading to new concepts and theories. The *ethnographic logic is analytic, not merely descriptive*, and fosters *new ways of seeing, studying, understanding, and (re)presenting* the social worlds studied. Agar sees logic, rather than methods or any particular parameters bounding a study, as a way to explore ethnographic spaces. Our volume also emphasizes the logic and transparent analytic representations of ethnographic inquiry across diverse sites, projects, and activities.

Abductive Logic

Agar proposes that the ethnographic logic is "first of all *abductive*, from the Latin for 'lead away'" (par.59), leading from old ideas, knowledge, and researcher points of view to new concepts and ways of seeing and understanding the groups and social life we study. Drawing on philosopher Charles Peirce, Agar (2013) argued that both inductive and deductive logics were closed systems and worked with already existing concepts the researcher brought to the study. In contrast, *abductive logic enables discovery of new ideas* and *tracing* of the social, cultural, linguistic, and other phenomena that precipitated and created new possibilities. In his book on Human Social Research (HSR, contrasted with Behavioral Social Science, BSS) called the *Lively Science* (from German translation of Geisteswissenschaft), Agar (2013) wrote,

> Abduction – and other nonmonotonic logics – fit the bill for HSR. They allow for surprises and creation and revision. Learning where new concepts come from was one of Peirce's main interests. He noticed that deduction and induction were *closed* with reference to the concepts used by a researcher. With deduction it's obvious. You start with the premises already in place. With induction it's a little more subtle. You notice X and Y, but the noticing is based on what you're already predisposed to see. In both cases, a researcher brings concepts into the science that were already in place, ready to wear, salient, as the psychologists like to say. Not with abduction. It's designed for learning something new, for reacting creatively to something you didn't expect.
>
> …. Abduction, the way I'm using it here, is about a *creative reaction to a surprise*. It is a logic that engages the unexpected and creates new concepts to imply it.
>
> *(p. 146)*

Abductive logic "leads away" from old ideas and searches for new possibilities. This abductive search for new ideas and ways of seeing is represented across chapters in this volume, and in the interactional ethnographic principles of stepping back from ethnocentrism (Green & Bridges, 2018; Heath, 1982) and creating boundaries based on following the data and discursive references of the participants (Bloome & Egan-Robertson, 1993; Green et al., 2012).

The nonlinear abductive search is anchored in the surprises Agar has called *rich points*, and you will encounter rich points for the ethnographer almost every chapter of this book. Rich points are unexpected moments impregnated with potentials for new discoveries. As Agar (2013) puts it,

> rich points… means is that something surprising happens that catches a researcher's attention. The reason it is "rich" – whatever words or

actions it might refer to – is because it usually signals differences in lived experience and intentionality between researcher and subject.

(p. 149)

In ethnography, rich points are everywhere (Agar, 1994, 2006) and can happen at any time when an ethnographer, with their own disciplinary, theoretical, and life-experience-based ways of seeing and interpreting the world, enters the lifeworlds of others and seeks to understand the different points of viewing and living in those lifeworlds. As authors in this book demonstrate, who we are as researchers and educators (e.g., Girdzijauskienė; Katz & Wilson) and what theories and commitments drive us (e.g., Baker et al.; Guerrero et al.; Hong & Bloome) shape what and how we study and where we encounter the rich points. No research is objective or neutral; therefore, we aim to

- make transparent our positionalities, theories, histories, and interrelationships and
- systematically unfold our logic of inquiry

so, you, as readers, can follow our arguments and explore your own rich points and ethnographic spaces.

As Agar argues and authors in many chapters make visible (e.g., Baker et al.; Skinner), rich points, often signaled through discourse, provide anchors for abductive, iterative, and recursive explorations of the processes and meaning-construction taking place in a particular group or site in which an ethnographer engages with participants. *Discourse analysis*, at the core of interactional ethnographic studies, facilitates examining rich points in depth, uncovering referential traces to other times, places, events, resources, and people who influenced and are currently co-creating ways of acting, being, knowing, sense-making, and culturing in the particular group (e.g., Baker et al.; Bridges; Castanheira et al.). The focus on discourse and languaging processes also expose rich points stemming from often-invisible linguistic, social, and historical presuppositions we all bring to social and cultural encounters and research (Gumperz, 1982b; see also chapters by Hong & Bloome; Skukauskaitė & Rupšienė, among others). The abductive logic allows the researcher to trace back, forward, and in multiple other ways (e.g., Kalainoff & Chian; Skinner) from a rich point to explore what participants and the researcher brought to the situation, how they created the rich point, and how its layered meanings and contexts reveal new concepts about the complex *languacultural* (Agar, 1994) processes and practices or life. The concept of *languaculture* signals the inseparability of language and culture through which life and its meanings are created; languaculture is discussed in multiple chapters (e.g., Baker et al.; Skukauskaitė & Rupšienė; Katz & Wilson; Skinner). A rich point, exposed in meeting of the differences between the researcher's and participants' languacultures, opens doors for deeper understandings.

Iterative Logic

The backward, forward, and multidimensional tracing – from the discursive construction of a rich point to new concepts revealing languacultural processes and practices of life – is facilitated not only through abduction but also through iterative and recursive processes of ethnography. These processes are illuminated in most chapters of this volume. Solving one puzzle and understanding one rich point is not enough to understand ongoing languacultures of a group in which, and with which, we conduct our studies. Therefore, interactional ethnographers engage *with* participants as insiders (e.g., Baker et al., Skukauskaitė & Sullivan; Guerrero et al.) and bilanguacultural guides (Skukauskaitė & Rupšienė).

Ethnographic inquiry processes are iterative, from the Latin "repeat", indicating movement from one rich point to another, remaining open to new discoveries, while also noting and creating ever-increasing focal context for ethnographic analyses. As Agar (2006) explains, "*Iteration* means that the early applications of abduction in fact *change* the historical context and create a new one within which the next abduction will occur. And the change narrows the focus" (par.73). This is evident in most chapters in this volume, most explicitly in Kalainoff and Chian, Baker et al., and Skukauskaitė and Sullivan.

Iteration points to the need for an overtime engagement (Atkinson, 2017; Walford, 2008), careful observation of the changing patterns of culture-making and breaking (Collins & Green, 1992), and attention to discursive construction of referential boundaries and connections that signal meaningful actions and interpretations within the group and beyond (Bloome et al., 2005; Castanheira et al., 2000; Hong & Bloome, this volume). Ethnographers grounded in anthropology have demonstrated how iterative processes of the ethnographic logic are constituted through principles of cultural relevance, setting aside the researcher's "ethnocentric" points of view, foregrounding insider perspectives, and making connections and interpretations situated in layered contexts revealed through careful study of meanings signaled by members of the group (Green et al., 2012; Heath & Street, 2008; Kelly & Green, 2019b).

Ethnographers, like authors in this volume, also demonstrate how iterative processes often demand that we utilize multiple processes for generating data such as video and audio recording (see Bridges), interviewing (e.g., Skukauskaitė & Sullivan), varied forms of observation from distant to engaged participation (e.g., Guerrero et al., Katz & Wilson; Skinner), arts-based methods (Girdzijauskienė), and working with archives (Baker et al., Kalainoff & Chian, Castanheira et al.). By iterating or repeating the processes of observation, careful analysis, and meaning-making, ethnographers (re)construct contexts of relevance to insiders (Skukauskaitė & Girdzijauskienė, 2021), ground their interpretations in the data and theories, and create warranted claims inclusive of participant points of view. This grounded warranting is further aided by the recursive aspect of the ethnographic logic.

Recursive Logic

Recursive logic, from Latin "run back" or "run again" (Agar, 2006, par.78), entails processes that enable ethnographers to explore and explain sequences of events and rich points before returning to an earlier rich point, with a now expanded and more grounded explanation of the initial surprise. You can see such processes in chapters by Castanheira et al., Baker et al., Kalainoff and Chian, and Skinner, among others in this volume. Agar, as well as other ethnographers, have argued that usually many rich points happen at the beginning of field-work but the richness of these points may fade and become indiscernible as the researcher increasingly gets embedded and familiar with the site or group studied. Recursive logic allows the researcher to return to earlier rich points after exam-ining other languacultural processes and practices (see Baker et al. for a program of research that follows this recursive logic). Recursive logic also signals when we are "done" and have exhausted all possible explanations and trails, thus returning to the anchor rich point, and revealing its languacultural action and meanings.

Explaining the relationship between recursion and abduction in ethno-graphic logic, Agar (2006) wrote:

> Abduction in ethnography is also recursive. Sometimes we use abduc-tion right in the middle of abducting. A surprise happens and we pursue it on the way to constructing a new H that explains it. But as we pur-sue it, another surprise comes up, so now we need to pursue that. An embedded sequence of abduction occurs as we explain one surprise after another before we return to the original surprise. It's not of course so mechanical as that, but it is recursive in the sense of abducting in the process of abducting.
>
> *(par.78)*

This process of exploring sequences of events and new trails has also been conceptualized as backward and forward mapping (Dixon & Green, 2005; Green et al., 2003, 2017), interruption analysis (Green & Heras, 2011), mul-tifaceted design (Green & Bridges, 2018; Green et al., 2015), and multilay-ered analyses of contexts, processes, practices, and discursive construction of everyday events in a group in time and over time (Bloome et al., 2005; Kelly & Green, 2019b; Santa Barbara Classroom Discourse Group, 1992b; Skukauskaitė & Girdzijauskienė, 2021). You can see such multifaceted and conceptually driven IRA processes in all chapters in this volume.

The IRA ethnographic logic, as Agar refers to it, creates spaces for gen-erating new concepts, working with participants in collaborative, culturally and ethically responsive and responsible ways, and creating warranted claims about complex processes and practices of everyday life in specific languacultural groups. This book includes a variety of studies within the IRA logic, foregrounding *IE as the space in which discourse plays a crucial role in revealing rich points and constructing culturally responsive interpretations of the languacultural actions and meanings of, with, and for people with whom ethnographers work and study.*

Interactional Ethnographic Spaces

IE as a logic of inquiry, or epistemology, emphasizes the role of discourse in constructing and revealing languacultural processes and practices of everyday life in diverse settings. The roots of IE can be traced back to the 1970s and movements to deconstruct deficit models of students with diverse linguistic, cultural, academic, and social histories. These roots were grounded in interdisciplinary dialogues sponsored by the US government to develop understandings of how language functioned in classrooms to support (or not) overtime construction of knowledge by diverse learners in educational settings (Cazden et al., 1972; Green, 1983).

In the 1990s, three major directions led to IE being a named epistemology. The first was the founding of the Santa Barbara Classroom Discourse Group (Green & Dixon, 1993; Rex, 2006; Santa Barbara Classroom Discourse Group., 1992a, 1992b; Yeager this volume). The second was an invitation by Cummings and Wyatt-Smith (2000) in Australia to contribute to a special issue for *Linguistics & Education*, with other researchers who had developed conceptual approaches to studying the complex worlds of educational spaces of literacy-curriculum inquiry across levels of schooling. In this special issue, Castanheira et al. (2000) were asked to make transparent how an interactional ethnographic perspective could support a researcher in comparing and contrasting the lived experiences of literacy for one student across five classes. While not an ongoing ethnography, Castanheira et al.'s study drew on conceptual arguments about ethnography (Spradley, 1980/2016) and discourse processes (Gumperz, 1982a, among others), and utilized a contrastive ethnographic approach (Zaharlick & Green, 1991) to examine how varied interactions between and among teacher, students, and curriculum afforded different learning opportunities for the student and his peers. In these ways, Castanheira et al. (2000) saw how IE was an epistemology and provided principles for conceptualizing, studying, and understanding educational processes and practices at different levels of time and analytic scale.

The third intersection were developments in the study of literacies across languages and social domains grounded in work of Street (1984) and international movements on literacies as social constructions (cf. Bloome et al., 2018; Scribner & Cole, 1981; Street, 2001; Wyatt-Smith et al., 2011). Ethnographic studies of literacy learning and everyday life across social, cultural, and academic spaces are at the center of IE studies and have led to ways of rethinking what counts as literacies in changing worlds (cf., Bloome et al., 2005, 2018; Street, 2001). This area of literacy studies, complements and extends work on discourse in and across disciplines and social contexts nationally and internationally and thus, like discourse studies, is central to an IE logic of inquiry.

Building on this early work and the roots in interactional sociolinguistic (Gumperz, 1982b; Gumperz & Hymes, 1972) and anthropological perspectives (cf., Agar, 2006; Heath & Street, 2008) over the subsequent decades, the IE epistemology deepened and expanded as it engaged with new disciplines and theories (Green & Bridges, 2018; Kelly & Green, 2019b). Today, in conducting IE research, interactional ethnographers explore the multifaceted processes and practices through which people, in and through language-in-use and interaction, continuously create particular dimensions of their (langua) cultures-in-the-making.

Culture, from IE and related perspectives, is not a predetermined set of patterns, traditions or belief systems, as a common use of the term suggests; instead, culture is an active, ever-developing process, a verb (Heath & Street, 2008; Street, 1993), a dynamic action. In other words, we culture, or engage in *culturing*, as we act and react to each other (Bloome et al., 2005) and interact with the surrounding physical, natural, material, and human words (Hong & Bloome, this volume). A group of people acting and interacting over time in particular activities engage in *culturing* – creating ways of speaking, being, acting, seeing, and meaning-making particular to the group. These languaging-culturing processes and practices can be analytically uncovered through an ethnographic focus on actions and what people do, and say, when, in what ways, with whom and what materials, in what situations, with what actions, reactions, and consequences.

The discourse focus of IE also enables studying *how* those actions are enacted and become progressively consequential for individuals and different collective spaces (Castanheira et al., 2000; Putney et al., 1999). Tracing language-in-use, or discourse (Bloome & Clark, 2006), provides a grounded methodology and a point of access to explore how languaging-culturing relationships take place through the actions and perspectives of the insiders, moment by moment and over time, in different configurations of actors within and across social settings impacted by layered histories, policies, and other sociocultural factors (Bloome et al., 2005; Heath & Street, 2008; Kelly & Green, 2019b).

The complementarity of anthropologically and ethnomethodologically (Heap, 1991, 1995) informed *ethnographic logic* and *the discourse focus* stemming from literacy theories and interactional sociolinguistics creates an IE space for in-depth, longitudinal, and contextualized studies of complex langua-culturing processes in diverse sociohistorical settings. IE's multidisciplinary roots guide ways of conceptualizing, examining, knowing, and representing the multilayered, multimodal, and multifaceted actions and interactions of people co-creating their lives and meanings within and across times, spaces, and varied configurations of actors (Castanheira et al., 2000; Green et al., 2003). While offering a discourse-grounded orienting ethnographic logic, IE remains open to explanatory theories (Green & Bridges, 2018; Green, Brock et al., 2020; Kelly & Green, 2019a) which iteratively and abductively enter the interactional ethnographic research space to create culturally and disciplinarily responsive grounded warrants for groups and activities studied.

IE is a part of an ethnographic space guided by the IRA logic. IE and related perspectives grounded in micro-ethnographic analyses of the discursive construction of everyday life are making significant contributions to education and other social science disciplines (Beach & Bloome, 2019; Kelly & Green, 2019b; Skukauskaitė et al., 2015). As demonstrated across the chapters in this book, this international interrelated network of ethnographic researchers is showing ways of studying moment-by-moment and overtime processes in grounded, participant responsive, insider-perspective-accountable, methodologically rigorous, and transparent ways.

Orienting Principles of Interactional Ethnography

Over the decades of IE development and uptake across disciplines and countries, IE scholars have published sets of interrelated guiding principles (Green & Bridges, 2018; Green et al., 2003; Santa Barbara Classroom Discourse Group, 1992b; Zaharlick & Green, 1991). While the wording may differ and change based on the field and the goals of the volume in which IE work is published, at the core, the principles are driven by the anthropological perspectives and emphasis on discourse. Drawing on work of Heath (1982), Heath and Street (2008), and Agar (1994, 2004, 2006), in a 2012 chapter for a volume on research methodologies, Green et al. synthesized the IE principles as encompassing:

- *Nonlinearity of ethnography.* Starting from a position that ethnography is a non-linear IRA process (Agar, 2006), IE researchers engage in searching for and chasing rich points, engaging in backward and forward mapping, utilizing multiple data sources, constructing telling cases, and triangulating across data, theories, researchers, and perspectives.
- *Leaving aside ethnocentrism.* This principle directs our focus on the emic/insider point of views and anthropological commitment to cultural relevance and non-judgment. Leaving aside ethnocentrism demands that we step back from personal views, theories, and knowledge we bring; acknowledge the differences what we and the people in the local context know; and engage in reflexivity, member checking, and collaborations *with* participants and cultural guides.

- *Identifying boundaries.* This principle foregrounds the discursive and infer- ential nature of social actions and processes. It asks that we note language- in-use and follow referential trails from participant discourse and actions to identify relevant cases, documents, and focal areas for examination. This principle also draws on comparative perspective in anthropology and guides our work in constructing contrastive analyses within group and across groups; within one source of data and across multiple sources; within a day or data source and over time. We follow IRA logic, abducting to make sense of what and how insiders propose, recognize, and construct as socially significant within their situated activities and language-in-use moment-by-moment and over time.
- *Making connections.* This principle focuses on part-whole relationships and the holistic perspective in anthropology. It also draws on the notions of intertextual and intercontextual nature of social life conceptualized by education and literacy researchers (cf., Bloome, 1992; Fairclough, 1992). Connections we make include connecting people, community, and study histories; drawing on interrelated theories; and looking for interwoven threads of actions, language, and understandings over time and spaces. IE researchers also draw on multiple data sources to make warranted claims and cross-case comparisons that demonstrate patterns of meanings and activities across times, spaces, disciplines, and/or researchers.

Taken together, these principles guide IE researchers in *constructing new ways of knowing* grounded in local and situated processes and practices among people in their everyday social groups (Green & Bridges, 2018). The anthropological and discourse connections among these principles also lead IE researchers to *develop ways of (re)presenting* (Green & Bridges, 2018) social life in complex, non-linear, and multifaceted ways at different levels of analytic scale and angles of vision. The chapters in this volume enact and inscribe these ethnographic principles across various sites and phenomena studied. The chapters are kinds of telling cases that make visible the theoretical, methodological, and practical potentials of the ethnographic logic of inquiry.

Chapters as Telling Cases

Each chapter in this volume is both a stand-alone exposition of the ethno- graphic processes and practices of studying complex social and educational phenomena *and* is a part of the whole of this volume through which we, as authors and editors, make transparent conceptual and empirical potentials of interactional ethnographic logic of inquiry. The chapters are a kind of telling cases of ethnographic inquiry.

In the chapter on "Producing Data", in a seminal edited volume on *Ethnographic Research: A Guide to General Conduct*, anthropologist Clyde

Mitchell (1984) contributed a section, entitled "Case Studies". He defined a *telling case study* as:

> ...the detailed presentation of ethnographic data related to some sequence of events from which the analyst seeks to make some theoretical inference. The events themselves may relate to any level of social organization: a whole society, some section of a community, a family or an individual. What distinguishes case studies from more general ethnographic reportage is the detail and particularity of the account. Each case study is a description of a specific configuration of events in which some distinctive set of actors have been involved in some defined situation at some particular point of time.
>
> *(p. 237)*

Mitchell defines telling cases as those that allow authors to make "theoretical inferences" from a "specific configuration" of events, actors, situations, and times. He further argues that the "theoretical inferences" arise from a focused study of "particular circumstances surrounding a case" (p. 239). Through such systematic, in-depth studies of processes, practices, and circumstances in particular social situations, ethnographers can make "suddenly apparent" the "previously obscure theoretical relationships" (p. 239). To Mitchell's argument about the theoretical potentials of telling case studies, we would add the possibilities of making transparent conceptual and analytic logic of inquiry as well as practical implications of systematic empirical ethnographic studies.

Organization of the Parts and Chapters

We organized the volume in three parts to encourage explorations of what and in what ways the authors' individual telling case studies in each chapter contribute to the theoretical and analytic understandings individually and collectively. The chapters can be read individually, within parts, and reorganized to fit different logics and needs of the readers. We heuristically organized the chapters around:

- Conceptual foundations of IE as a languaculture and logic of inquiry (Part 1),
- Methodological choices in generating research data and engaging with participants (Part 2), and
- Constructing logic-in-use both in analyses of research data and in educational practice (Part 3).

The first part opens with Skukauskaitė's and Rupšienė's chapter in which they conceptualize IE as a languaculture and offer the concept of a bilanguacultural guide as a mediator for the ethnographer as learner (or any novice) seeking to learn IE logic of inquiry and enter the IE community. In the next chapter, Baker, Green, and Machtmes center their arguments on ethnographer as learner and demonstrate how the ethnographer constructs an over-time IE program of study to explore developing research questions shaped by participants, ethnographer experiences, and IE as a logic of analysis. In the third chapter in this part, Hong and Bloome offer a languaging perspective as a way to conceptualize and make visible the social and discursive construction of everyday life in an elementary classroom. Together, the three chapters make visible the anthropological, educational, and languaging roots and processes of IE as a languaculture and an inquiry process.

The second part of the volume encompasses chapters which focus on choices and processes in conceptualizing and collecting research records and working with participants in locally and culturally responsive ways. In the first chapter of this part, Bridges demonstrates how video technologies facilitate systematic inquiry and discourse analyses in interactional ethnographic studies. She offers conceptual arguments, practical methodological suggestions, and demonstrates how she and her teams have enacted video-enabled educational ethnographies in clinical studies within higher education. In the second chapter of the part, Skukauskaitė and Sullivan explore theoretical and methodological foundations of conversational interviewing and demonstrate how IE principles embedded in a conversational interview help researchers develop new concepts in collaborations with teacher and student research partners. The third chapter by Girdzijauskienė draws on ethnographic theories of culture and presents arts-based methods for constructing and analyzing data to uncover cultural levels and their meanings in artistic practices of a young musician. Like other authors in this part, Guerrero, Peña, and Dantas-Whitney emphasize the importance of equitable and collaborative relationships with participants. In unfolding their collaborative ethnography with children, Guerrero et al. demonstrate how stepping back from their expectations and following the insider meanings, ethnographers could uncover new, locally grounded, interpretations with and about the site studied. Taken together, the four chapters in this part offer ways of exploring relationships, processes, and tools, as well as dispositions and experiences, ethnographers need to conduct socially just, locally responsive, and participatory ethnographic studies that offer depth of understanding of complex educational and social processes and lives.

The third part focuses on the ethnographic logic-in-use in constructing and working with ethnographic archives, mapping complex processes of IE studies, anchoring analyses in rich points, and enacting ethnographic observation principles in educational practice. The first chapter by Kalainoff and Chian offers two telling cases which illuminate ways in which IE principles of conduct guided researchers as learners in (re)formulating and unfolding analytic processes as principled actions involved in ethnographic archiving. Offering the visual representations of their axis of development, the authors make visible often-invisible layers of work required in conducting studies in educational settings.

In the next chapter, Castanheira, Green, and Matchmes introduce guiding principles grounded in the Interactional Ethnographic logic of inquiry for mapping and transcribing the developing languaculture of a bilingual classroom. Looking through IE lenses with different descriptive powers, Castanheira et al. make transparent complex processes and practices through which the teacher, with students, co-construct classrooms as developing languacultures.

The third chapter in this part also unfolds an analytic logic-in-use for making visible the languacultural nature of a group of elementary students and their teacher engaged in an after-school Philosophy club. In this chapter, Kim demonstrates how rich points can serve as analytic anchors for backward and forward mapping to understand what, how, and why a rich point happens in local interactions among children, texts, and the teacher. Teacher education is the focus of the last chapter in this part. Here, Katz and Wilson unfold their processes of rethinking participant observation and ethnographic actions when encountering disconnects in their work as leaders in teacher education. Drawing on ethnographic foundations, they demonstrate ethnography as a way of acting in the field to understand differential perspectives of local actors. Together the four chapters in this part show the potentials of the ethnographic logic-in-use in mapping and unfolding complex languacultural processes of studying diverse classrooms and enacting teaching practices.

The last part of the book includes two commentaries. In the first, Yeager offers a reflective commentary about the ways she as a teacher, scholar, and education consultant has enacted IE principles in her work with children, researchers, teachers, and administrators. In the second commentary, Kumpulainen, an international scholar, situates her encounters with IE historically and explores contributions of IE to "possibility knowledge" and to studying in nuanced learning across contexts. Sharing her own work in Finland and Canada and her shift to studying socio-ecological justice from a post-human perspective, Kumpulainen also poses intriguing questions of how the continuously evolving IE logic of inquiry can respond to and address the complex concepts and problems of our precarious times.

We offer this volume as an introduction to the IRA logic of IE and the ways IE is enacted to study a variety of complex phenomena within and across social and cultural settings around the world. By reconstructing their IE-guided inquiry processes in different research contexts, the contributors have sought to open doors for all who are new to IE as a way of thinking and knowing, that is, as an epistemology. Through this grounded approach, readers have a unique opportunity to explore:

- How researchers contributing to this book *conceptualized* ethnography, discourse, and phenomena they study.
- How they *engaged in* discourse-based ethnographic research.

- How they *demonstrated* ways of warranting (i.e., reporting on) the processes and practices of their work and what was learned through their inquiry processes.

The chapters do not offer prescriptions on how to do ethnographic and interactional ethnographic work. Rather, the chapter authors invite all of us – readers and authors – to explore IE concepts, processes, and practices so we can engage in dialogic explorations of how we can learn with, from, and build on each other's work.

References

Agar, M. (1994). *Language shock: Understanding the culture of conversation.* Quill.

Agar, M. (1996). *The professional stranger: An informal introduction to ethnography* (2nd ed.). Academic Press.

Agar, M. (2004). We have met the other and we're all nonlinear: Ethnography as a nonlinear dynamic system. *Complexity, 10*(2), 16–24.

Agar, M. (2006). An ethnography by any other name… *Forum Qualitative Sozialforschung/ Forum: Qualitative Social Research, 7*(4). http://www.qualitative-research.net/fqs

Agar, M. (2013). *The lively science: Remodeling human social research.* Mill City Press.

Anderson-Levitt, K. (2006). Ethnography. In J. L. Green, G. Camilli, & P. B. Elmore (Eds.), *Handbook of complementary methods in education research* (pp. 279–296). Lawrence Erlbaum.

Anderson-Levitt, K. M., & Rockwell, E. (2017). *Comparing ethnographies: Local studies of education across the Americas.* American Educational Research Association.

Atkinson, P. (2017). *Thinking ethnographically.* Sage.

Beach, R., & Bloome, D. (Eds.). (2019). *Languaging relations for transforming the literacy and language arts classroom.* Routledge.

Bloome, D. (1992). A special issue on intertextuality. *Linguistics and Education, 4*(3–4), 255.

Bloome, D., Carter, S. P., Christian, B. M., Otto, S., & Shuart-Faris, N. (2005). *Discourse analysis and the study of classroom language and literacy events: A microethnographic perspective.* Lawrence Erlbaum.

Bloome, D., Castanheira, M. L., Leung, C., & Rowsell, J. (Eds.). (2018). *Re-theorizing literacy practices: Complex social and cultural contexts.* Routledge.

Bloome, D., & Clark, C. (2006). Discourse-in-use. In J. L. Green, G. Camilli, & P. B. Elmore (Eds.), *Handbook of complementary methods in education research* (pp. 227–242). Lawrence Erlbaum & Associates for AERA.

Bloome, D., & Egan-Robertson, A. (1993). The social construction of intertextuality in classroom reading and writing lessons. *Reading Research Quarterly, 28*(4), 305–333.

Castanheira, M. L., Crawford, T., Dixon, C. N., & Green, J. L. (2000). Interactional ethnography: An approach to studying the social construction of literate practices. *Linguistics and Education, 11*(4), 353–400. https://doi.org/10.1016/s0898-5898(00)00032-2

Cazden, C., John, V., & Hymes, D. (Eds.). (1972). *Functions of language in the classroom.* Teachers College Press.

Collins, E. C., & Green, J. L. (1992). Learning in classroom settings: Making or breaking a culture. In H. Marshall (Ed.), *Redefining student learning: Roots of educational restructuring* (pp. 59–85). Ablex.

Cummings, J., & Wyatt-Smith, C. (Eds.). (2000). *Literacy and the curriculum: Success in senior secondary schooling.* Australian Council for Educational Research.

Dixon, C. N., & Green, J. L. (2005). Studying the discursive construction of texts in classrooms through interactional ethnography. In R. Beach, J. L. Green, M. Kamil, & T. Shanahan (Eds.), *Multidisciplinary perspectives on literacy research* (2nd ed., pp. 349–390). Hampton Press.

Eisenhart, M. (2017). A matter of scale: Multi-scale ethnographic research on education in the United States. *Ethnography and Education, 12*(2), 134–147. https://doi.org/10.1080/17457823.2016.1257947

Fairclough, N. (1992). Intertextuality in critical discourse analysis. *Linguistics and Education, 4*(3–4), 269–293.

Frank, C. (1999). *Ethnographic eyes: A teacher's guide to classroom observation.* Heinemann.

Green, J. L. (1983). Teaching as a linguistic process: A state of the art. *Review of Research in Education, 10,* 151–252.

Green, J. L., Baker, W. D., Chian, M., Vanderhoof, C. M., Hooper, L., Kelly, G. J., Skukauskaitė, A., & Kalainoff, M. (2020). Studying the over-time construction of knowledge in educational settings: A microethnographic-discourse analysis approach. *Review of Research in Education, 44,* 161–194. https://doi.org/10.3102/0091732X20903121

Green, J. L., & Bridges, S. M. (2018). Interactional ethnography. In F. Fischer, C. E. Hmelo-Silver, S. R. Goldman, & P. Reimann (Eds.), *International handbook of the learning sciences* (pp. 475–488). Routledge.

Green, J. L., Brock, C., Baker, W. D., & Harris, P. (2020). Positioning theory and discourse analysis: An explanatory theory and analytic lens. In N. Nasir, C. D. Lee, R. Pea, & M. M. De Royston (Eds.), *Handbook of cultural foundations of learning* (pp. 119–140). Routledge.

Green, J. L., Castanheira, M. L., Skukauskaitė, A., & Hammond, J. (2015). Exploring traditions studying discourse and interaction in classrooms: Developing transparency, reflexivity, and multi-faceted research designs. In N. Markee (Ed.), *Handbook of classroom discourse and interaction* (pp. 26–43). Wiley.

Green, J. L., Chian, M., Stewart, E., & Couch, S. (2017). What is an ethnographic archive an archive of? A telling case of challenges in exploring developing interdisciplinary programs in higher education. *Acta Paedagogica Vilnensia, 39*(2), 112–131. http://www.journals.vu.lt/acta-paedagogica-vilnensia/issue/view/1020

Green, J. L., & Dixon, C. N. (1993). Introduction to the special issue: "Talking knowledge into being: Discursive and social practices in classrooms". *Linguistics and Education, 5*(3–4), 231–239.

Green, J. L., Dixon, C. N., & Zaharlick, A. (2003). Ethnography as a logic of inquiry. In J. Flood, D. Lapp, J. R. Squire, & J. Jensen (Eds.), *Handbook of research on teaching the English language arts* (2nd ed., pp. 201–224). Lawrence Erlbaum Associates.

Green, J. L., & Heras, A. I. (2011). Identities in shifting educational policy contexts: The consequences of moving from two languages, one community to English only. In G. López-Bonilla, & K. Englander (Eds.), *Discourses and identities in contexts of educational change* (pp. 155–194). Peter Lang.

Green, J. L., Skukauskaitė, A., & Baker, W. D. (2012). Ethnography as epistemology: An introduction to educational ethnography. In J. Arthur, M. J. Waring, R. Coe, & L. V. Hedges (Eds.), *Research methodologies and methods in education* (pp. 309–321). Sage.

Gumperz, J. J. (1982a). *Discourse strategies.* Cambridge University Press.

Gumperz, J. J. (Ed.) (1982b). *Language and social identity.* Cambridge University Press.

Gumperz, J. J., & Hymes, D. (Eds.). (1972). *Directions in sociolinguistics: The ethnography of communication.* Holt, Rinehart & Winston.

Heap, J. L. (1991). A situated perspective of what counts as reading. In C. Baker, & A. Luke (Eds.), *Towards a critical sociology of reading pedagogy* (pp. 103–139). John Benjamin.

Heap, J. L. (1995). The status of claims in "qualitative" educational research. *Curriculum Inquiry, 25*(3), 271–292.

Heath, S. B. (1982). Ethnography in education: Defining the essentials. In P. Gillmore, & A. A. Glatthorn (Eds.), *Children in and out of school: Ethnography and education* (pp. 33–55). Center for Applied Linguistics.

Heath, S. B., & Street, B. V. (2008). *On ethnography: Approaches to language and literacy research.* Teachers College Press.

Kelly, G. J., & Green, J. L. (2019a). Framing issues of theory and methods for the study of science and engineering education. In G. J. Kelly, & J. L. Green (Eds.), *Theory and methods for sociocultural research in science and engineering education* (pp. 1–28). Routledge.

Kelly, G. J., & Green, J. L. (Eds.). (2019b). *Theory and methods for sociocultural research in science and engineering education.* Routledge.

McCarty, T. L. (2014). Ethnography in educational linguistics. In M. Bigelow & J. Ennser-Kananen (Eds.), *The Routledge handbook of educational linguistics* (pp. 23–37). Routledge. https://doi.org/10.4324/9781315797748.ch2

Mitchell, C. J. (1984). Typicality and the case study. In R. F. Ellen (Ed.), *Ethnographic research: A guide to general conduct* (pp. 238–241). Academic Press.

Putney, L. G., Green, J. L., Dixon, C. N., Durán, R., & Yeager, B. (1999). Consequential progressions: Exploring collective-individual development in a bilingual class-room. In P. Smagorinsky, & C. Lee (Eds.), *Constructing meaning through collaborative inquiry: Vygotskian perspectives on literacy research* (pp. 86–126). Cambridge University Press.

Rex, L. A. (Ed.). (2006). *Discourse of opportunity: How talk in learning situations creates and constrains– interactional ethnographic studies in teaching and learning.* Hampton Press.

Sancho-Gil, J. M., & Hernández- Hernández, F. (Eds.). (2021). *Becoming an educational ethnographer: The challenges and opportunities of undertaking research.* Routledge.

Santa Barbara Classroom Discourse Group. (1992a). Constructing literacy in class-rooms: Literate action as social accomplishment. In H. H. Marshall (Ed.), *Redefining student learning: Roots of educational change* (pp. 119–150). Ablex.

Santa Barbara Classroom Discourse Group (1992b). Do you see what we see? The referential and intertextual nature of classroom life. *Journal of Classroom Interaction, 27*(2), 29–36.

Scribner, S., & Cole, M. (1981). *The psychology of literacy.* Harvard University Press.

Skukauskaitė, A. (2021). Becoming an ethnographer: Living, teaching, and learn-ing ethnographically. In J. M. Sancho-Gil, & F. Hernández- Hernández (Eds.), *Becoming an educational ethnographer: The challenges and opportunities of undertaking research* (pp. 52–63). Routledge.

Skukauskaitė, A., & Girdzijauskienė, R. (2021). Video analysis of contextual layers in teaching-learning interactions. *Learning, Culture and Social Interaction, 29.* https://doi.org/10.1016/j.lcsi.2021.100499

Skukauskaitė, A., Rangel, J., Rodriguez, L. G., & Ramon, D. K. (2015). Understanding classroom discourse and interaction: Qualitative perspectives. In N. Markee (Ed.), *Handbook of classroom discourse and interaction* (pp. 44–59). Wiley.

Spradley, J. (1980/2016). *Participant observation.* Waveland Press.

Street, B. (1993). Culture is a verb. In D. Graddol (Ed.), *Language and culture* (pp. 23–43). Multilingual matters/BAAL.

Street, B. V. (1984). *Literacy in theory and practice.* Cambridge University Press.

Street, B. V. (Ed.) (2001). *Literacy and development: Ethnographic perspectives.* Routledge.

Walford, G. (2008). The nature of educational ethnography. In G. Walford (Ed.), *How to do educational ethnography* (pp. 1–15). Tufnell Press.

Wolcott, H. F. (2008). *Ethnography: A way of seeing* (2nd ed.). AltaMira Press.

Wyatt-Smith, C., Elkins, J., & Gunn, S. (Eds.) (2011). *Multiple perspectives on difficulties in learning literacy and numeracy.* Springer.

Zaharlick, A., & Green, J. L. (1991). Ethnographic research. In J. Flood, J. Jensen, D. Lapp, & J. R. Squire (Eds.), *Handbook on teaching the English language arts* (pp. 205–225). Macmillan.

PART 1

Languaculture in IE Programs of Research and Languaging in Focus

2

UNDERSTANDING INTERACTIONAL ETHNOGRAPHY AS A LANGUACULTURE WITH A BILANGUACULTURAL GUIDE

Audra Skukauskaitė and Liudmila Rupšienė

In this chapter we conceptualize *Interactional Ethnography (IE) as a languaculture* and explore the *role of a bilanguacultural guide* to help *a scholar new to IE* enter the group and learn the ways of being, thinking, and acting as members of the languaculture do. We first explain ways of thinking about the epistemology and research network of IE as a languaculture. We then describe the role of a languacultural guide as a key informant in ethnographic research. Building on the literature about key informants, we propose the concept of a bilangua-cultural guide and the roles the guide might play in languacultural encounters and collaborations. In the subsequent section we use a set of conceptual ques-tions from IE to demonstrate what a bilanguacultural guide may need to know and do to guide the new scholar in learning and becoming a member of the IE languaculture. We end the chapter with a set of suggestions for those seek-ing to enter new languacultures and for the bilanguacultural guides, both of whom, through their reciprocal learning and collaborations, can create access to new knowledge and networks.

Interactional Ethnography (IE) as a Languaculture

IE is an epistemological approach, a way of knowing, through which IE schol-ars conceptualize the phenomena they study as well as ways of studying and representing those phenomena in particular ways (Green et al., 2012). IE has its history, theoretical foundations, language, and ways of thinking, doing, being, knowing and (re)presenting the social worlds through the IE perspec-tive. IE is also composed of members with different histories and times within and beyond the group. These members have similar commitments to under-standing complex educational processes and practices, conduct and report

DOI: 10.4324/9781003215479-3

systematic research, and engage with cultural groups and research participants from participatory, collaborative, asset-based, and/or social justice stances. As can be seen across chapters in this volume, members of the IE network also speak and write utilizing common foundational texts and language. At the same time, many also bring additional explanatory theories to the common foundations, thus continuously shaping and expanding the living potentials of IE (Green et al., 2020; Kelly & Green, 2019). From these perspectives, IE can be seen as *a languaculture* – a cultural group who speaks, acts, and constructs meanings in particular ways.

In introducing the concept of languaculture in his book *Language shock: Understanding the culture of conversation*, Agar (1994) argued, "culture is in language, and language is loaded with culture" (p. 28); therefore it is not sufficient for an ethnographer to learn the grammar and vocabulary of the group they study, as early anthropologists believed. Languaculture is about communication and encompasses the social construction of meaning through discourse in particular groups and situations. He explained:

> the *langua* in languaculture is about discourse, not just about words and sentences. And the *culture* in languaculture is about meaning that include, but go well beyond, what the dictionary and grammar offer.
>
> *(1994, p. 96)*

Discourse, as "the way people talk in ordinary situations" (p. 95) both creates and reveals culture as "a conceptual system whose surface appears in the words of people's language" (p. 79). Bringing together language and culture in *languaculture,* Agar highlights how learning new perspectives and ways of living and researching among members who share common languacultural foundations (such as IE epistemology and history) involves constant meaning making and reframing of knowledge, expectations, and understandings within the languaculture as it encounters new perspectives, problems, and questions.

The languacultures are complex dynamic systems, dispersed among people, places, and times rather than clearly bounded "cultures" early anthropologists sought to study. As Agar argues, the concept of culture is a "mess" (Agar, 2006a) and not very useful in the "world of hybrids" of the 21st century (Agar, 2019). He proposes exploring languacultures as ever-changing systems, *connected through common goals, tasks, histories and discourse* (Agar, 2019) yet enacted in a variety of ways.

IE roots in the intersections of interactional sociolinguistics, anthropology, ethnomethodology, and education from the very beginning established *IE as a hybrid ethnographic space*, in which scholars could use common epistemological foundations and explore common goals in uncommon ways (Kelly et al., 2001; Rex, 2006; Santa Barbara Classroom Discourse Group, 1992b). As evidenced across this volume, authors draw on intersecting and complementary theories; engage in similar and diverging ways of constructing, analyzing, and representing data; and construct their arguments through discursive choices which reverberate across chapters. These commonalities, as well as differences, demonstrate how IE is a languaculture with its particular language and hybrid cultural patterns co-constructed among members of the group. As Green et al. (2015) argued, research communities such as IE are "discursive and social constructions" (p. 28) with particular frames of reference and expressive potentials (p. 31).

These frames of reference within a group overtime can become invisible to insiders, just as patterns of classroom activity become normalized and taken for granted by members of a class until an outsider, such an ethnographer, comes in and seeks to understand what is going on (Castanheira et al., 2001; Collins & Green, 1992). As authors across this volume demonstrate in their chapters, languacultural insiders such as students, children, teachers, and program designers, can become the languacultural guides who help newcomers, including researchers, learn ways of seeing, navigating, and understanding the languacultures in their situated contexts and activities.

Languacultural Guides in Ethnographic Research

Ethnography has a long history of relying on cultural guides, usually called *key informants* who provide ethnographers with access and insider perspectives on what is going on in a group or situation being studied (Spradley, 1979/2016). However, despite the importance of key informants for ethnographic research, there is still very little explicit literature about the roles, lives, and relationships informants and ethnographers develop as they engage in making visible the invisible patterns of the informant's culture. In one of the earliest collections about the informants who have aided anthropologists studying diverse cultures around the world, editor Joseph Cassagrande (1960) argued, "the successful outcome of field research depends not only on the anthropologists' own skills, but also on the capabilities and interest of those who teach them their ways" (p. x). Relationships ethnographers-as-learners form with the cultural guides influence what can be learned and understood, when, where, in what ways, and with what particular outcomes, processes, and contributions to the ethnographer, the informant, and their respective cultures or groups.

In this seminal volume, Cassagrande and the twenty anthropologists presenting personal memoirs about the people who have aided, guided, and collaborated with them, demonstrate how ethnographer-informant relationships involve the "process of mutual adjustment" (p. x) through which both the informant and the ethnographer learn about each other. The authors share insights into how the collaborations with the informants are shaped by the interpersonal interests, goals, and personalities of all involved. Over time, the mutual adjustments can transform into sustained, close, and reciprocal relationships through which an ethnographer enters the life of a cultural group while the informant learns about their own and the ethnographer's languacultures.

The early anthropologists tended to study far-away peoples and their cultures and often supported colonialist agendas (Beach, 2017; Marcus, 2021) while obscuring the humanity and complex lives and contributions of their cultural guides; nevertheless, Cassagrande and the twenty anthropologists in the 1960 volume present sensitive and complex portraits of their cultural guides. These informants, Cassagrande argues, "are the prismatic lenses, as it were, through which we see refracted the life we would observe" (p. xii). The guides bridge the cultural worlds and make possible the ethnographer's entry into and learning about, from, and with the members of the new languacultural group.

Without an insider languacultural guide willing to collaborate with an ethnographer, access to the group may remain closed or be limited to the ethnographer's own perspectives. As we demonstrate in this chapter and across this volume, entry into and learning of IE as a languaculture is possible through the openness of the community and willingness of the IE insiders to support and guide new members. In the next subsection, we share aspects of our story and how Audra became the languacultural guide for Liudmila who sought to understand IE as group and as an epistemology for studying educational phenomena.

Our Positionalities as Languacultural Guides and Learners

Audra has been engaged with IE for almost 20 years since her doctoral studies at the University of California, Santa Barbara (UCSB), under mentorship of Judith Green and Carol Dixon, two of the founders and leaders of IE. Working with Green and Dixon and following in the footsteps of the early members of the Santa Barbara Classroom Discourse Group, Audra learned the histories of how and why the group built on Green's earlier work in the 1970s and named their approach to studying life in classrooms IE (Castanheira et al., 2001; Rex, 2006; Santa Barbara Classroom Discourse Group, 1992b). Through dialogues, collaborations, coursework, reading, and writing, Audra saw the potentials of IE beyond classroom studies and applied the IE perspective and principles in her interview-based dissertation and subsequent studies in higher education settings.

As a professor of qualitative research methodologies in the US, Audra has taught IE as part of her Ethnography and Discourse Analysis courses and has published on IE individually and with colleagues. When, upon invitation of Lithuanian scholars, Audra started teaching brief qualitative methodology seminars in Lithuania, she introduced herself as an IE researcher and included IE perspectives and values in seminars on qualitative research, ethnography, interviewing, and others. Liudmila was one of the participants in a seminar on qualitative research Audra taught at Mykolas Romeris University in Lithuania, in 2014. Their conversations, collaboration, and learning of IE languaculture together developed after this encounter.

Liudmila is a professor of research methodologies and has been teaching quantitative and qualitative research to doctoral and master's degree students in Lithuania since 2004. Liudmila was mainly self-taught about research methodology from texts, having done a mixed method dissertation in 1996, under tutelage of a renown Lithuanian professor of quantitative methodology and educational philosophy. In addition to Lithuanian and Russian languages, she had learned German in school and had no formal education in English. However, when teaching research, she noticed most of the methodology textbooks were in English, so she needed to learn the language. Her first English methodology textbook around 2003 was a guide to the statistic software system SPSS, which she translated word for word from English to Lithuanian. She continued learning both methodology and English this way for the next decade, reading English texts and translating them for herself into Lithuanian, making sure she understood the content sufficiently to teach the information to her graduate students in Lithuanian. In 2007, Liudmila wrote the first methodology textbook on qualitative data collection and in 2008, with her former dissertation advisor Bronislovas Bitinas and another qualitative methodologist Vilma Žydžiūnaitė, published the first Lithuanian textbook about qualitative research methodologies.

Liudmila realized her own story of limited or no English knowledge was not uncommon among her peers and students she was teaching. She also understood learning methodology by reading books in a foreign language, even with developing language skills, was not enough to understand the concepts in depth or *how* to do research. Therefore, Liudmila started an initiative to invite international scholars to Lithuania to help graduate students and professors learn about the varied qualitative approaches still little known in Lithuania despite their popularity in the UK, the US, and other countries. By 2014, Liudmila had invited scholars from Canada and Norway who shared their knowledge in Lithuania. However, those presentations were in English, with translation, and sometimes depth and meaning were lost in translation.

When she met Audra, Liudmila realized the potentials of a collaboration with a scholar who not only had expertise in research methodologies and publishing in English but was also fluent in the Lithuanian language and could, therefore, reach broader Lithuanian audiences. Almost every year since that first encounter in 2014, upon Liudmila's and other Lithuanian insiders' invitations, Audra has participated in expanding the potentials of ethnographic and qualitative approaches in Lithuania (Skukauskaitė, 2021; Skukauskaitė et al., 2017).

Audra was born, raised, and educated in Lithuania, and was fluent in the Lithuanian language; she also still knew some of the Russian language, having grown up during the Soviet occupation. Audra had completed her graduate education in the US and has been teaching in the US universities for over 20 years, with 15 years teaching qualitative research methodologies in doctoral programs. Audra's knowledge of IE, the Lithuanian language, and the histories and environment of higher education in Lithuania positioned Audra as a languacultural guide with bilingual and bicultural expertise. She became a *bi*languacultural guide for Liudmila's (and other Lithuanian scholars') exposure to and entry into the languaculture of IE and the broader international networks.

Adding Bi- to the Languacultural Guide

We developed the concept of the bilanguacultural guide through many conversations and debates about research languages, cultures, texts, and terminologies in ethnography in general and IE in particular. As we explored what IE was and meant, what could and could not be understood, utilized, and adapted in Lithuania, we drew on multiple cultural, sociocultural, and linguistic resources and repertoires of knowledge. We used Lithuanian, English, Russian, and, at times, Greek and Latin roots of words to try to explain and/ or understand IE as an epistemology and a languaculture. We *translanguaged.*

Translanguaging refers to the use of linguistic features (e.g., lexical, paralinguistic, and other contextual cues) and modes of communication bilingual and multilingual speakers utilize to construct meaning in and through interaction (Lewis et al., 2012; Smith & Murillo, 2015). The concept encompasses the views of language as a contextual and dynamic *process*, or *languaging* (Beach & Bloome, 2019; see also Hong & Bloome, this volume). *Trans* in translanguaging refers to the possibilities and actions of traversing and using multiple linguistic and sociocultural resources to make new meanings. Translanguaging is an asset, rather than deficit-based view of multilinguals that flexibly can tap into varied repertoires of linguistic, cultural, and conceptual experiences to participate in co-creating their languacultural worlds. At least two languacultures are involved in the processes of translanguaging.

According to Agar (2006b), languaculture one (LC1) is the languaculture of the researcher or person who seeks to enter a new cultural group. In our case, Liudmila is the ethnographer-as-learner, seeking to understand the languaculture of IE. Liudmila, as the ethnographer, brings with her the cultural, historical, philosophic, linguistic, and academic repertoires of an educational researcher in Lithuania. She is a member of the Lithuanian higher education community, or LC1. IE is the target languaculture, or languaculture two (LC2). The languaculture of IE encompasses the histories, theories, actions, perspectives, and other aspects, as described in the previous section. It also includes the English academic language through which IE as a languaculture was developed and functions.

Audra is a member of the IE community and its languacultural processes, practices, and English discourse. In the discourse of anthropology, Audra is a key informant who can guide Liudmila to learning and understanding the languaculture of IE as LC2. However, unlike most other members of IE who have not lived the Lithuanian history and do not speak the language, Audra also is familiar with the Lithuanian higher education languaculture Liudmila represents. In this way, Audra becomes a *bilanguacultural* guide, not only a cultural guide. Figure 2.1 offers a visual representation of the interaction between languacultures one and two, with the role of a bilanguacultural guide connecting both.

In Figure 2.1, IE and its foundations in the English language are represented as LC2 and the Lithuanian language and higher education are represented as LC1. In the middle is the *bilanguacultural guide – a bilingual/multilingual person who is a member of LC2 but is also fluent or very familiar with LC1*. Therefore, the guide can mediate and translanguage between the two languacultures, with their linguistic and cultural nuances. In this chapter, Liudmila represents the LC1 researcher and Audra represents the bilanguacultural guide who is a member of LC2 and has experience in LC1. The middle ellipsis for the bilanguacultural guide is flushed more toward the LC2 on the right, to indicate Audra's greater familiarity with LC2 rather than the LC1 of Lithuanian higher education. She speaks the Lithuanian language, but her higher education, scholarship, and work is primarily in the US, thus she is less familiar with the systems and nuances Liudmila and other Lithuanian researchers encounter on a daily basis. Both Liudmila and Audra are multilingual speakers. Liudmila is the president of the Lithuanian Educational Research Association and wanted to understand IE as a languaculture with its research epistemology and a network of scholars.

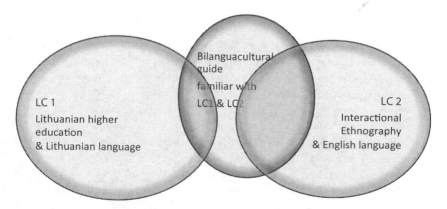

FIGURE 2.1 Bilanguacultural Guide as a Connector between LC1 and LC2

In exploring what a scholar new to IE would need to know, say, learn and do to understand IE and become a member of LC2 (Green et al., 2012), we drew on interpersonal, sociocultural, economic, and historical experiences and resources, as well as our academic expertise and multilingual communicative repertoires. Most of our collaborations were in Lithuanian, with frequent translations and back-translations of English to Lithuanian and vice versa, with occasional use of the Russian language due to Liudmila's knowledge of the Russian and Lithuanian academic lexicon. Through such translanguaging we realized the importance of engaging with a bilanguacultural guide when seeking to learn complex concepts and understand IE as a languaculture, not simply a methodological approach to educational research.

Over time and collaborations with a bilanguacultural guide, Liudmila developed deeper understandings of IE and began utilizing its principles in her own work and promoting it with her students. She created opportunities for more people from the IE languaculture, including multiple authors of this volume to come to Lithuania to lead seminars on IE and ethnography, discourse analysis, interviewing, narrative, video-enabled observation, and writing for publication. Additionally, with Audra and other colleagues at Klaipėda University, Liudmila co-designed a 4-year research grant in which Lithuanian scholars sought to apply IE principles to studying and improving the preparation of healthcare workers to work with people with disabilities. While the project did not become a full IE study due, in part, to other researchers' unfamiliarity with the languaculture of IE, both Liudmila and Audra expanded their understandings of both languacultures involved. They learned not only about the challenges and limits of working with ideas from LC2 in LC1 contexts but also the contextual, linguistic, sociohistorical, economic, and academic-funding aspects of the Lithuanian higher education system, or LC1.

While Liudmila was learning about IE, Audra was learning about the Lithuanian higher education and also about IE and the challenges it may pose to those seeking to understand and apply it in new, non-English dominant contexts. The bilanguacultural guidance became a mutual, reciprocal learning process, with both the ethnographer (Liudmila) and the BLCG guide (Audra) expanding their understandings of *both* languacultures. This book and the way the authors across the chapters present their processes and logics of working with IE epistemology and related ethnographic practices is one of the outcomes of this observed need to make IE languacultural processes and practices more transparent for those new to IE.

These understandings about IE as a languaculture and principled logic of inquiry developed through the many questions and ideas Liudmila, as ethnographer, asked and explored with Audra as the bilanguacultural guide. In the next section we demonstrate the kinds of questions an ethnographer (LC1 scholar) may want to ask and the insider guide may need to answer as they both learn the second languaculture – in this case, IE and its transferability and applicability to the Lithuanian context.

Learning LC2 of Interactional Ethnography *with* a Bilanguacultural Guide

To explore ways of learning IE with a bilanguacultural guide, we draw on questions developed by members of the IE community to study social life in classrooms and other social settings. Colloquially known within the IE languaculture as "the litany", these questions guide researchers in examining multiple dimensions of any languaculture of interest (Santa Barbara Classroom Discourse Group, 1992a, 1992b). The litany asks:

> within a developing languaculture, or "culture-in-the-making" (Castanheira et al., 2001):
>
> *Who can do and say what?*
> *To and with whom?*
> *When? Where? In what ways?*
> *Using what objects or artifacts?*
> *For what purposes?*
> *With what outcomes?*
> *and with what consequences?*
>
> for the group and its members.

These questions enable interactional ethnographers to study varied aspect of life and learning in ever-changing cultural groups such as classrooms or research communities. As a new member or an ethnographer enters and seeks to understand the group's languaculture, they could utilize these questions to engage in dialogues with insiders willing to guide the novice.

Table 2.1 organized around the "litany" questions shows the kinds of questions ethnographer-as-learner may ask and the actions the bilanguacultural guide may need to take to guide the new scholar and learn alongside them. In the first column of Table 2.1 we present the core question from the IE "litany", in the second column we demonstrate the questions the ethnographer as learner asks or needs to understand to answer the "litany" question about LC2. In the third column we provide an overview of actions and knowledge the bilanguacultural guide (BLCG) can share with the ethnographer/learner. The questions and actions are examples of the many questions Liudmila and Audra have explored over the past 7 years of our collaborations. Bolded in the table are some of the questions and responses we discuss below to demonstrate how a learner's questions and bilanguacultural guidance can deepen both scholars' understandings of IE.

TABLE 2.1 Ethnographer Questions and Bilanguacultural Guide (BLCG) Actions Framed through the IE Litany of Questions

IE litany prompts	Learner needs/questions	BLCG actions
1) who can do/does what?	• **Who are the members of IE?** • What are their positions and roles? • Who influenced whom? • What do IE researchers do? What do they study?	• **introduce to members who work in IE and related perspectives** • share your own and other members' intellectual histories • share books, articles, and core resources • explore with the ethnographer the kinds of questions IE members pose for research • show who else is involved in interdisciplinary fields and diverse sites
2) who says what?	• **What are key concepts and/or terms used in IE?** • What do these terms mean? • **How can they be translated?**	• **help understand the language IE members use and the nuances of that discourse** • share publications, what members of the community write (say in writing) • help identify which terms are of importance
3) to and with whom?	• Who are the people studied? • What are IE ethnographer's roles and relationships with participants? • How do IE researchers interact/relate to other scholars and traditions in related disciplines and languacultures (e.g., CDA, sociology)? • **In what conferences or networks do IE researchers present their work? Why?** • Who are the audiences for IE research?	• explain relationships *with* participants —with, collaborative nature of IE • conceptualize social contracts • **introduce ethical norms and expectations, including informed consent** • paint broader boundaries — introducing extended members in the international network • **invite a novice to come along and co-present**
4) when?	• **When and how did IE develop? What is its** history? • When is IE an appropriate approach for study? • **When do you begin an IE study?**	• **share the history and point to the people whose work provided a foundation for the IE** • provide examples of kinds of sites and questions IE members have explored • **describe cycles of inquiry, introduce the concept of logic-in-use** (cycles of activity; conceptualize what is the beginning)

(Continued)

TABLE 2.1 Ethnographer Questions and Bilanguacultural Guide (BLCG) Actions Framed through the IE Litany of Questions *(Continued)*

IE litany prompts	Learner needs/questions	BLCG actions
5) *where?*	• Where do they study? Is it only in classrooms? • How does IE apply to education? to other disciplines? • **Where do IE researchers work?** • Where do they participate and present?	• provide examples of where IE studies take place • **go together to places and/or people where IE is conducted** • involve the IE learner in conferences • co-author
6) *in what ways?*	• How do IE researchers gain access to sites? • **What methods are used?** • **In what ways do they construct their arguments for publication?**	• **explain methods used** (participant observing; ways of interviewing (pvz vipa interviu guide – we created and taught/learned how to apply IE in interviews for the project) • transcribing • analyzing • **demonstrate the genres**
7) *with what objects or resources?*	• **What tools do I need for collecting data?** • What books or resources can help me learn IE? • **What technological tools do I need? Can I use software** such as Atlas or Nvivo?	• **explain tools needed for IE** (video, audio recording, photo, artifacts) • **guide through a sample logic of inquiry to help the learner answer the question about technologies for themselves**
8) *for what purposes?*	• What is the goal of IE? • What questions can IE answer? • How do I formulate questions within IE?	• illuminate the overarching goals of IE, • help distinguish what IE researchers study (e.g., sharing relevant in articles)
9) *with what outcomes?*	• What are products of IE research? • **What does an IE dissertation look like?** • What are the pros and cons of working with IE epistemology?	• **share examples of IE publications** • **introduce the learner to the extended members of IE** • invite into and guide in the community • join in co-presenting and co-authoring • demonstrate how IE as an epistemology and way of life influences life beyond conducting studies
10) *or consequences?*	• **What are the challenges with IE?** • How hard is it to publish IE work? • How can I make it count for professional advancement? • What's the likelihood of receiving funding when doing IE?	• **Be honest and transparent** • Share members' CVs and career trajectories to demonstrate potential pathways • Show IE examples in books, journals, and other academic dissemination venues • Invite the new member to teach in their own contexts

In the next subsections we discuss some of the bolded questions, organized around two areas: access and logic of inquiry. We chose to leave the broader range of questions and actions in the table to help readers, learners, and cultural guides explore who can do and say what to support new members/ethnographers in learning ways of being, thinking, knowing, and acting in multifaceted languacultures such as IE. While the questions and responses in Table 2.1 revolve around IE, we have also utilized them in learning other perspectives and therefore believe they can be transferable to languacultural encounters across groups and fields. We invite readers to use the questions as guides in your own learning of new research traditions and languacultures, including as one potential way of reading this volume.

In our exploration of the litany, we group the questions and responses conceptually rather than explain each individually. In constructing the table, we noted three major areas of questions and concerns addressed across the litany prompts: access, logic of inquiry, and outcomes or consequences. Due to space limitations, here we explore the first two and encourage the reader to consider how they may respond to questions about outcomes. This book, as a whole, provides many examples of the potential outcomes to collaboration and knowledge construction within the IE languaculture. In this chapter, we first discuss the questions around *access to IE* and related networks, then present ways of learning about the IE *logic of inquiry*.

Gaining Access to IE and Related Knowledge and Networks

The litany prompts led us to uncovering novice's questions and bilanguacultural guide's explications around access to IE as a languaculture, with its people, knowledge, histories, and interrelationships. For example, when Liudmila asked "who are the members of IE?", "who influenced whom?" (litany prompt 1), "where do IE researchers work?" or "where do they participate and present" (prompt 5), she signaled a need to understand people, places, and networks of the languaculture. In guiding Liudmila as a learner of the IE languaculture, Audra first introduced Liudmila to *the people* within and adjacent to the community. Creating and gaining access also involved *sharing of resources* and introductions to the *larger network*.

Initially, creating access to IE involved dialogues and sharing of resources, particularly the IE researchers' *publications* such as books and articles. To facilitate access, Audra not only emailed copies of the articles and book chapters, but also created and shared with Liudmila a Google Drive folder for IE and related ethnographic materials. Such sharing created easier *access to the resources*, which may have been difficult for Liudmila to find on her own due to limited database availability in Lithuania and logistic and financial constraints in finding IE work published in edited books and international journals. Audra's bilanguacultural understanding of Lithuania's socioeconomic and higher education contexts made it possible for her to build more seamless opportunities for Liudmila to access foundational knowledge of IE.

Once Liudmila started learning more about IE and expressed an interest in extending the opportunities to others in Lithuania, Audra *shared the intellectual history of IE* and introduced her to Judith Green, one of the founders of IE. Upon Liudmila's invitation, Judith traveled to Lithuania from California, the US, and taught week-long seminars about IE three times since 2016 (Skukauskaitė & Girdzijauskienė, 2021). Moreover, Audra introduced Liudmila to *other members of IE and related groups* who also came to Lithuania to share their international experiences and expertise. Many of the authors of this volume have traveled to Lithuania to teach Lithuanian scholars about discourse analysis (Bloome from Ohio, US), video and participant observation (Bridges and Chian from Hong Kong), ethnography (Katz & Wilson from Ohio, US), and narrative (Guerrero from Colombia). In this way, through *conceptually linked seminars and people*, Liudmila and hundreds of Lithuanian scholars participating in the seminars have begun to gain access not only to IE but also to the broader international networks and fields of knowledge. They had opportunities to *see IE and related network members engaging in ethnographic research in diverse programs* (e.g., literacy, teacher education, medical education), *contexts and places* (internally displaced people's villages, K–12 and higher education classrooms), as well as *countries* (Hong Kong, Colombia, US).

Since in 2015 ethnography as a research approach was still relatively new in Lithuania, Audra and Liudmila, with support from Klaipėda University, also worked together to invite the international Rethinking Educational Ethnography network to hold their conference in Lithuania in 2016. The conference, and the resulting special issue of a research journal *Acta Paedagogica Vilnensis* published in Lithuania (Skukauskaitė et al., 2017), introduced more Lithuanian scholars to ethnographic approaches, including IE. International scholars also learned about a valuable publication venue.

Liudmila's and Audra's collaborations also led to Audra teaching multiple seminars on qualitative research, ethnography, and writing for publication at Klaipėda University as well as invitations for lectures at three other universities and the national education forum. As Audra created access for Liudmila to IE and larger international networks, so Liudmila, in her position in Lithuania as a key research methodologist as well as president of the Lithuanian Educational Research Association, opened doors for Audra to learn more about the Lithuanian higher education (LC1) and to give back to her country of birth. Over time, as anthropologists have attested in the past (Cassagrande, 1960; Spradley, 1979/2016), the ethnographer/learner's and informant/bilanguacultural guide's relationships became more mutual and reciprocal. These developing relationships also facilitated deeper understandings of IE as a logic of inquiry.

Understanding the IE Logic of Inquiry

Understanding the IE as a logic of inquiry involved two primary kinds of questions the bilanguacultural guide helped the ethnographer explore. The questions focused on *what IE is* and *what the terminologies* really mean, and *how* IE works or *how to design* an IE study. These questions often arose simultaneously though we separate them here to illuminate two interrelated aspects a novice needs to learn and the bilanguacultural guide needs to make present for the novice to begin understanding the languaculture (LC2) as members of the group do.

Exploring "What" Questions of IE Concepts

As a languaculture, IE embeds particular ways of speaking, writing, and conceptualizing key ideas. The more Liudmila read, heard, and discussed about IE, the more she started asking about the language and the nuances of terms used: "what are the key concepts?", "what do they mean?", and "how can they be translated into Lithuanian?" (litany prompt 2). The questions became particularly salient when she tried to translate the key ideas into Lithuanian and both of us realized direct translation made no sense. This led us *both* to realize that reading was not enough and deep understanding of LC2 (IE concepts in English) was necessary to find or create appropriate equivalents in the Lithuanian language and LC1 higher education context. Those were the discussions that led us to creating the concept of the bilanguacultural guide.

Both English and Lithuanian, IE knowledge and knowledge of research context in Lithuania, were needed to respond to such questions as: "how is ethnography an epistemology, not methodology?", "what is the difference between ethnography as a logic of inquiry and logic in use?", "what is a rich point?" Through translanguaging, reading, dialogues over time, with bilanguacultural guidance, we have come to agreement of how to conceptualize and translate these terms into the Lithuanian language and context. They may not encompass the full range of use across all IE publications by varied authors, but as an ethnographer/learner and a bilanguacultural guide, we sought to create foundational understandings Liudmila could use with her own students.

We have come to explain ethnography was an *epistemology* because it involved conceptualizing *ways of knowing and seeing* phenomena as well as *ways studying, or coming to know,* those phenomena. The *logic of inquiry* idea most closely related to the idea of *design, or theory-method relationships* and conceptual-methodological understandings of what, why, and how to study through the IE lens. Meanwhile, *logic-in-use* referred to the dynamic process the researcher was constructing in the field, making *decisions on the ground* while engaged in an IE study. Agar's (1994, 2006b) concept *of rich point* gave us a lot of translanguaging trouble. Translating it directly as "turtingas taškas" made no sense, so we had to explore the nuances of meaning and the use of the term in Agar's writing and ways IE scholars have taken up the concept. We have come to translate it as an "esminis taškas" (essential point) or "sankirtos taškas" (point of juxtaposition) to capture the meaning of rich point as moments where languacultural expectations meet to create opportunities for exploring the essence brought out through a juxtaposition of differential understandings.

Coming to the deeper understandings of the key concepts in IE involved translanguaging, reading, and conversations over time. It was not sufficient to share publications and identify the terms and their definitions. As the bilanguacultural guide, Audra needed to *explain the histories and goals* of IE (litany prompts 4, 8, and 9) and situate IE in the larger theoretical, disciplinary sociohistorical, and methodological movements occurring in the US at the time IE was developing. For example, IE was connected to social justice movements and goals to dismantle deficit-based models of education of diverse students, with an emphasis on language and literacy; interdisciplinary dialogues among sociolinguists, anthropologists, sociologists, and education scholars (Cazden et al., 1972); and linguistic and reflexive turns in ethnography and the social sciences (Clifford & Marcus, 1986; Green & Bloome, 1997).

Exploring "How" Questions of IE Methodology

In addition to introducing Liudmila to histories and social and academic contexts of IE development and terminologies, Audra, as a bilanguagultural guide, engaged *with* Liudmila in exploring those histories and concepts. Guide and ethnographer/learner became *co-learners* through dialogue, co-reading, and back-and-forth translations to explore nuanced meanings of IE concepts across various published texts. As we began to conceptualize studies we could design together and as Liudmila introduced IE and ethnography more generally to her students, questions of *how* to design and conduct IE studies became more prominent.

Some of the main *how* questions Liudmila asked included "What questions can IE answer?" (prompt 8), "where do they study?" (prompt 5), "what methods" (prompt 6) and "tools" or "resources" (prompt 7) IE researchers use in their studies? How and where to present or publish IE studies (prompts 3, 9, and 10)? What does an IE dissertation look like?" (prompt 9) and "what are the challenges" in doing and presenting IE work? (prompt 10). These questions led us to explore the logic of inquiry of IE studies, i.e., their design and interconnections of methodological choices and theoretical underpinnings.

Sharing example dissertations, studies, and insider knowledge, we explored the kinds of questions IE researchers asked in published studies, the sites studied, researcher and participant roles, and the methods used to generate, analyze, and represent data. For example, the bilanguacultural guide pointed to the prominence of discourse in IE studies to explore *how* people co-construct their social worlds, learning, and participation in languacultural groups. Audra and Liudmila also explored the ways IE scholars conceptualize time in the field and cycles of activity, the decisions researchers make for when, what, and how to observe and/or interview, or when the studies begin and end. Audra pointed to the need for considering and studying languacultural processes over time, through natural cycles of activity determined by the group studied rather than arbitrarily chosen by the researcher. We also talked about the need for video and audio recording in IE studies and the challenges this may pose for a Lithuanian context, where video in education research is not widely used and people generally are wary of observers due to the surveillance and snitching legacy from soviet occupation.

Understanding IE logic of inquiry and methodological processes involved dialogues with the insider – the bilanguacultural guide; published articles/chapters were not enough. Given that much of the methodological information is not present in published studies due to word limitations for any article or chapter, the bilanguacultural guide shared insider stories and knowledge and connected Liudmila to people, dissertations, and publications where the logic-in-use was more transparent. IE scholars seek to make transparent their theoretical-methodological decision processes, often in conceptually and/or methodologically focused publications such as this volume, or other more recent edited volumes such as Kelly and Green (2019) or Rex (2006).

Therefore, Audra guided Liudmila in exploring how we as readers and learners needed to look across studies within a scholar's program of study (rather than a single study alone) to understand the IE logic of inquiry more fully (see Baker et al., this volume, for an example). Dissertations are another great resource to see the more extensive explications of methodological decisions and the iterative, recursive, and abductive process of IE studies (see Kalainoff & Chian, this volume). Since Liudmila had limited availability of dissertations outside Lithuania or open-access sites, Audra shared her resources, thus leveraging access to academic scholarship. In exploring IE dissertations, articles, chapters, and scholarship across programs of study, Liudmila, with the bilanguacultural guide, developed deeper understandings of how to conduct IE studies. However, she also realized reading and conceptual understanding of methodology were not sufficient to develop expertise in IE logic of inquiry.

Learning-by-Doing: Enacting Ethnographic Principles in a Project

In working with a bilanguacultural guide over the years, Liudmila understood that to deepen and solidify her knowledge, and to expand the potentials for innovative research methodologies such as IE in Lithuania, she needed to *do* a study, not just read or discuss other studies. Therefore, Liudmila requested Audra to participate in co-designing a research study for a 4-year grant, inviting Judith Green to teach IE to the whole research team and consult along the way. The project received a European-Union funded grant and this volume is one of the outcomes of the project. Table 2.2 represents project tasks and the

TABLE 2.2 Ethnographic Principles Embedded in Tasks and Methods for a 4-Year, IE-Informed Study In Lithuania

Task	Ethnographic principles in use	Methods
Examine the help people with disabilities receive in the health care system in order to create a foundation (baseline) for improving specialist training for holistic care	• *Set aside ethnocentrism* to uncover varied emic perspectives • *Identify boundaries* of what is important to insiders • *Make connections* among various perspectives and policies • *Nonlinear* exploration and construction of knowledge based on discoveries of rich points and telling cases	• Develop consent forms for different stakeholders • Conduct conversational life history interviews (2–3 per participant) with people most familiar with the issues to be studied: people with disabilities, family members, and healthcare specialists • Develop surveys based on what is learned from the interviews; Survey members of the 3 groups: medical personnel; people with disabilities; their families/caretakers.
Analyze specialist training to provide holistic help for people with disabilities in the healthcare system.	• *Set aside ethnocentrism* to understand the preparation of healthcare specialists; do not judge or evaluate the programs but seek to understand them as they are • *Identify boundaries* of programs and classes to study by talking with insiders • *Make connections* among perspectives by including faculty, students, administrators both in higher education institutions and healthcare settings • *Make connections* with policy frameworks • Engage in *nonlinear abductive logic* and contrastive analyses of the varied perspectives of people and policies	• Conduct document and policy analyses about regulations and programs for specialist training • Conduct ethnographic interviews with students, faculty, administrators, others • Conduct on-site observations of specialist preparation
Through an ethnographic action research approach, improve the preparation of healthcare specialists to work with people with disabilities	• *Make connections* among varied perspectives and needs to design an action research project • Prioritize the needs of insiders and *set aside ethnocentrism* in designing action research with the insiders who want to make change • *Identify boundaries* of programs and perspectives in need of change by collaborating with the insiders • Utilize the abductive logic of ethnography to construct change in *nonlinear* and iterative need, participant and data driven ways	• Design and conduct an ethnographically informed action research to improve specialist training • Develop a pre- and post-survey of students and faculty engaged in action research

(Continued)

TABLE 2.2 Ethnographic Principles Embedded in Tasks and Methods for a 4-Year, IE-Informed Study In Lithuania *(Continued)*

Task	Ethnographic principles in use	Methods
Developing researcher competencies in the course of implementing the project	• *Make connections* among the seminars that emphasize varied aspects of ethnography • *Make connections* among scholars, universities, conferences and networks that help Lithuanian scholars develop research competencies • *Identify boundaries* based on epistemological alignment of outsider perspectives and insider needs • *Set aside ethnocentrism* and engage in reflexivity through exposure to different sites and perspectives on ethnography • Engage in *nonlinear thinking* by sharing rich points and collaborating on doing and writing research across years and project tasks	• Conduct interconnected seminar series led by international researchers who are part of an epistemologically aligned network • Participate in international internships/visiting scholar programs led by international researchers • International scholars (PI and co-PI) collaborate with Lithuanian scholars to design the project • Outsiders advise and guide based on knowledge generated by insiders on the ground
Utilizing knowledge, understanding, and developed research competencies for furthering science and practice (publications, dissemination, and future grant applications)	• Reflexively analyze own preferences and *set aside ethnocentric* needs by aligning publication interests with those of the funder requirements • *Identify boundaries* for knowledge creation and dissemination based on the guidelines of the funder as "insider" • Work *nonlinearly* across tasks and years to develop publications • *Make connections* among project tasks and team members to create collaborations for knowledge creation and dissemination • *Make connections* among present and future possibilities of the project	• Publish in high quality international journals and other venues that meet the requirements of the funder • Publish monographs, research studies, and textbooks as aligned in the project tasks • Divide publication tasks among project researchers

ethnographic principles underlying the ways we conceptualized the tasks and designed methods to address the tasks.

While the project did not go quite as intended due to factors and people beyond Liudmila's or Audra's influence (a discussion of which is beyond the scope of this chapter), the information in Table 2.2 demonstrates how IE principles (see introductory and other chapters in this volume) can guide conceptualizations of complex educational studies and choices of methods to answer the questions asked. For example, to accomplish tasks for this large-scale project, we began with in-depth interviews, policy analyses, and observations in relevant sites, but we also needed to develop surveys to understand the larger scope of the issue.

Instead of being driven by a priori theories, following ethnographic principles of *identifying boundaries* of relevance to participants and *making connections* across perspectives and documents, Liudmila designed surveys based on the interviews conducted with the different stakeholders (Rupšienė et al., 2021). Instead of one generic survey, the project team developed six different surveys with some related questions to retain the ethnographic principle of *cultural relevance* (Green et al., 2003) and to *honor the work and insights of insiders*, including people with disabilities, their families, and healthcare workers, who had shared their knowledge in the interviews. As Walford (2020) argues, "ethnography is not qualitative" and can encompass a variety of methods through which researchers explore cultural life and patterns in complex settings and phenomena. Chapters across this volume also demonstrate a variety of methods and tools used in IE-informed studies.

Enacting this study with IE-informed principles was not without challenges, but it did provide Liudmila, other Lithuanian researchers, and the people with whom they researched, an opportunity to design and enact a complex nonlinear project and thus *learn by doing* the innovative research approaches such as IE and their potentials and limits. In this way, instead of Audra as a bilanguacultural guide answering Liudmila's questions about consequences, opportunities, and challenges in IE (prompt 10, Table 2.1), Liudmila experienced them firsthand and thus developed an experiential, not only a conceptual, understanding of IE as epistemology.

Collaborating with a Bilanguacultural Guide: An Invitation

In this chapter, we explored the concept and potentials for collaborating with a bilanguacultural guide to develop deeper understandings of IE as epistemology and an approach to researching complex educational sites and phenomena. We demonstrated how, why, and in what ways the bilanguacultural guide can mediate the languacultural connections and help a researcher from the LC1 context (Lithuanian language and higher education) understand insider perspectives in LC2 (IE, English, and the US-based research) contexts, in this way supporting the process of an LC1 outsider becoming a member of LC2. In sharing Liudmila's and Audra's collaboration across languacultural contexts we demonstrated the potentials of a bilanguacultural guide to create access to new learning opportunities, to engage *with* ethnographers/learners in gaining deeper understandings of target languacultures such as IE, and to become a partner over time in scholarship, co-learning, and relationship-building. We share our perspectives based on our engagement with IE from the Lithuanian context and language, but the processes and ideas we uncover can be relevant to many other situations in which a non-English dominant LC1 encounters the English-dominant LC2. Our chapter provides a telling case of such encounters and demonstrates the potentials of the new concept of a bilanguacultural guide.

We end the chapter with an invitation for you as readers to consider when and in what ways you may serve as a bilanguacultural guide or may engage one to guide your entry into new languacultural communities. A few principles to consider:

- For an ethnographer/learner:

  - When working across languages and sociocultural contexts seek a bilanguacultural guide familiar with the group you are seeking to learn and understand; ideally the guide will also be familiar with your languaculture;
  - Ask a lot of honest questions;
  - Share the confusions, constraints, and challenges with your guide so together you can seek solutions and answers;
  - Invest the time and energy in learning over time

- For the bilanguacultural guide

  - Having become a member of your new languaculture (LC2), seek opportunities to help others learn and enter the LC2;
  - Share the histories and introduce the new member to the larger network;
  - Leverage your access and resources, fostering academic justice;
  - Engage in honest dialogues;
  - Commit to engaging over time;
  - Be open to learning both about LC2 and LC1.

- Both

  - Attend to discourse and language;
  - Do not take surface definitions or understandings at face value;
  - Engage in translanguaging to deepen understandings of concepts, processes, and practices;
  - Build the relationship over time;
  - Continue learning.

Suggested Readings

Anderson-Levitt, K. M. (Ed.). (2011). *Anthropologies of education: A global guide to ethnographic studies of learning and schooling.* Berghahn Books.

Atkinson, P. (2017). *Thinking ethnographically.* Sage. https://dx.doi.org/10.4135/9781473982741

García, O., & Otheguy, R. (2019). Plurilingualism and translanguaging: Commonalities and divergences. *International Journal of Bilingual Education and Bilingualism*, *23*(1), 17–35. https://doi.org/10.1080/13670050.2019.1598932

References

Agar, M. (1994). *Language shock: Understanding the culture of conversation*. Quill.

Agar, M. (2006a). Culture: Can you take it anywhere? *International Journal of Qualitative Methods*, *5*(2), 1–12. Retrieved 12/15/2009, from http://www.ualberta.ca/~iiqm/backissues/5_2/PDF/agar.pdf

Agar, M. (2006b). An ethnography by any other name... *Forum Qualitative Sozialforschung/Forum: Qualitative Social Research*, *7*(4). http://www.qualitative-research.net/fqs

Agar, M. (2019). *Culture: How to make it work in a world of hybrids*. Rowman & Littlefield.

Beach, D. (2017). International trends and developments in the ethnography of education. *Acta Paedagogica Vilnensia*, *39*(2), 15–30.https://doi.org/10.15388/ActPaed.2017.39.11455

Beach, R., & Bloome, D. (Eds.). (2019). *Languaging relations for transforming the literacy and language arts classroom*. Routledge.

Cassagrande, J. B. (Ed.). (1960). *In the company of man: Twenty portraits by anthropologists*. Harper & Brothers publishers.

Castanheira, M. L., Crawford, T., Dixon, C. N., & Green, J. L. (2001). Interactional ethnography: An approach to studying the social construction of literate practices. *Linguistics and Education*, *11*(4), 353–400. https://doi.org/10.1016/s0898-5898(00)00032-2

Cazden, C., John, V., & Hymes, D. (Eds.). (1972). *Functions of language in the classroom*. Teachers College Press.

Clifford, J., & Marcus, G. E. (Eds.) (1986). *Writing culture: The poetics and politics of ethnography*. University of California Press.

Collins, E. C., & Green, J. L. (1992). Learning in classroom settings: Making or breaking a culture. In H. Marshall (Ed.), *Redefining student learning: Roots of educational restructuring* (pp. 59–85). Ablex.

Green, J. L., Baker, W. D., Chian, M., Vanderhoof, C. M., Hooper, L., Kelly, G. J., Skukauskaitė, A., & Kalainoff, M. (2020). Studying the over-time construction of knowledge in educational settings: A microethnographic-discourse analysis approach. *Review of Research in Education*, *44*, 161–194. https://doi.org/10.3102/0091732X20903121

Green, J. L., & Bloome, D. (1997). Ethnography and ethnographers of and in education: A situated perspective. In J. Flood, S. B. Heath, & D. Lapp (Eds.), *Handbook of research on teaching literacy through the communicative and visual arts* (pp. 181–202). International Reading Association & MacMillan.

Green, J. L., Castanheira, M. L., Skukauskaitė, A., & Hammond, J. (2015). Exploring traditions studying discourse and interaction in classrooms: Developing transparency, reflexivity, and multi-faceted research designs. In N. Markee (Ed.), *Handbook of classroom discourse and interaction* (pp. 26–43). Wiley.

Green, J. L., Dixon, C. N., & Zaharlick, A. (2003). Ethnography as a logic of inquiry. In J. Flood, D. Lapp, J. R. Squire, & J. Jensen (Eds.), *Handbook of research on teaching the English language arts* (2nd ed., pp. 201–224). Lawrence Erlbaum Associates.

Green, J. L., Skukauskaitė, A., & Baker, W. D. (2012). Ethnography as epistemology: An introduction to educational ethnography. In J. Arthur, M. J. Waring, R. Coe, & L. V. Hedges (Eds.), *Research methodologies and methods in education* (pp. 309–321). Sage.

Kelly, G. J., Crawford, T., & Green, J. L. (2001). Common task and uncommon knowledge: Dissenting voices in the discursive construction of physics across small laboratory groups. *Linguistics and Education, 12*(2), 135–174. doi: 10.1016/s0898-5898(00)00046-2.

Kelly, G. J., & Green, J. L. (Eds.). (2019). *Theory and methods for sociocultural research in science and engineering education.* Routledge.

Lewis, G., Jones, B., & Baker, C. (2012). Translanguaging: Developing its conceptualisation and contextualisation. *Educational Research and Evaluation, 18*(7), 655–670. https://doi.org/10.1080/13803611.2012.718490

Marcus, G. E. (2021). *Ethnography through thick and thin.* Princeton University Press.

Rex, L. A. (Ed.) (2006). *Discourse of opportunity: How talk in learning situations creates and constrains– interactional ethnographic studies in teaching and learning.* Hampton Press.

Rupšienė, L., Ratkevičienė, M., & Saveljeva, R. (2021). *Žmonės su negaliomis sveikatos sistemoje: Aktualijos sveikatos darbuotojų edukacijos kontekste [People with disabilities in the health system: Critical issues in the context of health worker education].* Klaipėdos universiteto leidykla/Klaipėda University Press.

Santa Barbara Classroom Discourse Group. (1992a). Constructing literacy in classrooms: Literate action as social accomplishment. In H. H. Marshall (Ed.), *Redefining student learning: Roots of educational change* (pp. 119–150). Ablex.

Santa Barbara Classroom Discourse Group (1992b). Do you see what we see? The referential and intertextual nature of classroom life. *Journal of Classroom Interaction, 27*(2), 29–36.

Skukauskaitė, A. (2021). Becoming an ethnographer: Living, teaching, and learning ethnographically. In J. M. Sancho-Gil & F. Hernández-Hernández (Eds.), *Becoming an educational ethnographer: The challenges and opportunities of undertaking research* (pp. 52–63). Routledge.

Skukauskaitė, A., & Girdzijauskienė, R. (2021). Video analysis of contextual layers in teaching-learning interactions. *Learning, Culture and Social Interaction, 29.* https://doi.org/10.1016/j.lcsi.2021.100499

Skukauskaitė, A., Rupšienė, L., Player Koro, C., & Beach, D. (2017). Rethinking educational ethnography: Methodological quandaries and possibilities. *Acta Paedagogica Vilnensia, 39*(39), 9–14. https://doi.org/10.15388/actpaed.2017.39.11451

Smith, P. H., & Murillo, L. A. (2015). Theorizing translanguaging and multilingual literacies through human capital theory. *International Multilingual Research Journal, 9*(1), 59–73. https://doi.org/10.1080/19313152.2014.985149

Spradley, J. (1979/2016). *The ethnographic interview.* Waveland Press, Inc.

Walford, G. (2020). Ethnography is not qualitative. *Ethnography and Education, 15*(1), 122–135. https://doi.org/10.1080/17457823.2018.1540308

3

ON ETHNOGRAPHER-AS-LEARNER AND THEORY BUILDER

W. Douglas Baker, Krisanna Machtmes, and Judith L. Green

In this chapter, we introduce readers to the concept of the *ethnographer as learner* in ongoing studies in educational settings (Heath & Street, 2008; Walford, 2008). To introduce readers new to Interactional Ethnography (IE), and what is meant by IE as an epistemology, we reconstruct how Baker, guided by an IE logic-of-inquiry, engaged in nonlinear, iterative, recursive, and abductive processes to create a logic of analysis situated within a particular research contexts. By (re) constructing principles guiding decisions made within and across levels of analyses, we make transparent *ethnography as a nonlinear process* (cf. Agar, 1994; 2006).

By focusing on Baker's research decisions, grounded in an archive from a two-year study in an Advanced Placement Studio Art Class (Baker, 2001), we make visible different levels of analyses and cycles of research central to developing theoretical insights into the following re-occurring research question:

> What do students need to know and learn how to do in order to achieve goals set for them in particular educational contexts?
>
> *(cf. Baker, 2007)*

Thus, by reconstructing Baker's developing logic-in-use (Birdwhistell, 1977) in his ongoing study of what students needed to learn to be studio artists in this intergenerational studio art class, we unfold how each phase of the research led to the construction of a situated logic of analysis.

In unfolding Baker's iterative, recursive, and abductive decisions and research processes, we make transparent how Baker observed and generated a set of archived recordings of the class's everyday phenomena for analysis of different levels of scale. For example, as students and the teacher engaged in discursive and interactional processes, Baker drew on IE-guided theoretical

DOI: 10.4324/9781003215479-4

perspectives, and analysis processes, to construct warranted interpretations of recorded events. Processes undertaken included: assuming the role of ethnographer-as-learner, identifying rich points, tracing individuals across times and events and transcribing, as well as backward and forward mapping.

Our goal in tracing and (re)constructing the roots and inter-connected phases of Baker's developing logic of analysis is to make transparent what an iterative, recursive and abductive logic of analysis entails (Agar, 1994; 2006; Heath & Street, 2008). That is, we make visible how local and situated processes Baker examined enabled him to identify developing social, cultural, and linguistic as well as artistic processes that were being shaped by (Fairclough, 1992) participants as they engage in events of this class as a developing languacultures (Agar, 1994). Therefore, in focusing on reflexive processes and decisions Baker undertook within and across phases of analyses, we make transparent *principles of conduct* central to developing an IE logic-in-use.

On Constructing Transparency in Reporting on Ethnographic Research in Education

To provide further understanding of guiding principles central to an IE logic of analysis, we turn to guidelines proposed by Smith (1978) for reporting on ethnographic research in education (cited in Green, Baker et al., 2020). Smith framed the following phases central to making transparent roots and process for engaging in ethnographic studies:

- Identify the origins of the problem
- Identify major seminal bodies of work that frame methodological processes and issues
- Develop guiding models and theories, which requires developing awareness of competing theories that guide your research processes
- Identify the multiple phases required in designing and engaging in a study
- Construct ways of recording the researcher's thinking, decision making, and interpretive asides during phases of analyses
- Engage in conscious searching of records to construct data and literature to inform analyses as well as interpretation of records and analyses

(Green, Baker et al., 2020, p. 167)

Smith also identified what he termed the "new ethnography", which shifted the focus from a holistic study of a group or community to analyses of audio and videotapes of classroom events. This reformulation of ethnographic research, a direction he framed as *microethnography*, was presented in his book *The Complexities of an Urban Classroom* (Smith & Geoffrey, 1968). This direction situates IE in relationship to the work of Smith and developments of video-enabled recordings of classroom as social spaces (e.g., Baker et al., 2008; Bloome et al., 2005; Street, 2005; Zaharlick & Green, 1991). Microethnography ties together cultures-in-the-making with the ways people use language to create and participate in developing languacultures (Agar, 1994).

Developing Guiding Theories: Agar on Languaculture as LC1 and LC2

To introduce how Agar (2006) framed his developing understanding of *languacultures,* in this section, we introduce how Agar (re)formulated these concepts in an international seminar in 2005 attended by Baker, Green, and other authors of this volume (e.g., Bloome, Skukauskaitė, Katz, Castanheira, among others). In that seminar, Agar presented his current thinking about language, culture, and ethnography, as many of those attending had followed his publications (e.g., Agar, 1994; 1996) and were interested in the intersections among those concepts. In the published version of the seminar talk, Agar (2006) wrote:

> First of all, ethnographic research was described as equivalent to learning a second languaculture. Languaculture is a concept that I developed in a book called Language Shock (1994) to remind readers that actually using a language involves all manner of background knowledge and local information in addition to grammar and vocabulary. Ethnography, then, was defined as an encounter between two languacultures, abbreviated LC1 for the native languaculture of the ethnographer and the audience, and LC2 for the languaculture of the studied group.

He further argues that:

> I also argued that LC2 learning, like ethnography, is driven by *rich points,* [emphasis added] a concept from another book, The Professional Stranger (1996), that I named almost 20 years ago. Rich points are those surprises, those departures from an outsider's expectations that signal a difference between LC1 and LC2 and give direction to subsequent learning.
>
> *(Agar, 2006, pp. 1–6)*

In presenting how Baker and colleagues drew on, and adapted, Agar's arguments about *languaculture 1 and 2* for conceptualizing the research context, we make transparent the theoretical orientation Baker developed to guide his work as an *ethnographer-as-learner.*

Model Guiding Multiple Levels of Analysis

In this section, we make visible how Agar's argument provides a conceptual foundation guiding the work of Baker over the past three decades, as new questions arose that required further analyses. In Figure 3.1 we provide a *logic of*

> **RESEARCH QUESTION GUIDING MULTIPLE PHASES OF ANALYSIS:**
>
> *How did the teacher of the INTERGENERATIONAL Advanced Placement Studio Art class construct opportunities for learning a situated disciplinary knowledge?*

> **1.0 "PUBLIC CRITIQUE": A KEY PRACTICE WITHIN A COMMUNITY OF ARTISTS AS A TELLING CASE**

1.1 Initiating Questions ABOUT Public Critique

- How did members of the class construct the practice of "public critique," for what purposes, and for what desired outcomes?

- How did the students' language, actions and interactions with others, and material resources during public critique exemplify *principles of this community of studio artists*, i.e., students (and by extension the teacher) working as artists?

1.2 Creating a New Set of Data Representation

- Producing transcript representation organized in sequence units of analysis (see Green & Kelly, 2019 for most recent descriptions)

- Producing representation of results of semantic analysis and predominant discourse themes

1.3 Analyzing Data on Public Critique: Contrasting Two First-Year Students' Performances (first and second speakers as framed by the teacher for the group)

- Identify sequences of developing presentation on personal studio art project

- Creating a contrast table for two participants by using a template for presenting elements provided to class by the teacher to guide students' preparation for the presentation

- Identifying differences in performances of the two first-year students in the program in contrast with more experienced students (second, third and fourth-year students

> **2.0 CONSTRUCTING MAPS OF MULTIPLE SOURCES OF INFLUENCE ON OBSERVED DIFFERENCES IN PERFORMANCES: ANALYZING THE ONSET OF COMMUNITY PROCESSES AND PRACTICEES AS A TELLING CASE: SITUATING LEVELS OF ANLYSES IN THE HISTORY OF THE TEACHER, CLASS, AND STUDENTS**

2.1 Initiating Questions

- How did the teacher's discourse begin shaping a community of studio artists, including the times and spaces for students to learn, practice, and discuss conceptualizing and making art?

- How did the teacher's actions, particularly the activities offered to students, begin constructing opportunities for learning processes involved with working as studio artists on the first day of class?

  FOCUSED QUESTIONS FOR ENTERING ARCHIVE AND CONSTRUCTING DATA

  - How was time conceptualized in this class?
  - How did the social construction of time shape the language of and for the class?
  - How did the constructions of time and referenced events shape opportunities for learning?

2.2 (Re)presenting Data Constructed from Archive

- Identifying events and discourse recorded in fieldnotes, transcripts, and video recordings from Day One across first three months of class by creating maps describing participants' actions within event phases (e.g., chains of actions, proposed meanings/referential system, and subevents)

FIGURE 3.1 Logic-of-Inquiry across Levels of Analyses Grounded in Emerging Questions that Create Rich Points for Ongoing Analyses *(Continued)*

2.3 Analyzing Events

> (Re)viewing transcripts from the archive and
> constructing event maps for identifying how and what
> roles and relationships and demands and expectations
> were established through the discourse and
> interactional processes among participants

FOCUS QUESTION FOR ANALYSIS IN 2.0 OF
SECOND DAY

- How was a concept of studio art socially
  constructed?

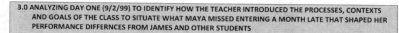

- How did the action of the class members reflect the
  concepts defined through verbal language?

3.0 ANALYZING DAY ONE (9/2/99) TO IDENTIFY HOW THE TEACHER INTRODUCED THE PROCESSES, CONTEXTS AND GOALS OF THE CLASS TO SITUATE WHAT MAYA MISSED ENTERING A MONTH LATE THAT SHAPED HER PERFORMANCE DIFFERNCES FROM JAMES AND OTHER STUDENTS

3.1 Initiating Questions Guiding Analysis of Day 1

- How were patterns of discourse and action constructed on Day Two (9/3/99)?
- How did constructed patterns inscribe particular ways of acting and working as artists for members of the class?

3.2 Creating a New Set of Data Representation

- Producing additional transcript(s) from archived video records of talk and interactions among participants at different levels of units of analysis (e.g., message units, interaction units, sequence units, and event units)
- Producing multiple-level event maps showing events and times as well as configuration of participants

3.3 Analyzing Cross Telling Cases: Tracing Processes Across Days Contrastively

- Situating developing activities from one event to another within the flow of activities developed in a day and across days
- Developing microanalysis of participants' actions and talk (discourse) to identify the nature of their contributions to the construction of the classroom collective text

FOCUSED QUESTIONS FOR NEW ANALYSES GROUNDED IN PROCESS IN
2.0

- How was a concept of studio art socially constructed in and through discourse, interactional processes, and engagement with material resources?
- How did the action of the class members reflect the concepts defined through verbal language(s)?

4.0 Further analyses to make transparent IE as an epistemology for tracing learning opportunities over times, events, and configurations of participants in different educational contexts

4.1 Analyzing Teacher Discourse to examine position theory as a telling case study for the *Handbook of the cultural foundations of learning.*

Shifting from focus on Maya's actions and presentation to teacher's support of Maya within the whole class developing Public Critique Event – Positioning theory and discourse analysis: An explanatory theory and analytic lens (Green, Brock et al., 2020)

4.2 Reformulating Embedded Layers of Analyses for seminal article on "Studying the overtime construction of knowledge in educational settings: A microethnographic discourse analysis approach" (Green, Baker et al., 2020) in the *Review of Research in Education*

cf. Castanheira et al. (2001)

FIGURE 3.1 *(Continued)*

analysis model that (re)presents processes undertaken to construct each study. The focus of each study (1.0, 2.0, 3.0, and 4.0) is presented in a *grey banner.* Under each banner are the questions explored, actions taken to construct a data set, and ways of analyzing data to construct warranted accounts of phenomena of interest. Figure 3.1, therefore, provides a graphic (re)presentation of Baker's *logic-of-inquiry* that he undertook with colleagues across levels of analyses grounded in emerging questions that created rich points for analyses (e.g., Baker & Green, 2007; Baker et al., 2008; Green, et al., 2012; Green, Baker et al., 2020; Green, Brock et al., 2020).

As indicated in Figure 3.1, Baker developed a conceptually grounded series of processes in constructing questions across studies in order to develop warranted arguments about what was being socially constructed within and across specific cycles of analysis to address new questions as they were identified. As demonstrated in Figure 3.1, the logic of analysis for developing studies involved:

- identifying initiating questions guiding the analyses undertaken,
- (re)presenting data constructed from archive, and
- analyzing events selected.

Visible across studies, multiple questions were identified to address the complex and developing levels of analyses.

In presenting Figure 3.1, we made transparent the logic behind analyses undertaken within and across studies so that readers new to IE as a logic of analysis could engage with this graphic (re)presentation as a guiding model for preparing ways of thinking about their own research projects. In (re)constructing how Baker (and colleagues) came to know x or y, we made transparent how emerging questions shaped a developing program of research.

Origins of the Problem: On Baker's History for Developing an IE Guided Logic-in-Use

Before turning to a discussion of specific studies and what was learned through each, we present the rationale for Smith's call for tracing the *origins of the questions guiding a research study.* In education, these origins are often grounded in the history of the researcher as a teacher, administrator, curriculum designer, or student in particular educational contexts. In publications, these origins are often invisible and appear to be objective, given the purposes and constraints of the volume in which the study appears. As we show, Baker's question guiding his research was grounded in his goal of understanding, as a teacher, the following: *what do students need to know and learn how to do in order to achieve goals set for them in particular educational contexts?*

Table 3.1 (re)constructs the origins of Baker's question and his actions taken to develop a research process for addressing this question. We include this

TABLE 3.1 Timeline (Re)constructing the Roots Leading to DB's Program of Research: Addressing KM's Questions

Date	Event/issue	Notes in response to requests for roots (origins) of the problem leading to published research
Phase 1 1986–1997	Baker teaches English at a high school: Interested in positioning students as writers and as readers of literature and creating a poetry club. Baker takes on role of basketball coach and is guided by a senior coach in supporting players to learn skills and understandings of how to be a member of a team and develop personal skills.	My orienting question: *What do students need to know and learn how to do in order to achieve goals set for them?*
Summer 1987	San Joaquin Valley Writing Project (SJVWP): Teachers as writers, etc. This model led to Baker position students as writers.	SJVWP, a site of the National Writing Project, in which I was a "fellow", where we shared practices and critically explored those practices with other teachers.
1987–1992	Baker works on and completes MA in Composition: Further study on how students can work as writers.	Based on my experiences as a writer and researcher on teaching writing, I created opportunities for students as writers that included: selecting their own topics (similar to the Studio Art teacher); participating in assessment practices (similar to public critique); etc.
Phase 2 Sept 1997– June 1998	Baker's first year at UCSB: Courses with JG: Literacy; classroom ethnography; classrooms as cultures	My focus during this year was on exploring theoretical frameworks for literacy, ethnographic perspectives for observing classroom interactions, and how members of a classroom construct what counts as x.
July 1998	Baker meets the English and Studio Art teacher through South Coast Writing Project (SCWriP), writing project in Santa Barbara	I joined SCWriP, a site of the National Writing Project, as a "Returning Fellow" and engaged with an English teacher and the Studio Art teacher, who were designing a common framework for teaching together, among others, to explore and learn from common interests and practices they introduced.
August 1998	Baker attends teachers' planning session: interested in opportunities students will have to learn across disciplines.	I did not understand all of the conversations between the two teachers: I later learned that the two teachers, with whom I had ongoing conversations and planned a study (Year 1), had different frameworks.

(Continued)

TABLE 3.1 Timeline (Re)constructing the Roots Leading to DB's Program of Research: Addressing KM's Questions *(Continued)*

Date	Event/issue	Notes in response to requests for roots (origins) of the problem leading to published research
Sept 2, 1998	First day of Year 1 (1998–1999): an interdisciplinary approach: Studio Art and English	The study we planned involved a common body of approximately 60 students from two different classes (Studio Art and English). I met with the two teachers in order to orient them to the ethnographic approach I would take with them to explore differences between the two teachers and courses. The 30 students in, each class switched classes for the two-period block. In a processing session, I identified "repetition" as a rich point, and it is a concept I returned to in 2001 during the post-fieldwork of analysis (Baker, 2001).
Feb/Mar 1999	Student tells DB: "if you want to know about this If class, you need to see [public] critique".	Kristen, the student, and I engaged in semi-structured interviews, and this was a first key moment.
Phase 3 Sept 2, 1999	First day of class: Year 2 in intergenerational Advanced Placement Studio Art class as focal study	How did the teacher initiate practices toward becoming studio artists? Public critique and the "creative process" were of particular interest.
Sept. 3, 1999	Second day of class: Year 2	Origins of critique formally begin: students respond to ideas, etc.
Sept–Oct 1999	Unanticipated conversations initiated by Kristen, a fourth-year student, who acted as Baker's cultural guide.	Kristen across dialogues and days (Sept. 10, 17, 23, October. 1, 8)
Sept–Oct 1999	"Friendly Critique" and drawing techniques and materials	First formal instance of "critique".
Sept–Oct 1999	"Gentle Critique"; drawing techniques and materials continue	Second formal instance of "critique".
Nov 17–19	"Deep Critique"	The sequence included one class period (on Nov. 16) for students to prepare for a formal, "deep" critique of a series of their drawings.

(Continued)

TABLE 3.1 Timeline (Re)constructing the Roots Leading to DB's Program of Research: Addressing KM's Questions *(Continued)*

Date	Event/issue	Notes in response to requests for roots (origins) of the problem leading to published research
Nov 17	Maya – first-year senior James – first-year senior Scott – second-year senior Kristen – fourth-year senior	James was originally chosen because I presumed, based on James's discourse, James was an experienced student demonstrating the expected discourse modeled by the teacher. I learned from the teacher James was a first-year senior. Maya had missed the first month, so her critique reflected what opportunities she missed.
2000–2001	Analysis for dissertation study Decision log: focused on compiling the parts of a dissertation. Fieldnotes were used extensively to create event maps, examine patterns, and decide what to transcribe.	Interviewed the English and Studio Art teacher; many meetings with JG – notes from meetings guide inquiry also. Analyses raise questions and Studio Art teacher *confirms* or *reshapes* Baker's assumptions based on his knowledge and analysis (e.g., My question about why Kristen did not use the expected language). This type of *triangulation* led Baker back to the process meeting after the first day of class, 1998, and the term "repetition".
2001–ongoing	Analyses to address issues of conducting video-enabled ethnography and IE research processes that served as illustrative cases Construction of data sets to address new and emerging questions related to the class-as-a-culture-in-the-making to create a telling case study of DB's logic-in-use in a *program of research*	Addressing questions about what guides and is involved in constructing warranted accounts of both: a) local members' knowledge in and for action in particular contexts, and b) to make transparent what underlies the decisions and actions central to engaging in an iterative, recursive, and abductive processes: the research process for studies in educational spaces for learning from, through and with members what is socially, culturally, interpersonally, and academically significant to learn to be studio artists in a community of study artists.

history given current calls to make transparent what drives a research program (cf. Samura & Alvermann, 2021). In this way, we introduce to readers a process they will need to consider when reporting on their own decisions about what to study, how and in what ways, and for what purposes, as they develop a program of research.

As we will show, this process also led to the selection of the site and to Baker's engagement with the Studio Art teacher and his guiding question. For members of our author team, Krisanna Machtmes, an experienced researcher who was new to IE, and Judith Green, a co-researcher on projects with Baker, Baker provided a (re)construction of the origins of his program of research, grounded in his journey from high school teacher to ethnographer-as-learner with participants in the intergenerational Advanced Placement Studio Art class (see Table 3.1).

The Roots of Baker's History From Learning as a Teacher to Ethnographer-as-Learner

In Table 3.1, Baker depicts three phases of an inter-contextual web (cf. Bloome & Egan-Robertson, 1993; Fairclough, 1992) of sources of influence that show how and for what purposes he developed an IE guided program of research. As indicated in Columns 1 and 2, the first phase of the history is grounded in his learning as a high school English Language Arts teacher. In each phase, Baker identifies roots of his guiding question and actions he took to learn from and with students, other teachers, and formal educational programs (MA and PhD).

In Column 3, Baker provides notes to coauthors to make transparent decisions and actions of his professional history that led to his becoming an IE grounded researcher. These notes also support readers new to IE in gaining deeper understandings of intellectual and theoretical roots of Baker's question and actions taken to construct an IE guided logic of analysis. Readers may want to consider how Baker's journey serves as a ground for (re)constructing the roots of their own research questions.

By including a timeline, identifying key events and issues, and offering notes to our author team, Baker provided a basis for learning from decisions and actions underlying his *guiding question* at the center of his program of research.

For example, Phase 1, representing the first chain of actions, spanned his history from 1987 to 1992. In the introduction to Phase 1, Baker documents his professional work and growing awareness of student learning processes as a teacher, coach, and mentor in different educational contexts. This history influenced how he formulated his guiding question for research (cf. Baker, 2007). In Phase 2, Baker (re)constructs actions and decisions in his doctoral program that led him to develop a language for, and ways to study, his guiding question in new contexts. In notes to his coauthors, he situates sources of influence that informed his theoretical and conceptual developments as a teacher and researcher.

In Phase 2, he also documents how he came to engage as a researcher with two teachers, an English Language Arts teacher and a Studio Art teacher, through his participation as *Returning Fellow* during the summer institute of the South Coast Writing Project (SCWriP), a site of the National Writing Project. He further identifies for his coauthors and readers anchor events and perspectives for his entry into the two teachers' classrooms. In Phase 3, Baker describes moments, decisions, and actions that grounded iterative, recursive and abductive processes of his reflexive logic-in-use we (re)construct in next section of this chapter.

Making Visible Previously Invisible Roots of Baker's Guiding Question

In dialogues with Baker about origins of his guiding question and his history presented in Table 3.1, Machtmes and Green encountered a previously unknown *rich point,* when new information about Baker's intellectual history was introduced that was not reported in research-oriented volumes they had read. During the dialogue about this point in his history, Baker identified an article (Baker, 2007) he had written for teachers in the *English Journal*, "When English Language Arts, Basketball, and Poetry Collide", which makes visible foundations of his guiding question.

The following excerpt from the *English Journal* article provides deeper grounding of the of Baker's *guiding question,* which Machtmes and Green came to view as critical to understanding what led Baker to IE as a logic-of-inquiry and analyses and the study of the intergenerational Advanced Placement Studio Art Class.

> During the first year, I taught six classes (189 students), coached boys' basketball, advised the Teachers for Tomorrow club and organized and taught SAT-preparation workshops. Many colleagues had similar schedules, and over the next couple of years I slowly learned of the increasing demands on the students' time inside and outside of school. By the fourth year I settled on two extracurricular activities, head coach for the junior varsity boys' basketball team and adviser of the Poetry Club...
>
> ...Before I could guide students to infer links of the disciplinary language, expectations, and practices of one context and apply them to another, I had to gain more experience in observing and living through the collision of basketball, poetry, and the English language arts classroom; I had to make the familiar in each setting strange (Green et al., 2003), discern underlying principles across contexts, and show the students (athletes or poets) how the intersections in their worlds provided opportunities for reflecting and learning. If I began with disciplines students chose, I could make fruitful connections with the disciplinary work of the classroom. (p. 38)

In this concluding section to this article, Baker introduced a new concept, *collision points*, in which differences in discourses and discipline-based practices of each site informed his decision to build on Agar's (1994, 1996) perspective on *languaculture* and *rich points*. As the sections that follow will make visible, *collision points* (clashes in frames of reference, Tannen, 1993) were critical in developing understandings of how the Studio Art teacher introduced students to ways of learning to work as artists in a community of studio artists. This article also demonstrated the importance of exploring publications designed for different audiences to understand more fully the goals of a research program.

Baker's Ongoing Journey to Learning With, and From, Participants: Ethnographer-as-Learner

In the section above, we created a basis for developing deeper insights into the context for how Baker assumed the role of ethnographer-as-learner to explore learning opportunities provided to students. In Phase 2 in Table 3.1, Baker extends his focus on his teaching to include his decisions and actions for learning with other teachers at two sites of the National Writing Project (NWP), and in his MA program in Composition Studies. In the following note, Baker captures how what he learned over an 11-year period (1986–1997) was consequential for student learning:

> Based on my experiences as a writer and researcher on teaching writing, I created opportunities for students as writers that included: selecting their own topics (similar to Art teacher); participating in assessment practices (similar to public critique), etc.

As indicated in Phase 2 of Table 3.1, Baker continued to unfold his journey as a researcher through his doctoral studies at UCSB, including courses on literacy and ethnographic research taught by Green (a coauthor). For this period, Baker identifies his goals as exploring theoretical frameworks for literacy, ethnographic perspectives for observing classroom interactions, and how members of a classroom construct what counts as x (e.g., what counts as a particular discipline-based literacy practice).

Also, as indicated in Phase 2, Baker points to a *recurring process*, his participation with the NWP, which led him to initiate a relationship with the two teachers who would become his research partners for "designing a common framework for teaching together, to explore and learn from common interests and practices they introduced". In framing these phases of his journey, Baker provided evidence of how he continued to grow the roots of his *guiding question* as he began to work as an ethnographer-as-learner with the two teachers as research partners.

On Unanticipated Learnings from Participants

During the SCWriP Summer Institute (July 1998), Baker engaged with the two teachers to explore their common goal of developing a common framework for teaching. The teachers met periodically with Baker near the conclusion of the Institute. However, as indicated in his entry in Phase 2, in August 1998, as he attended planning sessions with these teachers, he faced a *frame clash:*

> I did not understand all of the conversation between the two teachers: I later learned that the two teachers, with whom I had ongoing conversations and planned a study (year 1 of the original study, Baker, 2001), had different [theoretical and disciplinary] frameworks.

The awareness of gaps in his understanding and observation of a *frame clash* led Baker to engage as a researcher with the teachers across the 1998–1999 academic year to explore how students these teachers shared (in separate classrooms) were engaged in learning the representative disciplines. However, at the end of Year 1, the teachers elected to postpone the second year of their planned interdisciplinary approach. At this juncture, Baker sought and received permission from the Studio Art teacher to focus on her class, beginning in Year 2 of the study.

This decision led Baker to negotiate with the Studio Art teacher ways of entering her class from the first day, as students entered. In taking this action, he and the studio art teacher constructed a continuing opportunity for him to learn from her work with students what constituted the discourse, practices, and processes in learning to be studio artists, especially in relationship to the studio art practice of *public critique.*

The roots of Baker's interest in learning about public critique in Year 2 are captured in a semistructured interview he conducted with students in the two classes toward the end of Year 1 (see shaded section of Table 3.1). In that interview, one student told Baker that, "if you want to know about this [Studio Art] class, you need to see [public] critique". Although Baker had attended a public critique event during the final week of the first term (Fall 1998), the student's statement signaled the need to trace the roots of this studio art practice *if* he were to understand the importance of students presenting their work publicly in learning to engage as studio artists within this community of artists.

The information gathered from the interview and the decision to enter the Studio Art class in Year 2 led Baker to (re)formulate his guiding question in the following way:

> If 'deep critique' [a type of public critique in the class] is critical for students' development as studio artists, how does the teacher initiate and construct the practice with students?

Baker's interest in capturing the roots of this practice led to further negotiations with the teacher about ways of bringing a video camera into the developing class from the first day in the second year of his study (Table 3.1) as well as ways of engaging with students who initiated conversations with him.

On Negotiating Entry, Developing a Social Contract: Video as a Form of Fieldnote

In this section, we unfold ways in which the teacher and Baker created a process for entering the class that led to a *social contract* with the teacher about his role and physical positions in the classroom. The following excerpt from the chapter on "Video-enabled Ethnographic Research" (Baker et al., 2008) makes transparent Baker's process of entering and recording developing events as well as spontaneous interactions initiated by students and the teacher.

> When Doug entered with the video camera on the first day of school, he asked the teacher where she would like him to position himself and the video camera (they had negotiated the use of one camera). The teacher requested that the camera remain stationary and that Doug limit his movements in the classroom, since she viewed an ethnographer as a *fly on the wall* (her metaphor). Doug honoured the decisions of the teacher and placed (with her approval) the camera either at the back left or side left of the classroom; however, as the year progressed, informal discussions with students about art and the class became part of the ethnographic process, with implicit and explicit agreement of the teacher.
>
> *(p. 87)*

Within IE studies in classes, the entry process involves a *social contract* (along with the institutional research board approval) with the researcher, the teacher, the students, and others participating in a class, which is critical for establishing ethical, professional relationships and building trust (e.g., Tuyay et al., 1995).

On Students as Unanticipated Cultural Guides

Although Baker had intended to take the position of "fly on the wall", expected by the teacher, this position was renegotiated in an unanticipated conversation with one student, Kristen, a fourth-year student in the program. As the following informal conversation identified in a video record of Day 3 of Year 2 shows, Kristen approached Baker and offered her perspective on his actions in the class. This conversation began a process in which Kristen became Baker's *self-appointed cultural guide*. Kristen approached Baker and initiated the following dialogue:

KRISTEN: Can I ask you a question?
DOUG: Yes.
KRISTEN: Why do you just sit there and take notes? You look so bored.

In this dialogue, Kristen indicated she had been observing Baker and how he was engaging in the class, and noted she interpreted his actions as looking "bored". She implied he was missing what was important to know, understand, and do in learning how students were becoming studio artists, which as ethnographer-as-learner he was striving to understand.

This unanticipated interaction led Baker, as the following analysis of related instances will show, to develop a *researcher-cultural guide relationship* with Kristen. As indicated in Table 3.1, to identify how Kristen informed his understandings of what was significant to learn, Baker returned to his archive and examined his fieldnotes and video records to trace moments in which Kristen approached him and shared new insights about phenomena on which he should focus:

- September 17
  Kristen describes to Doug the value of sketchbooks and "learning to see" and urges him to purchase one and get started: "Art is learning to see different".
  She also describes development of student artists (and uses her experience in dance as a metaphor).
  Teacher adds to the dialogue in this interaction with an unanticipated comment: "[Kristen has] really developed over the past year; she's more comfortable as a leader". (Video: 0:59:57–01:09:00)
- September 23
  Kristen reminds Doug of a school event and encourages him to attend. She also works with another student on the latter's painting (Fieldnotes, 9–23)
- October 1
  Kristen describes the technique of "continuous line" and urges Doug to try it; and she describes her younger experiences drawing and receiving negative feedback (Fieldnotes, p. 9)
- October 8
  Kristen describes "texture and layering" (Video: 0:10:17–0:10:30)

To provide evidence for readers of the sources of these dialogic moments, and to situate the moments in the class, Baker included citations to where they were located in his fieldnotes and at particular points in a video record.

In (re)constructing these examples of unanticipated moments, in which Baker learned about particular processes from Kristen and the teacher, our author team came to a deeper understanding of how unanticipated *conversations of process,* such as the ones with Kristen, made transparent how Kristen perceived Baker as having more to learn *if* he were to understand the languaculture of the class as she did. Thus, through (re)examining Kristen's dialogues with Baker, we came to understand that participants in a social group often perceive someone external to their group, not as a "fly on the wall" (the teacher's initial, stated perspective) but as a person who needs insider support to learn ways of knowing, being, and doing everyday life in the class or other social space.

Thus, in creating an unanticipated position of cultural guide, Kristen confirms Agar's conceptualization of LC1-LC2, in which the ethnographer-as-learner is a learner of the second languaculture. Kristen's relationship with Baker also makes transparent how, through unanticipated interactions students (and teachers) (re) orient the ethnographer to what is socially, academically, and culturally important to understand from an insider perspective. In this chain of interactions, Baker demonstrates how he sought to minimize asymmetries of researcher/participant relationships with the teacher, and especially with students.

In (re)constructing Baker's chains of interaction with Kristen (and the teacher) through unanticipated dialogues, we demonstrated how Baker learned to *step back* from his assumptions about what he was seeing and hearing to begin a process of learning from, through, and with unanticipated dialogues in which students (and at times the teacher) observed that there were phenomena and processes he did not appear to know or interpret as members did. Additionally, as the next section shows, when such differences became visible to Baker in and through dialogues with insiders (teacher and students) as well as through further levels of analyses, Baker gained new insights into what he was (or was not) seeing, hearing or understanding.

Roots of Rich Points for Further Research Grounded in Conversations of Interpretation with the Studio Art Teacher

In the following section, we identify ways in which Baker's history led to deeper insights into decisions that led him to engage in multiple analyses when faced with a frame clash between his interpretations and the teacher's of the performances of two students in the event called Public Critique (November of the school year). By examining his decisions related to his research in the Studio Art class in Phase 3, of Table 3.1, we identified decision points unreported in the articles we had read. The sharing of this history demonstrated why reporting on the history of a research process and its roots is imperative for readers to understand sources of analytic decisions.

In Table 3.1, Phase 3, Baker describes a *conversation of interpretation* of student performances that he had with the Studio Art teacher during his post fieldwork phase of analyses.

In this interview, Baker made visible how and why he chose particular students as *tracer units* to understand what was involved in becoming a studio artist in this intergenerational community of artists. In Table 3.1, November 17, he wrote the following description of how he learned that his interpretation of the two students differed from that of the teacher:

> James was originally chosen as an anchor student because I presumed, based on his initial observation of James's discourse [during the event], James was an experienced student demonstrating the expected discourse modeled by the teacher. I learned from the teacher James was a first-year senior. I also learned that Maya was also a first-year senior who had missed the first month, so Maya's performance of self-critique reflected what opportunities [for learning to be a studio artist in this class] she had missed.

Without Table 3.1, therefore, those of us on our author team who were not part of the initial project (Machtmes and Green) would not have had a way of examining key decisions about the selection of particular actors to trace, or sources of frame clashes that led to particular events or chains of events for further analysis.

By creating this history for our author team, Baker provided a form of research log that laid a foundation for understanding origins of key elements of his decision-making process in and across phases of analyses. As indicated in Table 3.1, Phase 3, the research phase of his professional history, Baker inscribed elements of his process of selecting actors and deciding to step back from what he thought he knew from field observations. In the next section, we unfold how (re)constructing key moments of decisions and learnings from his analysis processes provided an anchor for making transparent recursive and abductive processes that shaped how differences in interpretation between Baker and the teacher became rich points for further analyses.

Contrastive Discourse Analyses: Maya and James as Telling Case Studies of Triangulating Differences in Performance

In this section, we (re)construct the analytic decisions stemming from Baker's growing understandings of the *limits to certainty* about his interpretation between what he assumed he was seeing and hearing in his role of ethnographer-as-learner in the field and that of the teacher's understandings (Baker & Green, 2007). Through (re)constructing how Baker engaged in an IE-guided process of discourse analysis of Maya's and James' performance in public critique, we make visible how the conversation with the teacher led Baker to (re)consider about what he thought knew and to gain a more grounded understanding of their performances and their histories in the class.

This process began by Baker entering his archive multiple times in response to frame clashes to assemble a data set from video records and fieldnotes in the archive to engage in a contrastive analysis of the discourse and actions of Maya and James during public critique (cf. Zaharlick & Green, 1991). In Table 3.2, we (re)construct the series of analytic decisions and actions Baker undertook

TABLE 3.2 Contrastive Analysis of Maya and James Performances in Public Critique

Column 1 Rubric elements	Column 2 Maya's transcript excerpt	Column 3 Maya's rubric references	Column 4 James's rubric references	Column 5 James's transcript discourse
Purpose/ questions	I guess my drawings will help me with shape and color (483–86)	X	X	I wanted to like express/how life is everywhere (1075–76)
Approach/ selection	[selected idea:] the beast in Lord of the Flies (497)	X	X	I wanted to look at the whole (1091)
Evolution/ process	[implicit, although does not mention process]	X	X	It's a long process/ like I worked.../ five/six/seven days straight (1128–32)
Technique	I just practiced with/like dark lines/and shading/ (508–11)	X	X	I started out/like with just ink/just black ink (1077–79)
Outcome/ presentation	I don't know if I/succeeded... but I tried ... who's to say (574–95)	X	X	[the daily work and details] all adds up at the end (1142)
Processes taught:		*Processes referenced*		
Processes for developing ideas	my first thought/when I got this idea (488–89); I don't know if I succeeded (575–77)	X	X	I wanted to like express/how life is everywhere (1075–76); long process (1128)
Process: technique	I just practiced with/like dark lines/and shading/... (508–11)	X	X	You can't just draw the whole thing all at once (1102)
Time required: developing idea	[implicit: M states that she began with an idea and explains evolution of it]	X	X	It's a long process/ like I worked.../ five/six/seven days straight (1128–32)

(Continued)

TABLE 3.2 Contrastive Analysis of Maya and James Performances in Public Critique *(Continued)*

Column 1 Rubric elements	Column 2 Maya's transcript excerpt	Column 3 Maya's rubric references	Column 4 James's rubric references	Column 5 James's transcript discourse
Practices taught:		*Drawing practices referenced*		
"Seeing" (9/30–10/1)			X	You need to examine every single part and see how they relate/ to each other (1099–1100)
Layering sequence (10/5–8)			X	You can't just draw the whole thing all at once (1102)
continuous line			X	I started out/like with just ink/…/ and drew the whole butterfly (1077–80)
texture			X	But it doesn't look/ like textured (1108–09)

Source: Adapted from Green, Brock et al. (2020, p. 133).

to contrast how Maya and James met the goals the teacher set for students in different ways, and how the contrastive discourse analysis formed a basis for further analyses of the sources of influence on their performances. As indicated in Table 3.2, this contrastive analytic process also involved exploring how the students prepared for critique by engaging with the elements of the rubric the teacher provided the day prior to their presentations.

As indicated in Column 1 in Table 3.2, the teacher designed and provided students with a rubric to prepare them for their presentations in public critique. In examining James' *References* to rubric elements (Column 3), what became visible was that James included all elements of the rubric in his public presentation of his series of drawings. In contrast, Maya, during her presentation, omitted three elements of the rubric (Column 3) – drawing on techniques the teacher had emphasized across time: "seeing" (9/30–10/1), layering sequence (10/5–8), continuous line and texture (10/5–10/8).

Baker's analysis did not stop with identifying elements of the rubric (Column 1); rather, he re-entered his fieldnotes to identify and report the dates in which concepts were introduced, thus making visible ones Maya missed by entering one month after the beginning of the class. By including this level of contrastive analysis, a form of triangulation (Green & Chian, 2018), Baker was able to identify differences in what James and Maya had access to for learning. This process also enabled Baker to make transparent how he constructed *warranted accounts* (Heap, 1985; 1991) for what was and was not included by each student during their performance during the public critique event.

As indicated previously, James' discourse more closely reflected discourse the teacher had used to introduce and describe the various drawing techniques. James's tone and apparent comfort in describing his "creative process" (another key concept described by the teacher) in constructing a series of drawings also reflected – and appeared to meet the expectations of the rubric, the other students, and the teacher. Moreover, James' chain of reasoning and reconstruction of his processes reflected the drawing techniques, discourse, and creative processes used and encouraged by the teacher beginning on Day 1.

For example, James starts with his goal and conceptual purpose of the series of drawings he had brought to anchor his presentation: "I wanted to like express/how life is everywhere". He continues with what he had envisioned for a final drawing and then begins to describe the purposes and processes of experimenting with the drawing techniques and materials the teacher had offered during the first two months of the academic year. He also identifies what is not possible to do from an artist's perspective, e.g., complete a final drawing without sketching out ideas, and begins to use technical terms (e.g., texture).

In contrast, Maya's tone appeared hesitant. In describing the techniques and materials she used, Maya's discourse was less specific, and she omitted aspects of the rubric. For example, she did not address drawing techniques (e.g., "seeing" and "continuous line") introduced in September, the month she missed before entering the class in October, even though the discourse in the class often referred to them. Maya's differences, when compared to James' presentation, created a rich point in which the teacher signaled to the class members (and by extension Baker) Maya's inexperience by *positioning* her as new to the class and to critique (cf. Green, Brock et al., 2020).

The contrastive analysis between Maya's and James' performances of public critique led Baker to step back once again and to return to research literature to seek ways of theoretically explaining how to understand sources contributing to each student's performance and how the teacher positioned them. This analytic observation exemplifies how a telling case, as Mitchell (1984) describes, can lead to (re)theorizing phenomena of study. For example, given prior opportunities to explore positioning theory, as an *explanatory theory* of the observed patterns in classrooms (cf. Baker & Green, 2011; McVee et al., 2011), Baker returned to this theoretical literature to create a foundation for (re)theorizing the patterns he had identified.

Through positioning theory, our author team was able to construct empirical understandings of how and why the teacher positioned Maya and James as the first two presenters of their self-critiques during the public critique event. While space precludes a full reconstruction of the discourse analysis of the teacher's positioning process, this section provides an example how a micro-ethnographic discourse analysis can lead to further (re)theorizing phenomena identified in a study.

Situating Public Critique in the History of the Class

In this section, we (re)construct the levels of analyses Baker constructed to address his guiding question for his research project as indicated in Table 3.1, Phase 3, in Notes: *How did the teacher initiate practices toward becoming studio artists?* Figure 3.2 provides a (re)construction of Baker's levels of analyses undertaken to build a deeper understanding of the class as a *languaculture-in-the-making*. Each level of history and analysis Baker identified are indicated through *time-lines* and a *swing out* format (a particular IE approach) to show part-whole relationships in and across times and cycles of activity. Figure 3.2, therefore, provides a foundation for examining how Baker engaged in iteratively and recursively *backward* and *forward mapping processes* (i.e., from November 17–19 to Day 1, and vice versa) to capture intertextual relationships among developing events in order to situate events in the history of the teacher and the class as a languaculture-in-the-making.

As (re)presented in Figure 3.2, to understand what Maya had missed by entering one month late into this community of artists, Baker (re)constructed how, on the first day of the class, the teacher introduced students to, and foregrounded future events, in which they would engage in learning how to work as studio artists. As indicated in the columns on *running record of phases* and *running record of events,* the teacher presented excerpts from letters written by former students to capture challenges current students would face as they sought to become studio artists. In this way, she introduced students new to this class to a community they were joining beyond the class and the Visual Arts Program.

In the following example, we focus on two sets of excerpts from the transcript of the teacher's reading from M's letter.

> The first surprising [instructional] technique that has become second nature to me is that [the teacher] gives us an introductory assignment before we receive any information regarding the overall topic matter. She does this so that we can ask the questions we'll have before she ever starts to confuse us with ideas we know nothing about. This way, we always start out knowing what we know and not knowing what we don't know.
>
> *(Sept. 2, Transcript of Class Meeting, Lines 757–768)*

LIFE HISTORY OF CLASS: TIMELINE OF INTERGENERATIONAL STUDIO ART CLASS (1997-2000)

Teacher – 29 years of teaching	1996-1997 (5% of students enter)	1997-1998 (12% of students enter)	1998-1999 (35% of students enter)	1999-2000 (53% of students enter)

ENTERING THE FIELD: TIMELINE OF THE ETHNOGRAPHY 1998-2000

Academic Year One (1998-1999)	Academic Year Two (1999-2000)

Event Map of First Day of Class

9/2 FIRST DAY OF SCHOOL: INITIATING CYCLES

Clock Time (Videotape time)	Running Record of Phases (phase numbers on left)	Running Record of Events (Line numbers) — Academic Year Two (1999-2000)
9:09-9:18 (00:00:01-00:10:01)	1. T preparing (talks to researcher) 2. T explaining letters from past students to present students	1. T preparing before students arrive (1-79)
9:18-9:22 (00:10:02-00:13:56)	1. T talking about class preparation 2. T instructing students to pick up two index cards and select a workbench	2. Students arriving, T greeting students at door (80-134)
9:22-9:30 (00:13:57-00:21:04)	1. Students writing two questions, etc. 2. T giving each student an envelope 3. Students passing back index cards	3. T taking roll and initiating "index card activity" (134-235)
9:30-9:44) (00:22:32-00:36:14)	1. *T presenting overview day and program 2. Introducing Disney video 3. Playing Disney video 4. Explaining links with video [Initiates cycles of friendly sharing: "tomorrow I'll have a short activity that's kind of a creative activity" (lines 332-334) (occurs on 9/3)]	4. T welcoming, presenting agenda and introducing self and program (236-686)
6 min. (00:28:28-00:34:28)		4a. Disney video (442-621
9:44-9:55 (00:36:15-00:47:24)	1. T reading letters from: D, M, A, C 2. T explaining connections 3. Handout; quoting Z. Hurston	5. T reading and commenting on excerpts from letters of past students (687-1063)
9:55-10:00 (00:47:26-53:01)	1. T assigning letter of intent 2. "Student agendas"	6. T assigning: Read letter from past student and write letter of intent (1064-1243)
10:00-10:09 (00:53:03-01:01:40)	1. T introducing sketchbooks 2. Notebooks: connection to AP and areas of concentration 3. Folders: Value of handouts 4. Fee: Cost of some of the materials	7. T presenting four needs for class (1234-1568)
10:09-10:15 (01:02:04-01:08:18)	1. Mini-chalk festival with kids 2. Visit from superintendent 3. Presentations from students who attended art summer school 4. "Film Festival"; 5. "Breakfast Club"; 6. "Fashion Show"	8. T discussing "highlights" of upcoming year (1569-1792)

HISTORY OF CYCLES OF CRITIQUE

Framing class James enters 9/2	Friendly Sharing 9/10, 9/13	Gentle Critique 9/22-24	Maya enters 10/11	Deep Critique 11/16-19

FIGURE 3.2 Timelines Leading to Cycles of Activity of Public Critique (Modified from Green, Baker et al., 2020)

In bringing M's language about what the teacher's approach enabled her to learn, the teacher makes present to current students how instructional techniques (M's language) of the teacher may be unanticipated processes and opportunities for learning what M (and others) did and did not know that would become part of their lives as artists in a community of artists and the class as a languaculture-in-the-making.

The final excerpt from M's letter provides further insights into the challenges that students would face and how M learned from these challenges to overcome "blocks in progress" over the course of her time in the program:

> I've always had artistic tendencies but [the teacher] has developed them in me. She helped me realize how to integrate art and an open mind into everything I do. The impossible is now always possible and I have learned how to accept confidence in myself and live through it. I've actually come to appreciate blocks in my progress [and] learned to learn from them.
>
> *(Sept. 2, Transcript from Class Meeting, Lines 847–857)*

By sharing letters from previous students, the teacher made possible for students in the current class to recognize how they would develop their own journeys to understanding what is involved in developing a "creative life" within and across the academic year and beyond.

On What Was Learned About Baker's Logic-in-Use about IE as a Logic-of-Inquiry and Analyses

In this section, we made visible dynamic and developing processes of inquiry that constituted Baker's logic-in-use that led to the (re)analyses from the archive of video records and related documents. By tracing roots of the opportunities that Maya missed but James had access to, Baker created a basis for warranting each level of analysis. By bringing forward the actual texts of the discourse indicated in Figure 3.2 on the first day, Baker provided deeper understandings of what was gained by James by entering on the first day and what was missed by Maya. Thus, each level of analysis (re)presented in Figure 3.2 provided warranted accounts of the sources of the differences Baker and colleagues reported in the contrastive analyses of Maya's and James' performances (Table 3.2).

In tracing the histories and making transparent the actual text of reported activities, Baker made present how and why levels of analyses are critical within an IE guided study to construct *evidence* of the sources of difference he identified through his process of triangulation. In this section, therefore, we have grounded the (re)construction of Baker's logic of analysis to make transparent what decisions and actions were critical for understanding Baker's processes of analyses. This section also shows how actual text (not coding) can provide a more grounded source of evidence for interpretations of what is being interactionally accomplished by participants in particular times, events and cycles of activity.

An Ending and a Beginning: Retheorizing Learning in Developing Educational Spaces

We conclude this chapter by presenting three additional explanatory theories that frame theoretical insights guiding the warrants for what Baker learned through his layers of analyses, (re)presented in Figure 3.2, and analyses presented in earlier sections of this chapter. First, in their seminal volume on micro-ethnography and discourse analysis, Bloome et al. (2005) demonstrated how in moment-by-moment and over time interactions, identity positions, power relationships, and literacy processes and events are being interactionally accomplished that are socially and academically significant in a particular community of learning.

By drawing on Bloome et al.'s arguments, Baker created a basis for readers to understand how undertaking multiple levels and angles of analyses of the developing languaculture-in-the-making were central to address his guiding question:

> What do students need to know and learn how to do in order to achieve goals set for them in a particular educational context.

By unfolding and theorizing what was possible for him to learn from the telling cases he created in each analysis, Baker made transparent his logic-in-use that led to warranted accounts of what was socially, culturally, linguistically, and academically relevant and significant for students to learn in becoming studio artists, as well as for Baker in taking the role of ethnographer-as-learner in this community of studio artists.

Second, by tracing Maya and James across events in the class and situating their histories in the layers of, and from, the first day, we make visible how Baker grounded his interpretations in the work of John Gumperz (1982) on discourse processes from interactional sociolinguistics. In his work on conversational inferences, Gumperz identified how people bring *linguistic, cultural, and social presuppositions* about what is relevant to say, share, and/or do from prior contexts to contexts in which they seek to accomplish particular goals and/or to participate, whether in a class or in other social spaces.

This conceptual argument provided theoretical understandings about the sources of frame clashes that Baker experienced as he became aware of what he learned, or was not understanding, when observing the moment-by-moment interactions in real time. In unfolding the iterative, recursive and abductive processes he undertook to explore the sources of influence on Maya's and James' performance differences, Baker made transparent why stepping back from what he assumed was being proposed or undertaken in particular moments in time in the class was critical. The process of stepping back, as we have shown, created a foundation for Baker to explore further *how the teacher initiated and constructed the practice of public critique with students.*

Thus, by tracing the history of both Maya's performance and the teacher's actions to support Maya, Baker demonstrated the importance of tracing the history of specific students and the event itself. Additionally, by tracing the teacher's discourse and actions from the first day and across times and events, Baker provided evidence that the teacher brings a history of the students' work to a given context, just as students bring their own history to new events.

The final theoretical argument we view as central to understanding Baker's program of research, as reflected in his personal history and in his analysis in this class, is a theoretical argument that Bakhtin (1986) proposed in his chapter on "Speech Genres".

> Sooner or later what is heard and actively understood will find its response in the subsequent speech or behavior of the listener. In most cases, genres of complex cultural communication are intended precisely for this kind of actively responsive understanding with delayed action. Everything that we have said here also pertains to written and read speech, with the appropriate adjustments and additions.
>
> *(p. 60)*

In foregrounding this argument, Bakhtin captures the dynamic and ever-developing nature of speech genres, speaker-hearer relationships, and other forms of communication. He also frames why looking, or analyzing one moment, will not provide a complete understanding of what individual learners and the collective have had opportunities to "learn" (cf. Alexander, 2015).

Final Thoughts

In this chapter, by (re)constructing Baker's decisions and actions to understand what *counts as learning* in the studio art class, we identified areas and processes IE researchers seek to (re)theorize through ongoing IE programs of research. As we have made transparent by (re)constructing Baker's logic-in-use, the researcher, like participants, *needs to undertake a series of interconnected iterative, recursive and abductive processes of reasoning and analyses.*

The examples in Baker's journey, therefore, provided a ground for understanding that *reporting on learning in particular moments in a class provides a limited picture of how learning in a developing languaculture is an ongoing-process* for the collective and individuals-within-the-collective. Thus, this argument forms a foundation for IE researchers, through iterative, recursive, and abductive *reasoning* and *analytic* processes to recognize the *need to (re)theorize learning not only of students but also of the teacher* as she/he introduces students to ways of knowing, being, and engaging in discipline-based sites for learning as well as the researcher.

Suggested Readings

Bloome, D., & Egan-Robertson, A. (Eds.), *Students as researchers of culture and language in their own communities* (pp. 115–139). Hampton Press.

Murnen, T., & Rex, L. (2007). Video records and interactional ethnography: Mapping the social construction of authorship. *Pedagogies, 2*(3), 179–190.

Nasir, N., Lee, C. D., Pea, R., & McKinney de Royston, M. (Eds.), *The handbook of the cultural foundations of education.* Routledge.

References

Agar, M. H. (1994). *Language shock: Understanding the culture of conversation.* William Morrow Paperbacks.

Agar, M. H. (1996). *The professional stranger: An informal introduction to ethnography.* Emerald.

Agar, M. (2006). Culture: Can you take it anywhere? *International Journal of Qualitative Methods.* doi: 10.1177/160940690600500201.

Alexander, R. J. (2015). Dialogic pedagogy at scale: Oblique perspectives. In L. Resnick, C. Asterhan, & S. Clarke (Eds.), *Socializing intelligence through academic talk and dialogue* (pp. 429–439). American Education Research Association.

Baker, W. D., & Green, J. (2007). Limits to certainty in interpreting video data: Interactional ethnography and disciplinary knowledge. *Pedagogies: An International Journal, 2*(3), 191–204. https://doi.org/10.1080/15544800701366613

Baker, W. D., Green, J., & Skukauskaité, A. (2008). Video-enabled ethnographic research: A microethnographic perspective. In G. Walford (Ed.), *How to do educational ethnography* (pp. 77–114). Tufnell Press.

Baker, W. D. (2001). Artists in the making: An ethnographic investigation of discourse and literate practices as disciplinary processes in a high school advanced placement studio art classroom. Unpublished doctoral dissertation. University of California-Santa Barbara.

Baker, W. D. (2007). English language arts, basketball and poetry collide. *English Journal, 96*(5), 37–41.

Baker, W. D., & Green, J. L. (2011). A microethnographic approach to exploring positioning theory as educational action. In M. B. McVee, C. H. Brock, & J. A. Glazier (Eds.), *Sociocultural positioning in literacy: Exploring culture, discourse, narrative and power in diverse educational contexts* (pp. 95–103). Hampton Press.

Bakhtin, M. M. (1986). *Speech genres and other late essays* (V. W. McGee, trans. University of Texas Press.

Birdwhistell, R. (1977). *About Bateson: Essays on Gregory Bateson.* Dutton.

Bloome, D., Carter, S. P., Christian, B. M., Otto, S., & Shuart-Faris, N. (2005). *Discourse analysis and the study of classroom language and literacy events: A microethnographic perspective.* Lawrence Erlbaum.

Bloome, D., & Egan-Robertson, A. (1993). The social construction of intertextuality in classroom reading and writing lessons. *Reading Research Quarterly, 28*(4), 305–333. https://doi.org/10.2307/747928

Fairclough, N. (1992). *Critical language awareness.* Longman.

Green, J., Baker, W. D., Chian, M., Vanderhoof, C., Hooper, L., Kelly, G., Skukauskaité, A., & Kalainoff, M. (2020). Studying the over-time construction of knowledge in educational settings: A microethnographic-discourse analysis approach. *Review of Research in Education, 44*(1), 161–194. https://doi.org/10.3102/0091732X20903121

Green, J., Brock, C., Baker, W. D., & Harris, P. (2020). Positioning theory for learning in discourse. In N. Nasir, C. Lee, R. Pea, & M. Royston (Eds.), *Reconceptualizing learning in the 21st century: The handbook of the cultural foundations of learning* (pp. 119–140). Routledge.

Green, J., & Chian, M. M. (2018). Triangulation. In B. Frey (Ed.), *The SAGE encyclopedia of educational research, measurement, and evaluation* (vol. 4, pp. 1717–1720). Sage. https://dx.doi.org/10.4135/9781506326139.n711

Green, J., Dixon, C. N., & Zaharlick, A. (2003). Ethnography as a logic of inquiry. In J. Flood, D. Lapp, & J. Squire (Eds.), *The handbook of research on teaching the English language arts* (pp. 201–224). Erlbaum.

Green, J., Skukauskaitė, A., & Baker, W.D. (2012). Ethnography as epistemology: An introduction to educational ethnography. In J. Arthur, M. I. Waring, R. Coe, & L. V. Hedges (Eds.), *Research methodologies and methods in education* (pp. 309–321). Sage.

Gumperz, J. J. (1982). *Discourse strategies.* Cambridge University Press.

Heap, J. (1985). Discourse in the production of classroom knowledge: Reading Lessons. *Curriculum Inquiry, 15*(3), 245–279. https://doi.org/10.1080/03626784.1985.110759

Heap, J. L. (1991). A situated perspective of what counts as reading. In C. D. Baker & A. Luke (Eds.), *Towards a critical sociology of reading pedagogy* (pp. 103–139). John Benjamin.

Heath, S. B., & Street, B. V. (2008). *On ethnography: Approaches to language and literacy research.* Teachers College Press.

McVee, M. B., Brock, C. H., & Glazier, J. A. (Eds.). (2011). *Sociocultural positioning in literacy: Exploring culture, discourse, narrative, and power in diverse educational contexts.* Hampton Press.

Mitchell, C. J. (1984). Typicality and the case study. In R. F. Ellen (Ed.), *Ethnographic research: A guide to general conduct* (pp. 238–241). Academic Press.

Samura, D., & Alvermann, A. (2021). *Ideas that changed literacy practices: First person accounts from leading voices.* Stylus Publishing.

Smith, L. M. (1978). An evolving logic of participant observation, educational ethnography, and other case studies. *Review of Research in Education, 6*(1), 316–377. https://doi.org/10.3102/0091732X006001316

Smith, L. M., & Geoffrey, W. (1968). *The complexities of the urban classroom.* Holt.

Street, B. V. (2005). Foreword. In D. Bloome, S. Power Carter, B. M. Christian, S. Otto, & N. Shuart-Faris (Eds.), *Discourse analysis and the study of classroom language and literacy events: A microethnographic perspective* (pp. ix–xii). Lawrence Erlbaum.

Tannen, D. (1993). *Framing in discourse.* Oxford University Press.

Walford, G. (2008). *How to do educational ethnography.* Tufnell Press.

Tuyay, S., Floriani, A., Yeager, B., Dixon, C., & Green, J. L. (1995). Constructing an integrated, inquiry-oriented approach in classrooms: A cross-case analysis of social, literate, and academic practices. *Journal of Classroom Interactions, 30*(2), 1–15.

Zaharlick, A., & Green, J. (1991). Ethnographic research. In J. Flood, J. Jensen, D. Lapp, & J. Squire (Eds.), *Handbook on teaching the English language arts* (pp. 205–225). Macmillan.

4

LANGUAGING THE SOCIAL CONSTRUCTION OF EVERYDAY LIFE IN CLASSROOMS

Huili Hong and David Bloome

People act and react to each through languaging and related semiotic processes. Once people are viewed as the context for each other (Erickson, 2004; McDermott et al., 1978), the questions to ask about them shift from questions of individualized characteristics, motivations, intentions, and cognitions to questions about how they are together, how they interactionally and socially construct who they are, what they are doing, and how what they are doing is connected to broader social and cultural processes (inclusive of the power relations constitutive of those social and cultural processes). This is no less true of classrooms than of any other social setting with the exception that classrooms are defined and designated as a social space of and for educational processes.

These educational processes are both *explicit* and *implicit, oriented to stability* and *to change, proffered by societally* and *governmentally established, empowered, and delegated groups,* as well as *sought by the people targeted for education* (e.g., children, students more generally, and their families and communities). These educational processes – which can be defined as a *"calculated intervention in learning processes"* (Spindler & Spindler, 1987, p. 3) – need to be

- recognized across multiple scales from the individual student interacting with another individual or group (e.g., a teacher or peers) to
- interactions among diverse communities, social institutions, and socioeconomic classes engaged with educational institutions.

Educational processes are neither magical nor ethereal; they are *socially, materially, and visibly constructed* with and through people acting and reacting to each other over time and across spaces.

DOI: 10.4324/9781003215479-5

This chapter draws on a *languaging perspective* (Beach & Bloome, 2019; Becker, 1988; Volosinov, 1973), which conceptualizes *language as a verb* and focuses on *how people together language meaning, social relationships, and shared ideological contexts*. From a languaging perspective, to ask of a classroom event, "What is happening here?", requires also asking a series of interrelated questions:

- How is it happening?
- What are the histories of the literacy event or languaging behavior that is happening?
- Who is involved?
- How being teacher and students is socially and discursively acted and reacted?
- What learning, knowledge, and the participants' personhoods are being constructed?
- What curriculum and hidden curriculum are being presented, constructed, and practiced in and through the teacher–student social collective languaging?

In this chapter, the notion of *hidden curriculum* calls attention to the teacher–student languaging as an integral part of classroom everyday life that is socially, historically, and politically situated and practiced daily but usually without being recognized or examined in–depth (Cornbleth, 1984; Alsubaie, 2015). For the most part, educational processes happen through languaging, classroom conversations, and other communicative processes, including *producing written work* and *other semiotic productions, across modalities* (e.g., paper and pen, digital/screens, painting, etc.).

From a philosophical perspective, the *"how* is the *what"* (Wentzer & Mattingly, 2018, p. 150); people live their lives in the doing (the interactional social constructing) rather than in the accomplishment and nominalization of the social event (e.g., accomplishing the doing of a "reading lesson"). Implied in such a philosophical perspective – *"how* is the *what"* (Wentzer & Mattingly, 2018) – are two precepts. First, people are inherently connected to each other. Such a philosophical precept has been argued from different perspectives. For example, Buber (1970), for example, has argued that there is no *"I"*, only *"I-You"*, and *"I-It"*. As Schaefer (2020) notes:

> [Buber] highlighted the way that relationships and dialogical interactions between human beings not only give meaning and purpose to our lives-they are constitutive of life itself. Human beings, Buber taught, are shaped by and through their relationships with others, without whom their lives would be meaningless, empty affairs.
>
> *(p. 6)*

From a complementary perspective, scholars such as Power-Carter et al. (2019) and Dillard (2012), among others, have taken up the African philosophy of Ubuntu (see Battle, 2009; Venter, 2004) to similarly foreground the inherent connectedness of people to each other and to the communal context. Power-Carter et al. (2019) write:

> Ubuntu emphasizes the connectedness of Black people and their experiences rather than a more individual and/or Eurocentric paradigm of knowing. Ubuntu espouses an awareness of self in relation to others (Garmon & Mgijima, 2012; Nussbaum, 2003). Dillard [2012] notes, "operationally Ubuntu suggests that each individual's full personhood is ideally expressed in relationship with others (p. 85)." Interdependence and caring for others are central to this philosophy (Venter, 2004; Battle, 2009).

The second precept is that there is no separation between people and languaging. Becker (1988) elaborates that the shift from *language to languaging* is to changing our thinking of language as a finished product to our thinking of language as an ongoing process. It moves from seeing language as something apart from time and history to something is being done, changed, and evolved continuously. As such, language is a *verb*, a set of actions that people take with each other.

These two philosophical precepts align well with interactional ethnography as described by Castanheira et al. (2000), and Skukauskaitė and Green (in press) and its foundations in theories of language and culture by Gumperz (1986, 2001), Hymes (1974), and Agar (2006). What a languaging perspective adds is a focus on what has been called the "in-between" (cf., Bertau, 2014).

In this chapter, we describe how we employ a languaging perspective in our exploration of everyday life in classrooms. Scholars have taken up a languaging perspective in the study of classroom education in diverse ways (see Beach & Bloome, 2019). Our approach incorporates an ethnographic approach involving long-term participant observation, foregrounding an emic orientation, attending to the relation of parts and wholes, and focusing on cultural and social processes. We provide an illustrative case focusing on how a first-grade teacher and her students languaged everyday life and relationships among themselves within a classroom event and between that classroom event and other social events and social contexts.

Methodological Framework/Logic of Inquiry

Given the limited space in this chapter, we only discuss a few select methodological concepts. A more detailed discussion can be found in Bloome et al. (2022) and in Beach and Bloome (2019). First, everyday life in classrooms is constituted and shaped by the teacher-student and student-student interactions, manifest through verbal, prosodic, and nonverbal contextualization cues (cf., Gumperz, 1986).

Contextualization cues are the material and "visible" means through which people are taken by interlocutors as signaling and contextualizing the evolving meanings and their explicit and implicit propositions; social significances, including social relationships and social capital, and cultural import such as cultural ideologies. With a shared understanding of the co-constructed contextualization cues, the participants can recognize and hold each other accountable for their moment-to-moment languaging action as a sequence of actions and reactions. The meanings, social significances, and cultural import socially constructed in one particular languaging action and reaction may be referenced and thematically connected to other meanings, social significances, and cultural import languaged in other social events and contexts.

Second, shaping relational-keys, teacher-student languaging is not only performed emotions, styles, and tones (Beauchemin, 2019) but is also an embodiment of the material characteristics of languaging that constitute, reflect, and refract everyday life, social realities, and ideologies in and out of classrooms (Volosinov, 1973). The participants, including the participant observers and embedded researchers, can recognize the connections between and across contexts and further build chains of meanings across interrelated social events and across evolving social relationships.

Third, rather than focus on the participants as individuals, the focus is shifted to the "in-betweenness" (Bertau, 2014) of people acting and reacting to each other in and through their languaging in interrelated social events and contexts. Researchers need to document and thickly describe (cf., Geertz, 1973) the naturally occurring languaging processes in and across particular social events. As part of the methodological process of documenting and thickly describing, researchers need to attend to what is signaled by contextualization cues. We note that the phrase "what is signaled" refers not to a person's intentions, but rather to how a set of contextualization cues, such as a performed utterance, is subsequently taken up by others. This is to claim that the meaning, social significance, and cultural import lie in the "in-betweenness" of the languaging actions and reactions (see Bloome et al., 2022, for detailed discussion). Often the meaning, social significance, and cultural import of people's languaging actions and reactions lie just below the surface of participants' consciousness. They are nonetheless jointly languaging into being a shared set of cultural norms and values, epistemologies, and social ideologies including ideologies of personhood. As such, a significant contribution of discourse analysis of languaging everyday life in classrooms is addressing issues about how personhood is defined within and across educational events, institutions, and communities, as well as how personhood may be re-defined. Personhood is defined as a generally held understanding of what a person is, what is inherent in being a person, what characteristics and qualities a person possesses, and what rights and responsibilities are considered to be part of being a person (Bloome et al., 2022).

The illustrative case below from a first-grade classroom provides an illustration of how languaging indexes multiple scales of literacy events, hidden curriculum, spatial and temporal frames, social contexts, relationships, personhood, and ideologies. Following Heath (1980), we define a literacy event as a social event "in which a piece of writing is integral to the nature of the participants' interactions and their interpretive processes" (p. 3). As we will show later, this particular literacy event is connected to other classroom events past and future, to social events outside the classroom both near and distant in time and space, and well as to broader social, cultural, economic, and political contexts. These connections are not given but are socially constructed and materially realized through the teacher-student languaging. Our microethnographic discourse analysis of this literacy event illustrates how the teacher and students language relationships between one particular classroom event to other social events and social contexts. The illustrative case below also highlights how the dialectic relationships between theoretical frames and actual engagement in research and analysis may yield potential re-conceptions of essential education constructs such as learning, teaching, instruction, curriculum, literacy, time, and personhood.

Illustrative Case

Research Context and Participants

Our research site is a first-grade classroom in Greenwood Elementary School (all names pseudonym) which serves K-6 students in a low-income area in the US. Ms. Sterling was the teacher. There were twenty students in her class. At the time of the research, Ms. Sterling had almost 20 years of teaching experience. She usually starts the school day with a circle time for the students to share their experiences in or outside of school. This morning routine often integrates some math and science learning through talking about the weather, environment and temperature changes, and the numbers related to their schooling days. Their morning learning focuses on phonics, reading, and writing, with a lunch break in between. In the afternoon, one hour is set up for math and another for special arts. Prior to the end of the school day, the students have recess before their dismissal.

During the yearlong data collection, one of the researchers (Hong) made two to three visits to Ms. Sterling's class each week and spent the whole morning observing the classes as a participant observer. During school visits, the researcher had many chances to work with the children at the teacher's or the children's requests. To capture the teacher-child social and discursive construction of their everyday life in classroom, the naturally occurring classroom interactions during reading and writing workshops were audio and video recorded. One of the researchers wrote fieldnotes and collected children's artifacts and classroom documents during the course of the yearlong research project. She kept data analytic and reflection memos during the data collection and analysis processes.

Ethnographic Data

Data selected for this chapter were drawn from a 140-minute research visit made in the spring semester. It was also the spring after Barak Obama was re-elected and inaugurated as the U.S president. The classroom literacy event on which we focus below occurred on a Tuesday morning. The day started with the teacher's checking of the students' homework. Based on their established routine, they proceeded with their morning circle time (usually about 5 to 10 minutes) to greet each other and share their feelings. Then, the teacher led the students go through their school calendar. The teacher asked the students to count the numbers (by ones, twos, fives, tens, hundreds) and dates. After that, the teacher did a read-aloud of *Duck for President* written by Cronin (2012), an American author known by her click clack book series for young readers. This first-grade class has previously read other books from this series.

The read-aloud was followed by their routine "Daily 5", five learning stations set for small group learning: (1) read to self, (2) read to someone, (3) work on writing, (4) listen to reading, and (5) word work. During their daily-five choice times, the teacher worked with a small-guided reading group. Guided reading is a type of small-group instruction. The students read the whole or part of a teacher-selected text at their instructional reading level. The teacher provides explicit teaching and support for reading increasingly difficult texts. During the students' reading, the teacher monitors the students' reading behavior, fluency, comprehension, and responds to their strengths and needs.

After the 30-minute daily five, the students watched a movie clip about the "President" on Brain Pop Junior, an American animated educational site for young children. The video clip presented how the US became a country and then addressed a few key questions in child-friendly language:

> Why do we have a president?
> What is the president's job?
> Who can become president?

After that, the teacher and the students created a chart on the whiteboard to map out all the facts they heard from the video.

The selected transcript below is from this part of the reading block. Later, the teacher led the students to review their concept map (also called fact or anchor map by the teacher at different times) and to read another book together before the students began independent writing. For the writing task, the teacher gave the students the prompt, "What would you do if you were a president?" The teacher expected students to draw on their concept map and write down one statement, three facts about the president, one wrap-up sentence, and add illustrations.

Data Analysis

Below, we take a close look at a few minutes of classroom life during the class discussion of the Brain Pop Junior video. Because we had conducted the broader yearlong ethnographic study and had extensive records, we are able to analyze the languaging in these few minutes of classroom life embedded in multiple social and cultural contexts at multiple scales. Our data analysis starts with transcribing the audio clip into a transcript with the purpose of showing the turn-taking in the teacher-student discussion about the video they had just seen. The transcript is parsed into message units, defined as "the minimal unit of conversational meaning" (Green & Wallat, 1979, p. 164). The boundaries of message units are recognized by contextualization cues (prosodic and nonverbal cues; cf., Gumperz, 1986). The transcript is then further divided into interactional units which Green and Wallat (1981) define as an interactionally coherent set of message units also recognized through contextualization cues.

Once we parsed the transcript in message units and interactional units, we could analyze it on a moment-by-moment basis, focusing on how people (such as the teacher and students) act and react to each other and in so doing language meaning, social significance, and cultural import into being. For example, consider the interactional unit 1 below. (Please refer to the appendix for the keys to the symbols used in our transcripts.)

101 Teacher: Sunny, what FACT did you hear?
102 Sunny: They live in the White House↑.
103 Teacher: Okay.
104 Teacher: Presidents↑ live in the WHITE HOUSE.

The teacher names Sunny as the student who is responsible for answering her question (line 101). Sunny is responsible individually. Based on interactional patterns from other classroom events, *if* another student had taken Sunny's turn-at-talk, it is reasonable to assume that the teacher would have intervened, stopped the take-over, and returned the turn-at-talk to Sunny. While such an action may seem minor, given that the data collected across events in this classroom over the yearlong study shows a recurrent pattern, we can ask what cultural import this pattern of languaging has. What cultural ideologies are being reflected and constituted? And, *if* data from studies of other classrooms reveals pervasive recurrence of this pattern of languaging, questions could also be asked about the cultural import of this pattern of languaging in schooling as a social institution within the community or nation studied.

Notice that by responding, Sunny validates the teacher's initiation. That is, one cannot assume that merely because the teacher initiates the interaction that her message unit is taken up the way the teacher intended or the way that might seem given by the utterance itself. Rather, what needs to be examined is how the people there (in this case, Sunny and the other students) take up and respond to the teacher's utterance. Following Green and Wallat (1981) and Bloome et al. (2022), such an analysis can be called a *post hoc* analysis since the meaning, social significance, and cultural import is not in what a speaker intended but rather is in how interlocutors take up a message unit or other communicative actions. It is in this sense that the students' responses are the primary focus for our analysis.

In Sunny's response (line 102), Sunny gives one "fact" from the video clip they have just heard. It does not matter if what Sunny says is actually a fact. It is publicly and interactionally languaged as a fact because the teacher validates it as a fact with "Okay" (line 103) and then restates the "fact" (line 104). Although one must be careful not to overstate the impact of any one interactional unit, the interaction of Sunny and the teacher regarding a "fact" raises questions about how a definition of "fact" is being languaged and more broadly how an epistemology is being languaged into being.

The interaction between the teacher and Sunny may seem to be "natural" and perhaps unremarkable. Nonetheless, what is happening – what is being languaged into being – needs to be analyzed and unpacked. Often cultural processes, power relations, social relationships, and relational-keys operate just below the level of overt consciousness. It is because they are nearly "invisible" that they may be powerful. For example, consider the pattern of interaction in Interactional Unit 1 above. That pattern is known as an Initiation-Response-Feedback (I-R-F, see Sinclair & Coulthard, 1975, for an extensive discussion of this interaction pattern) or Initiation-Response-Evaluation (I-R-E, see Mehan, 1979, for an extensive discussion of this pattern).

In such IRF/E languaging, the teacher determines the topic, and makes the student (or students) responsible for responding within a particular category of responses. That is, Sunny's response is taken as derived from the video; otherwise, a problem would have been noted and the teacher, Sunny, and other students would have engaged in repairing apparently different communicative frames. After Sunny responds, the teacher has the authority for validating knowledge. Both Sunny and the other students may be held accountable for being able to produce that validated knowledge. Such an interactional pattern, an I-R-F/E pattern, is associated with schooling. It would be strange to engage in such an interactional pattern outside of schooling. Therefore, engaging an I-R-F/E pattern of acting and reacting indexes schooling and the various cultural ideologies accompanying schooling.

The teacher continues the instructional conversation by asking the students, "What else did we hear about presidents?" One student responds by telling the teacher that presidents have to be 35 years old. The teacher expands on the requirements for being president and then asks a series of questions addressed to the class as a whole rather than to just one student as occurred in line 101 above.

Interactional Unit 2

117 Teacher: CA:N a president just be a MAN? ↑
118 Students: NO
119 Teacher: No↑
120 Teacher: = >It can be a man or a woman<.

Interactional Unit 3

121 Teacher: Do they have to have a certain skin color? ↑
122 Students: NO
123 Teacher: =NO.
124 Teacher: Okay.

Interactional units 2 and 3 follow the I-R-F/E interactional pattern and, as such, also index schooling. The teacher's initiations – the questions in line 117 and 121 – were not directly derived from the video or the read-aloud text. Based on yearlong participation in the classroom and informal chatting with the teacher, we understand these questions index two social-political events. The first one was Hilary Clinton running for president as a candidate in Democratic presidential primaries. The other is Barack Obama's election as the first African American President. Broadly speaking, interactional units 2 and 3 are consistent with the general topic of the American presidency. However, analysis of the languaging, considered within the context of the broader ethnographic study, suggests that more is happening here.

Looking only at the propositional meaning (cf., Frederiksen, 1975) in lines 177, 120, and 121, the content would appear to be about whether the presidency is limited to people of a particular race and gender. At the time, these topics were broadly discussed in the popular media. Yet, it is unclear what is happening in interactional units 2 and 3 and whether the propositional meaning is taken-up by the students in more than a superficial and perfunctory manner.

The prosody and syntax of the questions in lines 117 and 121 might be taken up by the students as suggesting a particular response "No" regardless of the propositional content. What we mean by "being taken up" here is the students' social and discursive reactions based on their interpretation of the teacher's languaging actions. It could be that the students are, indeed, responding to the propositional content; it could be that they have only a limited, superficial, understanding of the propositional content. Or, it could be that they are responding to the prosodic and syntactic contextualization cues and co-constructing the doing of and the getting through a lesson with the teacher (a procedural display, cf., Bloome et al., 1989). In interactional units 2 and 3, there is no evidence to warrant one of those interpretations over the others.

Further, there is no evidence in subsequent events in that classroom or in interviews with the teacher that would warrant a particular interpretation over the other. What we can say about what happened in those two interactional units is

a. that the teacher and students successfully engaged each other in an interaction that can count as doing a classroom lesson, engaging in a procedural display,
b. that the teacher validated knowledge that a particular race and gender are not requirements for being a president, and
c. that the class made visible a shared accountability for how to respond to questions about race, gender, and the presidency based on the textual evidence in their chosen reading texts and video.

Might individual students have had different thoughts about the meaning, social significance, and cultural import of the questions in lines 117 and 121 and about the class's response?

From the perspective of microethnographic discourse analysis, such a question is a non-sequitur. A more appropriate question would be, "What public response(s) did one or more of the students make to the teacher questions?" followed by, "What do those responses warrant as an evidence-based interpretation of what is happening in that social event at that moment?" followed by, "What were the responses to the responses to the teacher's questions and what do those responses warrant as an evidence-based interpretation of what is happening in that social event at that moment?"

A few moments later, the teacher begins another interactional unit with, "Another very very big thing" (line 130).

Interactional Units (IU) 4, 5, 6 and 7

IU4

130 Teacher: Another very very big↑ THING ↓
131 Teacher: >Cou:ld I walk into the White House and say HEY I am here?<
132 Teacher: =I would like to be °president°.
133 StudentS: =No

IU5

134 Teacher: =What has to happen?
135 Student: Run XXX (inaudible)

IU6

136 Teacher: What do people have to DO? ↑
(Inaudible students' responses)
137. Student: °Maybe give money or something like that? ° ↑
138. Students: =NO

IU7

139 Teacher: So, >if I go, if I go to the White House and say here's a
    20-dollar
bill.<
140 Teacher: =Can I be president today? ↑
141 Teacher: =>Would that work? ↑<
142 Students: Nope

To this point in the lesson, the students have been responding to the teacher's questions and statements with strong voices and a prosody suggestive of engagement and enthusiasm. We take the way in which the teacher rendered "very very big thing" (line 130) as a response to the tone of the classroom conversation so far. "Very" is heavily emphasized both times and all in a way that is exaggerated and might be characterized as a bit mocking.

The teacher follows line 130 by accentuating the vowel in "Could" and she stylizes "I am here" with an accentuated colloquial word "HEY". The students respond with "No" but rendered with an elongated vowel and accompanying prosody we take as evidence that they have taken up the teacher's utterances at that moment as playfulness. That is, the teacher and students together have socially constructed playfulness where before – although the instructional conversation was pleasant, included active and enthusiastic engagement by the students – it was not interactionally constructed as playfulness.

In interactional unit 4, the teacher and students are not only languaging a tone for the classroom event and for their being together, they are also languaging a relational-key (cf., Beauchemin, 2019). Beauchemin defines a relational-key as:

> Language action that people make towards and with one another to constitute the evolving, momentary state of relationships among them. Drawing from the field of music, relational key can be likened to how

a particular song or string of notes creates a mood or atmosphere in a room to constitute the construction of relationships between people.

(p. 199)

A relational-key is languaged into being by the teacher and students in interaction with each other. The relational-key here is not just the "footing" (cf., Goffman, 1979) or framing of the social relationships of the teacher and the students but also of the social event (or the part of the social event) in which they are participating. That is, it is not just that the teacher and students are being playful in lines 130 to 133 but that relational-key also redefines the I-R-F/E sequence they are enacting. What would appear on the surface to be an I-R-F/E sequence is perhaps better described as the teacher and students play-acting an I-R-F/E sequence.

This playful relational-key requires the teacher and the students to acknowledge each other as already knowing the "script" for what they are play-acting. There are, in interactional unit 4, at least two "scripts". The first is the script of a classroom I-R-F/E sequence; the second is the script of a person walking into the White House and saying, "I am here". Of this, we can ask, what cultural capital and what cultural import must be indexed by the teacher and the students to make it possible for the teacher and students to language this footing of playfulness, these scripts, this relational-key?

The prosody of Ms. Sterling's utterance in line 132 is different from that of lines 130 and 131 (her earlier utterances), and the response of one of the students, "Run", is rendered in a prosody similar to previous I-R-F/E sequences rather than the playful prosody of line 133. As such, the student's response on line 135 validates a shift in the relational-key, perhaps reconstructing the relational-key of I-R-F/E sequences earlier in the lesson.

After interactional unit 5, the teacher appears to initiate another I-R-F/E sequence by asking, "What has to happen?" There are many inaudible responses from the students. One of them responds with audible uncertain: "Maybe give money or something like that?" This response is not derived from their video or reading texts but intertextualizes what the students know about presidential campaigning. Meanwhile, his response is quickly rejected by his peers by a quick and loud "NO".

We do not know whether his peers know the presidential protocol or not. However, the peers apparently deny this answer because it is not from what they read or watched or from what the teacher said. This languaging process indexes a relational-key and identity issue about who is the authority of information or what counts as the reliable facts. Of course, had we had a video recording and were able to examine the nonverbal actions of the students and the teacher, we might be better able to warrant with evidence an interpretation of what happened in response to line 136.

Regardless, the teacher does not further respond to any of the students but follows line 136 by saying, (line 139-140) "So if I go to the White House and say here's a 20-dollar bill | Can I be president today?" The prosody of these message units is similar to that of lines 130 to 133, in which the teacher and students languaged a relational-key of playfulness. And the response of a student to the teacher's question, "Would that work?" (line 141) publicly validates a relational-key of playfulness. They are, again, together enacting multiple scripts.

A few moments later in this instructional conversation, the teacher and students are working together to construct what they called a "fact/anchor map" (similar to a conceptual web). As they begin to do so and the teacher asks the students, "What do we put there?" (in the anchor map), the following interaction occurs.

Interactional Unit 8

150 Teacher: So, presidents, uhm…
151 Teacher: What do we put there?
152 Teacher: Okay, presidents (starting to write on their anchor map).
153 Student: President Obama won
154 Teacher: >He won the race<
155 Teacher: =That is why he is the president.

As the teacher was starting to write facts on the anchor map (line 151 – "What do we put there?"), a student, without being designated a turn by the teacher – says aloud "President Obama won" (line 150). The student's response intertextualized what happened in real life and what they have been reading and writing about that week, namely the presidency. The teacher validated his answer – and the intertextual connection the student made. However, the teacher adds that President Obama "won the race | That is why he is president" (line 154 and 155). The teacher's addition connects their current discussion (what to include in the anchor map), the texts from outside the classroom about the election of Barak Obama, and the text of the book they had been reading and the video they had watched.

It is unclear whether all of these intertextual connections are recognized by the students or, if they are recognized, or whether the intertextual connections have any meaning, social significance or cultural import. Had there been continued discussion of these intertextual connections there might, perhaps, be evidence that might warrant an interpretation about the uptake of these proposed intertextual connections. What we do know is that intertextual connections are socially constructed in and through instructional conversations. From the languaging perspective we take here, this is a key issue since the set of interactionally validated intertextual connections constitutes a shared "universe" of texts that are appropriate to juxtapose and, in such juxtapositions, to socially construct shared meanings, social relationships, and cultural ideologies.

From Data Analysis and Findings to Grounded Theoretical Hypotheses and Grounded Theoretical Constructs

In the previous section, we illustrated a microethnographic discourse analysis of only a few minutes in one classroom. If we were presenting an empirical study exploring and perhaps re-conceptualizing essential educational concepts, we would have analyzed a larger number of events across classrooms (and perhaps across diverse social spaces in and out of schools) selected in a systematic way (for further discussion see Baker, Machtmes, & Green in this volume, Bloome et al., 2022; Erickson, 2004; Markee, 2015; McDermott et al., 1978)

Please note that the analysis is not designed to provide a summative evaluation of the teacher's intention, teaching approach, or effectiveness (at least, as evaluation is typically defined). Instead, we focus on what is happening and what it means to the students there and in the moment and how "what it means" is taken up by the students in various learning tasks and different social events and contexts. The languaging approach we have taken, the ethnographic perspective, and the time commitment in participant observation in this classroom provide an emic participant perspective. The ethnographic design of the overall study enables us to describe and infer what is happening, what meanings, social significances, and cultural import are being socially constructed by the teacher-student languaging behaviors.

Conclusion

In this chapter, we drew on a yearlong ethnographic study in a first-grade classroom and explore the social and discursive construction of the everyday life in the classroom through a languaging perspective. We focused on a small bit of one classroom event in order to illustrate what a languaging approach, embedded in a larger ethnographic study, would have to offer the study of classroom life. Necessarily, given the limited space in this chapter, the discussion has been brief. We have provided references for further exploration.

In this chapter, we have shown *how*, as people act and react to each other through languaging and related semiotic processes, they *socially constructed structures* for their interactions with each other and for their *interactions with social institutions* such as schooling. The IRE/F teacher-student interaction pattern was one such structure. Such structures are not given but socially constructed; the power of these structures is in how they are taken up by teachers and students as they *construct knowledge, social relationships, relation-al-keys,* and *cultural ideologies,* all of which both reflect and refract what has gone before and what will come later as well as the social and material contexts in which they are required to enact daily life together (cf., Bakhtin, 1981; Volosinov, 1973).

The discussion above also highlighted how the teacher and students languaged *power relations, what constitutes knowledge* and *knowing, personhood,* and *social, cultural, and political ideologies* at multiple levels (including person-to-person, institutional, and societal). In discussing the presidency, issues of race and gender were raised. Yet, it is unclear how those issues were taken up by students.

As a whole, the students responded appropriately and moved the classroom lesson forward. The complex and difficult issues of personhood and history of the students and the teacher were left incomplete and without subsequent social construction. Let us be clear; this is not a criticism of the teacher – leaving it so may have been appropriate. What is at issue here is recognizing that part of the *hidden curriculum of classroom education* is the languaging of shared definitions of personhood.

Explicitly, the teacher-student interaction in the selected event centered on *what counts as* facts, knowledge, and knowing. Their interaction makes clear how facts are defined, selected and taken up in their teaching and learning and reflected in their social, cultural, and political ideologies at different levels. Their languaging process also foregrounds a kind of *cultural import of collectivism rather than individualism,* and *text-based evidence instead of real-life experiences,* evidenced in how they collectively constructed a shared fact map by only drawing from their class's anchor texts. Furthermore, their discussion intertextualizes the relevant classroom events and social political events (presidential election, the presidential candidates' qualification, age, residency, gender, color, voting, election results and consequences, a president's job, cabinets, budget, etc.). This is evidence of another aspect of the hidden curriculum of classroom life; *the languaging what texts can be connected to what other texts in what situations, how, and by whom* (what Bloome & Egan-Robertson, 1993, call intertextual substance, process, and rights).

In sum, a languaging perspective on the social construction of classroom life

1. provides researchers with a way to make arguments about what is happening, warranted by the material and empirical evidence of social interaction among teachers and students, and
2. enables researchers to generate grounded theoretical constructs about the social construction of meaning, social relationships, and cultural import as well as reconceptualizations of fundamental educational constructs including curriculum, teaching, and learning.

Select Principles of Practice to Guide a Languaging Approach to Discourse Analysis and Ethnographic Research in Classroom Settings

In presenting the following principles, we connect them to the theoretical arguments that guide the researcher's practice.

1. Even if the phrase "everyday life" is ambiguous, focusing on ordinary people's daily lives and activities indicates a combined interactional ethnographic, languaging, political, and philosophical perspective.

   This principle is designed to assert, justify, and demonstrate the significance of the uniqueness of people's lives, being the beings, and being-togetherness as they face the historical times in which they find themselves through their languaging.

2. A languaging perspective applied to discourse analysis and ethnographic research incorporates both "micro" and "macro" viewpoints, looking at local events (micro) and wider social contexts (macro).

   This principle is grounded in an understanding that people are constantly languaging the social event they are in and social relationships among the participants, as well as responding to past (and anticipated) events, various social institutions, and broader social, cultural, and political ideologies, whenever they act and react to each other.

3. A languaging perspective applied to discourse analysis and ethnographic research needs to be adapted to the particular circumstances, contexts, and situations of the educational setting of a targeted social event or set of social events.

   This principle is grounded in an understanding of the situated nature of discourses. Our languaging is a social collective behavior and process that shape and constitute social relationships, contexts, and realities.

4. From a languaging perspective applied to discourse analysis and ethnographic research, there can be multiple valid analyses of a segment of classroom life.

   This principle does not mean that any analysis is valid. Each analysis needs to be warranted by material evidence as the languaging process is materially realized (primarily through the contextualization cues).

Suggested Readings

Alsubaie, M. A. (2015). Hidden curriculum as one of current issue of curriculum. *Journal of Education and Practice*, 6(33), 125–128.

Beach, R., & Bloome, D. (Eds.) (2019). *Languaging relations for transforming the literacy and language arts classroom*. Routledge.

Beauchemin, F. (2021). Literacy practices as social: Relational-keys in literacy events. *English Teaching: Practice & Critique, 20*(3), 328–340.

Hammersley, M., & Atkinson, P. (2019). *Ethnography: Principles in practice* (4th ed.). Routledge.

Madsen, L. M., Karrebæk, M. S., & Møller, J. S. (2016). *Everyday languaging.* De Gruyter.

References

Agar, M. H. (2006). Culture: Can you take it anywhere? *International Journal of Qualitative Methods, 5*(2), 1–12.

Bakhtin, M. (1981). *The dialogic imagination.* University of Texas Press.

Battle, M. (2009). *Ubuntu: I in you and you in me.* Church Publishing, Inc.

Beach, R., & Bloome, D. (Eds.). (2019). *Languaging relations for transforming the literacy and language arts classroom.* Routledge.

Beauchemin, F. (2019). Reconceptualizing classroom life as relational-key. In R. Beach & D. Bloome (Eds.), *Languaging relations for transforming the literacy and language arts classroom* (pp. 23–48). Routledge.

Becker, A. L. (1988). Language in particular: A lecture. In D. Tannen (Ed.), *Linguistics in context: Connecting observation and understanding* (pp. 17–35). Albex.

Bertau, M.-C. (2014). Introduction: The self within the space–time of language performance. *Theory & Psychology, 24*(4), 433–441.

Bloome, D., Carter, S. P., Christian, B. M., Madrid, S., Otto, S., Shuart-Faris, N., & Smith, M. (2008). *On discourse analysis in classrooms: Approaches to language and literacy research.* Teachers College Press.

Bloome, D., & Egan-Robertson, A. (1993). The social construction of intertextuality and classroom reading and writing. *Reading Research Quarterly, 28*(4), 303–333.

Bloome, D., Power-Carter, S., Baker, W. D., Castanheira, M., Kim, M., & Rowe, L. (2022). *Discourse analysis of languaging and literacy events in educational settings: A micro-ethnographic perspective.* Routledge.

Bloome, D., Puro, P., & Theodorou, E. (1989). Procedural display and classroom lessons. *Curriculum Inquiry, 19*(3), 265–291.

Buber, M. (1970). *I and thou.* (W. Kaufman, trans.). Touchstone.

Castanheira, M. L., Crawford, T., Dixon, C. N., & Green, J. L. (2000). Interactional ethnography: An approach to studying the social construction of literate practices. *Linguistics and Education, 11*(4), 353–400.

Cook-Gumperz, J. (2006). *The social construction of literacy* (2nd ed.). Cambridge University Press.

Cornbleth, C. (1984). Beyond hidden curriculum? *Journal of Curriculum Studies, 16*(1), 29–36.

Cronin, D. (2012). *Duck for president.* Simon and Schuster.

Dillard, C. B. (2012). Learning to (re)member the things we've learned to forget: Endarkened feminisms, spirituality, and the sacred nature of research and teaching. *Black studies and critical thinking, 18.* Peter Lang.

Erickson, F. (2004). *Talk and social theory: Ecologies of speaking and listening in everyday life.* Polity.

Frederiksen, C. H. (1975). Representing logical and semantic structure of knowledge acquired from discourse. *Cognitive Psychology, 7*(3), 371–458.

Garmon, C. W., & Mgijima, M. (2012). Using Ubuntu: A new research trend for developing effective communication across cultural barriers. Communication Faculty Publication, Western Kentucky University. Paper 1. Retrieved from http://digitalcommons.wku.edu/comm_fac_pub/1

Geertz, C. (1973). *The interpretation of cultures: Selected essays.* Basic Books.

Goffman, E. (1979). Footing. *Semiotica, 25*(1–2), 1–29.

Green, J., & Wallat, C. (1979). What is an instructional context? An exploratory analysis of conversational shifts across time. In O. Garnica & M. King (Eds.), *Language, children and society* (pp. 159–188). Pergamon Press.

Green, J., & Wallat, C. (1981). Mapping instructional conversations – a sociolinguistic ethnography. In J. Green, & C. Wallat (Eds.), *Ethnography and language in educational settings* (pp. 161–207). Ablex.

Gumperz, J. J. (1986). *Discourse strategies.* Cambridge University Press.

Gumperz, J. J. (2001). International sociolinguistics: A personal perspective. In D. Schiffrin, D. Tannen, & H. E. Hamilton (Eds.), *The handbook of discourse analysis* (pp. 215–228). Blackwell Publishers.

Heath, S. (1980). The functions and uses of literacy. *Journal of Communication, 30*(1), 123–133.

Hymes, D. (1974). *The foundations of sociolinguistics: Sociolinguistic ethnography.* University of Pennsylvania Press.

Markee, N. (Ed.) (2015). *The handbook of classroom discourse and interaction.* Wiley Blackwell.

McDermott, R. P., Gospodinoff, K., & Aron, J. (1978). Criteria for an ethnographically adequate description of concerted activities and their contexts. *Semiotica, 24*(3–4), 246–275.

Mehan, H. (1979). *Learning lessons: Social organization in the classroom.* Harvard University Press.

Nussbaum, B. (2003). African Culture and Ubuntu. *Perspectives, 17*(1), 1–12.

Power-Carter, S., Zakeri, B., & Kumasi, K. (2019). Theorizing and languaging blackness: Using the African philosophy of Ubuntu and the concept of Sawubona. In R. Beach & D. Bloome (Eds.), *Languaging relations for transforming the literacy and language arts classroom* (pp. 195–215). Routledge.

Schaefer, Y. (2020). A life of dialogue. *Jewish Review of Books,* Winter, 1–8. Found at https://jewishreviewofbooks.com/articles/6097/a-life-of-dialogue/ on 4/20/2020.

Skukauskaitė, A., & Green, J. (in press). Ethnographic spaces and possibilities: Interactional ethnography and focus. In A. Skukauskaitė & J. Green. *Interactional ethnography: Designing and conducting discourse-based ethnographic research.* London: Routledge.

Sinclair, J. M., & Coulthard, M. (1975). *Towards an analysis of discourse: The English used by teachers and pupils.* Oxford University Press.

Spindler, G., & Spindler, L. (1987). Issues and applications in ethnographic methods. In G. Spindler & L. Spindler (Eds.), *Interpretive ethnography of education* (pp. 1–7). Lawrence Erlbaum Assoc.

Venter, E. (2004). The notion of Ubuntu and communalism in African educational discourse. *Studies in Philosophy and Education, 23*(2–3), 149–160.

Volosinov, V. N. (1973). *Marxism and the philosophy of language* (L. Matejka & I. R. Titunik, trans.). Harvard University Press.

Wentzer, T. S., & Mattingly, C. (2018). Toward a new humanism: An approach from philosophical anthropology. *HAU: Journal of Ethnographic Theory, 8*(1–2), 144–157.

Appendix: Key to Symbols Used in Transcript

↑ Marked shift in pitch up
↓ Marked shift in pitch down
> word < increased speaking rate
(.) indicates final falling intonation
= indicates no pause
UPPERCASE indicates louder words.
: elongated sound
Underline indicates emphasis.
(.) indicates final falling intonation
((word)) enclose comments.
°word° indicates quieter words

PART 2

Constructing and Engaging with Research Records and Participants

5

VIDEO-ENABLED EDUCATIONAL ETHNOGRAPHIES

The Centrality of Recordings in an Interactional Ethnography

Susan Bridges

Recordings are the beating heart of an Interactional Ethnography (IE). In this chapter I take readers unfamiliar with IE through the principles and practices of the collection of recordings, specifically video recordings, and how they are consulted for analysis within an ethnographic archive. First, I situate the recording of learning events within a conceptual and methodological framework, highlighting how IE sits within an interpretivist paradigm and how recordings support a microethnographic discourse analysis (ME/DA) (Green & Bridges, 2018; Green et al., 2020). Second, I explicate how, from an IE perspective, the researcher designs a study using digital recordings, with considerations for video and audio capture, transcription, and archiving to support analysis. This is grounded in my IE research in university professional education programs (medical, dental, speech language, and initial teacher education) where I have continued to draw on the IE logic of inquiry to shape empirical studies from video and other artifacts housed in purpose-designed digital archives.

In each study, my research teams and I have explored learning designs and learner engagement across a range of inquiry-based professional educational contexts in higher education. These include researching technology-enabled problem-based learning (PBL) in undergraduate Dentistry (Bridges et al., 2012, 2015, 2016), Speech Language Pathology (Lai et al., 2020), and Medicine (Bridges, Hmelo-Silver et al., 2020); as well as interprofessional team-based learning (TBL) across undergraduate health professions programs (Bridges, Chan et al., 2020); and inquiry-based postgraduate initial teacher education (Chian et al., 2021). I share these contexts to support readers in understanding how IE as video-enabled research process can and does support studies across a broad range of educational spaces.

DOI: 10.4324/9781003215479-7

In the final section, I draw on our Bridges, Hmelo–Silver et al. (2020) publication on educational technologies in problem-based medical education as a telling case study (Mitchell, 1984) to provide an overview of the guiding principles I employ with my research teams when adopting IE for empirically grounded studies of learning *in situ*. The overarching goal of this chapter is to make transparent how adopting IE's logic of inquiry supports interdisciplinary research teams in exploring social interactions within and across professional learning contexts to construct an evidence base for theory building.

Conceptual and Methodological Frameworks

For IE researchers, the collection of recordings and associated learning artifacts supports the microethnographic discourse analysis of talk and actions within the moment and over time. The IE approach to working with video recordings provides an empirical basis for the formulation of warranted accounts of learning *in situ*. My research in university professional education settings is shaped by epistemological and ontological groundings in interpretivism from a sociocultural and linguistic theory perspective. Central to the research process is assembling of interdisciplinary teams. Using the guiding logic of IE not only provides a framework for our research design but also supports joint analyses of the social, discursive and cultural processes recorded on video and audio records. Conducting an IE study with an interdisciplinary team, as illustrated in this chapter, has enabled me to gain new insights and our team to achieve transdisciplinary understandings of learning processes across a range of contexts.

Video's Role in IE and Epistemological Groundings: On Video as Partner in Analysis

While many may view the camera as a "tool" for collection and the recording itself as "data", IE researchers take a different view (Green et al., 2007). We do not claim to capture the "reality" of an entire phenomenon but rather consider the camera as a "partner" providing one or more lenses with which we can capture particular aspects or moments as they occur in the learning space (Baker et al., 2008; Skukauskaitė et al., 2007). While a recording allows us to capture a learning event as a "slice of life" (Hymes, 1977), we need to ask questions about how the researcher and the camera lens are positioned in terms of views of reality (e.g., Dyer & Sherin, 2016).

Epistemologically, in creating a research process, researchers need to consider both the nature of knowledge from the theories that guide the research and how we can know about the knowable through our research perspectives (Carr, 1995). Within an IE epistemology (Green et al., 2012), we see knowledge as (co)constructed in both the learning environment and in the research process (see Practice Point #2 below on interdisciplinary team-based analysis process). Given this perspective on the nature of reality as a social construction in and through the discourse and interactions among participants in developing cycles of activity (Green & Meyer, 1991; Baker & Luke, 1991), this chapter focuses on how an IE logic of inquiry supports what researchers, who adopt this perspective, are able to know and seek to understand through adoption of, and interactions with, recordings.

These ontological and epistemological stances lead us to methodological considerations such as how an educational ethnographer should go about finding out what counts as knowledge as well as ways of knowing, being and interpreting what is being interactionally proposed and constructed by participants in the local educational spaces being studied (See Baker & Luke, 1991; Green & Wallat, 1981; Heap, 1995; Heath & Street, 2008; Green & Bridges, 2018). Before moving to methodological considerations, let us briefly examine the conceptual foundation for how we view the site of a study.

Conceptualizing Classrooms as Site of Video-Enabled Microethnographic Discourse Analysis (ME/DA)

Microethnography refers to studies in which the ethnographer makes video records of everyday events that are analyzed through particular forms of discourse analysis. This approach has also been referred to as video-enabled ethnography (Baker et al., 2008; Smith, 1978). What is captured/recorded on video records is grounded in a conceptual view that participants in classrooms (or other social spaces) develop texts (spoken, written, digital, visual) as well as actions that shape ways of being, knowing, and doing everyday events of a developing class (or other social groups) (Green et al., 2012; Derry et al., 2010). From this perspective, IE, as an interdisciplinary logic of inquiry, engages researchers in ME/DA analysis to construct warranted accounts of how everyday life in a class is discursively and socially constructed.

Agar's conceptualization of *languaculture* is at the center of an IE logic of inquiry and forms a foundation for how IE researchers (and others) have come to understand what is captured on a video recording as "a slice of life" (Hymes, 1977), not the whole of the developing languaculture of a group. Digital recordings, therefore, form the foundation for examining particular aspects of a developing languaculture and are not data prior to the IE researcher undertaking the analysis of these recorded bits of life. These conceptual arguments have grounded my research in different higher education programs and spaces since my first published chapter using IE to explore PBL and the role of technologies in blended learning environments (Bridges et al., 2012). In what follows, I detail the chain of actions undertaken to guide an IE study.

On the Chain of Actions in an IE Logic of Inquiry

As noted above, IE researchers have long relied on analysis of video recordings to construct theoretical insights into how the talk and actions among participants within and across learning contexts provide ways of constructing warranted accounts of the complexities of the *situated dynamics* of learning (Heap, 1995; Green & Harker, 1988). At the center of the dynamic and developing process of an IE study is the principled collection of digital recordings and artifacts that create opportunities for constructing what Agar (2006) framed as an *ethnographic space,* a space that supports the researcher in iterative and recursive consultations of the records in the archive (see also Kalainoff & Chian, this volume). Once we collect the records from the study site, we engage with the video recordings in multiple ways, including transcribing video recordings and identifying related artifacts of learning events. We connect the collected artifacts to the video recordings to provide a foundation for interpretive processes aimed at uncovering emic ways of knowing, being, and doing everyday life in learning contexts. Through these processes we construct warranted accounts and/or to identify questions for further analyses (e.g., Gee & Green, 1998; Green et al., 2012; Baker et al., 2008; Green & Bridges, 2018).

The IE logic of inquiry involves principled decisions and actions about what to record, and how to undertake the task of addressing the questions of interest to the researcher. Figure 5.1 illustrates the developing decisions and actions my research teams undertake to construct, what I call the *flow* of our research as adopted in our studies in university professional education settings (medical, dental, speech language, and initial teacher education). The figure signals key moments in an IE study from the initial guiding question to archiving recordings and archive consulting processes within the developing IE-guided logic of inquiry. As represented from the placement and direction of arrows in Figure 5.1, this logic of inquiry is iterative and recursive (Agar, 2006). By this, we mean that one decision leads to particular ways of observing, collecting, and consulting video and other records in a developing context; then, what is learned in one context can require further exploration of a phenomenon in other contexts (Green & Bridges, 2018).

As indicated in Figure 5.1, the interconnected flow of conduct of the research process (the logic of inquiry) begins by defining a *guiding question* with which to enter the field. For example, in a General Research Fund (GRF) study of undergraduate health professions education, the guiding question was: *How and when are educational technologies used in and across PBL learning contexts?* As elaborated in the Bridges, Hmelo-Silver et al. (2020) study discussed below, this question formed a foundation for exploring over time what counts as learning in the PBL problem being studied. The *guiding question* also drives the process of *data collection*, which also includes *site access* and *participant recruitment.*

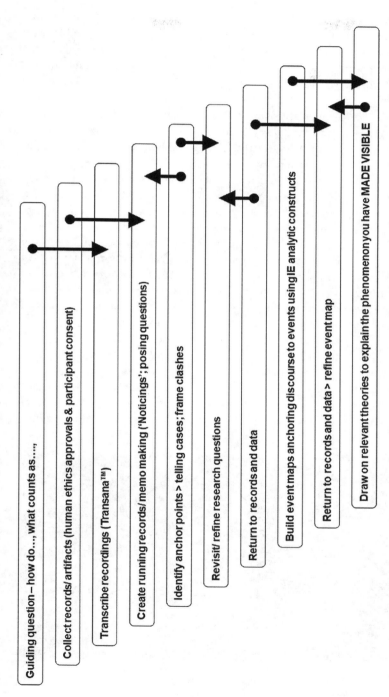

Guiding question – how do..., what counts as....,

Collect records/ artifacts (human ethics approvals & participant consent)

Transcribe recordings (Transana™)

Create running records/ memo making ('Noticings'; posing questions)

Identify anchor points > telling cases; frame clashes

Revisit/ refine research questions

Return to records and data

Build event maps anchoring discourse to events using IE analytic constructs

Return to records and data > refine event map

Draw on relevant theories to explain the phenomenon you have MADE VISIBLE

FIGURE 5.1 The Flow of the IE Analytic Process as Actions for Constructing Warranted Accounts of Learning Processes

Prior to formally entering the site and beginning the phases of observing, recording, archiving, and analyzing records, the researcher must address all ethical concerns and obtain formal permission from the Human Subjects committees. On recruitment to your study, consenting participants grant informed permission for observing and recording particular events or slices of life in which they participate.

Once the permissions are obtained, in the next phase of the developing process, we begin video and audio recording and generate records of observations, artifacts, and other materials relevant to the guiding question. In our research process, we then *transcribe* the video recordings and create a structured *running record* of the talk and actions of participants/actors in the moment (see Figure 5.2 and Castanheira & Green, this volume). As we engage in this chain of actions, we also make researcher "memos" as we notice points where wonderings arise in the act of transcribing the video records as well as in periods of observing *in situ*. Memos are generally made when we face a puzzling moment, where the ethnographer wonders what is happening and/or what led to or leads from this moment (Agar, 2006). Through such actions and notes on what is being accomplished, we begin to identify potential telling cases and identify *frame clashes* and *rich points* to serve as anchors for further analyses (Agar, 2006; Tannen, 1993; Skinner; Baker et al., this volume).

As also indicated by the upwards arrows in Figure 5.1, as we identify rich points, we then return to the archive to re-consult the video recordings and transcripts previously constructed to begin the process of tracing, not only how the rich points came to be, but their *trajectory* over time and across events. In IE studies, this is referred to as *backwards and forwards mapping* (see Kalainoff & Chian, this volume), which leads to refining the original question and to

FIGURE 5.2 Problem-Based Learning in a University Tutorial Room (Bridges, Hmelo-Silver et al., 2020)

posing research sub-questions for new levels of analysis. As I will illustrate in the following section, central to this phase of analytic work is the building of event maps and identifying key sections of transcript for further discourse analysis (Baker et al., 2008; Skukauskaitė & Girdzijauskienė, 2021). Through this process, the original transcripts are further refined as we revisit (re-view) original videos and analyze related artifacts.

Finally, grounded in the patterns identified through these analytic processes, we return to educational theories to provide both *explanatory power* for what has been made visible and to form the basis of re-theorizing the phenomena of study. While Figure 5.1 illustrates a rather seamless flow of iterative and recursive activity (Agar, 2006; Green & Bridges, 2018), I acknowledge that video-based ethnography is a complex and sometimes "messy" process. In the following sections, I unfold a series of principles and practices for the collection of digital recordings, specifically video recordings, and how they are consulted for analysis within an ethnographic archive/space.

Conceptualizing Video as a Partner within a Multimodal Research Setting

In each of my interdisciplinary research studies, I sought to understand the interplay between the planned, enacted, and experienced curriculum in higher education as evidenced through analysis of the micro moments of learning as it unfolds *in situ* in video recordings of the life of learners and learning communities. In addition to presenting transcribed talk, the use of video enables multimodal representations with associated de-identified video frame grabs (Flewitt, 2011). For example, Figure 5.2 from the Bridges, Hmelo-Silver et al. (2020) study on PBL and educational technologies in undergraduate medical education, shows how people in the undergraduate medical education site (university tutorial room) are positioned, how they have multiple sources to draw on (mobile devices, whiteboards, large screens), and how the presenter (in this case a student sharing an idea) has a white board as well as a digital space for making transparent how multimodal resources become central to understanding the medical problem being proposed (Kress, 2010; Flewitt, 2011).

To de-identify the frame grab image, as in Figure 5.2, I adopt a simple editing process in Microsoft Word using the built-in function of "Format Pictures" to make adjustments using a global template selected from those offered under "Artistic Effects". My preference is a "sketch" style which allows enough contextual features (human and non-human configurations) while masking identities. Adding arrows to your image can, for example, indicate line of gaze or gesture. Higher-end image editing software may render a better result but this approach in basic word processing has been reliable across my studies.

As you can see from this section on conceptual and methodological frameworks, video-based recordings have played a foundational role in my studies in the following ways:

a.   as a "partner" in the IE process with each decision regarding placement providing a new "lens" to capture the lived experiences of learners and educators;
b.   as an anchor(s) for multiple layers of joint viewings and transcript analyses by interdisciplinary research teams providing insights and warranted interpretations across both emic and etic perspectives;
c.   as a basis for identifying "rich points" and "frame clashes" that provide the starting point for tracing across a larger archive of recordings and artifacts (the ethnographic space) to investigate the consequential nature and cumulative effect of such events for learning within a purposeful educational design (PBL or TBL cycles; dialogic feedback; etc.).

After examining the conceptual and methodological frameworks for video-enabled educational ethnographies, let us now consider design issues for an IE.

Designing the Role of Video: Recording, Transcribing and Archiving

Video-based approaches may include fixed view (tripod or wall mounted), overhead (ceiling mounted indoor and drone outdoor), portable (hand-held cameras and mobile devices), and wearable (head mounted cameras, google glasses, etc.) recording devices (see Estapa & Amador, 2016; Dyer & Sherin, 2016). After gaining trust, participant consent, and access to the site for making recordings, the educational ethnographer must address the following key questions to understand how decisions about placement and positioning of the camera mediate what can be analyzed from the recording of the events captured on the video record.

1. What phenomenon (lived experience) do you wish to record?
2. What video and audio recording devices (fixed or mobile) will best capture this phenomenon?
3. How will your placement of the recording equipment capture this?
4. Who will control the video in-situ?
5. How will the files be archived for later analysis?

Before we can interpret digital recordings and make sense in and of our ethnographic space, we must first collect quality recordings. In this section,

I provide an overview of the range of video recording devices and processes used in my research in different contexts which may assist readers in considering what devices will support your research. I then address issues related to building and maintaining an archive of the collected records and related artifacts.

Video and Image Capture

Camera placement is critical to a successful recording in classrooms (Castanheira et al., 2000; Derry et al., 2010). For a relatively low-technology approach, depending on room size, I usually set up two or three video cameras on tripods placed diagonally opposite in a room. However, as Baker et al. (this volume) show, what is possible in a given site depends on the negotiation with the instructor of a class. In our study of PBL and educational technologies in medical education (Bridges, Hmelo-Silver et al., 2020), the PBL tutorial was in a smaller university tutorial room with a medium sized tutorial group (8–12 people), so I decided to set up two diagonally opposite cameras to capture the Interactive Whiteboard and provide views of all participants' faces (see Figure 5.2). While videos are often made with an ethnographer in situ controlling the camera and making observations, in this study, rather than having one or two video ethnographers in this small physical space, I gave control for switching the video device on/off to the group members and then the research staff left the room. Passing recording autonomy to consenting participants supports trust-building and has worked well in the university context.

The size of the space, therefore, along with who records the developing events, also informs the decisions about devices to use and where to position them. For example, in a setting with more space, I include an observer. In one large-scale (300+ students) TBL project, we used recordings from ceiling-mounted overhead cameras as well as the floor-level tripod mounted cameras (Bridges, Chan et al., 2020). In contrast to decisions about where to place the recording devices and which to use in classroom settings, in a recent inquiry-based project on environmental sustainability education with secondary teachers and students and university marine ecologists, we used a combination of static tripod mounted cameras with wearable recording devices (Lo et al., under review). In this outdoor site, multiple static tripod mounted cameras were erected parallel to the shoreline to capture the span and landscape of the site and provide a holistic view. Key participants wore Glass™ by Google fitted as spectacles which provide a point-of-view (POV) recording capturing what the wearer sees, says, and hears. They also carried pen microphones in their pockets as a back-up audio recording.

This brief overview highlights some of the ways that sites for video recording shape decisions about what can be recorded as well as what to record, in what ways, using what particular recording devices. Readers will need to include such considerations if they elect to engage in video-enabled research.

Audio Recording

Given our focus on discourse analysis, audibility is key. While not used by all IE researchers, in my studies, lapel microphones that feed to the camera were added to provide high fidelity recordings. For example, if fitted to the classroom teacher, these microphones provide clearly audible recordings of, for example, a study of teacher orchestration of different groups within the class. In the 2020 study of PBL in medical education, we used two audio sources with the camera's built-in microphone complemented with a conference recording system placed in the center of the larger round table (see Figure 5.2). This high-fidelity audio recording is used as a secondary file stored in the project archive to support transcription of the video recording where audibility may be compromised.

Transcription

Speech recognition systems have improved greatly in recent years with companies such as YouTube™ and Zoom™ providing automatic captioning and speech-to-text records. In considering the vast array of transcription software tools that continue to evolve, IE researchers should heed the advice of Skukauskaitė et al. (2007):

> The challenge, therefore, facing researchers using video-enabled research is not one of finding the "perfect" tool, because none exist, but rather to create a theoretically and methodologically driven approach to the analysis of the questions under study.
>
> *(p. 135)*

If we follow Ochs' (1979) argument that the video is not the data nor is the transcription software a tool, then in an IE study, the act of transcribing is a process of producing data and the act of transcription is central to what is available to be interpreted (Ellen, 1984; Skukauskaitė, 2014). In my studies, selected video files for analysis are first transcribed in Transana™ to support the identification of rich points which then form the anchor for analysis. As we iteratively and recursively refine analysis, we re-consult the original videos and refine the transcriptions. In an interdisciplinary team, this process not only assists in verifying what is (re)presented on the transcript in ways that the study requires to be inscribed to support particular analyses (see Figure 5.3) but also enables interpretations grounded in the multiple perspectives of the viewer – educator/disciplinary specialist/learning scientist, etc.

Timeline (2015-16)					
Year 2 MBBS					
Semester 1			Semester 2		
Block A	Block B: Cardiovascular System	Block C	Block A	Block B	Block C
Cases #1-4	Cases #1-4	Cases #1-4	Cases #1-4	Cases #1-4	Cases #1-4

Case 1 - Paediatric cardiovascular · Focus Learning Outcome: Graphical representation of VSD cardiac cycle

Swing out table 1a: Tutorial 1 (T1) (Oct 19)

Time	PBL Phase
0:00:00	Climate setting (new group): Self-introductions
0:05:10	**Establishing group norms:** Roles and responsibilities. *Technology management:* Recording using a google doc shared on central, large screen; scribe plus group online collaborative
0:07:36	Problem Scenario: Case 1 Sequential disclosure (Part 1, Patient presentation): *Technology management:* Facts & ideas on central shared screen via Google Doc
0:13:42	Generating alternative hypotheses: differential diagnoses; "Congenital heart disease" raised
0:33:00	Scaffolding hypothesis generation: "VINDICATE tool" for differential diagnoses "Septal defect links to the oxygen problem"
0:39:29	Problem Scenario: Case 1 Sequential disclosure (Part 2"History taking"): Identifying knowledge gaps, Cleaning up the (ideas) board: "We can write out congenital septal defect"
0:44:45	Problem Scenario: Case 1 Sequential disclosure (Part 3, Physical examination): Identifying knowledge gaps: "What do we hear if there's septal defect?"
1:19:40	ARTEFACT 1: "Can you explain it in the diagram for that?" (Whiteboard drawing – heart sections) ARTEFACT 2: "If we can bring up the diagram on screen" (Anatomical image of heart with VSD) ARTEFACT 3: "Pressure difference" (Cardiac cycle graph) ARTEFACT 4: "Left and right ventricles"
1:44:45	Problem Scenario: Case 1 Sequential disclosure (Part 4, Further investigations): ARTEFACT 5: "Different P wave... characteristic correspond to the right or the left atrium enlargement" (P Wave morphology)
1:53:18	**Identify learning issues/ objectives for Self-directed Learning (SDL):** Group norms (5 min powerpoint presentations)

Swing out table 1b: Tutorial 2 (T2) (Oct 26)

Time	PBL Phase
0:00:00	**Group norms:** Roles and responsibilities; Reporting SDL_processes
0:03:40	**Case 1: Applying new knowledge to problem:** Group 1 sharing "LO1: Why only left atrial enlargement will lead to biphasic P wave?" (S11, S2, S3, S5, S8)
00:7:49	Group 2 sharing "LO2: What to differentiate a louder component? pulmonary? aortic?" (S4, S1, S9) ARTEFACT 6: Youtube video "the second heart sound" (S1)
00:34:14	Group 3 sharing "LO3: Is there a diagram for VSD cardiac cycle?" (S7, S6, S10) ARTEFACT 7: "Shape of the curve"? (S7)
0:45:56	Problem Scenario: Case 1 Sequential disclosure (Parts 5-7, Treatments, Follow-up visits): Generating alternative hypotheses - Differential diagnoses; Identifying knowledge gaps; Sharing prior knowledge
1:55:00	Case 1 Sequential disclosure (Part 8: Treatment): Identify learning issues/ objectives for Self-directed Learning (SDL): "LO0 LO3 from T1 (Graphical representation of VSD cardiac cycle) (S11)"

Swing out table 1c: Tutorial 3 (T3) (Oct 29)

Time	PBL Phase
0:00:00	**Group norms:** Roles and responsibilities
0:03:00	**Case 1: Applying new knowledge to problem:** LO3 from T1 (Graphical representation of VSD cardiac cycle) (S11)" ARTEFACT 8: "VSD Chart" (S11)
0.8:30	Problem Scenario: Case 1 Sequential disclosure (Part 9): Resolve case; Reveal planned LOs with student-devised Los and contrast
	ARTEFACT 9: Revised VSD chart shared with PBL group (S11)

Self-directed Learning (SDL)

Information Classification: General

FIGURE 5.3   Event Map of Visualizations across Tutorials (Bridges, Hmelo–Silver et al., 2020)

Maintaining a Digital Archive

The development and logical maintenance of a research project archive becomes central to the analytic process as team members jointly and separately consult the archive to access recordings, transcriptions and related artifacts and files. In my large-scale study of PBL and educational technologies, we used a relatively low-technology approach using Excel to build a password protected digital spreadsheet. This included details about events (time/and place), actors, observer notes, and hyperlinks to a secure (internal) server storing all digital files (original recordings, Transana™ files and transcribed text, photographs, curriculum, and student learning artifacts). We developed the following columns in the Excel file as an index for the first round of recordings and are presented here as an example of a contextually grounded archiving process:

> Column 1 – Individual student identifier (number)
> Column 2 – Individual student name
> Column 3 – Student group identifier (curriculum/year/group e.g., BDS1.4)
> Column 4 – Inquiry Cycle (local identifier – number or name)
> Column 5 – Recordings start date (for longitudinal tracing)
> Column 6 – Tutorial/session time
> Column 7 – Number of complete problems/cases filmed
> Column 8 – Recordings start date (for longitudinal tracing)
> Column 9 – Location # (server URL; add columns per recording)
> Column 10 – Researcher notes (devices used/artifacts/memos).

This indexing process was then expanded over a 3-year period and enabled my team to identify key events for analysis as well as potential "tracer" individuals and groups, whose participation could then be followed across time, events, configuration of participants, and intertextually tied cycles of activity (Castanheira et al., 2000). This approach to creating an index for archiving video records and related artifacts and fieldnotes, therefore, provides a foundation for forward and backward mapping of inter-related (intertextually tied) events as the researcher seeks to undertake multiple levels of analysis (Putney et al., 2000; Skukauskaitė & Girdzijauskienė, 2021; see also, Baker et al.; Kalainoff & Chian, this volume). The goal of forward and backward mapping is captured by Kumpulainen and Rajala (2017) in the concept of *chronotopes*. Kumpulainen and Rajala (2017) provide the following definition for chronotopes in interactional research:

> The notion of chronotope originates from the works of Mikhail Bakhtin (1981), a dialogic literary scholar, who used the concept to describe the contextual grounding of events in a literary narrative, that is, the unity of time and space. Here, space and time are not seen as neutral abstractions

or as a background or a passive context in which activity occurs but as socially constructed, intrinsically interconnected and imbued with cultural meanings and practices, values, and ideology (Morson & Emerson, 1990). Chronotopes are actively constructed in social interactions within and across sociocultural sites (Renshaw, 2013).

(p. 92)

In this definition, Kumpulainen and Rajala frame a way of understanding that the identification and analysis of rich points and mapping of intertextual relationships provides support for interpretations of the embedded nature of particular moments in a developing research narrative which is grounded in multiple levels of analysis. The logic of the index will differ across studies; however, as evident in the chapters presented in this volume, the indexing of times, dates, actors, and activities is key to supporting analysis.

At the micro level, the inclusion of time stamps on transcripts provides a form of evidence constructed by the researcher to mark where the participants were constructing particular processes, practices, and discipline-based knowledge. That is, the inclusion of time stamps provides a basis for detailing where the recording occurs in a planned *sequence* of activities and curricula. It also provides a basis for assembling different levels of analysis to construct warranted accounts of the developing languacultural processes, practices, and discipline-based epistemic knowledge participants construct in and across events and cycles of activity (e.g., Green & Bridges, 2018; Skukauskaitė & Girdzijauskienė, 2021).

The above sections have framed the conceptual basis and *flow* of my IE studies. In what follows, I demonstrate the principles and practices I employ to create recordings for my digital archive as a basis for interpretive analysis.

A Conceptual Logic Guiding Analysis Processes

In this section, I identify a series of *practice points* undertaken by particular members of a research team. Each *practice point* is designed to foreground particular conceptually guided actions of the analyst or team of analysts. I draw on Bridges, Hmelo-Silver et al. (2020) as a telling case study to exemplify these practice points.

Practice Point #1: The Video Recording as a Mediator of Interpretive Expertise

While recordings are key to a video-enabled approach, as shown in the preceding sections, central to Interactional Ethnography (IE) is our approach to analysis as a *process of interpretation* to uncover the referential and intertextual nature of classroom life both in time and over time (Dixon et al., 1992). The process of revisiting and reviewing digital records is time-consuming but critical. First, it enables the IE researcher-as-analyst to view the recorded slice(s) of the lived experiences of teachers and learners in formal and informal learning environments through different lenses. Second, it enables the researcher to construct warranted accounts of developing teaching and learning processes through these lenses. Putney et al. (2000) framed three core analytic constructs for IE that were central to guiding my earliest studies and which relate to the concept of chronotopes introduced in the previous section:

1. Analyzing the *historical and over-time relationship* between and among texts (intertextuality) and contexts (intercontextuality) uncovered through forward and backward mapping from a key event;
2. Tracing *whole-part, part-whole relationships* from descriptions of the actions and discourse of members; and
3. Analyzing the *consequential progression* of how knowledge constructed in one context becomes socially and academically consequential to another.

Critical to analyzing video recordings in teams is developing trust with partners, especially since the sensitivity of live teaching and learning "performance" can be particularly challenging when co-viewing with participants and examining both teachers and students' perspectives as well as that of the researcher. To contextualize this practice point, I reconstruct the research process of my team's publication, "Dialogic intervisualizing in multimodal inquiry" (Bridges, Hmelo-Silver et al., 2020).

Contextualizing Analyses from the Point of View of Different Analysts

The telling case study of one PBL cycle in undergraduate medical education in Bridges, Hmelo-Silver et al. (2020) is situated within a larger project archive (~300 recorded hours) focusing on the use of educational technologies in PBL across three undergraduate health professions programs (Medicine, Dentistry, and Speech Language Pathology) (see Figure 5.1's guiding question). Our focus was on how multimodal texts shape and were shaped by particular technological, discursive, and interactional affordances (Kress, 2010).

This focus also guided our search for patterns of interaction to address how these interrelationships were created through the lens of multimodality and social semiotics (Lemke, 2009). The goal of including multimodality analysis processes was to consider the relationship between student-generated texts and collaborative learning in technology-supported PBL in undergraduate health professions education. We selected this particular telling case study for in-depth analysis due to the rich variety of educational technologies adopted, including a range of devices used and screen-based activities such as online searching and Interactive Whiteboard sharing (Jin et al., 2015). Our final research sub-question for the PBL study in this site was,

> How and in what ways do members of blended PBL tutorials co-construct complex knowledge of proposed medical concepts through intervisual and intertextual dialogic relationships as they engage with a developing series of texts across a PBL cycle of inquiry moment-by-moment and over time?

This question guided the analytic work of the interdisciplinary team in which medical educators, curriculum designers, and educational researchers from sociology and psychology, undertook a process of multiple, joint analyses of videos, Transana™ files and transcripts. In this process, team members brought different ontologies and epistemologies to the processes of analyses. Their professional knowledge informed team members about a series of different theoretically guided interpretations of the same video record.

Figure 5.3 in the following section represents a mapping of the visual texts and associated classroom and interview discourse that evolved within and across the PBL cycle of activity (face-to-face and self-directed learning). As you engage with Figure 5.3, consider how the different lenses (i.e., perspectives from interdisciplinary colleagues) contribute to the complex processes being re-constructed by participants through the lens of the different members of the team. For example, our medical team member identified the disciplinary learning outcome and linked it to collected curriculum documents. Our PBL team experts drew on their expertise in designing problems and cases and identifying facilitation processes. Team members with a background in literacy theory contributed to conceptions of texts. These multiple perspectives and layers of expertise contributed to developing a complex narrative of what participants were experiencing, based on evidence proposed and afforded to them in the developing phases and events of the tutorial process across multiple days and sites.

Practice Point #2: The Iterative and Recursive Process of Team-Based Video Analysis

In this *practice point,* I make visible how an IE logic of analysis involved identifying the boundaries of units for analysis as well as the referential and observed links between units to construct theoretical understandings of the phenomena under study (Heath, 1982; Green et al., 2012). Identifying the intertextual links, as Figure 5.3 shows, involved multiple levels of analytic scale, each grounded in what members of my team identified as central to understanding what was being proposed and recognized by members of the PBL tutorial group (seen in subsequent speech and actions), and acknowledged by the facilitator of the session as well as their peers (Bloome et al., 2005). We, therefore, examined the boundaries of units of analysis through consideration of participants' speech and actions as well as what they were orienting to and holding each other accountable to/for within and across times in this developing languaculture of medicine in this PBL tutorial (Green & Bridges, 2018; Bloome et al., 2005). Green et al. (2020) capture this process in the following argument:

> By tracing the actions of particular actors and analyzing the sequence of events through particular theoretical lenses, the anthropologically guided ethnographer seeks to develop valid connections among actions, objects, actors, and activities to construct theoretical understandings of what is being interactionally, socially, discursively, and situationally accomplished by participants. The process that the ethnographer engages in, therefore, is one of analytic induction (not deduction, or a priori defined phenomena); that is, by undertaking a set of analytic processes, the ethnographer seeks to make theoretically valid (i.e., grounded) connections between and among the phenomena analyzed (Corsaro & Heise, 1990).
>
> *(pp. 164–165)*

The conceptual argument about analytic induction processes provided a basis for my team to construct events of developing intertextually (and intervisually) tied cycles of learning activities and for identifying rich points for recursive analyses that formed the basis for constructing a potential narrative (warranted accounts) of learning processes. Figure 5.3 provides a graphic (re)presentation of how identifying units of analysis in developing events in each site of the tutorial processes supported our construction of analytic maps of developing events within the IE logic. An IE event map, as in Figure 5.3, provides a basis for identifying and (re)presenting what we have previously described as

> the chronological relationship between texts and talk which assists in identifying how knowledge developed with texts in one context becomes academically and socially consequential to learning across other contexts.
>
> *(Bridges, Hmelo-Silver et al., 2020, p.292)*

This multi-sited *event map* situated the three recorded tutorials and stimulated recall interview within the time scale of the Year 2 undergraduate medical curriculum. The swing-out tables provide a breakdown with timestamps of the major phases of activity of a problem-based cycle (see Lu et al., 2014). The timestamps provide a clear signpost for reference during the interpretive analysis. For example, we signaled "the rich point at 1:22:45" when one medical student was asked by his peers to "explain it in a diagram" (Bridges, Hmelo-Silver et al., 2020, p. 295). The inclusion of the recorded time stamp of when this rich point occurred and reflected in the actions of participants in the "embodied actions" column with image and description provided an anchor for tracing forward and backward in time, what this student engaged in as he sought to construct his professional narrative. The developing oral narrative of his medical diagnostic reasoning as evident in the transcribed talk was making explicit both his and his peers' understanding of the identified heart problem (ventricular septal defect, VSD). The developing narrative was also a visual one as the students sought to identify how VSD could be graphically represented as it manifested in the PBL case under discussion. Anchoring these events to time also formed a boundary for tracing his subsequent actions in the three face-to-face sessions as well as tracing how he explored what he did not understand in the digital contexts between tutorials.

Practice Point #3: Drawing on Explanatory Theories in the Light of the Phenomenon Surfaced

The IE process of analysis enables the researcher to make visible particular phenomena occurring in a learning environment. Given the Bridges, Hmelo-Silver et al. (2020) study's focus on text-discourse-meaning relations, we drew on three distinct fields of existing theory. We recognized that examining *visual* text-discourse-meaning relations in an inquiry-based learning cycle, such as PBL, requires new approaches to both spoken and written language. Existing literacy theory related to "intertextuality" supported tracing of discourse and text, multimodal semiotics provided a lens to view embodied actions, and art history theory enabled insights in the role of "intervisual ties" across a series of visual texts. Given this study's focus on "developing texts", the embedding of the key visual texts as images in the event map (Figure 5.3) captures their evolution across events and over time. The visuals became central to signposting the instances where microethnographic-discourse analysis (ME/DA) was undertaken to gain deeper understandings of what was being interactionally and discursively accomplished. Excerpts re-present the talk and actions identified as rich points being traced across the event map. In this study, we represented excerpts in four columns:

1. **Time** (Tutorial T3; Transana™ time stamp 0:8:31)
2. **Speaker** (identifiers) (e.g., F: Facilitator; S11: Student + identifier)
3. **Transcript of the developing discourse as message units**[1] (e.g., Would that be easier/to show it on the chart/Are you talking about these many changes in pressure and volume/)
4. **Embodied actions** as aligned to the event to indicate paralinguistic features such as proxemics, orientation to group members/whiteboards/screens, gestures, gaze, etc. (e.g., S11 taps screen to move PowerPoint to next slide, Artifact 8).

Instances of analytic interest followed up in the interpretative narrative are signaled with an arrow (→).

As indicated above, this analytic slice of life occurred at 8 minutes and 31 seconds in the third tutorial session (T3/0:8:31). To construct an interpretive narrative (analytic induction) of this set of interactions, we built on Wegerif's (2007) arguments about dialogic learning with digital technologies which highlighted that educational technologies are a "tool for opening up and resourcing the kind of dialogic spaces that enable people to think, learn, and play together" (p. 7). We also capitalized on my team's prior understandings in the field of the learning sciences, particularly learner agency, educational technologies, and inquiry-based learning in the computer-supported collaborative learning. Sociocultural understandings of learning supported our investigation into the dialogic relationship between social activity and collective-individual cognition (Mercer & Howe, 2012). Sociolinguistic theories of multimodality as linked to social semiotics provided further *explanatory windows* into the intertextual phenomena uncovered as students created, accessed, curated, and developed a range of interpretations of texts presented to them (Figure 5.3) as well as texts created by other students. An IE approach, therefore, enabled our interdisciplinary research team to take a series of steps (e.g., discourse analyses and re-consulting literature) to construct a grounded basis for warranted theory-building.

Practice Point #4: Building Concepts/Theories for New or Unique Phenomena Identified

While the explanatory theories captured aspects of the intervisual phenomenon we identified and (re)presented in the event map (Figure 5.3) and discourse analysis, these were partial (re)presentations of our research process as well as the processes being co-constructed by students within and across the three tutorial spaces. Taken together, theoretical insights from these existing fields provided *explanatory power* for parts of the phenomenon made visible. However, they did not fully capture the complexities of combining in-the-moment reasoning with and through multimodal, visual texts across multiple forms of physical and virtual spaces (Suthers, 2006). The analytic induction and the selection of explanatory theories led to our proposing the concept of *dialogic intervisualizing* to characterize:

> the dynamic interplay between and among information problem-solving processes, textual negotiations and purposeful, facilitated dialogue for deep knowledge co-construction within and across collaborative, computer-supported learning activity in an inquiry cycle.
>
> *(Bridges, Hmelo-Silver et al., 2020)*

As we demonstrated in the sections above, we achieved this argument about intervisualizing the dynamic interplay among processes in the tutorial through a collaborative, interdisciplinary analysis in our IE research team. By co-viewing and co-analyzing the developing texts and processes being constructed within the group and over time, our disciplinary expert, in this case an expert medical educator, not only identified knowledge co-construction on VSD; as the medical curriculum member on our team, he also provided expert and detailed information about the learning design of this PBL cycle, including learning goals and the various resources made available to students. This member's intimate understanding of the discipline and the history of the students grounded in earlier PBL cycles, helped contextualize what they were, or were not, understanding as was visible in their group discussions.

In closing, my goal in this illustrative telling case study of analytic processes in Bridges, Hmelo-Silver et al. (2020) was to provide a means for readers to gain insights into how we laid a foundation for making warranted interpretations and re-theorizing what was learned through our analyses. As such, the above four practice points, as applied to this telling case, illustrate how a video-based IE draws on ethnographic and discourse-based approaches to capture and analyze the interactive processes of facilitated learning and thus provide new insights into the dialogic, material, and socially constructed nature of learning with technologies in problem-based medical education.

Summary

In this chapter, I have provided the conceptual and methodological foundations for a video-enabled Interactional Ethnography (IE). I have outlined a series of design principles and practices for the collection of digital recordings, specifically video and audio recordings. I also demonstrated how they are consulted for analysis within an ethnographic archive/space. I have revisited my interdisciplinary team's recently published video-based study of PBL in medical education (Bridges, Hmelo-Silver et al., 2020) as a telling case study to illustrate the central processes involved in collecting, analyzing and (re)presenting what was learned from working with digital recordings in an interdisciplinary IE. In guiding researchers new to IE and the use of digital video recordings, I have proposed four key practice points as the basis for archive building and interpretive analyses:

1. The video recording as a mediator of interpretive expertise
2. The iterative and recursive process of team-based video analysis
3. Drawing on explanatory theories in light of the phenomenon surfaced
4. Building new concepts/theories to explain new or unique phenomena identified through the analysis of the complex and dynamic processes of learning in educational spaces.

Suggested Readings

Fischer, F., Hmelo-Silver, C. E., Goldman, S. R., & Reimann, P. (Eds.). (2018). *International handbook of the learning sciences*. Routledge.
Goldman, R., Pea, R., Barron, B., & Derry, S. J. (Eds.). (2007). *Video research in the learning sciences*. Lawrence Erlbaum.
Jewitt, C., Bezemer, J., & O'Halloran, K. (2016). *Introducing multimodality*. Routledge.

Note

1 Drawing on Gumperz and Herasimchuk's (1972) it is a sociolinguistic approach to contextualization cues in the construction of meaning (see Kelly and Green 2019).

References

Agar, M. (2006). An ethnography by any other name. *Forum: Qualitative Sozialforschung/ Forum: Qualitative Social Research, 7*(4), Article 37. http://www.qualitative-research. net/fqs
Baker, C., & Luke, A. (Eds.) (1991). *Research methodologies and methods in education*. Sage.
Baker, W. D., Green, J., & Skukauskaitė, A. (2008). Video-enabled ethnographic research: A microethnographic perspective. In G. Walford (Ed.), *How to do educational ethnography* (pp. 77–114). Tufnell Press.
Bakhtin, M. (1981). *The dialogic imagination: Four essays*. University of Texas Press.
Bloome, D., Carter, S. P., Christian, B. M., Otto, S., & Shuart-Faris, N. (2005). *Discourse analysis and the study of classroom language and literacy events: A microethnographic perspective*. Lawrence Erlbaum Associates.
Bridges, S., Botelho, M., Green, J. L., & Chau, A. (2012). Multimodality in problem-based learning (PBL): An interactional ethnography. In S. Bridges, C. McGrath, & T, L. Whitehill (Eds.), *Problem-based learning in clinical education* (pp. 99–120). Springer.
Bridges, S. M., Chan, L. K., Chen, J. Y., Tsang, J. P. Y., & Ganotice, F. A. (2020). Learning environments for interprofessional education: A microethnography of sociomaterial assemblages in team-based learning. *Nurse Education Today, 94*, 104569. https://doi.org/10.1016/j.nedt.2020.104569
Bridges, S. M., Green, J., Botelho, M. G., & Tsang, P. C. S. (2015). Blended learning and PBL: An interactional ethnographic approach to understanding knowledge construction in-situ. In A. Walker, H. Leary, C. E. Hmelo-Silver, & P. A. Ertmer (Eds.), *Essential readings in problem-based learning: Exploring and extending the legacy of Howard s. Barrows* (pp. 107–130). Purdue University Press.
Bridges, S. M., Hmelo-Silver, C. E., Chan, L. K., Green, J. L., & Saleh, A. (2020). Dialogic intervisualizing in multimodal inquiry. *International Journal of Computer-Supported Collaborative Learning, 15*(3), 283–318. https://doi.org/10.1007/s11412-020-09328-0
Bridges, S. M., Jin, J., & Botelho, M. G. (2016). Technology and group processes in PBL tutorials: An ethnographic study. In S. M. Bridges, L. K. Chan, & C. Hmelo-Silver (Eds.), *Educational technologies in medical and health sciences education* (pp. 35–56). Springer.
Carr, W. (1995). *For education: Towards critical educational inquiry*. McGraw-Hill.

Castanheira, M. L., Crawford, T., Dixon, C. N., & Green, J. (2000). Interactional ethnography: An approach to studying the social construction of literate practices. *Linguistics and Education, 11*(4), 353–400. https://doi.org/10.1016/s089858 98(00)00032-2

Chian, M. M., Bridges, S. M., & Lee, D. P. L. (2021). Synergistic co-teaching: Surfacing the invisible flows of dramaturgy in practice in initial teacher education. *Learning, Culture and Social Interaction, 31*, 100573. https://doi.org/10.1016/j. lcsi.2021.100573

Corsaro, W. A., & Heise, D. R. (1990). Event structure models from ethnographic data. In C. Clegg (Ed.), *Sociological methodology* (pp. 1–27). Basil Blackwell.

Derry, S. J., Pea, R. D., Barron, B., Engle, R. A., Erickson, F., Goldman, R., Hall, R., Koschmann, T., Lemke, J. L., Sherin, M. G., & Sherin, B. L. (2010). Conducting video research in the learning sciences: Guidance on selection, analysis, technology, and ethics. *Journal of the Learning Sciences, 19*(1), 3–53.

Dixon, C., de la Cruz, E., Green, J., Lin., L., & Brandts, L. (1992). Do you see what we see? The referential and intertextual nature of classroom life. *The Journal of Classroom Interaction, 27*(2), 29–36.

Dyer, E. B., & Sherin, M. G. (2016). Instructional reasoning about interpretations of student thinking that supports responsive teaching in secondary mathematics. *ZDM – Mathematics Education, 48*(1–2), 69–82. https://doi.org/10.1007/ s11858-015-0740-1

Ellen, R. F. (Ed.). (1984). *Ethnographic research: A guide to general conduct*. Academic Press.

Estapa, A., & Amador, J. (2016). Wearable cameras as a tool to capture preservice teachers' marked and recorded noticing. *Journal of Technology and Teacher Education, 24*(3), 281–307.

Flewitt, R. (2011). Bringing ethnography to a multimodal investigation of early literacy in a digital age. *Qualitative Research, 11*(3), 293–310.

Gee, J. P., & Green, J. L. (1998). Discourse analysis, learning, and social practice: A methodological study. *Review of Research in Education, 23*, 119–169. https://doi. org/10.2307/1167289

Green, J. L., Baker, W. D., Chian, M. M., Vanderhoof, C., Hooper, L., Kelly, G. J., Skukauskaitė, A., & Kalainoff, M. Z. (2020). Studying the overtime construction of knowledge in educational settings: A microethnographic-discourse analysis approach. *Review of Research in Education, 44*(1), 161–194.

Green, J. L., & Bridges, S. M. (2018). Interactional ethnography. In F. Fischer, C. E. Hmelo-Silver, S. R. Goldman, & P. Reimann (Eds.), *International handbook of the learning sciences* (pp. 475–488). Routledge.

Green, J. L., & Harker, J. O. (Eds.). (1988). *Multiple perspective analyses of classroom discourse* (Vol. 28). Ablex.

Green, J. L., & Meyer, L. (1991). The embeddedness of reading in classroom life: Reading As a situated process. In C. Baker, & A. Luke (Eds.), *Research methodologies and methods in education* (pp. 309–321). Sage.

Green, J. L., Skukauskaitė, A., & Baker, W. D. (2012). Ethnography as epistemology. In J. Arthur, M. Waring, R. Coe, & L. V. Hedges (Eds.), *Research methods and methodologies in education* (pp. 309–321). Sage.

Green, J., Skukauskaitė, A., Dixon, C., & Cordova, R. (2007). Epistemological issues in the analysis of video records: Interactional ethnography as a logic of inquiry. In R. Goldman, R. Pea, B. Barron, & S. J. Derry (Eds.), *Video research in the learning sciences* (pp. 115–132). Routledge.

Green, J., & Wallat, C. (1981). Mapping instructional conversations. *Ethnography and Language in Educational Settings*, *5*, 161–205.

Gumperz, J. J., & Herasimchuk, E. (1972). The conversational analysis of social meaning: A study of classroom interaction. In R. Shuy (Ed.), *Sociolinguistics: Current trends and prospects* (pp. 99–134). Georgetown University Press.

Heath, S. B. (1982). Ethnography in education: Defining the essentials. In P. Gilmore & A. A. Glatthorn (Eds.), *Children in and out of school: Ethnography and education* (pp. 33–55). Center for Applied Linguistics.

Heath, S. B., & Street, B. V. (2008). *On ethnography: Approaches to language and literacy research. Language & literacy (NCRLL)*. Teachers College Press.

Heap, J. L. (1995). The status of claims in "qualitative" educational research. *Curriculum Inquiry*, *25*(3), 271–292. https://doi.org/10.1080/03626784.1995.11076182

Hymes, D. (1977). Critique. *Anthropology & Education Quarterly*, *8*, 91–93.

Jin, J., Bridges, S. M., Botelho, M. G., & Chan, L. (2015). Online searching in PBL tutorials. *Interdisciplinary Journal of Problem-Based Learning*, *9*(1). https://doi.org/10.7771/1541-5015.1514

Kelly, G. J., & Green, J. L. (2019). *Theory and methods for sociocultural research in science and engineering education*. Routledge.

Kress, G. (2010). *Multimodality: A social semiotic approach to contemporary communication*. Routledge.

Kumpulainen, K., & Rajala, A. (2017). Negotiating time-space contexts in students' technology-mediated interaction during a collaborative learning activity. *International Journal of Educational Research*, *84*, 90–99. https://doi.org/10.1016/j.ijer.2016.05.002

Lai, H. Y. Y., Wong, A. M. Y., & Bridges, S. M. (2020). How can screen sharing support knowledge co-construction in technology-enhanced problem-based learning? In S. M. Bridges & R. Imafuku (Eds.), *Interactional research into problem-based learning* (pp. 297–326). Purdue University Press.

Lemke, J. L. (2009). Multimodal genres and transmedia traversals: Social semiotics and the political economy of the sign. *Semiotica*, *173*(1–4), 283–297.

Lo, S. C. T., Bridges, S. M., Yip, V. W. Y., Williams, G. A., Chan, K. K. H., Chen, G., Leung, J. S. C., Russell, B., Not, C., & Goodwin, A. L. (under review). *Sociomateriality of apprenticeship learning in ecological fieldwork* [Poster abstract submitted for presentation]. International Conference of the Learning Sciences, Hiroshima, Japan.

Lu, J., Bridges, S. M., & Hmelo-Silver, C. (2014). Problem-based learning. In R. K. Sawyer (Ed), *The Cambridge handbook of the learning sciences* (2nd ed., pp. 298–318). Cambridge University Press.

Mercer, N., & Howe, C. (2012). Explaining the dialogic processes of teaching and learning: The value and potential of sociocultural theory. *Learning, Culture and Social Interaction*, *1*, 12–21.

Mitchell, C. J. (1984). Typicality and the case study. In R. F. Ellen (Ed.), *Ethnographic research: A guide to general conduct* (pp. 238–241). Academic Press.

Morson, G. S., & Emerson, C. (1990). *Mikhail Bakhtin: Creation of a prosaics*. Stanford University Press.

Ochs, E. (1979). Transcription as theory. In B. Schieffelin (Ed.), *Developmental pragmatics* (pp. 43–72). Academic Press.

Putney, L., Green, J. L., Dixon, C., Duran, R., & Yeager, B. (2000). Consequential progressions: Exploring collective individual development in a bilingual classroom.

In C. Lee & P. Smagorinsky (Eds.), *Constructing meaning through collaborative inquiry: Vygotskian perspectives on literacy research* (pp. 86–126). Cambridge University Press.

Renshaw, P. D. (2013). Classroom chronotopes privileged by contemporary educational policy: teaching and learning in testing times. In S. Phillipson, K. Y. L. Ku, & S. N. Phillipson (Eds.), *Constructing educational achievement: A sociocultural perspective* (pp. 57–69). Routledge.

Skukauskaitė, A. (2014). Transcribing as analysis: Logic-in-use in entextualizing interview conversations. In *Sage research methods cases*. Sage. doi:10.4135/9781446 27305014532202.

Skukauskaitė, A., & Girdzijauskienė, R. (2021). Video analysis of contextual layers in teaching-learning interactions. *Learning, Culture and Social Interaction, 29*, 100499. https://doi.org/10.1016/j.lcsi.2021.100499

Skukauskaitė, A., Liu, Y., & Green, J. L. (2007). Special issue on analysing video records of classroom events: From observable moments to multiple levels of scale. *Pedagogies: An International Journal, 2*(3), 131–137.

Smith, L. M. (1978). An evolving logic of participant observation, educational ethnography, and other case studies. *Review of Research in Education, 6*(1), 316–377. https://doi.org/10.3102/0091732X006001316

Suthers, D. D. (2006). Technology affordances for intersubjective meaning making: A research agenda for CSCL. *International Journal of Computer-Supported Collaborative Learning, 1*(3), 315–337. https://doi.org/10.1007/s11412-006-9660-y

Tannen, D. (Ed.). (1993). *Framing in discourse*. New York: Oxford University Press.

Wegerif, R. (2007). *Dialogic education and technology: Expanding the space of learning (vol. 7)*. Springer Science & Business Media.

6

CONVERSATIONAL INTERVIEWING GROUNDED IN INTERACTIONAL ETHNOGRAPHIC PRINCIPLES

Audra Skukauskaitė and Michelle Sullivan

Locating the Conversational Interview in a Larger Project

This chapter is based on a project in which we explored who, what, and in what ways supported a teacher and her students working on an invention project at a high school in Oregon. The project is part of a larger program of research and collaboration with people and organizations involved in invention education – an educational approach in which students engage in invention processes which range from identifying complex problems in need of solution to developing and publicly presenting technological prototypes of the solution (Couch et al., 2019b; Invention Education Research Community, 2019). This program of research is informed by Interactional Ethnography (IE) (Green & Bridges, 2018; Green et al., 2012), which guides our questions, processes, and goals of uncovering insider perspectives about complex educational practices co-constructed by diverse actors in multilayered local and larger contexts (Green & Heras, 2011; Skukauskaitė & Girdzijauskienė, 2021).

In the smaller project derived from this larger program of research, we focused on one team in Oregon and sought to explore the internal and external networks supporting invention education from the perspective of students and teachers who had received an InvenTeam grant from the Lemelson-MIT (LMIT) Program at the Massachusetts Institute of Technology (MIT) (Skukauskaitė et al., under review). The LMIT InvenTeams initiative supports invention education in high schools across the US, providing grants for teams of students, teachers, and mentors engaged in creating technological solutions to real-world problems (Couch et al., 2019a; Invention Education Research Community, 2019). In 2018, upon LMIT staff's invitation, two InvenTeams volunteered to collect records of their work during the year. Oregon's McKay High School InvenTeam was one of

DOI: 10.4324/9781003215479-8

the teams in which a student volunteered for the student-historian (student-ethnographer) role and used an LMIT-provided video camera and hard drive to generate video records and write a historian notebook (a kind of ethnographic fieldnotes) about what took place during their InvenTeam work (Skukauskaitė et al., 2019). The video records and historian notebook were our primary data sources for the analyses and conversational interviews explored in this chapter. Our work was a collaboration between a team of university-based researchers: a professor (A) and two doctoral students (C & M), and two InvenTeam participants: the teacher (K) and the student-historian (J). Professor A had previously worked on research with the staff of the Lemelson-MIT program, whom we also consulted during this project.

Utilizing records collected by the InvenTeam, we engaged in weekly conversational interviews with the teacher and the student-historian over the course of a six-month period. The teacher, K, was the primary participant-partner and attended every meeting; the former student-historian, J, joined as her schedule permitted. The interviews were nonlinear and mainly followed the flow of the conversation rather than predefined questions. In the early interviews, we invited the participant-partners to view the video segments and help us as outsiders and learners understand what we saw on the video from their insider points of view. These video-facilitated interactions then led to more conversational interviews in which we explored a variety of supports for the InvenTeam.

In this chapter we focus on one aspect from this over time work with members of the Oregon InvenTeam – the processes of conversational participatory interviewing informed by interactional ethnographic principles. Through this focus on the processes and potentials of conversational interviewing, we construct a telling case of how IE principles can be employed in conversational interviews when working with records collected by others who serve as insiders, or cultural guides.

Conceptualizing Conversational Interviewing in IE Studies

Interactional ethnographers seek to understand complex social worlds from the perspectives of the insiders who socially and discursively co-construct patterns and meanings of their lives within situated cultural groups over time. Interactional ethnographers work *with* participants and pay careful attention to the language-in-use through which members of groups co-construct ways of acting, being and knowing in their groups or teams. The focus on language-in-use, or discourse, enables interactional ethnographers to explore how processes, meanings, and social, material, semiotic, and activity systems (Gee & Green, 1998) within groups are created in and through interactions moment-by-moment and over time. Attention to discourse enables uncovering varied sociocultural and linguistic resources (Bloome et al., 2005; Gumperz, 1992) and funds of knowledge (Gonzalez et al., 2005; Saenz & Skukauskaité, under review) participants bring to social situations and signal as relevant to contextualize their actions and meanings.

Focusing on the discourse of conversational interviews, we explore how participants, in an ongoing IE-informed project, interactionally co-construct grounded interpretations of their developing understandings and practices situated in their cultures-in-the-making (Collins & Green, 1992). To conceptualize conversational interviewing, we first introduce the IE principles and then step back to provide the larger contexts shaping the role of interviewing in ethnographic research more broadly. We link IE to ethnographic and interviewing literature by: 1) introducing IE principles, 2) examining conversational interviewing in ethnography, 3) conceptualizing interviews as purposeful conversations, 4) demonstrating the relationality potentials in conversational interviews, and 5) illuminating the role of discourse in co-constructing and analyzing conversational interviews. Through these five subsections we lay the foundation for conceptualizing and employing conversational interviews in interactional ethnographic studies and beyond.

Interactional Ethnographic Principles for Conversational Interviewing

Our exploration of conversational interviewing is grounded in interconnected IE principles such as:

- *stepping back from what we know* (Green & Bridges, 2018) to seek *emic understandings* and develop relationships with participants;
- *identifying boundaries* (Green et al., 2012) by following referential trails or tracing units of study (such as people, texts or events) through which cultural practices can be revealed (Castanheira et al., 2001);
- *making connections* (Green et al., 2012) through contextualizing participant discourse and *backward and forward mapping* to uncover the roots and routes of insider actions and knowledge;
- constructing a *holistic perspective* (Green et al., 2003) through triangulation (Green & Chian, 2018) and intertextual and intercontextual analyses at multiple levels of scale (Green et al., 2015; Skukauskaité & Girdzijauskiené, 2021);
- engaging in *nonlinearity* (Green et al., 2012) through employing an abductive, iterative and recursive logic of inquiry, which leads to
- developing new understandings and (re)presentations (Green & Bridges, 2018) of phenomena under study.

These principles are embedded in the ways we conceptualize and enact conversational interviews with our research partners and participants. Throughout the chapter, we use italics to highlight the IE principles and related concepts central to constructing the iterative, recursive, and abductive processes of conceptualizing, analyzing, and presenting conversational interviewing and its possibilities.

Conversational Interviewing in Ethnography

Conversational interviewing is one method in a plethora of interviewing options available to ethnographers and other researchers. Interviewing is one of the most common methods for generating data in wide range of qualitative studies (and other forms of research) (Brinkman & Kvale, 2015; Roulston, 2022). Methods of interviewing may range from more formal semi-structured interviews to photo-, artifact-, video-, or task-elicitation interviews, walk-alongs or place-based interviews, to brief informal conversations sparked by observations in the field. Ethnographic interviewing, unlike the one-time semi-structured interviews dominating qualitative research, requires deeper contextualization, ongoing access, relationship-building over time (Heyl, 2007), and the holistic understandings of the languacultures in which inter-views take place. In ethnography, interviews are part of "being there" (Heath & Street, 2008; Heyl, 2007; Walford, 2008) and often occur in relation to over time observation and/or engagement with the participants in a variety of spaces and activities; therefore, even more formal semi-structured interviews tend to be more conversational in ethnographic research.

Conversational interviewing allows the researcher to engage dialogically with the interviewee in co-constructing knowledge and meaning during the interview process (Skukauskaitė, 2017). Since ethnographic inquiry devel-ops over time, ethnographic interviews are typically not one-time events but ongoing conversations which can be initiated and/or guided by the research-ers and/or participants (Heyl, 2007). Key informants and other participants become partners who influence the study's developing logic-in-use (ongoing decision-making processes during the course of a study) and can (re)shape its directions. In this way, *conversational interviews are responsive to the people and local situations* and facilitate meaning construction over time. Bakhtin (1979/1986) argued that "actively responsive understanding" in communication anticipates over time change and deepening understandings:

> Sooner or later what is heard and actively understood will find its response in the subsequent speech or behavior of the listener. In most cases, genres of complex cultural communication are intended precisely for this kind of actively responsive understanding with delayed action.
>
> *(p. 60)*

The "delayed action" may include research partners' reflexivity; connec-tions among events, ideas, and people; and subsequent questions or topics for interview conversations. (We will explore such "delayed action" in the section related to event map in Table 6.1.) The delayed actions are possible

TABLE 6.1 Event Map of a 22-Minute Segment of a Conversational Interview

Event #	Time Stamp	Speakers	Event	Subevent	Analytic notes re Conversational Interviewing in IE
1	00:00 → 00:16	A, K	Rapport building	• Greetings	**Relationship building,** checking in;
	00:17 → 01:43	K, M, A		• Talking about pets	Participant initiates topics
	01:51 → 02:04	K, M, A		• Asking about our week	Participant asks researchers
2	02:05 → 04:12	K, C, K, A, K	Constructing current context in school	• What is happening in school re COVID plans • C relating to K as a teacher • Expressing fatigue	**Contextualizing;** making connections; relationship building; human connection
3	04:14 → 05:11	K, A, K, A, M, A, C, A, M, A	Discussing logistics for research	• Dialogue about student–historian • Research explanations	**Ethnographic interview explanations;** positioning of researchers and participants; positioning participant as guide/leader
4	05:13 → 06:54	K, C, K, C	Video–facilitated interviewing (image on screen)	• Talking about classroom setup • Talking about how/why she painted • Talking about installed components/pegboard	**Contextualizing through video;** calling for emic perspective; participant as expert & guide
5	06:56 → 07:25	A, K, A, K, A	Research explanations	• Explaining that we planned to start here • Asking for further description	**Research explanations;** situating in rich points
6	07:25 → 08:43	K	Sharing philosophy	• Discussing personal philosophy • Discussing school philosophy • Talking about students	**Following participant lead;** creating space for the insider to make discuss what is important to her

(Continued)

TABLE 6.1 Event Map of a 22-Minute Segment of a Conversational Interview *(Continued)*

Event #	Time Stamp	Speakers	Event	Subevent	Analytic notes re Conversational Interviewing in IE
7	08:43 → 12:10	K, A	Explaining learning space	• Pointing out space dedicated to InvenTeam • Talking about flexibility of space • Verbally mapping space	**Contextualizing dialogue in local space**; inviting insider sharing of her space for outsiders; researcher positionings as learners
8	12:11 → 13:36	K	Talking about stress	• Using space to deal with difficult days • Shifting to present situation • Shifting back to past	Participant demonstrating **contrastive relevance**; **contextualizing teacher work in times and space**
9	13:40 → 16:00	A, K, A, K, A, K, C	Expanding on preparedness for InvenTeam facilitators	• Asking for suggestion for future IT facilitators • Talking about advice given • Learning from experience • Comparing self to others	Employing **ethnographic questions** for further explanation; K positioning herself as expert;
10	16:01 → 17:10	C, K, A	Discussing the role of teacher as facilitator	• Expressing difficulties in teaching • Describing the perceptions of others	Interjection from researcher leads to new topic; **Nonlinear co-construction of flow**

(Continued)

TABLE 6.1 Event Map of a 22-Minute Segment of a Conversational Interview *(Continued)*

Event #	Time Stamp	Speakers	Event	Subevent	Analytic notes re Conversational Interviewing in IE
11	17:11 → 17:42	K, A, C, K, C, A, K	Exploring impact	• responding to A's statement about possible impact of someone reading about the InvenTeam • Current impact of project (& paper)	Co-constructing new understandings; **contextualizing in larger fields;** allowing new topic to occur and unfold nonlinearly
12	17:44 → 20:36	K	Introducing the roles and relationships with school principal	• Communication with principal about project and paper • History of principal • Introduction of principal's predecessor • Past role of principal as a support • conflict at school perception of others need for cooperation • principal as team/community resource	**Participant insider leads** to new topic; Researchers employ **active listening** to hear emic POV
13	20:37 → 21:56	K, C, K, C, K	Making suggestions to InvenTeam teachers	• Making suggestions to future facilitators	Positionings within and beyond the research partnership; **contextualizing in larger fields**

in conversational interviewing because such conversations are iterative, over time, and purposeful.

Purposeful Conversations

Conversational interviews are both friendly conversations and interviews. Partners in an interview know they are engaged in a purposeful event in which they explore a range of interrelated topics and co-construct knowledge of interest to the researchers and the participants. While friendly chit-chat and exchange of views and experiences can and does take place in ethnographic interviewing, interviews as purposeful research interactions tend to reduce or forego the "socially accepted rules of conversation and reciprocity" (Walford, 2007) for the goals of seeking insider understandings in the locally situated contexts. Spradley (1979/2016), in one of the early systematic volumes on ethnographic interviewing, identified a set of similarities and differences between everyday conversations and ethnographic interviews. He argued,

> It is best to think of ethnographic interviews as a series of friendly conversations into which the researcher slowly introduces new elements to assist informants to respond as informants. Exclusive use of these new *ethnographic elements*, or introducing them too quickly, will make interviews become like a formal interrogation. Rapport will evaporate, and informants may discontinue their cooperation. At any time during an interview it is possible to shift back to a friendly conversation. A few minutes of easygoing talk interspersed here and there throughout the interview will pay enormous dividends in rapport.
>
> *(pp. 58–59)*

Spradley identified three ethnographic elements which inextricably transform a friendly conversation into an ethnographic interview: *explicit purpose, ethnographic explanations,* and *ethnographic questions.* Unlike everyday conversations which do not have to have an explicit purpose in constructing knowledge about a particular topic, conversational interviews revolve around *a purpose* and involve the researcher posing questions through which the ethnographer "gradually takes more control of the talking, directing it to those channels that lead to discovering the cultural knowledge of the informant" (p. 59).

Writing in 1978–1979, Spradley described the researcher-informant roles more hierarchically and statically than they are viewed in ethnographic research nowadays. He did not yet have access to knowledge about varied ways of diffusing power differentials, knowledge sharing, and constructionist perspectives on knowledge creation and participatory research. Nevertheless, Spradley's argument about ethnographic interviews being more than, and different from, friendly conversation remains germane and has been reiterated in varied ways by numerous scholars writing on ethnographic and qualitative interviews (e.g., Brenner, 2006; Brinkman & Kvale, 2015; Roulston, 2010).

In addition to having an explicit purpose, ethnographic interviews involve *ethnographic explanations* (Spradley, 1979/2016) about the project and informed consent, recording, roles and positionings of the researcher and participants, formats and goals for the interviews, notetaking, reasons for particular kinds of questions and interactions, among many other explanations the researcher shares throughout the ethnographic project. These explanations are not one-time events but can be brought up throughout the ethnographic project as the researchers and participant-partners learn about and with each other and (re) negotiate access and directions for the individual interview conversations and the study as a whole.

Spradley argued the ethnographic interview further differs from a friendly conversation in the kinds of *ethnographic questions* the researcher asks and how the questions are structured. In his book on *Ethnographic Interviewing*, Spradley (1979/2016) introduced more than 30 descriptive, structural and/or contrast questions ethnographers can employ in seeking to understand participant meanings about their cultural worlds. In a friendly conversation both partners may ask each other questions or may transition from topic to topic without in-depth exploration; in contrast, in an ethnographic interview conversation, the researcher will need to employ a variety of questions and interviewing skills (e.g., listening, back-channeling, empathizing, probing) to develop in-depth understandings about the perspectives, experiences, actions, and meanings participants enact in their social worlds. Turn-taking, reciprocity, abbreviating, and assuming common knowledge are employed less in ethno-graphic interviews than they would be in everyday conversations (Spradley, 1979/2016; Walford, 2007). Nevertheless, conversational ethnographic inter-views become opportunities for dialogue, learning, and discovery not only for the researcher but also for participant research partners. Conversational interviewing creates spaces for knowledge co-construction, power-sharing and diffusion, and relationship building.

Relationality in Conversational Interviews

At the core of conversational interviews are relationships grounded in mutual *respect* and commitment to *beneficence* and *justice* – the three underlying prin-ciples for the ethical conduct and protection of human subjects in research (National Commission for the Protection of Human Subjects of Biomedical and Behavioral Research, 1979). Enacting mutual respect, beneficence, and social justice, interactional ethnographers build relationships in which research partners and participants influence what can be uncovered and how to under-stand the phenomena studied. IE principles of *stepping back from the known* and *seeking emic understandings* of participant perspectives *in the contexts of relevance* to insiders guide the interactional ethnographer's logic of inquiry, ongoing co-negotiated access, and relationality with research partners.

As interactional ethnographers working *with* our research partners, we seek to create opportunities through which the research interactions can be beneficial to all involved in a variety of ways. Understanding what is beneficial to whom and in what ways develops through over time engagement and developing relationships. For example, our partner teacher shared that for her some the benefits of the research partnership with us included: an opportunity to remember and reflect on a difficult year of action in which time for reflection was scarce; connecting with other adults, especially during the isolating times of the COVID-19 pandemic; sharing her expertise; seeing the importance and potential impact of her work beyond her local situation; and feeling heard and validated as a teacher and a human being with complex perspectives, emotions, needs, and accomplishments.

Conversational interviewing revolves around *the relationship* between the interviewer and the participant. The relationship develops *over time* and can be in constant flux, as research partners interact and position themselves and each other in particular ways relative to the topic and developing relationships. The researcher may initiate the contact and access to the site but as the project develops, trust and relationships grow, participant-partners can take on more of the leadership role in introducing the topics and guiding the researchers to aspects of social life of significance to the partners. The IE principles of *stepping back from the known, seeking an emic perspective,* and exploring participant languacultures *holistically* by *making connections,* encourage the researchers to create opportunities for participants to lead and initiate topics in *nonlinear* ways. In stepping back from our role and its implicated power as researchers, we as interactional ethnographers *position ourselves as learners* (Agar, 1996; Heath & Street, 2008). In this way, we open up spaces for our partners to show us what they deem important in their social worlds in relation to the interests the researcher may have initiated but participating research partners have (re)constructed anew.

In positioning ourselves as learners and encouraging participants to initiate topics and lead us into and through their social worlds and their meanings, we aim at diffusing the power differentials of researcher-participant roles seen in more formal semi-structured interviews where the researcher asks questions and the participant answers. In conversational ethnographic interviewing guided by IE principles, we seek to learn *with* and *from*, not merely *about* our research partners and their social worlds. While IE research projects may start with more defined researcher-participant roles, the over time relationship building and the conversational nature of ethnographic interviewing enables the repositioning of roles, relationships, expertise, and insiderness (who is an insider to what; Skukauskaitė & Girdzijauskienė, 2021) in relationship to the social contexts, relationships, and topics of study, as demonstrated across multiple chapters in this volume. The underlying role and implicated power of the researcher (Briggs, 2002) never fully goes away, but is mitigated through purposeful *stepping back* and *sharing of the research process* with participant-partners. How this sharing occurs and what is signaled as relevant by whom, becomes visible through analysis of discourse.

Discursive Co-construction of Roles and Meanings in Conversational Interviewing

One of the distinguishing features of IE is its *focus on the discursive construction of meaning in and through interaction and contextualization cues*. Focusing on the way people in interaction use language and signal meanings enables IE researchers to follow the referential trails in moment-by-moment conversations, as well as over time, within any interview and in the larger project. In this way, we enact the IE principle of *creating boundaries* for analyses based on what insiders mark as important. Discourse analysis of what and how participants signal to each other also guides the ways we engage with the IE principle of *making connections*. Discourse is an anchor that leads us to exploring meanings, documents, and ideas co-constructed through moment-by-moment interaction. In the event map and discourse analysis of one segment from our interview below, we demonstrate how attention to moment-by-moment meaning construction can lead to discoveries of unforeseen topics of importance to the participants and thus also to IE researchers.

Underlying the discourse analysis and IE researcher interests in *how*, not only *what*, participants co-construct as important, is Bakhtin's (1979/1986) premise that *people speak with an implicated hearer* in mind. The speaker constructs expectations for the hearers both present in the conversation and implied as potential audiences. For example, in our interview, the teacher talked with us not only as a research team, but also as individuals with particular backgrounds and relationships to her. She connected with one of our team members (C) as a fellow teacher and also implied other, future, teachers who would be facilitating invention education with their students.

As speakers speak with present and distant implicated hearer(s), and as hearers listen to the current speaker as well as speakers of the past (Bakhtin, 1979/1986), they signal how meaning is to be heard, understood, and (re) presented to others. Through such multilayered interactions, hearers and speakers engage in what Gumperz (1995) called "mutual inferencing", or meaning-making based on contextualization cues signaled in the conversation. Contextualization cues are auditory, visual, technological, and other signals through which speakers and hearers make sense of the flow of the conversation. The cues could be pauses and their length; shift in pitch or volume; pacing of the speech; eye gaze shifts; physical actions; lexical signals; and semantic shifts, among others (Green & Kelly, 2019; Gumperz, 1992). In our work in the Zoom environment, contextualization cues also included muting/

unmuting, video on or off, physical proximity to camera, configurations of gazes toward/away from the camera, a raised hand icon or an actual raised hand, screen sharing, etc. These cues, while taken for granted and almost invisible in the flow of the conversation, provide analytic clues for focusing attention and boundary-making during analysis.

Contextualization cues in discourse also signal what is socially relevant and significant (Hymes, 1974) for the participants in the conversation. Drawing on Bakhtin's dialogic theories and Kristeva's concept of intertextuality, Bloome and colleagues (2005) argued that, in acting and reacting with each other, people propose a variety of potential directions and meanings. For meanings to become socially significant, once the cues are proposed, they need to be recognized, acknowledged, and then entered into the active *co-construction of social significance and accomplishments within a particular group* (including a research team). The four-part discursive actions of (1) *proposing*, (2) *recognizing*, (3) *acknowledging*, and (4) *marking as socially significant specific aspects of interactions* help IE researchers recognize the *emic perspective, construct boundaries* of relevant events, and follow the intertextual trails to *making connections* which help contextualize the moment-by-moment interaction to construct a *holistic understanding*.

In this conceptual part of the chapter, we introduced conversational interviews in IE studies, explored them as purposeful conversations involving relationship building and discursive co-construction of meanings focused on insider perspectives. Throughout the section, we wove IE principles at the core of conversational interviewing into IE studies. In the next section, we explore a co-constructed conversational interview between three university-based researchers and a teacher-partner as they explored insider perspectives about working on an InvenTeam.

We chose this interview for this chapter because it enabled us to illuminate the conversational interview aspects discussed above. It is also representative of the many other nonlinear conversations we had throughout the project. We first present an event map of the beginning of the interview and analyze how the events represent various aspects of conversational interviewing. Then we employ discourse analysis to demonstrate how a rich point encountered in the conversation was co-constructed and how it led to new topics and ethnographic explorations. In this way, we demonstrate how ethnographic conversational interviewing enacts IE principles in the interview and analysis.

Conversational Interview in Action

The conversational interview took place on June 5, 2020, as part of an IE-informed study about the work of teachers, students, and others in invention education in one InvenTeam. Participants in this interview conversation included three members of a university-based research team (A, C, and M) and the InvenTeam teacher (K) who partnered with us on the research as an insider. For this interview the research team pre-selected a video segment we wanted the teacher to view to help us understand what was going on in her classroom. This video segment was paused and visible via the screenshare feature in Zoom. The conversational interview lasted about two hours. In our analyses, we focus on 22 minutes of the interview. The first step in our analyses to uncover how a conversational interview was co-constructed involved developing an event map of the whole interview sequence and then selecting the segment of focus for this chapter.

Constructing the Event Map

Table 6.1 includes an event map of the first 22 minutes of this interview. An event map is a type of structuration map which provides a big-picture overview of what has occurred in a given period of time (Green & Meyer, 1991). It is constructed by following contextualization cues signaled by participants in interaction (Green & Kelly, 2019), noting shifts in activity, speakers, and/or topics to mark a new event and its constituent subtopics, or subevents. Event maps allow us to explore *how* a conversation is socially co-constructed through an often-nonlinear sequencing of topics, positionings, and participant and/or researcher actions. We demonstrate this in the analyses below.

In Table 6.1, events (numbered in the first and listed in the fourth column) represent the major topics of the conversational interview, while subevents (column 5) indicate the subtopics, or elements the major events encompass. In the last, shaded, column we include analytic notes relating to conversational interviewing and IE principles.

As indicated in Table 6.1, the first event focuses on building rapport. The event begins in a conversational tone and includes three sub-events: initial greetings, talking about pets, and asking about each other's week. As indicated in column 3, Speakers, researcher A starts the first event, but the teacher-partner K initiates the next two subevents, in which researchers M and A also participate. K's first utterance, "I just popped in and I was like, oh my gosh who's in my classroom right now", refers to the video cued and paused on a shared screen in the Zoom call (see Figure 6.1). In this utterance, the discursive choices of informal language ("popped in", "I was like", "oh my gosh"), marks the conversational register of the interview, while her gaze directed to the video also signals the researchers' intention to direct a conversation toward K's classroom (picked up directly in Event 4).

Event 2 shifts to a new topic K initiates. This event continues the process of relationship building but refocuses on contextualizing the conversation to the pandemic and K's school's response. In the first subevent of Event 2, K shares her frustration about her school's plans regarding COVID-19, which leads to the next subevent, in which one of the researchers, C, relates to the frustration and positions herself as a former fellow teacher. In the third subevent of

Event 2, the teacher-partner expresses fatigue, connecting the larger context of the pandemic with the challenges of teaching. As indicated in the Speakers column, K initiates the event and the conversation weaves back and forth among K, C, K, A, and K, signaling a conversational space being created among the teacher-partner K and co-researchers C and A.

The first two events focused on relationship building, making connections, contextualizing, and positioning of self and others in the research partnership and professionally. Event 3 shifts from a friendly conversation to the ethnographic interview, with its *ethnographic explanations* (Spradley, 1979/2016) of the research logistics, roles, and positionings in research. As in Event 2, it is the teacher-partner who initiates Event 3 (marked by K in the first position of speakers for Event 3). She changes the subject to the discussion of logistics for research and participant roles. She positions herself as a guide by stating she will check on the student-historian who had not yet arrived in the Zoom call (she joins later in the meeting). The conversation then shifts to research explanations, as seen by mainly researchers A, M, and C co-constructing this event. In this way, Event 3 moves from a conversation to an ethnographic interview, which then continues in Event 4.

Event 4 develops from the research explanations begun in Event 3. On the shared Zoom screen, researcher C had cued a segment of the video from K's classroom. The video frame shows a focused view of one part of the room. Without prompting by the researchers, K directs her gaze to the video and begins talking about the class setup (Subevent 1), explains how and why she painted the walls the way she did (Subevent 2), and what she installed on a pegboard (Subevent 3) to support student access to tools for invention. Figure 6.1 is a

FIGURE 6.1 Teacher Partner's Classroom Space – Screenshot of Paused Video Projected on Zoom Through Screenshare

screenshot of the video, with labels identifying the items and spaces K described to the researchers.

In Event 4, the teacher as an insider provides a grand tour of her classroom, guiding researchers to her emic point of view and contextualizing it in the goals she had for the students. K leads the conversation, with C providing brief responses and playing/pausing the video. At a pause, researcher A adds an explanation of why we started with that video and asks for further, in-depth descriptions, so researchers can learn to see the classroom the way the teacher does. This research explanation constitutes Event 5 and ties to Event 3 (both shaded, to show connection), where research explanations had begun. This weaving of participant-partner-initiated dialogue and researcher explanations and (re)positionings as learners demonstrates how a conversational interview both *creates spaces for the participant-partner to lead* and for the researchers to add research explanations when necessary. In this way, the researchers make transparent to the participant the reasons behind particular questions while the participant-partner has the freedom to choose what insights and in what ways to share in the interview conversation. Transparency of ethnographic explanations and freedom of choice for the participant enact the principles of relationality, respect, and power diffusion we presented above as important for conversational interviewing.

This diffusion of power and the participant-partner's take-up of leadership in the conversation is visible in Events 6–8, all initiated by K. Events 6 and 7 pick up on discursive actions initiated in Event 4, in which the teacher had begun to talk about her classroom. In Event 6 she shares her philosophy of teaching. In Event 7 she refers back to the on-screen video to map her classroom space and explain the ways she creates the learning spaces for her students. Here she is the languacultural guide taking the ethnographers-as-learners on a tour of her teaching space.

In Event 8, K contextualizes the work she did with the team in both time and space: in Subevent 1, she discusses how she had used her space to deal with difficult days, and in Subevent 2, shifts her focus back to the present, revealing how therapeutic it has been for her to discuss her InvenTeam year with us. This leads her to another temporal shift in Subevent 3, where she moves back to talking about the physical space, and how she used parts of the space to take needed breaks of "alone time" when needed.

Events 9 and 10 are initiated by the researchers. In Event 9, researcher A asks a structural ethnographic interview question: whether the teacher-partner would make suggestions for future facilitators to create a space to take a break. The teacher-partner shares about advice she was given (Subevent 2) and expresses having learned from her mistake of not heeding that advice (Subevent 3). In Subevent 4, she also shares about the difficulties she had not comparing herself to others who had been in her position before. This leads into a conversational interjection from one of the researchers, C, which shifts to Event 10.

In Event 10, C speaks about the role of the K–12 teacher as a facilitator and shares her own experience as a teacher, reiterating her positionality and identification with K as a teacher, first expressed in Event 2. This shift from insider perspective of K about her classroom to C self-positioning as a fellow teacher rather than only as researcher in this project, *re-introduces conversational elements into the flow of the interview.* C, as well as A, in Event 10 express the support for the importance of K's work and state her impact is beyond her school, through research with us. This conversation then opens another line of thought teacher-partner leads in Event 11.

In Event 11, the teacher-partner and researchers explore the impact of her work through publications and presentations from the research project, which leads to Event 12, in which K introduces her communication with the school principal and the principal's role. This interview segment ends with K initiating suggestions for other teachers. Events 11–13 are initiated by the teacher, in response to an ethnographic follow up question by the researcher in Event 9 and a conversational interjection by another researcher in Event 10.

Taken together, these thirteen events demonstrate the *nonlinear, iterative, and recursive nature of conversational interviewing,* in which *participant-partners and researchers co-construct the flow, positionings, and deep, contextualized understandings* about the work of the teacher and her students. The event map represented in Table 6.1 allowed us to demonstrate:

- *how* the conversational interview was co-constructed event-to-event,
- *who* led the *shifts* in topics and thus events,
- *what ties connected* events and *what got socially accomplished* through intertextual connections (Bloome & Egan-Robertson, 1993) among discourses, spaces, and experiences within the interview and across time.

Given that the teacher-partner initiated nine of the thirteen events in this segment, the event map also provides evidence for ways of enacting the ethnographic principles of *seeking emic understandings*; following referential trails *to note the boundaries of what participants signal as important*; and *creating connections* among events and knowledge co-constructed.

The weaving of *elements of the friendly conversation* in Events 1, 2, 8, and 10, the *ethnographic research explanations and questions* (Events 3, 4, 5, 9), and the empathetic, relational aspects of human interaction *among* and *with* partners demonstrate *how the relationality, diffusion of power, and conversational spaces of ethnographic interviews enable the participant, alongside the researchers, to build connections* with each other as well as among events, times, and spaces. In this way, ethnographers-as-learners and the participant-partner develop deeper understandings not only of *what* happened during the InvenTeam year, *how* it happened, *where* and *in what contexts*, but also *how people felt and experienced* the events and *what it meant for them* at the *time* and *in reflection*.

In this section, we demonstrated how a conversational ethnographic interview is enacted with IE epistemological principles providing the foundation for the relationality, connections, contextualizing, and diffusion of researcher-participant power relationships with the ethnographic focus on insider perspectives. Giving the participant-partner space to lead the conversational interview creates opportunities for deeper understandings, reflexivity, and knowledge construction in ways responsive and responsible to our research partners as well as the larger research and educational communities.

We understand that such forms of interviewing in which we give *space for the participant to lead* as we wander together among topics which sometimes seem disconnected may be disconcerting and uncomfortable, especially for beginning scholars who may want to have more control and know what to do beforehand. However, we encourage embracing the discomfort (Skukauskaitė et al., 2018), trusting the process, and working *with* the research partners to discover together what is important to the insiders in the ethnographic spaces we seek to understand. Remaining *open* and not redirecting a conversation to what the researcher planned may lead to new rich points and discoveries. In the next section, we show how one such conversation occurred and led us to explore an unanticipated, but highly relevant, idea about the role of a school principal in the InvenTeam process. The conversation encompasses Events 11 and 12 in the event map above.

Enacting a Conversational Interview with the Teacher-Partner: Initiating and Leading Unanticipated Topics

In this section, we explore a transcript of Events 11 and 12 to demonstrate how the conversational interview is co-constructed and how the space for the participant to lead takes all members of the interview to unforeseen topics. Table 6.2 is a transcript of three minutes of the interview. The transcript is in message units (Green & Kelly, 2019; Green & Wallat, 1981), with some of them summarized to conserve space and maintain the focus on the interactional sequences analyzed. Column 1, Time Stamp, indicates time and demonstrates the flow of the conversation; Column 2 indicates shifts in speakers. We provide the transcript in Column 3, in which we numbered message units to facilitate analysis. The fourth column groups message units into sequence units which tie a set of message units together thematically (Green & Kelly, 2019) to show how participants co-construct particular semantic meanings as they act and react to each other (Bloome et al., 2005).

In the last column we include some notable contextualization cues enacted in this conversation. One of the main contextualization cues − regular micro-pausing while co-constructing the flow of a conversation − is embedded in the shifts from one MU to the next. Contextualization cues noted include longer pauses, laughing, addressee directionality, intonation, self-corrections,

TABLE 6.2 Transcript of Events 11 and 12

Time stamp	Speaker	Transcript, based on message units	Sequence unit	Contextualization cues
17:11 → 17:13	K	1. I	1	Pause after "I"
		2. people.		Pause after "people"
		3. wait.		Rising intonation
		4. people are gonna read this?		
		5. are you sure [A]?		
	A	6. *(inaudible) yes*		K laughing
17:18 → 17:20	K	7. people read what you write		K laughing
		8. you're right		
		9. you're right		
17:22 → 17:23	A	10. *you'll be writing with us*		Falling intonation — statement
17:24 → 17:31	C	11. *I just cited you in the paper that I'm writing in the lit review*	2	
		12. *[K] and [J] are both in the citation page*		
17:31 → 17:33	K	13. oh my gosh.		Interjection, emoting
17:33 → 17:38	C	14. *(inaudible) in [State]*		(Directed to K)
		15. *just so you know*		
		16. *you're (inaudible) cited now*		
		17. *seriously*		18 − Falling
		18. *dead serious*		intonation, stop
17:39	K	19. *really cool*		
→ 17:43	A	20. *cite personal communication*		(To C)
17:44 → 18:02	K	21. well	3	Pause after "Well"
		22. we also		holding floor; short
		23. like		MUs 21–26, choppy
		24. it is a really exciting thing		talk signals developing ideas
		25. and I was able.		(thinking out loud)
	K	26. last week I sent my principal a text		
		27. and I said		
		28. hey just so you know		
		29. this is happening		
		30. and we are moving forward with this		
		31. so he was super excited about it		

(Continued)

TABLE 6.2 Transcript of Events 11 and 12 *(Continued)*

Time stamp	Speaker	Transcript, based on message units	Sequence unit	Contextualization cues
18:03 → 18:18	K	32. um 33. he came in 34. goodness 35. he's been at [High School] 36. I think this is his second full year 37. second 38. no third full year 39. I don't know 40. I could look it up 41. um 42. and he came in after a principal who was like 43. beloved	4	Pause after "he came in" slight pause, indicating thinking Self-correction short MUs –show process of constructing what to say in the moment
18:19 → 19:02	K	44. –71. conversation about the previous principal and the new principal, compared to the past principal, with opinions of colleagues about both	5	
19:03 → 19:14	K	45. um 46. I- 47. I knew 48. throughout the entire InvenTeam experience 49. that I needed him on board though 50. because I knew the role that 51. that advocacy role 52. that he would play	6	"um" – Holding floor from previous turn while shifting and developing the topic further
19:15 → 19:19	K	53. um 54. and there were my colleagues 55. would often 56. um 57. maybe like hassle me 58. and make fun of me a little bit	7	Longer pause after "often" Pause after "um" "um"/"maybe"/"like": Hedging, constructing ideas
19:21 → 19:31		59. they're like oh [K] 60. you're just stroking his ego 61. and I was like 62. no		Longer MU in 90-developed idea, statement of belief

(Continued)

TABLE 6.2 Transcript of Events 11 and 12 *(Continued)*

Time stamp	Speaker	Transcript, based on message units	Sequence unit	Contextualization cues
19:32 → 19:44	K	63. this is stuff I'm doing that I need him on board	8	Repeated "like" – fillers while developing thought
		64. because whether it be like		Pause after "signatures like"
		65. the process		
		66. that was the school district		
		67. or something that I needed		
		68. something within the building		
		69. or I needed certain paperwork		
		70. or signatures		
		71. like		
		72. I		
		73. I needed him to know what was going on		
19:45 → 19:51	K	74. and I think for a lot of people	9	Pause after "don't see" Pause after "those"
		75. if they don't see		
		76. Those		
19:52 → 19:58		77. it's		
		78. It's almost like that placeholder		
		79. like the principal		
		80. regardless of if they're good or the bad		
		81. they're the placeholder		
19:58 → 20:04		82. that is their role in the school		
		83. is to lead the school		
		84. and to support their students and teachers		
20:04 → 20:17	K	85. so	10	
		86. throughout the entire InvenTeam process		
		87. I was trying to just like		
		88. drip information for him		
		89. so that when he was in the community		
		90. he could talk about it,		
		91. or when he was at district office,		
		92. he could talk about it.		

(Continued)

TABLE 6.2 Transcript of Events 11 and 12 *(Continued)*

Time stamp	Speaker	Transcript, based on message units	Sequence unit	Contextualization cues
20:18 → 20:30	K	93. um 94. because 95. I felt like people didn't understand 96. how cool of a thing we were doing 97. and I just was like 98. they don't 99. ... 100. nobody gets it yet 101. like they still don't 102. ... 103. do they understand what's happening		Pause after "they don't" Pause after "they still don't"
20:32 → 20:36	K	104. um 105. so that was 106. that was really helpful for me 107. to be able to do that		Pause after "so that was"

Glossary of transcript notation symbols:

Symbol	Visual	Denotes		Example
Parentheses	( )	Transcription notes		(inaudible)
Brackets	[...]	Replaces proper nouns / identifying information		Participant names, location names
Ellipses	...	Used to denote longer pauses		MU 99, 102
Question mark	?	Rising intonation		MU 5
Period	.	Marked pause with a falling intonation		MU 2, 3
Italics	*italics*	Distinguishing researcher speech from that of the teacher. Teacher text in regular font to indicate her primary role as the core contributor, with researchers in supportive roles for the flow of K's talk		

verbal fillers, etc., all of which show *how* the conversation is being co-constructed. We provide the notations for the cues underneath the transcript in Table 6.2.

The conversation in this transcript follows Event 10 (Table 6.1), in which one of the researchers (C) and the teacher (K) discussed the role of teacher as facilitator and how that role is often misunderstood by others, who view it as "babysitting" rather than purposeful, informed guidance. Researcher A redirects the conversation and emphasizes the positive impact of the teacher's work by saying, "The lasting impact on your students, but also on us, and who knows who else that will read some of the work we eventually write".

Event 11, Sequence 1, begins by teacher K attempting to continue her prior thought "I/people" (MUs 1-2 in Table 6.2), then abruptly stopping herself with a pause (.) and a statement "wait" (MU3). She then addresses A's statement in the previous event, by using rising intonation: "people are gonna read this?/ are you sure, A?" This *delayed response* (Bakhtin, 1979/1986) results in shifting the conversational focus from the InvenTeam and teacher role with students (Events 9 and 10, Table 6.1) to the broader impact of our work together.

In MU 10, A confirms K's prior statement "people read what you write" (MU7), but repositions K as part of the group, an "us:" "you'll be writing with us". By not accepting "people read what you write" as being about her or her role as a professor, A diffuses the researcher-participant power positionings and includes all partners of the research team as writers whose work people will read. This sequence demonstrates how the researcher and participant (re) position themselves and the other, and how active listening, relationality, and empathy play a role in shifting the conversation from K's and C's doubts about teacher facilitator roles to the larger impact such roles enable.

In Sequence 2, C recognizes and acknowledges the thematic shift to teacher impact and discursively enacts a specific example in which the teacher K and the student-historian J have already made an impact in C's academic writing (MU11-12). In MU13, K emotes "oh my gosh" to which C then adds a confirmation of truthfulness "you're cited now/ seriously/ dead serious" (MU16–18). K acknowledges and accepts this co-constructed truth with "really cool" (MU19), which, after A's side note to C about how to cite "personal communication", leads to Event 12 and Sequence 3.

Sequence 3 begins with five message units (21–25) which are short, self-aborted bursts of speech, indicating K holding the floor (turn at speaking) (Edelsky, 1981), while constructing her thoughts. In MU26, K shifts the topic to a conversation about her principal, which continues for the rest of Event 12. In Sequence 3 she continues the idea of impact co-constructed in Sequences 1–2 but now, instead of doubt (MU 4–5: "people are gonna read it?"; MU 13: "oh my gosh") and acceptance (MU 19: "really cool"), K *demonstrates her own agency in constructing the impact of this work*. She states her action of sending her school principal a text (MU 26) to tell him about our collaborative work and then receiving his response, "super excited about it" (MU 31).

Introducing her interaction with the principal relating to the impact of our work then leads K to talking about her principal (Sequence 4), prior principal (Sequence 5), and her vision about the role of a principal in supporting her and her InvenTeam students (Sequences 6–10). In Sequences 7 (MU 53–62), 9 (MU 74–76, 80), and 10 (MU 95–102), K implicates the colleagues and other nay-sayers who do not "understand what's happening" (MU 103), connecting these sequences to Event 10; however, instead of using their views as a negative, she contrastively shows her own agency in envisioning and utilizing the school principal to support her work with students. In Sequence 8, K talks about how she constructed her own purposes for the principal, envisioning the principal's role (Sequence 9) as a "placeholder" (MU 81) to "support their students and teachers" (MU 84). She further demonstrates how she took a set of actions (Sequence 10) to keep the principal informed ("drip information to him"; MU 88) so he could help others understand "how cool of a thing we were doing" (MU 98).

In these three sequences (8–10), the teacher-partner talked into being the role of the principal, contrastively responding to the implicated perspectives of her colleagues and demonstrating her own agency as a facilitator of the InvenTeam. As indicated in the speaker column, once K brought up the idea of the principal in Sequence 3, the researchers did not interrupt. They *stepped back* and allowed the teacher to think even through moments when it was not clear what she might say, as indicated by short, tentative bursts of speech (e.g., MU 21–23, 39–41, 76–77), self-corrections and redirections (e.g., MU 24, 34, 42, 77–78), and longer pauses (MU 99, 102).

By not stepping in, allowing the teacher-partner to introduce the topic of the principal, and *listening* to how the topic unfolded, we gained valuable, unexpected insights. The ideas the teacher co-constructed with us as audience in this conversation included: the context of the school, the perspectives of the colleagues, K's vision about the role of the principal, her actions in advocating for her students, and her understanding of the school principal as a role, not a particular person. As ethnographers, we had no prepared questions about school principals or colleague perspectives on the work of an InvenTeam teacher. However, K's initiation of this topic became a rich point which enabled us to understand her insider perspective of what and whom she viewed as important supports in varied ways for her work with students on an InvenTeam. This conversation led us to adding principal as one of the key supports InvenTeams needed locally (Skukauskaitė et al., under review).

Trusting the Process of Conversational Interviews: Conclusions

In the previous two sections, we demonstrated how the conversational interview was enacted through a sequence of events (Table 6.1) and conversational sequences (Table 6.2). The interview was both an informal conversation, with its back-and-forth talk, informal chatting, and life-sharing, as well as a formal interview, with ethnographic explanations, recording, and overarching purposes of knowledge construction through the interview. In this last part of the chapter, we offer conclusions synthesizing the role of conversational interviews in interactional ethnographic research.

First, as our analyses demonstrate, conversational interviewing in IE supports us in gaining access to participant *emic points of view* we seek to uncover in ethnographic research. The analyses also make visible how the ethnographers-as-learners *step back from what they know or want to know* to create spaces for relationship building and *nonlinear* explorations of topics participants choose to foreground (Green & Bridges, 2018). We also emphasize that a conversational interview in ethnographic research is not a one-time event but a sequence of *contextually grounded* conversations *over time*.

Second, through our analyses we also demonstrated how conversational interviewing enacts the IE principles of *making connections* and *identifying boundaries* (Green et al., 2012) by following participant discursive actions *in context moment-by-moment* and *over time* (Kelly & Green, 2019). Our focus on language-in-use during the interview conversations, construction of message unit transcripts with contextualization cues, mapping of events and actions, and detailed analyses at multiple levels of scale enabled us to uncover many layers of meanings brought to, and co-constructed in and through, the ongoing interactions (Kelly & Green, 2019; Skukauskaitė & Girdzijauskienė, 2021). These multilayered analyses also enabled our team of IE researchers to discover the *rich points*, to follow them through, and to learn not only *what* was important to the insiders but also *how* this importance was co-constructed discursively and relationally (Skukauskaitė, 2017).

Third, through our analyses we illuminated how conversational interviewing creates opportunities for relationship building, power diffusion, and co-creation of knowledge *not about*, but *with* the people. Through active listening, dialogue, and ongoing positioning and repositioning of ourselves and our partners, we engaged in reflexive action, or *reflexivity*, that opened doors to new ways of interacting and knowledge construction. Throughout the chapter, we provided examples of how *conversational interviewing* can serve as a key resource for IE researchers as they study discursive co-construction of social life in various groups and situations. Other chapters in this volume offer additional and complementary perspectives on ways of engaging in the epistemological processes and discoveries constituting IE. We end the chapter with a set of suggestions to consider when envisioning and conducting conversational interviews within ethnographic studies.

Suggestions for Developing Conversational Interviewing in IE Studies

- One single interview is not enough in ethnographic research. We need *multiple* conversations, *over time*, to develop depth of understanding of the *emic perspectives* in *context*.
- Utilize *varied sources* of information to *prepare* for interviews, to *make connections* during interviews and analyses, and to *contextualize* interviews.

Video and audio records, fieldnotes, artifacts from the field and archived materials can be utilized as anchors for analyzing *interview conversations*.

- Work *with* the *participant-as-partner*, not a subject to use for your research interests. Encouraging participant expertise may help *build a relationship of trust* through which you will get closer to the *insider perspectives* you seek in ethnographic research.

- *Let go of the need to control* the interview: *step back* and *let the participant lead* even if, in the moment, the direction may not seem related to your purpose. You may discover knowledge and topics you didn't expect, and they will enrich your study and/or your understandings of your own role, as well as of interviewing processes and potentials.

- *Look for connections* – often nonlinear – during the analysis. Show the complexity of the ideas explored through the *nonlinear, iterative, and recursive* pathways of conversational interviewing.

- *Step back* from what you know or think you want to know. *Listen. Follow. Empathize. Create spaces* for *human connection* as well as for connections among ideas.

- Create *an event map to see the big picture* of how the interview is co-constructed and what topics and actions connect with others.

- Construct multiple levels of analyses to uncover not only *what* is talked about, but also *how* meanings are actively co-constructed in and through the interaction. *Look for rich points* for further analyses.

- *Engage the participant in looking back* at the records or data generated previously so they can expand, provide deeper insider perspectives, as well as reflect when looking back.

- Continuously engage in *reflexivity,* considering your actions, perspectives, and the way they shape what is happening in the research. Create spaces for participants and research partners to engage in reflexivity, too. Reflexivity about our experiences and our work in research can open doors not only to deeper relationships but also to deeper understandings of contexts and networks shaping what meanings are co-constructed and how they are enacted throughout the research process.

Suggested Readings

Mishler, E. G. (1986). *Research interviewing: Context and narrative.* Harvard University Press.
Roulston, K. (2022). *Interviewing: A guide to theory and practice.* Sage.

References

Agar, M. (1996). *The professional stranger: An informal introduction to ethnography* (2nd ed.). Academic Press.
Bakhtin, M. M. (1979/1986). *Speech genres and other late essays* (V. W. McGee, trans). University of Texas Press.

Bloome, D., Carter, S. P., Christian, B. M., Otto, S., & Shuart-Faris, N. (2005). *Discourse analysis and the study of classroom language and literacy events: A microethnographic perspective.* Lawrence Erlbaum.

Bloome, D., & Egan-Robertson, A. (1993). The social construction of intertextuality in classroom reading and writing lessons. *Reading Research Quarterly, 28*(4), 305–333.

Brenner, M. E. (2006). Interviewing in educational research. In J. L. Green, G. Camilli, & P. B. Elmore (Eds.), *Handbook of complementary methods in education research* (pp. 357–370). Lawrence Erlbaum.

Briggs, C. L. (2002). Interviewing, power/knowledge, and social inequality. In J. F. Gubrium & J. A. Holstein (Eds.), *Handbook of interview research: Context and method* (pp. 911–922). Sage.

Brinkman, S., & Kvale, S. (2015). *Interviews: Learning the craft of qualitative research interviewing* (3rd ed.). Sage.

Castanheira, M. L., Crawford, T., Dixon, C. N., & Green, J. L. (2001). Interactional ethnography: An approach to studying the social construction of literate practices. *Linguistics and Education, 11*(4), 353–400. https://doi.org/10.1016/s0898-5898(00)00032-2

Collins, E. C., & Green, J. L. (1992). Learning in classroom settings: Making or breaking a culture. In H. Marshall (Ed.), *Redefining student learning: Roots of educational restructuring* (pp. 59–85). Ablex.

Couch, S., Skukauskaitė, A., & Estabrooks, L. B. (2019a). Invention education and the developing nature of high school students' construction of an "inventor" identity. *Technology & Innovation, 20*(3), 285–302. https://doi.org/10.21300/20.3.2019.285

Couch, S., Skukauskaitė, A., & Green, J. L. (2019b). Invention education: Preparing the next generation of innovators. *Technology & Innovation, 20*(3), 161–163. https://doi.org/10.21300/20.3.2019.161

Edelsky, C. (1981). Who's got the floor? *Language in Society, 10*(3), 383–421. https://www.jstor.org/stable/4167262

Gee, J. P., & Green, J. L. (1998). Discourse analysis, learning, and social practice: A methodological study. *Review of Research in Education, 23*, 119–169.

Gonzalez, N., Moll, L. C., & Amanti, C. (Eds.). (2005). *Funds of knowledge: Theorizing practices in households, communities, and classrooms.* Laurence Erlbaum Associates.

Green, J. L., & Bridges, S. M. (2018). Interactional ethnography. In F. Fischer, C. E. Hmelo-Silver, S. R. Goldman, & P. Reimann (Eds.), *International handbook of the learning sciences* (pp. 475–488). Routledge.

Green, J. L., Castanheira, M. L., Skukauskaitė, A., & Hammond, J. W. (2015). Developing a multi-faceted research process. In N. Markee (Ed.), *The handbook of classroom discourse and interaction* (pp. 26–43). Wiley/Blackwell.

Green, J. L., & Chian, M. M. (2018). Triangulation. In B. B. Frey (Ed.), *The SAGE encyclopedia of educational research, measurement, and evaluation* (pp. 1718–1720). SAGE. http://dx.doi.org/10.415/9781506326139.n711

Green, J. L., Dixon, C. N., & Zaharlick, A. (2003). Ethnography as a logic of inquiry. In J. Flood, D. Lapp, J. R. Squire, & J. Jensen (Eds.), *Handbook of research on teaching the English language arts* (2nd ed., pp. 201–224). Lawrence Erlbaum Associates.

Green, J. L., & Heras, A. I. (2011). Identities in shifting educational policy contexts: The consequences of moving from two languages, one community to English only. In G. López-Bonilla & K. Englander (Eds.), *Discourses and identities in contexts of educational change* (pp. 155–194). Peter Lang.

Green, J. L., & Kelly, G. J. (2019). Appendix A: How we look at discourse: Definitions of sociolinguistic units. In G. J. Kelly & J. L. Green (Eds.), *Theory and methods for sociocultural research in science and engineering education* (pp. 264–270). Routledge.

Green, J. L., & Meyer, L. A. (1991). The embeddedness of reading in classroom life: Reading as a situated process. In C. Baker & A. Luke (Eds.), *Toward a critical sociology of reading pedagogy* (pp. 142–160). John Benjamins.

Green, J. L., Skukauskaitė, A., & Baker, W. D. (2012). Ethnography as epistemology: An introduction to educational ethnography. In J. Arthur, M. J. Waring, R. Coe, & L. V. Hedges (Eds.), *Research methodologies and methods in education* (pp. 309–321). Sage.

Green, J. L., & Wallat, C. (1981). Mapping instructional conversations: A sociolinguistic ethnography. In J. L. Green, & C. Wallat (Eds.), *Ethnography and language in educational settings* (pp. 161–195). Ablex.

Gumperz, J. J. (1992). Contextualization and understanding. In A. Duranti & C. Goodwin (Eds.), *Rethinking context: Language as an interactive phenomenon* (pp. 229–252). Cambridge University Press.

Gumperz, J. J. (1995). Mutual inferencing in conversation. In I. Markova, C. Grauman, & K. Foppa (Eds.), *Mutualities in dialogue* (pp. 101–123). Cambridge University Press.

Heath, S. B., & Street, B. V. (2008). *On ethnography: Approaches to language and literacy research*. Teachers College Press.

Heyl, B. S. (2007). Ethnographic interviewing. In P. Atkinson, S. Delamont, A. Coffey, J. Lofland, & L. Lofland (Eds.), *Handbook of ethnography* (pp. 369–383). Sage.

Hymes, D. (1974). *Foundations in sociolinguistics: An ethnographic approach*. University of Pennsylvania Press.

Invention Education Research Community. (2019). *Researching invention education: A white paper*. https://lemelson.mit.edu/node/2511

Kelly, G. J., & Green, J. L. (2019). Framing issues of theory and methods for the study of science and engineering education. In G. J. Kelly, & J. L. Green (Eds.), *Theory and methods for sociocultural research in science and engineering education* (pp. 1–28). Routledge.

Roulston, K. (2010). *Reflective interviewing: A guide to theory & practice*. Sage.

Saenz, C., & Skukauskaitė, A. (under review). Engaging Latina students in the invention ecosystem. *Technology & Innovation*.

Skukauskaitė, A. (2017). Systematic analyses of layered meanings inscribed in interview conversations: An interactional ethnographic perspective and its conceptual foundations. *Acta Paedagogica Vilnensia, 39*(2), 45–60. https://doi.org/10.15388/ActPaed.2017.39.11466

Skukauskaitė, A., Estabrooks, L., Morales Rodriguez, J., & Hull, K. (2019). High school student-historians documenting invention education processes: Opportunities and challenges from insider perspectives. *Forum on Ethnographic Investigations with Children and Youth*, Western Oregon University, Momouth, OR, May 30–131, 2019.

Skukauskaitė, A., & Girdzijauskienė, R. (2021). Video analysis of contextual layers in teaching-learning interactions. *Learning, Culture and Social Interaction, 29*. https://doi.org/10.1016/j.lcsi.2021.100499

Skukauskaitė, A., Noske, P., & Gonzales, M. (2018). Designing for discomfort: Preparing scholars for journeys through qualitative research. *International Review of Qualitative Research, 11*(3), 334–349. https://doi.org/10.1525/irqr.2018.11.3.334

Skukauskaitė, A., Saenz, C., Sullivan, M., Hull, K., & Rodriguez, J. M. (under review). Networks supporting problem-based invention education. *Interdisciplinary Journal of Problem-Based Learning.*

Spradley, J. (1979/2016). *The ethnographic interview.* Waveland Press.

National Commission for the Protection of Human Subjects of Biomedical and Behavioral Research (1979). *The Belmont report: Ethical principles and guidelines for the protection of human subjects of research.* https://www.hhs.gov/ohrp/regulations-and-policy/belmont-report/read-the-belmont-report/index.html

Walford, G. (2007). Classification and framing of interviews in ethnographic interviewing. *Ethnography and Education, 2*(2), 145–157. https://doi.org/10.1080/17457820701350491

Walford, G. (2008). The nature of educational ethnography. In G. Walford (Ed.), *How to do educational ethnography* (pp. 1–15). Tufnell Press.

7

UNCOVERING CULTURAL LEVELS EMBEDDED IN STUDENT ARTS-BASED PRACTICES

Rūta Girdzijauskienė

Lithuanian philosopher Vydūnas said: "People are never as beautiful as when they create". For me as a longtime music educator that has been the motto of my professional career. Art-based practices transport students from everyday life to a world of ideas and imagination, changing their daily behavior and ways of expression. Artistic emotions, expression, and persuasiveness are what viewers or listeners enjoy and admire. The outcomes of artistic activity – a drawing, a dance, a musical piece, or a performance – are usually chosen as the object of research in which the results of creating are analyzed.

No less important are the process aspects of arts-based practices: how works of art are created, what determines the diversity of creation, and how the personality and experiences of the creator are embodied in specific works. The components of cultural and social artistic creation processes receive the attention of researchers much less often than the finished artistic products. When the contextual aspects of creativity are ignored or paid insufficient attention, both the creative outcomes and the processes cease to be examined as multidimensional and systemic human activities. As researchers, we need to explore how and under what circumstances the work of art was created, what was the target audience, and how and by whom it was evaluated, in what situations and social contexts, for what purposes, and with what outcomes for the artist and their worlds.

In this chapter I undertake an examination of student arts-based practices and processes in a specific sociocultural context. Sixteen-year-old Tomas agreed to reflect on his journey through a creative process, revealing the influence of the cultural contexts on his art. His case became a "telling case" (Mitchell, 1984; Andrews, 2017) that enabled me to take a broader look at arts-based practices and gain insights into their processes "when specific contextual circumstances are taken into account" (Mitchell, 1984, p. 239). Anchoring my

DOI: 10.4324/9781003215479-9

analyses in Tomas' art and reflections, in this chapter I explore three cultural levels and the ways they affect student artistic processes.

I chose the perspective of interactional ethnography as the logic of my study (Castanheira et al., 2001; Green & Bridges, 2018), focusing on the interaction between members of the community and the role of language in the development of cultural norms, meanings, and knowledge. When students sing, compose music, dance, play, or draw, the meanings, personal attitudes, reasons for performances, and many other things remain unknown or hidden. The interactional ethnographic perspective guided my conversational interviews (Skukauskaitė, 2017) with Tomas and helped reveal the multilevel cultural nature of arts-based practices. In our conversations, Tomas reflected on a collage and music he created and explored how interactions with other people and groups across different contexts over time influenced his art and art identities.

Throughout the study, I followed the main principles of ethnographic research (Green et al., 2003; 2012): *ethnography as a nonlinear system, leaving aside ethnocentrism, identifying boundaries of what is happening,* and *building connections.* In realizing the first principle – ethnography as a nonlinear system – I constructed an ethnographic logic-in-use to examine what cultural influences affect student arts-based practices. The second principle led to the emic perspective as I sought to look at art-based practices through the eyes of Tomas. Identification of boundaries was the easiest principle to follow as I bounded the study around Tomas' participation in the National Students' Music Olympiad in the spring of 2021. Though arts-based practices were directly related to the time and place of that event, I uncovered how those practices related to the past and future as well as local and global events and different groups of people. And finally, while building connections, I sought to understand arts-based practices as a holistic phenomenon, characterized by specific cultural attributes of the age group of upper secondary grade students. I related the data obtained from the study of student arts-based practices to the existing knowledge about the levels of culture, thus "connecting different cultural activities, actions, and meanings" (Green et al., 2012, p. 314).

The first part of the chapter is dedicated to the theoretical and methodological substantiation of my research. In the second part, I introduce Tomas as a young creator and explicate the context as well as the methods of data collection and analysis. The third part presents the results of the study and reveals the multiplicity of cultural layers in arts-based practices.

Theoretical and Methodological Grounding

The present study, aiming to explore student arts-based practices, is grounded in the understanding that "social reality is constructed based on the specific perspective of the individual" (Matsunobu & Bresler, 2014, p. 23). I collected and interpreted data on the artistic practices of young people located within cultural contexts and influenced by different levels of culture. I started with an analysis of cultural levels based on an anthropological conception of culture that focuses on the expression of an already existing culture from the perspectives of community members.

Using interactional ethnographic conceptualizations of classrooms and other educational settings as rich cultural sites (Green & Bloome, 1997), I paid attention to the subtleties of social and cultural life reflected in Tomas' discourse, practices, and art. Interactional ethnography combines anthropological views of culture and language. Therefore, to explore the cultural levels of arts-based practices signaled in Tomas' language, I used discourse analysis. Arts-based methods provided a way to collect and analyze data on the integral representation of different cultural levels within student artistic practices.

Levels of Culture and Its Influence on Student Actions

Culture is a complex and multidimensional phenomenon that is difficult not only to analyze but also to define. One of the most commonly used descriptions defines culture as "the complex whole which includes knowledge, belief, art, law, morals, custom, and any other capabilities and habits acquired by man as a member of society" (Tylor quoted in Beldo, 2010, p. 144). All these elements of culture affect individual action at different levels because an individual interacts with other actors in cultural surroundings. Therefore, from the anthropological point of view, there is no point in talking about a concept of culture that would be common to all people and situations (Agar, 2006). In a particular context and at a particular moment, a person is related to different cultures. That is why "culture is always plural" (Agar, 2006, p. 9).

There have been numerous attempts to show the multilevel nature of culture. Karahanna et al. (2005) argued that an individual's behavior was influenced by supranational (regional, ethnic, religious, linguistic), national, professional, organizational, and group levels of culture. Erez and Gati (2004) described culture from the macro to the individual level and distinguished global, national, organizational, group, and individual layers of culture. Kottak and Kozaitis (2012) distinguished three cultural levels that influenced an individual's behavior: international, national, and subcultural. Those three levels of culture became my basis for analyzing student arts-based practices.

International culture transcends national or certain group boundaries and is understood as a set of customs, capabilities, and habits characteristic of most humankind. Artistic practices such as dance, music, and visual art are common across all cultures. However, each nation has its own traditions of artistic practices. In some countries, the dominant genre of national artistic practices is singing, in others, dance, and in still others, handicrafts or sculpture.

The purpose of artistic practices also differs. In South Africa, for example, singing is an expression of freedom and protest (Barrett, 2008). In Central Asia and the Middle East, singing is strongly associated with religious practices (Schaefer, 2000). National culture has distinctive features, yet it is not homogeneous: each national culture is made up of the subcultures of smaller groups. In the context of this chapter, I would like to reject the negative connotation of the term subculture as deviance or resistance. Subcultures in this case do not manifest themselves through resistance and shared identities, but as the interconnectedness of people, places, and products (Bennett, 2011). In the same national culture, subcultures differ in accordance with the place of residence of a particular group of people, their religion, their socioeconomic status, their age, or racial differences. Individual subcultures are formed in the family, in a group of friends, or in a group of people practicing certain activities.

All individuals are more or less influenced by a national culture that is relatively stable, because it forms over a long period of time and encompasses the basic features of artistic practices. Subcultures are the most dynamic, as the composition of a group of people who make up a subculture and the values they recognize can change over time. A person may be affected by different subcultures at different levels (such as family and groups of friends). Irrespective of the number of cultures the individual represents, belonging to any of them is a way for people to say what they consider themselves to be at one time or another and how they see their lives (Bennett, 2011). Without understanding the specificity of a particular culture or subculture, it is impossible to understand the actions and behavior of individuals or the similarities and differences among people or groups of people (Sewell, 2005).

International, national, subcultural, and personal cultural levels are interrelated and intertwined. Their influence is often invisible and hidden. Understanding them becomes possible through the density of the description of details, contexts, and individual behavior (Geertz, 1973). An ethnographic approach can help to explore and explain how culture participates in artistic practices and in interpretations of works of art and multidimensional artistic symbol systems.

Ethnography and Discourse Analysis to Explore Cultural Levels of Arts-Based Practices

Ethnography seeks to know and understand people and their behavior in culture. Cultural context is important and must be taken into account to understand human behavior. Whereas in the past ethnographic research sought to know other cultures, contemporary ethnography seeks to understand people's behavior in the cultures in which they live (Agar, 2006; Green & Bridges, 2018). Contemporary ethnographers study how people themselves understand

and account for their lives in everyday situations in cultural groups (Green et al., 2012). Understanding of ethnography as a particular intellectual way of approaching a cultural phenomenon of interest, rather than a script of actions or methods, allows for flexible and creative adaptations of ethnographic principles to smaller-scale studies (Agar, 2004), such as the one reported in this chapter.

Ethnography also seeks to illuminate elements of sociocultural life which have not been a subject of awareness and conscious understanding (Matsunobu & Bresler, 2014). Many meanings and experiences are not directly expressed or easily seen in particular interactions; therefore, ethnographers engage in observations over time and conversations with insiders to uncover those often invisible aspects of everyday life. As Green and Bloome (1997, p. 9) argue, the task of an ethnographer is to understand and describe how any particular "cultural practice is constructed within and across the events and patterns of activity that constitute everyday life." Understanding of culture from the insider perspective is an essential condition for ethnographic research. Ethnographers argue that an individual's behavior and culture are interrelated, and that group members hold and create knowledge within their society (Spradley, 1979/2016). Therefore, an ethnographer needs to step back from their points of view, abandon preconceived notions about one or another culture, and seek to come as close as possible to the insider's understanding (Green et al., 2003).

Language is central to culture and cultural studies because it is through language that cultural meanings and knowledge about people and their social worlds are formed and communicated (Agar, 2006; Barker, 2004). Language is inseparable from culture; it is the most common form of action through which cultural knowledge, meanings, beliefs, and values are expressed. Language is the way to get to culture (Agar, 2006). On the other hand, language is not just a carrier of knowledge. As Vygotsky (1986) argues, language involves the reorganization of knowledge, where thoughts come into existence through language. In other words, through language, not only do people acquire cultural knowledge, beliefs, and values, but they also convey their own worldviews (Kroeber & Kluckhohn, 1952; Sherman et al., 2019).

Even though art is often based on non-verbal symbols, human response to art is always multimodal, i.e., it combines visual-aural-verbal expressions (Barone & Eisner, 2012). Both the creator and the viewer or listener use discourse to explain artistic signs or symbols, thus combining language and images, sounds, gestures, dance, and other symbolic art forms (Eisner, 2008). Through language, artists, viewers, and researchers can focus on the meanings and emotions of a work of art, linking them to personal experiences. Language helps understand and explain artistic symbol systems, and relate art interpretations to the author, the work, and its purpose and meaning. In the context of this article, language reveals the social contexts in which discourse is embedded (Bloome et al., 2005).

I used discourse analysis to show how a work of art relates to the creator's environment and personal experience and how different cultural levels interact during the creative process and in the presentation of its outcome. Artistic practices enable any creator to use not only rational thinking but also intuition and sensory experience to express values, feelings, emotions, and ideas (Eisner, 1991, 2008; Barone & Eisner, 2012). Meanwhile, discourse analysis helps make that multifaceted experience audible and visible through the interpretation of artistic creation. The aural-visual-verbal expression of artworks, focusing on meanings, emotions and expressions, is the essence of the arts-based method used in the present study.

Arts-Based Research to Explore Student Artistic Practices

A visionary in the field of arts and education Elliot Eisner (2008) states that there are many ways to see and interpret the world. Arts are one of them. Using the systems of music, drama, dance, and art symbols, we as humans manipulate images and concepts to define and create reality. Through the arts we can see things and phenomena from different perspectives, get to know ourselves and reveal our subjective life to others, as well as better understand and explain the world we live in. Arts-based practices function as a powerful mechanism for reaching the deepest, richest, and most abstract aspects of our existence within a culture (Eisner, 1991, 2008). When social scientists encounter the arts, they create studies in which arts offer researchers an opportunity to gain a different research perspective, to see multidimensionality and complexity, to emotionally engage individuals and groups, and to overcome limitations in verbal expression and logical thinking (McNiff, 2008; Barone & Eisner, 2012; Wright, 2012).

Artists use artistic symbol systems to make their experiences public and invite the viewer or listener to understand what is created (Wright, 2012). Interpretation involves recognizing artistic symbol systems and reflecting on the meanings of artistic work. Interpretation is not neutral. It is shaped by the situation and the context as well as personal experiences. It is conditioned by our beliefs, values, knowledge of the world and the experience of being in it as members of particular communities. The same work of art can be interpreted differently depending on the viewer's or listener's experience grounded in a particular culture. As Wright (2012) argues, we look at the world as well as at works of art through our cultural glasses.

Arts-based research encompasses numerous methodological and epistemological approaches, however, the choice of any of them implies one constant: in order to conduct arts-based research, one or several arts are to be employed (Greenwood, 2019). The present research made use of the practices of two fields of art, performing and visual arts. Performing arts were represented in Tomas' composition and song performance. Tomas conveyed his creative process through creating and discussing a collage, "where stories are shared graphically and become the mode of representation for the research" (Butler-Kisber, 2018, p. 114). Collage inquiry became the main research method, enabling Tomas and me to converse about his artistic practices from different perspectives, to reveal subconscious experiences, and to present unique insights (Butler-Kisber & Poldma, 2010). For me as a researcher, conversations around the collage were a way to catch the subtle moments of the creative process, to understand the role of the cultural context in Tomas' artistic activities, and to describe how different cultural levels coexisted in arts-based activities.

Methodology

Context and Research Site

After the pandemic broke out in the spring of 2020, many activities, including artistic ones, moved into virtual space. Exhibitions, concerts, performances, artistic educational events, competitions, and festivals flexibly adapted to the new situation. The Music Olympiad of Lithuanian students, in which 16-year-old Tomas participated, was also conducted virtually.

The National Student Music Olympiad, organized since 2012, is an event in which students aged 14–18 compete in four areas: music sign reading, a creative task, singing, and performing their own composition. The creative task is different every year. In 2021, the participants of the Olympiad were asked to create a collage on the topic "Music and I". The participants were free to choose which song to perform and what kind of musical composition to write. The students submitted music recordings and provided brief descriptions of the recordings and their compositions.

The Olympiad is a competition in which student performances are judged by a jury of professional musicians. Singing and composition performances in the pre-pandemic period used to take place as an open competition, where all students, their teachers, parents, and others interested in students' work could watch the performances in music halls and interact with each other. The virtual Music Olympiad in 2021 prevented live interaction. My discussions with the jury members and teachers after the Olympiad revealed that the absence of live music and the inability to share impressions and insights was a major limitation. The importance of human interaction to feel and understand what it meant for students to participate in events of this kind, what and why students played, sang, and created became evident. The invitation of one participant to research and in-depth conversations about his arts-based practices provided an opportunity both for the researcher and the participant to get closer to those social and cultural settings that influenced the processes and outcomes of musical creation.

Tomas

Sixteen-year-old Tomas (pseudonym) lives and studies in a small Lithuanian town. It is far away from big cities, so Tomas rarely attends major cultural events. The musical and cultural life of his town is not rich, with most of the events taking place at his school. Tomas lives with his parents and one-year younger brother. None of the family has substantial experience in musical or cultural activities, and they do not participate in artistic group, or contribute to the organizing of community events. The parents are civil servants; the brother is interested in sports.

Tomas took part in the Olympiad for the first time; however, he had performed with student groups at his school. He has played the piano since early childhood and sang in the school choir for two years. At the beginning of the school year, the music teacher invited Tomas to participate in the Olympiad and demonstrate his abilities. The musical piece written for the Olympiad was Tomas' first composition, and the song performed was his first solo performance. Tomas also created a collage for the first time.

A total of 37 students who had won city and regional rounds throughout Lithuania took part in the Olympiad. I chose Tomas as a participant for several reasons. Tomas' singing stood out for its expressiveness and choice of a song that ideally matched his voice. He also performed the composition much more expressively than most of the participants. The descriptions he had submitted about the song and the composition were quite extensive, containing rich details and revealing a personal relationship with the music performed. A final decision to focus on him was his collage, characterized by a clear compositional structure and images related to cultural contexts.

When I telephoned Tomas and explained the nature of the study, he was surprised and interested: he said he had never thought about his participation in arts-based practices and no one asked him any questions. With the consent of Tomas and his parents, our journey into the ethnographically informed world of arts–based research began.

Data Collection

Tomas sent the recordings of his singing and composition as well as their descriptions to the organizers of the Olympiad before the event. I had access to Tomas' song, composition, collage, and recording of his performance at the competition through my position as one of the organizers of the Olympiad. There were no specific requirements for the performance of the song or the composition. Creating a collage for the Olympiad took place for the first time. All the participants of the Olympiad received an e-mail two weeks before the event, in which the collage technique was explained, with references to more information about creating a collage. The assignment was as follows:

> Create a collage on the topic *Music and I*. You can use photos, pictures, pieces of cloth, and other various items. The collage is to consist of at least 10 pieces. Glue everything on a piece of paper and take a picture or arrange the images on your computer screen and save them as a picture. On a separate sheet, describe the idea of the collage and what each collage image means.

Tomas's collage (Figure 7.1) consisted of 23 images. Tomas used the photo of the concert hall as the basis for the composition and incorporated the other 22 images in a meaningful way.

To get to the *emic* perspective of the collage and his other performed artistic practices, I talked with Tomas twice; the total time of our conversations was 1 hour and 40 minutes (55 and 45 min, respectively). Due to the pandemic, I conducted both interviews on a Zoom platform after considering possible limitations: lower speech expressiveness, lack of non-verbal communication signs, and shorter and faster responses involving fewer explanations and details (Weller, 2017). When preparing for the interview, I thought of ways to facilitate communication. I asked Tomas whether he felt comfortable communicating on Zoom, whether he understood audio and video control functions, and whether he had a reliable Internet connection to ensure quality

FIGURE 7.1 Collage *Music and I* by Tomas

communication. We started the conversation with a discussion about Tomas' life – his studies, leisure time, and hobbies. These topics helped to overcome the initial discomfort and establish a relationship. I suggested Tomas take his time and that silences or pauses during a conversation, especially a virtual one, could be expected.

During the first virtual meeting, I asked Tomas to tell me about himself. Afterwards, I invited him to listen to the recording of his song and describe it, focusing on the meanings he sought to convey through singing. In this first interview conversation (Skukauskaitė, 2017; Skukauskaitė & Sullivan, this volume), we also listened and talked about his musical composition. The second conversation was dedicated to the collage. Tomas first described his work in general terms, and then talked about the individual images, their meanings, the connection with the available experience, and the reasons for one or another image being in the particular place of the collage. Finally, Tomas commented on the way he created the collage.

Data Analysis

I performed the data analysis in two stages: first I analyzed the artistic practices Tomas presented, and afterwards I worked with the data obtained during the interviews. In the first stage, I used the videos of the song and the composition Tomas performed as well as his collage and its description. Table 7.1 represents data collected and my analytic focus, which also guided the conversations with Tomas.

Collage creating was my focus. Although singing and music composition were not the objects of this study, the information I received helped me get

TABLE 7.1 Data of Arts-Based Practices and Analytic Prompts for the Conversation

Arts-based practices	Data collected	Scope	Analytic foci and prompts for the conversation
Singing	Recording of the song	1″50 min.	Motives for choosing the song. Links between choosing and performing the song
	Description of the song and its performance	70 words	Personal meaning of the content of the song. Social meaning of the song and its performance
Music composition	Recording of the music composition	2′15 min.	The idea of the composition, the links with personal experience
	Description of the music composition	193 words	Motives for writing the composition
Creating of a collage	The collage	1 photo	Meanings of the images used and their composition
	Description of the collage	210 words	The process of creating the collage

TABLE 7.2 Example of the Story Grid for Analyzing the Transcript of the Conversation about Tomas' Collage

No.	Collage image	Connotations	Quotes from the description of the image	Level of culture
1.	Stage	Joy Disappointment	*For me, music is a stage. Not a stage of great significance on which world-famous music stars sing. Where audiences of thousands gather... Here I show what I have learned, what I can do, how I make music. Sometimes it's a joy. Sometimes, if I fail, it's frustration.*	International Personal
2–8	People	Closeness Loneliness	*These are people close to me. Here's mom, here's dad, brother... They know how important music is to me. But I wouldn't say they're very interested. They are just happy for me. And I sometimes feel alone...*	Family subculture Personal

to know Tomas better, to understand what one or another musical activity meant to him, and how and under what circumstances he wrote and performed his music.

To start the analysis of the collage, I numbered all the images. Then I created a story grid, revealing the unity of insights and explanations of the images (van Schalkwyk, 2010). All the images Tomas used in his collage are listed in column 2 of Table 7.2. Column 3, connotations, indicates meanings Tomas attributed to the images. The quotes from the descriptions of the images are presented in column 4. In analyzing the images and the way Tomas described their literal and symbolic meanings, I discovered levels of cultural contexts and marked them in the last column of Table 7.2. Table 7.2 is an example, not a full analytic table (available upon request).

The detailed way in which Tomas discursively constructed his explanations of the images and what they meant to him led me to uncover an underlying theme of cultural influences on Tomas' artistic practices. As described further in the Results section, Tomas contributed to distinguishing the cultural levels of the arts-based practices. He helped me understand, from his point of view, how the meanings a young performer created for his art were situated in intersecting contexts and shaped by varied interactions with people locally and globally.

Researcher Position

In ethnography, the researcher needs to examine their positionality so that they can step back from what they know in order to learn about the cultures studied from the participant points of view. To this study, I brought knowledge and experience in performative arts, music education, and organizing of the national music competitions such as the Music Olympiad. My experience in music practices accumulated through singing in various groups and writing songs for children. Through these experiences, I had firsthand understandings of how different people and contexts can affect artistic practices. My work in organizing the National Student Music Olympiad in Lithuania allowed me to be in the field and see the events Tomas attended through the eyes of an insider. As a music teacher for over 30 years, I could understand what it meant for a 16-year-old boy to participate in arts-based practices and how to support Tomas' reflections in sensitive ways. I did not aim to be an objective outsider, but rather acknowledged how my subjectivity played a role in knowledge construction (Matsunobu & Bresler, 2014). While my subjectivity influenced all stages of work with the data, I did my best to maintain a conscious, critical, reflexive, and analytic perspective throughout the research process.

Results

Interactional ethnographic principles enabled me to uncover layers and meanings of arts-based practices co-constructed through the conversational interviews with a young musician. Stepping back from what I know and seeking *emic* understanding, in this section, I explore the cultural levels of arts-based practices I uncovered in Tomas' work and discourse. I describe the influences of the international, national, and subcultural levels of culture on Tomas' artistic practices.

The Influence of International Culture

The international level of culture manifests itself through global culture, "which transcends national borders and exists in many different places around the world" (Robertson, 1992, p. 114). Global music culture is available to everyone through a wide variety of media and social networks. Even in the most remote places, with an Internet connection one can get to know and participate in representations of global music culture.

Although Tomas lived in a small remote town, he was familiar with the global pop culture and referenced it when reflecting on the image of the stage in his collage. The stage was the first image Tomas described. He juxtaposed his own experience with what he knew about the concerts of popular music stars. A segment of the transcript (lines 1–8) reveals the meaning of the stage for Tomas:

1. "For me
2. music is a stage.
3. Not a stage

4. of great significance
5. in which world-famous
6. music stars
7. sing
8. where thousands of spectators gather…"

Tomas associated music with a specific place, a stage. He began the description of the stage from his personal viewpoint – "for me" (line 1), implying that not everyone may see music as a stage (2). The stage of Tomas' artistic practices differed from the concert venues "of great significance" (4) and "world-famous" (5), where "music stars" performed (6) in front of "thousands of spectators" (8). Through these discursive choices, Tomas described the attributes of global music pop culture, implicitly contrasting those attributes to his stage and the venue of his performance.

Tomas identified singing as the primary pathway to fame in music when he stated that "music stars sing" (7). Singing as a major part of musical performance in popular culture encompasses almost 90% of all events. In the conversational interviews, he revealed that participation in the Music Olympiad and singing solo made him think of singing professionally. Two collage images were related to his ideas: a road paved and a field on both sides of the road. When discussing the images with the researcher (R), Tomas (T) talked about a singer's career:

R: You sang solo for the first time …
T: … and I really liked it.
    I would love to be
    like Sheeran or Timberlake …
R: They are famous singers …
T: … and sing very well.
    I've got a long way to go …
R: A long way?
T: A long way
    to full stadiums
    and Grammy awards …
    I still have no idea
    where that road can take me.
    So far, I am in an empty field.

After publicly singing solo for the first time in his life, Tomas admitted he really enjoyed it. He compared his music making to world-renowned singers Ed Sheeran and Justin Timberlake. When considering a possible career as a singer, Tomas dreamt of international stages, full stadiums, and Grammy Awards. At the same time, however, he understood he had a long and difficult way to go to international recognition ("I still have no idea where that road can take me"). To describe the uncertainty of the beginning of the road, Tomas chose the metaphor of an empty field ("I am in an empty field").

These two examples show how the global pop music culture pervaded the thoughts of a young man living in a small town. When revealing his relationship to music, Tomas named elements of global pop culture such as full stadiums, thousands of spectators, music stars, and Grammy awards. His role models were also singers at the top of the global popularity. Global culture naturally coexists with other levels of culture, such as national culture of music.

The Influence of National Culture

National culture is the norms, behaviors, beliefs, customs, and values that characterize a particular nation (Hofstede, 2001). National culture manifests itself through language, religion, art, traditions, customs, and history (Erez & Gati, 2004; Kottak & Kozaitis, 2012). One can judge whether an individual belongs to the national culture by his or her lifestyle and the admission that he or she belongs to that culture. In exploring his arts-based practices, Tomas referenced national culture twice in his narrative: when discussing the images of instruments and the song he performed.

The image of the piano in the picture represented Tomas's history of playing the instrument since his childhood. His musical piece was also written for piano. However, the image of the piano occupied a peripheral place in the collage. It was the four guitars that caught the eye. The transcript of the conversation revealed the meaning of the guitar and Tomas' view of its relation to the national culture:

R: There are images of four guitars on the stage …
T: Folk instruments (smiles)
R: The guitar is a Lithuanian folk instrument?
T: Because the guitar is popular.
    everybody
    wants to play the guitar.
    Unfortunately,
    not the kanklės [psaltery], birbynė [chalumeau], or skudučiai [panpipes].
R: What about you, what other music instruments do you play?
T: Only the piano.
    But I'd like to learn to play some others …
    maybe even the skrabalai [pitched wooden bells] …
    like Šilinskas.
    It would be cool.

Tomas jokingly called the guitar a Lithuanian folk instrument because this instrument was popular with young people. He stated everybody wanted to play the guitar. Tomas then explained with a smile why there were four guitars on the stage, arranged in different places: *so that there would be enough for everyone, big and small*. Tomas compared the guitar with the *kanklės, birbynė,* and *skudučiai* and regretted (*unfortunately*) that students did not want to learn to play those Lithuanian folk instruments. Tomas was acquainted with Lithuanian folk instruments and noted their unpopularity with young people.

Tomas indicated an interest in learning to play the *skrabalai* (wooden bells). It is a vertical wooden percussion instrument popularized on TV and in social networks by Regimantas Šilinskas, a folk musician who often played on TV. Šilinskas played both solo and in various ensembles and performed melodies of popular songs together with rock bands or chamber ensembles. Being a popular folk instrument performer seemed an interesting potential career to Tomas (*it would be cool*). National culture in this case merged dynamically with global culture representations, such as rock music and TV shows.

The image of an Oriental fighter in the background of the stage was related to the Lithuanian folk song Tomas performed during the Olympiad. Tomas commented on the fighter image in detail:

> It takes strength to sing a folk song. I sing folk songs only at school, during music lessons. We do not sing folk songs with friends or in the family. I had to find my own arguments for why and what I am doing while singing. Also ... singing a folk song in public is not fun. I was wondering what my friends would say ... Singing a folk song is not cool ...

In this quote, Tomas touched upon two national culture-related meanings. The first was the disappearance of a tradition of folk singing in Lithuania. In Tomas' environment, a folk song was rarely heard (*we do not sing folk songs with friends or in the family*). Tomas only sang folk songs during music lessons. Therefore, performing a folk song was not an easy task (*I had to find my own arguments*). Second, folk singing is not valued among young people. When preparing for the performance, Tomas wondered how his choice would be accepted by friends because *singing a folk song was not cool*. Therefore, the decision to perform a folk song required strength, which was given prominence through the image of an Oriental fighter.

The Lithuanian singing tradition is unique. Its uniqueness is determined by the sociocultural context and a singing-based system of music education (Girdzijauskienė, 2021). Tomas' narrative testified that his environment was not conducive to maintaining the tradition of folk singing. The most important cultivator of the singing tradition was the school, where singing, and especially folk songs, occupied a special place in the curriculum (Girdzijauskienė, 2012). The fading tradition of singing as part of the national culture was revealed through the attitudes and values of Tomas' family and his classmates. The influence of the subculture of smaller groups (family, peers, classmates, musicians) on Tomas' arts-based practices is discussed in the next section.

Influences of Sub-cultures

Generations, gender, religion, region, language, and occupation are "markers of what people now routinely call culture" (Agar, 2006, p. 3). Those markers could mingle in different ways and vary from person to person, from time to time. Two people living in the same country, in the same city may be belong to subcultures comprised of different genders, belief systems, age groups, interests or professions. Each of these subcultures influences the individual's practices and values because, as Bloome and colleagues (2005) argue, people act and react with each other in everyday life.

While engaging in arts-based practices Tomas interacts with many people from different subcultures. Family, friends and professional musicians with various values and dispositions influence Tomas' decision-making processes and the ways he imagines himself as a musician. Collage images of the stage and the audience facilitated our talk about interaction with individuals from different subcultures and their influence on Tomas' arts-based practices. In describing his associations of music as a stage, in addition to references to global culture, Tomas highlighted the influence of his teacher, who had encouraged Tomas to participate in the Olympiad as a solo vocalist, despite his misgivings regarding his musical abilities:

> ... I never sang solo before, I'm not convinced that I have a good voice. But my teacher said that I could. She is a singer, so she knows best. I trust her opinion. There's really no one else I could ask. Choosing a folk song was also the teacher's suggestion. She said the jury likes folk songs ... I could get more points.

Tomas' teacher is a professional vocalist who often performs at various venues and has participated in a TV music project. Her faith in Tomas' abilities was important to Tomas because she is both a teacher and a musician. The teacher was the first, and so far the only professional musician with whom Tomas has had the opportunity to interact. He trusted her unconditionally regarding his musical abilities as well as in his choice of the performance repertoire.

Jury members were another group of musicians important in this context. The committee consists of professional, nationally renowned musicians. Even though Tomas is not acquainted with the jury members, he learned about their preferences (valuing folk songs) from his teacher. Tomas repeats the teacher's view that the committee likes folk songs and that a suitable song may result in more points. There is nothing in the Olympiad regulations about folk music, yet it is quite plausible that the teacher's view is the result of her conversations with colleagues and previous Olympiad participants. Both the teacher and the jury members are musicians whose values influence Tomas' arts-based practices.

The family is another subculture to which Tomas belongs. When speaking about the collage image of the audience in his performance venue, Tomas imagines his family members among them. In this excerpt Tomas describes the attitudes of his family regarding his music practices.

T: These are people
   close to me...
R: They are sitting with their backs to us.
T: Here's mom, here's dad, my brother...
   They know
   how important music is to me.
   But they don't understand,
   why I'm participating in the Olympiad,
   how difficult it is to
   sing and play alone.
R: Are they opposed to you participating?
T: No, they're not opposed.
   They are just happy for me.
   I sometimes feel
   that I am alone...

Tomas names his mother, father and brother as people close to him, but who do not understand. Tomas is the only member of the family who studied music from childhood and participated in arts. As Tomas explained, the family has not experienced music and it is hard for them to understand the challenges Tomas encounters when he sings and plays. And so, Tomas feels alone. On the other hand, his family supports him and is happy for him. Although musical values are not fostered in the family, there is no opposition to Tomas' decision to participate in the Olympiad. Family members are happy for him and are the first audience members Tomas mentions in his imagined audience.

Another subculture Tomas mentions twice is friends. Describing his imagined audience, he mentions that there are a few friends who are interested in what Tomas does. Much like his family, they support him, but in Tomas' opinion *they are not much interested in singing or playing, because they are utter jocks.* The music that Tomas performs comes under the category of academic music. According to Tomas, *everybody wants to play the guitar... Singing folk songs is not cool.* When getting ready for performances Tomas thinks about what his friends will say. Although the surrounding musical culture of his friends differs from the serious music Tomas performs, he makes no mention of opposition. These two subcultures co-exists side by side, they are not at odds.

In summary, collage was an effective arts-based research tool for showing the variety of cultural layers that influence young people. Collage enabled dialogues about aspects of culture and Tomas' life and artistic practices. The images anchored reflections through which Tomas, with the researcher, revealed what would ordinarily be unknowable and hidden from an audience member. I end this chapter with some final thoughts about interactional ethnography is a useful epistemology to explore cultural levels of students' arts-based practices.

Final Thoughts

The perspective of interactional ethnography enabled me to explore how processes and meanings of arts-based practices have been created by a young musician Tomas through interactions with different groups of people in different cultural contexts. Reflections on his collage testified to his musical practices being affected by global and national cultures and different subcultures. All those cultures intermingled because Tomas himself related to different cultures, depending on his place of residence, nationality, age, time period, etc.

The global, national, and local subcultures influenced Tomas' arts-based practices. Interactions with people across those cultural levels provided him with confidence, encouraged him to make decisions, imagine himself as a musician in the future, and consider the career prospects of a musician. The collage made visible the moments of the young musician's inner life experienced during arts-based practices. It helped Tomas and the researcher develop deeper understandings of how arts-based practices were socially constructed by members through their actions and interactions.

In the study, I sought to look at arts-based practices through the eyes of a young person and see what was not visible to an outsider who did not share in the activities of the Music Olympiad and did not know people or their history or the site for performance. Conversations with Tomas helped me understand what mattered in the young musician's arts-based practices and what social and cultural influences affected those practices. Tomas' conversations with me were a valuable way for him to consider the role music played in his and other young people's lives. He considered the values characteristic of his immediate environment and the wider context; explored what it meant to be a musician and envisioned a future musical career. When parting, Tomas said, *Thank you, now I have something to think about. I know what I want to do next.* The conversation deepened and changed the minds and attitudes of us both.

Principles for Exploring Artistic Processes and Practices

Based on this study, I would like to suggest some recommendations to a researcher seeking to understand student arts-based practices in-depth:

- Utilize various sources of information to understand relationships between individuals' lived experiences and multilevel cultural influences in their artistic activities. Just listening to and/or observing the creative work is not enough to be understand the multifaceted nature of arts-based practices;
- Provide young people with opportunities for reflective explorations of their arts-based practices. When students sing, compose music, dance, play, or draw, the meanings, personal attitudes, reasons for performances, and many other things remain hidden not only from the audience but also from the students themselves;
- Accept students as equal study participants to get to the emic perspective of their performance. Look at the arts-based practices through the eyes of an insider to explore how interactions with other people and groups across different contexts over time influence the students and their artistic work;
- Don't be afraid to use your insider knowledge to contextualize conversations with the participants of the study and deepen the analysis of the data. Your personal experience can be very valuable during the conversation with the students, helping them to reveal the circumstances, contexts, and outcomes of creating art;
- Consider how arts-based research can be expanded for ethnographic inquiry. Arts-based practices could be a way of revealing students' subjective life to others as well as of better understanding and explaining the world we live in.

Suggested Readings

Barker, C. (2004). *The sage dictionary of cultural studies*. Sage.
Holdhus, K., Murphy, R., & Espeland, M. I. (Eds.). (2021). *Music education as craft: Reframing theories and practices*. Springer.
Knowles, J. G., & Cole, A. L. (2008). *Handbook of the arts in qualitative research: Perspectives, methodologies, examples, and issues*. Sage.

References

Agar, M. (2004). We have met the other and we're all nonlinear: Ethnography as a nonlinear dynamic system. *Complexity, 10*(2), 16–24.
Agar, M. (2006). Culture: Can you take it anywhere? *International Journal of Qualitative Methods, 5*(2), 1–16.
Andrews, P. (2017). Is the "telling case" a methodological myth? *International Journal of Social Research Methodology, 20*(5), 455–467.

Barker, C. (2004). Language. In C. Barker (Ed.), *The SAGE dictionary of cultural studies* (pp. 107–108). Sage.

Barone, T., & Eisner, E. W. (2012). *Arts based research*. Sage.

Barrett, M. J. (2008). *The value of choral singing in a multi-cultural South Africa*. Unpublished PhD Thesis. University of Pretoria.

Beldo, L. (2010). Concept of culture. In H. J. Birx (Ed.), *21st century anthropology: A reference handbook* (pp. 144–152). Sage.

Bennett, A. (2011). The post-subcultural turn: Some reflections 10 years on. *Journal of Youth Studies, 14*(5), 493–506.

Bloome, D., Carter, S. P., Christian, B. M., Otto, S., & Shuart-Faris, N. (2005). *Discourse analysis and the study of classroom language and literacy events: A microethnographic perspective*. Lawrence Erlbaum.

Butler-Kisber, L. (2018). *Qualitative inquiry: Thematic, narrative and arts-based perspectives*. Sage.

Butler-Kisber, L., & Poldma, T. (2010). The power of visual approaches in qualitative inquiry: The use of collage making and concept mapping in experiential research. *Journal of Research Practice, 6*(2), M18.

Castanheira, M. L., Crawford, T., Dixon, C. N., & Green, J. L. (2001). Interactional ethnography: An approach to studying the social construction of literate practices. *Linguistics and Education, 11*(4), 353–400.

Eisner, E. W. (1991). *The enlightened eye: Qualitative inquiry and the enhancement of educational practice*. Macmillan Publishing Company.

Eisner, E. W. (2008). *The arts and the creation of mind*. Yale University Press.

Erez, M., & Gati, E. (2004). A dynamic, multi-level model of culture: From the micro level of the individual to the macro level of a global culture. *Applied Psychology: An International Review, 53*(4), 583–598.

Geertz, C. (1973). Thick description: Toward an interpretive theory of culture. In C. Geertz (Ed.), *The interpretation of cultures* (pp. 3–30). Basic Books.

Girdzijauskienė, R. (2012). The peculiarities of development of creativity of pupils of senior forms while performing, creating, listening to, describing and evaluating music. *The Space of Creation, 10*, 8–18.

Girdzijauskienė, R. (2021). The craft of music teaching in a changing society: Singing as meaning, education, and craft – reflections on Lithuania. In K. Holdhus, R. Murphy, & M. Espeland (Eds.), *Music education as craft: Reframing theories and practices* (pp. 77–87). Springer.

Green, J. L., & Bloome, D. (1997). Ethnography and ethnographers of and in education: A situated perspective. In J. Flood, S. B. Heath, & D. Lapp (Eds.), *Research on teaching and literacy through the communicative and visual arts* (pp. 181–202). Macmillan.

Green, J. L., & Bridges, S. M. (2018). Interactional ethnography. In F. Fischer, C. E. Hmelo-Silver, S. R. Goldman, & P. Reimann (Eds.), *International handbook of the learning sciences* (pp. 475–488). Routledge.

Green, J. L., Dixon, C. N., & Zaharlick, A. (2003). Ethnography as a logic of inquiry. In J. Flood, D. Lapp, J. R. Squire, & J. Jensen (Eds.), *Handbook of research on teaching the English language arts* (pp. 201–224). Lawrence Erlbaum Associates.

Green, J. L., Skukauskaitė, A., & Baker, W. D. (2012). Ethnography as epistemology: An introduction to educational ethnography. In J. Arthur, M. J. Waring, R. Coe, & L. V. Hedges (Eds.), *Research methodologies and methods in education* (pp. 309–321). Sage.

Greenwood, J. (2019, February 25). Arts-based research. *Oxford research encyclopedia of education.* https://oxfordre.com/education/view/10.1093/acrefore/9780190264093.001.0001/acrefore-9780190264093-e-29

Hofstede, G. (2001). *Culture's consequences: Comparing values, behaviors, institutions and organizations across nations.* Sage.

Karahanna, E., Evaristo, J., & Srite, M. (2005). Levels of culture and individual behavior: An integrative perspective. *Journal of Global Information Management, 13,* 1–20.

Kottak, C. P., & Kozaitis, K. A. (2012). *On being different: Diversity and multiculturalism in the North American mainstream.* McGraw-Hill.

Kroeber, A. L., & Kluckhohn, C. (1952). *Culture: A critical review of concepts and definitions.* Harvard University Peabody Museum.

Matsunobu, K., & Bresler, L. (2014). Qualitative research in music education. In C. M. Conway (Ed.), *The Oxford handbook of qualitative research in American music education* (pp. 13–31). Oxford University Press.

McNiff, S. (2008). Arts-based research. In R. G. Knowles & A. L. Cole (Eds.), *Handbook of the arts in qualitative research* (pp. 29–40). Sage.

Mitchell, J. (1984). Typicality and the case study. In R. Ellen (Ed.), *Ethnographic research: A guide to general conduct* (pp. 237–241). Academic Press.

Robertson, R. (1992). *Globalization: Social theory and global culture.* Sage.

Schaefer, J. (2000). Songline: Vocal traditions in world music. In J. Poter (Ed.), *Cambridge Companion in singing* (pp. 9–27). Cambridge University Press.

Sewell, W. (2005). The concept(s) of culture. In W. Sewell (Ed.), *Logics of history* (pp. 152–174). University of Chicago Press.

Sherman, B. J., Bateman, K. M., Jeong, S., & Hudock, L. A. (2019). Dialogic meta-ethnography: Troubling methodology in ethnographically informed qualitative inquiry. *Cultural Studies of Science Education, 16*(1), 279–302.

Skukauskaitė, A. (2017). Systematic analyses of layered meanings inscribed in interview conversations: An interactional ethnographic perspective and its conceptual foundations. *Acta Paedagogica Vilnensia, 39*(2), 45–60.

Spradley, J. (1979/2016). *The ethnographic interview.* Waveland Press, Inc.

van Schalkwyk, G. J. (2010). Collage life story elicitation technique: A representational technique for scaffolding autobiographical memories. *The Qualitative Report, 15*(3), 675–695.

Vygotsky, L. S. (1986). *Thought and language.* MIT Press.

Weller, S. (2017). Using internet video calls in qualitative (longitudinal) interviews: Some implications for rapport. *International Journal of Social Research Methodology, 20,* 613–625.

Wright, S. (2012). Ways of knowing in the arts. In S. Wright (Ed.), *Children, meaning-making and the arts* (pp. 1–27). Pearson.

8

COLLABORATIVE ETHNOGRAPHY *WITH* CHILDREN

Building Intersubjectivity and Co-constructing Knowledge of Place

Alba Lucy Guerrero, Ivonne Natalia Peña, and Maria Dantas-Whitney

This chapter introduces collaborative ethnography, an ethnographic approach complementary to interactional ethnography (IE) and its focus on emic perspectives, discursive construction of knowledge, researcher reflexivity, and analyses of sociocultural contexts impacting people's actions and interactions in social groups. Collaborative ethnography is a form of research where participants act as interlocutors and co-producers of knowledge and where investigators seek to learn from and with people who belong to specific social groups. In this chapter, we highlight the intersubjective and interactional nature of the research process and explore how internalized meanings and knowledge can be made visible through analysis of discursive constructions of daily life, while stepping back from familiar understandings (see related work in chapters by Baker et al.; Skukauskaitė & Sullivan; Hong & Bloome, this volume). Researchers in collaborative ethnography, similar to IE, believe social knowledge is jointly constructed *with* participants, who are conceived as active knowing subjects capable of making decisions about the research process, and whose understandings are incorporated in all stages of the investigation.

In particular, we showcase a research study focusing on notions of place and territory. We examine the process of knowledge production during fieldwork in collaboration with children who live in the outskirts of a large urban area in Colombia, in contexts of vulnerability and violence. The study was conducted by the College of Education and the Youth Research Center at the *Pontificia Universidad Javeriana* (Pontifical Javeriana University) in a primary school sponsored by the Jesuit Refugee Services, between 2015 and 2017. Participants were students from third and fourth grades at the school, located in the *Altos de la Florida* (Floral Heights) sector of the municipality of Soacha, near Bogotá. Eighty percent of the population in this area is displaced

DOI: 10.4324/9781003215479-10

by the Colombian armed conflict. Families live in a situation of poverty, in territories known colloquially in Colombia as "invasions", that is, illegal and unregulated neighborhoods and settlements due to the illegitimate and unauthorized appropriation of land. The area has limited access to basic services and is exposed on a daily basis to different forms of violence and insecurity caused by unofficial armed groups (paramilitaries and guerrillas), criminal organizations, and common crime.

The methodological design of the study was centered on ethnographic encounters that utilized different expressive forms which children developed, such as dramatic performances, games, and the production of a book with their own stories. For us as the researchers, it was necessary to attempt to reduce the asymmetries that exist in adult-children interactions and to establish a dialogue through a relationship of "coevalness" (Fabian, 1983), enabling an intersubjective construction of meanings where we view the children as agentive authors of their own life stories (Guerrero & Milstein, 2017).

In collaborative ethnography, the gradual construction of intersubjectivity occurs as researchers and participants share time and space, and perform activities together (Fabian, 1983). Researchers engage with participants as interlocutors and partners in dialogue, learning from their perspectives and experiences, allowing themselves to be guided by their actions, and constantly reflecting on situations and circumstances that may be puzzling or surprising to them (Blommaert & Jie, 2010). This approach to performing ethnography, similar to interactional ethnographic relationships with participants as demonstrated across other chapters in this volume, comes in sharp contrast to more traditional ethnographic methods, where participants become the distant, exotic others who are simply observed by researchers and considered objects of the investigation without a sense of agency or individuality, and whose voices are often marginalized (Ramos, 2017).

Focusing on collaborative ethnography, we examine the intersubjective nature of the process of knowledge construction with children as both interlocutors and creators of knowledge. Engaging with children as interlocutors entails exchanging, negotiating, and building ideas through collaborative dialogue and joint participation in activities. For our analysis, we utilize the epistemological logic proposed by Michael Agar (2006), who states that ethnography must be understood as a dynamic system of knowledge production that is nonlinear, generative, iterative, recursive, and abductive. In discussing the concept of "abductive ethnography", Agar (1996, p. 35) emphasizes that the work of the ethnographer is not to derive hypotheses from theoretical propositions, nor is it to adjust the information gathered during fieldwork according to predetermined theoretical propositions. For Agar (1996), ethnography is neither inductive nor deductive, it is abductive. This means that its logic of investigation is characterized by the development of new theoretical propositions that arise from encounters and interactions that occur in the field. In this way, Agar posits that a necessary condition for a study to be ethnographic is that, at the end of the study, new concepts or understandings will emerge that were not contemplated in the original design of the investigation.

Drawing on the abductive logic of ethnographic research, we describe the way in which, during fieldwork and through interactions between children and researchers, new understandings about the concept of territory emerged. Our discussion is carried out through the analysis of specific situations that arose during fieldwork when the children challenged the researchers' views about them and their territory, thus generating alternative interpretations and insights.

The Production of Knowledge With Children as a Collaborative Logic of Inquiry

Ethnographic inquiry focuses on identifying and understanding the dynamics of a cultural environment from the point of view of its members (Guber, 2001). Interactional ethnography (IE) as a logic of inquiry emphasizes the particular role of discourse in the construction of everyday life in various settings by tracing interactions across time and events. Castanheira et al. (2001) state:

> The interactional ethnographer, therefore, must look at what is constructed in and through the moment-by moment interactions among members of a social group; how members negotiate events through these interactions; and the ways in which knowledge and texts generated in one event become linked to, and thus a resource for, members' actions in subsequent events.
>
> *(p. 358)*

Although our study is not framed within a micro analysis of discourse and actions among participants proposed in IE, it does share the perspective that practices are constructed by and made available to members, in and through their everyday actions in situated interactions (Green et al., 2020). Drawing on the collaborative ethnography logic of inquiry (Rappaport, 2004), we encourage nonacademic participants (in this case, children) to be involved in the research process. We consider the collaborative ethnographic approach as a "space of possibility" (Agar, 2006) that allows us to understand *with the other* the complexity of everyday social life, including language use and actions within a particular space and time (Green et al., 2020). We conceive research as an interactive and communicative form, committed to collaboration, through intersubjective and contemporary relationships between the researcher and participants (Fabian, 2012; Baker et al., Skukauskaitė & Sullivan, this volume). Guerrero et al. (2017) state that collaboration implies a constant negotiation during fieldwork:

> [collaborative ethnographic] research – in addition to involving documentation, analysis, explanation and interpretation – requires interaction

and communication, which makes ethnography a type of inquiry that modifies the knower and also impacts those with whom we meet. [...] Thus, the production of ethnographic knowledge is intimately and directly linked to the relationships that researchers establish with the individuals and groups that reside and work or transit the places where we conduct fieldwork.

(p. 15)

Drawing on the assumption that the production of knowledge is intersubjective and occurs through interactions between researchers and participants, in this study the children acted as co-researchers who contributed ideas and co-constructed knowledge together with the investigators. Recognizing children as subjects of knowledge empowers them to express how they understand their lives and the contexts in which they live (Milstein et al., 2011). Thus, the methodological design privileged ethnographic encounters between researchers and children to develop understandings about the children's perspectives of the world.

Ethnographic Research in Collaboration with Children

Research approaches in social sciences and education have tended to privilege the perspectives of adults. However, as noted above, the study presented in this chapter prioritizes perspectives developed through a collaboration between adult researchers and children. This collaborative approach is part of a movement that emerged in the eighties in the fields of Anthropology and the New Sociology of childhood. The movement questions the invisibility of children's voices and recognizes them as agentive subjects with capacity for influencing the social, cultural, and political dynamics of their own contexts (Prout & James, 1990). This approach also entails a methodological turn in research with children that has been developed by a number of scholars (Gandulfo, 2016; Guerrero et al., 2017; Milstein, 2006; Silva et al., 2021), who highlight the importance of involving children as interlocutors and/or partners in data collection and analysis.

The idea of creating spaces to listen to the voices of children has also been recognized in international and national legislations, accentuating the need to position children as subjects who can influence their environment and demand the protection of their rights. The United Nations Convention on the Rights of the Child (The United Nations, 1989) redefined the status of children by acknowledging their civil and political rights through Article 12, on the right to express their views freely, and the right to be heard in any judicial and administrative proceedings affecting the child. Incorporating the voices of children in social research involves a gradual and complex process, which implies that researchers have a genuine interest in comprehending children's points of view as qualified members of their communities who can speak about culture and society. James (2007) refers to the challenges imposed by "giving voice" to children in social inquiry. On the one hand, the author suggests that "giving them voice" does not simply mean allowing children to speak, but rather recognizing the unique contributions they offer to our understanding and theorizing about our social worlds (James, 2007), which poses great challenges in regards to translation, interpretation, and mediation of their voices. On the other hand, there is a risk in talking about "children's voices" as a univocal categorization of undifferentiated voices, without understanding the diversity of children's perceptions and experiences, which can contribute to children's invisibility and silencing. In this way, James (2007) underscores the need to capture children's individual voices and make them visible, while at the same time understanding them within the collective. Ethnography enables this contextualization and connection between individual voices, the collective, and the sociocultural environments in which children and others speak and act (Kelly & Green, 2019).

It is also important to problematize the relationship between researchers and participants, especially children. Guerrero and Milstein (2017) point out that to build a truly collaborative relationship between child and adult researchers, it is necessary to minimize the asymmetries that exist in the relationship. For intersubjectivity to be achieved, it is important to establish a dialogue between equals. This "equality" refers to the understanding of the child as a subject of knowledge, that is, as a builder of knowledge. According to Mayall (1996, cited by Balen et al., 2006) the term "knowledge subject" implies an effort to move beyond the construction and reconstruction of children's experiences based on adult-centered ideals. This process entails accepting the experiential meaning of children's social worlds, and a desire to both describe and understand the social practices that shape and constitute their existence.

According to Agar (2006), ethnography seeks to learn from and with people who belong to a specific social group, to understand their internalized meanings, and to build social knowledge that can be made visible through the analysis of discursive constructions of daily activities. This analysis presupposes an estrangement from meanings that are familiar to the researcher, or stepping back from ethnocentrism and the known (Green & Bridges, 2018). Consequently, in the case of collaborative ethnography with children, their conceptions about life must be incorporated in the analysis as a fundamental element for the understanding of their social worlds.

As mentioned earlier, for Agar (2006) ethnography is abductive because the knowledge that is built during the research process is intersubjective. Agar describes the logic of ethnographic knowledge construction in terms of resolutions, whose starting point is the "frame" of understanding the researcher possesses before arriving in the field (languaculture 1, LC1, as described in Skukauskaitė and Rupšienė and other chapters in this volume).

This frame of understanding is shaped by the researcher's prior life experiences and beliefs. According to Agar (2006), upon reaching the field, the researcher encounters a number of events, conversations, and situations that arise in interaction with people in the community and constitute the ethnographic experience. These encounters then become the data and artifacts used in the research process and provide crucial information to modify the initial frame of understanding.

All this information is conceptualized by Agar (2006) as connecting "strips", which represent ethnographic events. For these strips to transform the initial frame of understanding and configure a new one, it is necessary to experience a "rich point", which is a specific moment of amazement and surprise when new meanings are revealed to the researcher, which they did not know or did not understand and which challenge their previous beliefs (see also Skinner's chapter). From this challenge, a new "frame" of understanding is generated that incorporates these new meanings and reflections. Subsequently, the researcher will be confronted with other connecting "strips" and, eventually, will experience another "rich point", which will provoke the configuration of a new "frame" of understanding, and so on. In this way, an intersubjective process of knowledge construction emerges within the ethnographic practice (see Figure 8.1).

In this chapter we attempt to provide transparency to the process of intersubjective knowledge construction through collaborative ethnography, following Agar's (1996) model described above. To achieve this goal, we discuss a specific study conducted in collaboration with children living in a community on the outskirts of Bogota, Colombia. We describe in concrete detail the process of joint knowledge construction related to the locality and territory.

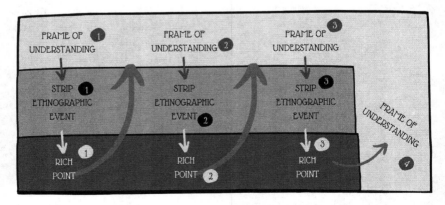

FIGURE 8.1   Building Ethnographic Knowledge through Interactional Events (Based on Single-strip Resolution, Agar, 1996, p. 34)

Context of the Study

This study was conducted with a group of children who live in an area called *Altos de la Florida* (Floral Heights), in the municipality of Soacha, located in the periphery of Bogota, the capital of Colombia. Since the purpose of this chapter is to illuminate the logic of inquiry guiding our research process (Green et al., 2020), we analyze our process of intersubjective knowledge construction carried out with the children about their concept of place and territory. To contextualize our analysis, we first provide an overview of Colombia's historical, social, and political situation. This contextualization is important, since ethnography contributes to the understanding of the "global" in relation to the "local" and vice versa.

Colombia has had a long history of internal armed conflict, characterized by confrontations between government security forces and guerrilla groups, which have been exacerbated by the intervention of paramilitary groups supported by the government, and the prevalence of criminal activities such as drug trafficking, extortion, kidnappings, homicides, massacres, smuggling, and torture. Such activities have resulted in the recruitment of children and teenagers and have forced the displacement of families, who attempt to flee areas of violence.

Two important events intensified Colombia's situation of armed conflict: first, the demobilization of paramilitary groups belonging to the AUC (*Autodefensas Unidas de Colombia* [United Self-Defense Forces of Colombia]) in 2003, which had little effect on the de-escalation of violence, but brought serious consequences such as the formation of independent criminal gangs. The second event was the signing of the peace agreement between the national government and the oldest guerrilla in the world, the FARC (*Fuerzas Armadas Revolucionarias de Colombia* [Revolutionary Armed Forces of Colombia]) in 2016, which initially resulted in a significant decrease in violence.

However, Colombia has seen another recent surge in violence, precipitated by a number of murders of human rights defenders, social leaders, land restitution leaders, and former FARC combatants. This increase in violence has coincided with the resurgence of paramilitary groups, criminal gangs, and FARC dissidents, who now compete for control of territory and criminal activities, especially in regions such as the Pacific, Antioquia and Catatumbo, as reported by organizations such as the Norwegian Council for Refugees (NCR, 2018), the *Programa Somos Defensores* (We are Defenders Program) (2018) and the *Consejo de Seguridad de las Naciones Unidas* (United Nations Security Council) (2017). Thus, Colombia is now said to be experiencing a period of "post-conflict", referring to the critical current situation of violence enveloping the country after the signing of the peace agreement.

The pervasive violence in Colombia has contributed to the phenomenon of massive internal displacement, causing almost 8 million people to leave their homes and settle in the largest cities of the country and the surrounding municipalities, as reported by the *Observatorio Global del Desplazamiento Interno* (Internal Displacement Monitoring Center – IDMC) (2020). This situation has made Colombia the country with the biggest number of internally displaced persons in the world. The city of Bogotá has the highest rate of the displaced persons, closely followed by the surrounding municipalities, as is the case of Soacha, which is a district of about 650,000 inhabitants, with a poverty rate of 67%, and 15.4% unemployment (Alcaldía Municipal de Soacha (Soacha Municipal Mayor's Office), 2021).

The municipality of Soacha is known for its high rates of violence. Residents coexist with urban cells of paramilitary and guerrilla groups, criminal gangs, and common criminals. Sectors of Soacha are strategic corridors for drug and arms trafficking, as well as for smuggling and other illegal activities. One of these sectors is *Altos de la Florida* (Floral Heights), located at the foot of a hill in the central mountain range of the Andes. It was in this location that our study was conducted with 24 children between the ages of 9 and 10.

To gain access to the site, we proposed the project in partnership with Jesuit Refugee Services, a humanitarian organization which offers educational services to vulnerable populations and sponsors a private school in this area. This Jesuit foundation facilitated our communication with the school directors, who approved our research proposal. We discussed the selection of children participants with the teachers in charge of third and fourth grades. At first, the teachers recommended children with academic and behavioral difficulties, thinking that the research project could become a school support strategy. However, during several conversations with the teachers, we emphasized the collaborative nature of our research approach, and it was finally agreed that the most important criteria for participation would be the children's desire to be part of the project. We presented our research proposal to the children during a workshop, and 24 of them volunteered to participate and affirmed their assent. Their participation also was authorized by their parents and guardians through informed consent protocols. To maintain confidentiality, we used pseudonyms for all participants. Thus, we only worked with children who wanted to contribute to the project. The study comprised ethnographic encounters designed and planned in collaboration with the children, reflecting their interests and motivations, and allowing them to examine their lives, experiences, and hopes for the future.

The Research Process

Figure 8.2 summarizes our logic of inquiry during the research process, as we revised our conceptualizations about the territory *Altos de la Florida* (Floral Heights) in collaboration with the children as our interlocutors, based on Agar's (1996) theoretical framework. As we began the study, our perspectives

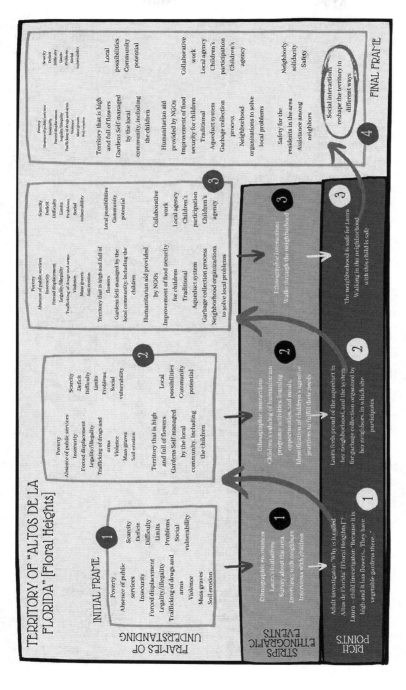

FIGURE 8.2 Co-production of Knowledge about the Territory Altos de la Florida (Floral Heights) in Collaboration with Laura (Based on Agar, 1996)

about *Altos de la Florida* (Floral Heights) were influenced by what we had heard about all the violence and poverty in the area, as well as our observations while visiting with a priest who worked there coordinating the Jesuit Refugee Services organization. Thus, these preliminary views shaped our initial "frame" of understanding about the place, which is clearly evidenced in the following fieldnotes of one of the researchers:

> We walked through the four sectors of *Altos de la Florida*. After climbing approximately one block from the school, we were told that at that point, the authorized neighborhoods ended, and the illegal settlements began. In the entire area, including within the legal neighborhoods, the streets were unpaved.
>
> The poverty in these neighborhoods is evident. Due to illegality, homes do not have public services. Natural gas is now being installed in a low area, but that is the only service available. Along the way there are tank trucks that bring water up the hill and fill large cisterns, apparently communal, which contain the only water available to residents. The sun is inclement, the heat is suffocating, and the land is arid; it is more sand than land. The sand flies through the air carried by the wind and the vehicles. It goes into our noses. It causes us to cough frequently. Our eyes burn. As we keep walking, the climb becomes more difficult due to these conditions.
>
> In the streets we see houses with different characteristics. In sectors 1 and 2 houses made with brick and tiles are common. In sector 3 this type of house begins to mix with others made with materials such as zinc tiles and wood. In sector 4 it is rare to see brick houses; most of them are made of wood and there are several *cambuches* [makeshift homes precariously built with recycled, rustic or waste materials, which can be temporary or permanent]. In this sector several houses are also under construction.
>
> Very few children are seen on the streets, which is understandable because we guess they are at school. The children we see are with their mothers or caregivers, who look untidy and unkempt. It is common to see adult residents in these conditions.
>
> We see many animals in the streets, especially dogs. Most of them are in very precarious conditions, malnourished and with skin diseases.
>
> The priest, a member of the Jesuit Refugee Services, tells us that many of the men work in *Abastos* [Bogotá's main farmers' market square]. They have to leave their homes at midnight to get to the market early and *cotear* [carry large bundles of food]. Many prefer to walk the entire way, to save money on transportation.

Problems related to drug and arms trafficking are common here. Trafficking is controlled by paramilitary organizations and criminal gangs. Another important characteristic of this area is the high percentage of displaced people. We heard that many people who have been displaced from their homes due to violence, first moved to depressed zones in Bogotá where they also encountered violence, so they had to migrate once again to reach this area of Soacha.

Up on the mountain, there is an area that, according to what they tell us, has been appropriated by a family, "Los Ramírez." They reclaim their lands from time to time and displace the families that have already settled there. Here, new families have to pay large sums to get permission to "raise a roof."

Climbing to the top of the mountain, we arrive at a place where there are three large crosses. Near the crosses there are large rocks and deep holes, which do not look natural. The priest tells us that, for reasons associated with territorial control, drugs and weapons, many people were murdered in this sector. Their bodies were raised to the top of the mountain and buried. The holes are graves where the authorities found bodies. A large cross was erected here, as the site was declared a holy place. Then, two more crosses were erected to accompany the initial one. From the crosses we can look down and see the entire municipality.

Walking to the other side of this view, turning our gaze towards the rural landscape of the mountain range, we can see the contiguous mountain named *Altos de Cazucá* [the border zone between Bogotá and Soacha, known as a dangerous place]. The desolate trails that lead to Cazucá are easily seen. We can clearly see the entrance to *Ciudad Bolívar* [Bogotá area] and, therefore, to the capital. These trails are used for drug and arms trafficking.

From another view, we can observe the terrible erosion caused by extraction of raw materials by factories that produce brick and cement. The soil is dead and without vegetation. A land invaded by countless trucks that constantly go up and down the mountain to take the extracted products to large companies that do not give back to the community that they directly affect. They just exploit the land for their enrichment.

(Field Journal, February 18, 2015)

As can be seen from the fieldnotes above, our description of the place was marked by an emphasis on the conditions of social vulnerability of its residents due to the situations of violence, insecurity, and poverty in the area, which was reinforced by our observations during our visit. This "frame" of understanding (Agar, 1996) shaped our initial interactions with the children of the group who collaborated with us (Figure 8.2, frame 1 – initial frame).

In our first ethnographic encounters with the children, we focused on establishing a relationship of trust, so that they could freely express themselves. From the beginning, the research questions explored by the team were proposed by both the children and the adult researchers. One of the girls, 9-year-old Laura, was very interested in researching aspects of her territory. For this reason, she developed a series of questions related to her neighborhood. For example, there is a tree near her house, and she wanted to find out why people call it "the tree of love". In collaboration with one of the researchers, Laura developed the methodology to answer her questions. Her design included conducting interviews with neighbors, elaborating a map to mark the sites she considered most important, and taking a walking tour of the neighborhood to show the area to the researcher, including the path she took from her school to her house. This series of interactions make up what Agar calls a "strip" (Figure 8.2, strip 1).

The process began with the elaboration of the map of the neighborhood by Laura and a few other girls. During this activity, we asked them why the place is called *Altos de la Florida* (Floral Heights), to which Laura responds:

> "It is because it is high and it has flowers." Shirley, another girl from the neighborhood, called her out, and questioned her, hinting that there are no flowers. However, Laura tells her that there are, because they grow vegetable gardens… Laura knows that there really are no flowers in *Altos de la Florida*; however, she proudly talks about the cultivation of vegetables in gardens. At no time did she express shame for her neighborhood.
> *(Field Journal, May 14, 2015)*

Laura's answer was quite surprising to us because we knew how arid the terrain was, and because our perspectives about the area had focused solely on its difficult circumstances and scarcity of resources. Laura's statement appeared to be a defining point, a "rich point" in Agar's terms (Figure 8.2, rich point 1), because it questioned and disrupted our frame of understanding, revealing a new frame (Figure 8.2, frame 2), that of Laura's, which incorporated a new perspective about the place that was "high and full of flowers", a place that to our eyes seemed only dusty and unpleasant. Massey (1994) argues that spaces are not determined by their physical characteristics but are socially constructed and signified in everyday interactions. Laura's affirmation then responds not to an objective reality but to an interpretation she builds using the existence of communal vegetable gardens where several neighbors and she herself actively work. It should be noted that these gardens are highly valued by the families in the neighborhood, since they contribute to improving the community's difficult conditions of food insecurity and offer a different aesthetic to the area (Figure 8.2, frame 2).

Another aspect also valued by the children was the presence of humanitarian organizations in their territory. As mentioned above, living conditions were precarious. In particular, food scarcity was prevalent and generated great concern among the residents. During our visits to the school we observed that several children, including Laura, often arrived without having had breakfast, and many times, were not able to eat lunch because their families couldn't provide. For this reason, the children viewed the humanitarian aid organizations as important resources which helped them meet their needs for food, particularly on the weekends. On one of our visits, Danna and Laura commented:

> It's better that you go up on Saturday because it's cooler, there are more things to do and you can learn more," said Danna. We asked them about the difference between going up on a weekday or on a weekend, then Laura replied: "I can take you to visit all the aid organizations, which are very cool. The first one is 'World Vision,' where Victor is the person in charge. There they give us notebooks and gifts, but you have to register and they give you a name and a code. The second one is 'His Children International.' And the third coolest is *'Camino a Emaús'* [Road to Emaús], which is where I work… The cool thing about these foundations is that they teach important things in life and some give us breakfast and others give us lunch on Saturdays … 'World Vision' gives us gifts once a year, and 'His Children' gives us a snack on Fridays when we leave school at 3pm, and breakfast and lunch on Saturdays. So, you know, if they come up on Friday: snack. On Saturday: breakfast and lunch.
>
> *(Field Journal, July 24, 2015)*

Through these interactions with the children, we discovered that in many cases they decided on their own to participate in the programs offered by these NGOs. The children were well aware of the benefits they could obtain from each organization, and when/how they could access those benefits. This made us question our preconceived ideas about the intervention of many of these NGOs in vulnerable territories, with assistance strategies that often do not offer long-term solutions that transform communities. For these girls, the presence of these aid organizations allowed them to meet their immediate nutritional needs and make decisions about activities to structure their days, as well as discover other interests and create opportunities to get together with peers in a space other than the school (Figure 8.2, strip 2).

Together with other experiences in the field, these exchanges made us aware of strategies children used when facing adversities such as hunger. The children planned and enacted strategies to fulfill the needs their families could not meet, which reflected their collective sense of agency.

Another realization which altered our initial view of the territory involved the collective actions performed by the residents to counter situations of vulnerability due to the unauthorized and unregulated nature of the settlements in the area. Thus, conditions such as lack of water services and poor waste management had led families to build an aqueduct to provide access to drinking water and to organize a system for waste disposal. The children were fully involved in these efforts, performing tasks assigned to different members of the community. As Laura stated, they were proud of their community's organization, and valued their roles in implementing solutions to problems. This became evident in a conversation with Laura, which resulted in another "rich point" in our research journey (Figure 8.2, rich point 2):

> Laura begins to talk to us about something else that is important to her, because we never asked about it, and that is water. She tells us that there are two dimensions. What she means is that there is a high zone and a low zone (taking into consideration their location on a mountain). She mentions that at the top of the mountain there are three water tanks, and that the middle, the smallest one, belongs to her family. The big ones belong to the neighbor who has chickens.

According to Laura, the aqueduct system consists of a small hose that comes from above, and they have to open a tap to fill the tanks [...] Laura finishes with her explanation of the aqueduct system in the neighborhood, and continues describing the system her mother invented for her house, with a wooden crate and a covered container located in their kitchen. Her mother created a support structure and placed a filter on it, which allows them to use a glass to drink water. They also have other containers with additional filters that are filled with a dripping device (Field Journal, April 15, 2016).

Laura knows the community solutions designed to meet the collective needs of families, and also understands and collaborates on solutions developed in her own home. She describes another strategy developed in her neighborhood for garbage collection. According to her, they have placed *chus* (receptacles) every few blocks, where the families must deposit their waste. Laura explains that each *chu* "has tiles and sticks to hold it up, and a door that opens where children deposit the garbage" (Field Journal, November 5, 2015). Children are often in charge of garbage collection. Laura affirms that this system occurs because:

LAURA: They make us clean
RESEARCHER: Who makes you clean?
LAURA: The men who own the different blocks in the neighborhood, like Don Alex Torres, who drives around giving orders with a megaphone
RESEARCHER: To children or adults?
LAURA: For everyone to help. And we begin to collect and deposit everything in the *chu*.

(Field journal, November 5, 2015)

Laura builds her own understandings about the dynamics operating in her neighborhood and creates explanations about them. Thus, for her a community leader like Don Alex acts like the boss of the blocks, because the residents obey him, and this system works to prevent the area from getting contaminated with garbage. Once again, this realization allowed us to modify our frame of understanding about the relationships these children establish with their territory and how they position themselves in it (Figure 8.2, frame 3).

Another "rich point" that modified our frame of understanding about this territory had to do with our conceptualization of safety and security. For us researchers, this area seemed dangerous and unsafe, due to the presence of organized crime and common crime. However, our perception of insecurity was revised by Laura's views about the dynamics of her neighborhood. On the one hand, Laura knew that the investigators should never go up to the neighborhood alone, because "something could happen to them". To be safe, it was necessary for her to accompany them because she lived there. She moved alone in different parts of the neighborhood without concern because she knew where she could walk and where she couldn't. On the other hand, Laura considered her neighborhood to be safe (Figure 8.2, rich point 3).

RESEARCHER: And why is there a baby Jesus here?

LAURA: Because in these parts there used to be a lot of robberies, so they placed the baby Jesus here, so that he can bless them, that is, so that they stop stealing. That's why he is there.

RESEARCHER: And what do you think? Is it safe or not?

LAURA: It is safe.

RESEARCHER: Yes? For sure?

LAURA: For sure.

(Field Journal, May 14, 2016)

Furthermore, Laura states that her neighborhood is safe because when someone is about to be robbed "people help you". In this way, it is evident that her perception of security also depends on the collective solidarity among neighbors. Her sense of belonging to the territory and the community's actions to protect her from dangerous acts, provide the basis for her perception of safety. This rich point was significant in transforming once again our frame of understanding. It allowed us to appreciate the local dynamics and to understand the interactions the children have with their environment and with the other people who inhabit it. Our conceptualization of the territory was now very different from the initial ideas we had when we first arrived in *Altos de la Florida* (Floral Heights) (Figure 8.2, frame 4 – final frame).

The different rich points we experienced during the research process through our collaboration with Laura, allowed us to gradually modify our frame of understanding about the territory of *Altos de la Florida* (Floral Heights). Sosa (2012, pp. 7–11) remarks:

> The conceptualization of territory is understood from its concrete possibilities in the process of transformation of human groups. However, it is also the result of the representation, construction, and appropriation that these groups carry out, as well as the relationships that impact them in a dialectical symbiosis, in which both the territory and the human group are transformed in the historical journey [...] In this sense, the territory is not only a portion of land delimited with its biophysical complexity (relief, environmental conditions, biodiversity). It is, above all, a socially constructed space, that is, historically, economically, socially, culturally and politically [constructed] [...] From this perspective, territory is structured and organized in its spatiality through relationships between human beings and its other elements. This structuring and organization depend on factors, such as landscape configuration, that affect the spatial distribution of human activities and influence the appropriation and transformation of the space.

This perspective of territory highlights the importance of the relationship between the people of a community and their physical space. When we reflect on our initial frame of understanding about this territory, we realize that we had prioritized the relational dynamics established by groups that operate on the margins of the law, especially those linked to armed conflict and organized crime. In addition, we had also emphasized structural conditions of social inequality related to poverty and the illegality of the settlements in the area. Regarding the residents, we not only highlighted their vulnerability but also the circumstances of displacement experienced by many families.

Emergence of New Perspectives and Understandings

Our way of interacting with the children, especially Laura, allowed us to move from a perspective of this territory based on vulnerability and deficit, toward the intersubjective construction of a perspective based on collective action and ingenuity. Ultimately, we became aware of the vast possibilities afforded by individual and collective agency. We came to understand that, through their sense of agency, the children in the neighborhood were able to appropriate their territory, organize as a community to seek solutions to their immediate problems, improve their living conditions, and overcome the limitations imposed by the territory, in spatial-geographic, social, economic, and political terms.

Although this new perspective of the territory does not disregard the presence of violence related one way or another to the Colombian armed conflict, we note that the children from *Altos de la Florida* (Floral Heights) were able to resignify these problems through their lived experiences. This perspective does not ignore the fact that the children's lives and their relationship to their territory are affected by crime and violence, which influence their everyday actions and behaviors, as well as their relationship to the place. The children are aware of the risks they face, and make everyday decisions based on this knowledge.

Through the gradual transformation of our frame of understanding, guided by several rich points described above, we came to comprehend the children's positioning within the dynamics of their territory: They are subjects of knowledge who actively participate in community efforts to improve local conditions. In this sense, the notion of children as subjects of knowledge is directly connected to their recognition as political subjects, capable of making decisions that impact their own lives and communities, and becoming reproducers as well as change agents of their local culture.

In this way, through the research process, our conceptualization of the children as subjects of knowledge was also transformed, not only through our theoretical framework which guided us to incorporate the children's knowledge in our reformulations of our notion of territory but also implicitly through the way the children interacted with the territory and with us.

Principles of Practice Guiding Collaborative Ethnography

As we have demonstrated through the description of the study above, a collaborative ethnographic approach can contribute to the field of IE in several ways: 1) It focuses on interactions between researchers and participants (in this case, children) to produce knowledge collaboratively, rather than only through interactions among the members of a particular social group researchers observe; 2) it incorporates participants' perspectives, actions, and experiences in the design, development, analysis, and/or writing of the research; 3) it positions researchers and participants as equally valuable contributors to the research experience, minimizing hierarchical relations of power; and 4) it attempts to build intersubjectivity between the researchers and participants, with researchers engaging in constant self-reflection and inevitably being personally transformed by the research experience through changes in their worldview and/or ways of thinking.

It is important to highlight that all ethnographers practice some kind of collaboration, and that these principles and actions are indeed present in many studies adopting an ethnographic perspective, including interactional ethnographies, as demonstrated across chapters in this volume (e.g., Baker et al.; Skukauskaité & Sullivan; Yeager). However, in collaborative ethnography, the act of collaboration is explicitly and deliberately emphasized at every stage of the research process. In other words, collaborative ethnography "moves collaboration from its taken-for-granted background and positions it on center stage" (Lassiter, 2005, p. 15).

Based on our experience, we offer the following recommendations to guide beginning researchers who would like to conduct collaborative ethnographic research:

- Engage in constant reflection about your role and positionality throughout the research process, attempting to minimize asymmetrical relationships of power; open spaces for participants to express their perspectives, needs and desires.
- Interactions with participants must be above all collaborative and "coeval" in nature (Fabian, 2012). This implies conceiving of participants as equals in an intersubjective time and space; in other words, as subjects of knowledge who possess agency and who may contribute to all aspects of the research process, including planning, design, data collection, and/or analysis.
- Pay close attention to unforeseen events and unexpected occurrences which may surprise you during the research process. Carefully reflect on how these "rich points" may alter your current "frame" of understanding (Agar, 1996), and be open to changing your perspectives and expanding your perspectives throughout your time in the field.
- Carefully analyze both micro- and macro-level forces that affect the context and the participants of your study. As Agar (1996) remarks, "frames allow both lateral connections [...] and hierarchical connections between local observation and political economy and history" (p. 36).

Suggested Readings

Barley, R. (2020). "Why have you not written my name?" Collaborative research with children. *magis, Revista Internacional de Investigación en Educación, 13*(1), 1–21. https://doi.org/10.11144/Javeriana.m13.whwn

Milstein, D., Clemente, A., & Guerrero, A. L. (2019). Collaboration in educational ethnography in Latin America. *Oxford Research Encyclopedias Education.* https://oxfordre.com/education/view/10.1093/acrefore/9780190264093.001.0001/acrefore-9780190264093-e-565

Rappaport, J. (2008). Beyond participant observation: Collaborative ethnography as theoretical innovation. *Collaborative Anthropologies, 1*, 1–31. doi:10.1353/cla.0.0014.

References

Agar, M. (1996). *The professional stranger: An informal introduction to ethnography* (2nd ed.). Academic Press.

Agar, M. (2006). Culture: Can you take it anywhere? *International Journal of Qualitative Methods, 5*(2), 1–12.

Alcaldía Municipal de Soacha (Soacha Municipal Mayor's Office). (2021). *Indicador Socio-Económico.* https://www.alcaldiasoacha.gov.co/NuestroMunicipio/Paginas/Indicador-Socio-economico.aspx

Balen, R., Blyth, E., Calabretto, H., Fraser, C., Horrocks, C., & Manby, M. (2006). Involving children in health and social research: "Human becomings" or "active beings"? *Childhood, 13*(1), 29–48.

Blommaert, J., & Jie, D. (2010). *Ethnographic fieldwork.* Multilingual Matters.

Castanheira, M. L., Crawford, T., Dixon, C. N., & Green, J. L. (2001). Interactional ethnography: An approach to studying the social construction of literate practices. *Linguistics and Education, 11*(4), 353–400. https://doi.org/10.1016/S0898-5898(00)00032-2

Consejo de Seguridad de las Naciones Unidas. (2017). *Informe del Secretario General sobre la Misión de Verificación de las Naciones Unidas en Colombia.* https://colombia.unmissions.org/sites/default/files/informe_trimestral_sec_gnal_mision_de_verificacion_de_la_onu_en_colombia.pdf

Fabian, J. (1983). *Time and the other: How anthropology makes its object.* Columbia University Press.

Fabian, J. (2012). Cultural anthropology and the question of knowledge. *The Journal of the Royal Anthropological Institute, 18*(2), 439–453. http://www.jstor.org/stable/41507968

Gandulfo, C. (2016). 'Hablan poco Guaraní, saben mucho'. Una investigación en colaboración con niños y maestros en un contexto bilingüe de Corrientes, Argentina. *Signo y Seña, 29*, 79–102. http://revistascientificas.filo.uba.ar/index.php/sys/article/view/2807

Green, J. L., Baker, W. D., Chian, M. M., Vanderhoof, C., Hooper, L., Kelly, G. J., Skukauskaitė, A., & Kalainoff, M. Z. (2020). Studying the over-time construction of knowledge in educational settings: A microethnographic discourse analysis approach. *Review of Research in Education, 44*(1), 161–194. https://doi.org/10.3102/0091732X20903121

Green, J. L., & Bridges, S. M. (2018). Interactional ethnography. In *International handbook of the learning sciences* (pp. 475–488). Routledge.

Guber, R. (2001). *La etnografía: Método, campo y reflexividad.* Norma.

Guerrero, A. L., Clemente, A., Dantas-Whitney, M., & Milstein, D. (2017). *Bordes, límites y fronteras. Encuentros etnograficos con niños, niñas y adolescentes.* Pontificia Universidad Javeriana.

Guerrero, A. L., & Milstein, D. (2017). Dialogar y producir alteridad. un episodio de trabajo de campo con una niña en Colombia. In A. Guerrero et al. (Eds.), *Bordes, límites y fronteras. Encuentros etnograficos con niños, niñas y adolescentes* (pp. 157–176). Editorial Pontificia Universidad Javeriana.

Internal Displacement Monitoring Center – IDMC. (2020). Global report on internal displacement 2020. https://www.internal-displacement.org/global-report/grid2020/

James, A. (2007). Giving voice to children's voices: Practices and problems, pitfalls and potentials. *American Anthropologist, 109*(2), 261–272.

Kelly, G.J. & Green, J.L. (2019). *Theory and methods for sociocultural research in science and engineering education.* Routledge.

Lassiter, L. E. (2005). *The Chicago guide to collaborative ethnography.* University of Chicago Press.

Massey, D. (1994). *Space, place and gender.* Polity Press.

Milstein, D. (2006). Y los niños, ¿por qué no?: Algunas reflexiones sobre un trabajo de campo con niños avá. *Revista De Antropología, 9,* 49–59. http://www.redalyc.org/articulo.oa?id=169014140004

Milstein, D., Clemente, A., Dantas-Whitney, M., Guerrero, A. L., & Higgins, M. (2011). *Entre espacios y tiempos compartidos: Encuentros etnográficos con niñ@s y adolescentes.* Editorial Pontificia Universidad Javeriana.

NCR – Consejo Noruego para los Refugiados [Norwegian Council for Refugees]. (2018). *Catatumbo en crisis humanitaria. Comunicado oficial.* http://www.nrc.org.co/2018/04/20/comunicado-cluster-de-proteccion-colombia/

Programa Somos Defensores (We are Defenders Program). (2018). *Piedra en el Zapato. Informe anual 2017. Sistema de Información sobre Agresiones a Defensores y Defensoras de los DDHH – SIADDHH.* Bogotá. https://choco.org/documentos/informe-anual-2017-piedra-en-el-zapato.pdf

Prout, A., & James, A. (1990). A new paradigm for the sociology of childhood? Provenance, promise and problems. In A. James & A. Prout (Eds.), *Constructing and reconstructing childhood: Contemporary issues in the sociological study of childhood* (pp. 7–33). Routledge Falmer.

Ramos, A. C. (2017). *Denial of coevalness as an epistemic injustice.* Unpublished master's thesis. University of Tartu. http://hdl.handle.net/10062/56492

Rappaport, J. (2004). *Más allá de la escritura: La epistemología de la etnografía en colaboración.* Georgetown University & Gajat.

Silva, R. C. M., Dantas-Whitney, M., Clemente, A., Guerrero, A. L., & Milstein, D. (2021). *Dos momentos inesperados e interesses surpreendentes: (Re)invenção e (re)descoberta na etnografia colaborativa com crianças e jovens/De momentos inesperados e intereses sorprendentes: (Re)invención y (re)descubrimiento en la etnografía colaborativa con niñas, niños y jóvenes.* Pedro & João Editores. doi: 10.51795/9786558693604.

Sosa, M. (2012). *¿Cómo entender el territorio?* Cara Parens.

The United Nations. (1989). Convention on the rights of the child. *Treaty Series, 1577,* 3.

PART 3
Constructing Logic-in-Use

9

UNFOLDING PRINCIPLED ACTIONS FOR ETHNOGRAPHIC ARCHIVING AS AN AXIS OF DEVELOPMENT

Melinda Z. Kalainoff and Monaliza Maximo Chian

Our goal in this chapter is to introduce ways of developing archives and engaging with archived records within interactional ethnographic (IE) research projects. By (re)constructing the decisions and actions taken by two novice ethnographers in their dissertation research, we unfold a principled set of actions for constructing and engaging with an archive over iterative, recursive, and abductive cycles of analyses at the center of an IE logic-of-inquiry (Green et al., 2020).

The first telling case study (Mitchell, 1984) of archiving processes traces Kalainoff's (first author) decision-making processes from the moments of conceptualizing a potential problem for study to identifying a study site, entering the site after Institutional Review Board (IRB) approval, and engaging in multiple layers of record collection and analyses in her pilot and dissertation studies. This telling case focuses on how engaging with the archive through multiple cycles of analyses supported her in developing understandings of ways in which participants in an undergraduate General Chemistry course co-constructed problem-solving practices in an innovative studio learning environment designed to integrate lecture and laboratory modes in the same physical space within each class session of the course.

This process of inquiry and analysis led to constructing a graphic (re)presentation of the learning processes of the ethnographer as they moved between the known and unknown across cycles of analysis to develop emic (insider) understandings of problem solving in the chemistry class. This graphic (re)presentation, as we unfold below, forms an *axis of development* (Kalainoff & Clark, 2017) to make transparent the overtime research process within and across cycles of analyses we use to construct warranted accounts of the phenomena under study.

The second telling case demonstrates how the axis of development Kalainoff framed, served as a resource in two ways for Chian (second author) in reporting

DOI: 10.4324/9781003215479-12

her research process in understanding the processes in developing, implementing, and refining an integrated curriculum in higher education. Specifically, the study involves tracing the decisions, actions, and considerations necessary in integrating long-term futures thinking (LTFT) in the context of an undergraduate major in organizational communication at a regional university. First, the axis of development provided a basis for identifying how Chian's study, like Kalainoff's, was guided by the principles of an IE logic-of-inquiry and analysis. Second, it enabled Chian to construct her own axis of development to show the processes and actions across cycles of analyses she undertook to gain insider understandings of an ongoing innovative project where she served as the lead ethnographer on an analysis team (Chian, 2016, 2020).

In the next section, before presenting Kalainoff's telling case, we present a set of principles for engaging in ethnographic research guiding Kalainoff's and Chian's approach to collecting records in the field and archiving them to support analyses upon leaving the field. After introducing the concept of *axis of development*, Kalainoff presents a first-person description of the phases of her research study to address her overarching questions. Following that, Chian describes how she adapted Kalainoff's axis of development to make transparent the cycles of analysis of her study.

Introducing the Principled Actions for Constructing and Engaging with an Archive

In this section, we introduce principled actions for constructing and engaging with an archive. These actions are conceptually guided by principles of conduct derived from Heath and Street (2008) and Agar (2006), as presented in Skukauskaitė and Green's introductory chapter of this book. As an overview of both telling cases whose details will be presented in subsequent sections, here we introduce the principles and how they guided Kalainoff and Chian.

Table 9.1 presents the overarching questions guiding each telling case and the principles of conduct (Column 1), the principled actions associated with each (Column 2), and the actions Kalainoff (Column 3) and Chian (Column 4) took to address each principle of conduct.

As indicated in the relationship between Columns 1 and 2, the principled actions for constructing and engaging with an archive follow each principle of conduct, creating an *if–then logic* central to the two telling cases that follow. For example, *if* the goal of the ethnographer is to step back from ethnocentrism (Heath, 1982) as they engage with records in the archive to construct datasets for analysis, *then* the analyst does not predefine what records are needed in advance; rather, they identify questions and relevant records for each cycle of analysis. This way the principles of conduct and principled actions lay a foundation for the iterative, recursive, and abductive processes undertaken to address the overarching question(s).

TABLE 9.1 Summarizing and Contextualizing the Principled Actions for Constructing and Engaging With an Archive

IF: principles of conduct (Heath & Street, 2008)	THEN principled actions for constructing and engaging with an archive	Case specific actions/decisions/insights	
		Telling Case 1: Kalainoff's study	Telling Case 2: Chian's study
Framing overarching and orienting (emerging) questions of the study	**Deciding on what types of records to collect and archive from the site** **When engaging in analysis, the researcher asks a parallel question: What records from the archive form a foundation for addressing the orienting/overarching questions to construct warranted accounts of the developing phenomena of interest?**	Overarching Q1: What's happening as the instructor seeks to integrate lecture and lab? Overarching Q2: In the studio learning environment how are problem-solving practices proposed and taken up by students?	Overarching Q1: How did the instructional team integrate organizational theory with long-term futures thinking (LTFT) in an undergraduate bachelor's organization theory program? Overarching Q2: What were the phases of developing integration processes across classes (n=8)?
Stepping back from ethnocentrism	**Documenting the history of the site and how actors (including the ethnographer) came to the site in space and time** **Not predefining variables of particular phenomena of interest. Rather, deciding on what records to collect and what theories will guide the analyses**	• Kalainoff's prior experience as an instructor in an undergraduate General Chemistry course required that she deliberately step back from her prior knowledge to build grounded interpretations of this learning environment through evidence constructed from archived records	• Chian was external to the disciplines when she entered an ongoing research project and unknown context. • Chian had no prior knowledge of LTFT or organizational communications disciplinary content requiring that MC build grounded interpretations of the disciplinary context

(Continued)

TABLE 9.1 Summarizing and Contextualizing the Principled Actions for Constructing and Engaging With an Archive (*Continued*)

IF principles of conduct (Heath & Street, 2008)	THEN principled actions for constructing and engaging with an archive	Case specific actions/decisions/insights	
		Telling Case 1: Kalainoff's study	*Telling Case 2: Chian's study*
Learning *from* and *with* participants	**Archiving records collected in the field on which observed events are recorded (video, fieldnotes, and other) for re-entry at a later time** Interrogating records in processes of records collection and data construction for assessing the *analytic potential* of the records for what is possible to know (and, for an existing archive, how the archive came to be) Assembling data sets from the records for analysis to construct warranted claims of the phenomena of study	• Adding records to the archive that document the rich points of the study (personal communications, an email from the instructor, discussing disciplinary content that students found challenging) • Expanding the records collection in Phase 2 to include the lab–partner interactional space and student learning outcomes • Including summary of ongoing conversations between Kalainoff and the instructor as partner in the study in the fieldnotes	• Taking inventory of the types, purpose, and amounts of records in the existing archive and gaining understanding of their analytic potential • Identifying other resources to understand the contexts or background of the project or to answer emerging questions or rich points and frame clashes; this added 100 email chains (and other forms of records) representing the significance of partnering with cultural guides – i.e., insiders • Conducting multiple virtual interviews with participants
Making connections among developing layers or levels and angles of analyses as well as across developing questions	**Building an indexing or referential scheme (naming of digital files and annotations within fieldnotes) that reflects the nature of the phenomenon under study for ease in tracing phenomena through intertextual (Bloome et al., 2005) ties across time, events/activity, configurations of actors and interactional spaces during analyses** Identifying and tracing phenomena of interest across layers/levels of analyses and across developing questions	• Constructing an indexing scheme that was modified for additional records-types and dimensions of the developing study • Anchoring the analysis in a particular lab exam problem (identified by the instructor) and backwards tracing of disciplinary content and practices made visible in archived records • Organizing and annotating fieldnotes as a guide to other records in the archive	• Anchoring the analysis to identify characteristics of "the best integrated course to date" (as identified by the instructor), analyzing materials in the course and contrasting one course with prior iterations of the course • Re-entering the archive to construct datasets to address emerging questions that arose from the previous analysis

(*Continued*)

TABLE 9.1 Summarizing and Contextualizing the Principled Actions for Constructing and Engaging With an Archive *(Continued)*

IF principles of conduct (Heath & Street, 2008)	THEN principled actions for constructing and engaging with an archive	Case specific actions/decisions/insights	
		Telling Case 1: Kalainoff's study	Telling Case 2: Chian's study
Representing the iterative, recursive, and abductive process of collection and analyses as an axes of development to construct warranted accounts of the phenomena of study	**Conceptualizing the analytic processes undertaken by the ethnographer-as-learner in developing understandings in each cycle of analysis** **Reconstructing the analytic processes for each cycle to show the relationship between cycles and how one cycle informs the next as the researcher seeks to develop theoretical inferences grounded in the analyzed phenomena of study**	• Identifying over time patterns in the analytic processes and the role of frame clashes and rich points in this process; building explanatory theories of analyzed phenomena under study within and across cycles of analyses	• Making visible the additional cycles of analysis, actions, and decisions when entering an existing program of research and existing archive

Axis of Development: A (Re)presentation of Cycles of Analyses

In this section, we introduce the conceptual basis of an axis of development (see Figure 9.1) and how representing it graphically makes transparent the developmental processes involved in ethnographic archiving and constructing datasets for analysis of archived records to address emerging questions. Thus, the axis of development is a conceptually grounded way of graphically (re)presenting the cycles of collection and analyses undertaken in ethnographic studies.

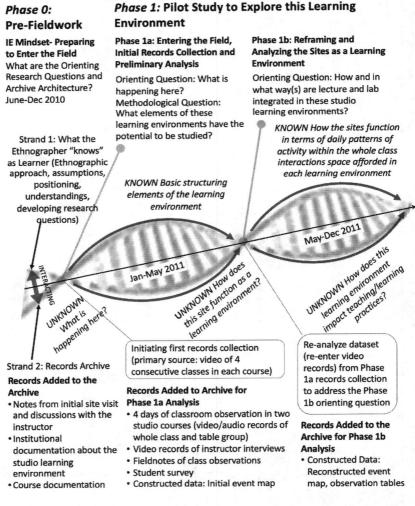

FIGURE 9.1   Axis of Development of Kalainoff's Research Process *(Continued)*

Phase 2: (Re)entering the Field to Explore Problem Solving Practices

Phase 2a: Reentering the Field for 2nd Records Collection and Preliminary Analysis
Orienting Question: How and in what ways does the studio learning environment shape teaching/learning practices in these science courses?

Phase 2b: Engaging with the Archive as a Partner to Develop the Logic-in-use
Overarching Question: In what ways does the learning environment afford or constrain problem solving practices as demonstrated through tracing of the anchoring phenomenon in the General Chemistry course?

KNOWN *Structuring of the two courses in terms of repeated patterns of activity in the whole group interactional space and potential to study patterns within table group and lab group interactional spaces*

Feb 2012 – May 2013

Jan 2012

UNKNOWN *How are problem solving practices co-constructed in this General Chemistry course?*

Through the anchoring phenomenon, redirect research question(s) to show how problem-solving practices are proposed and taken up over time, events, activity, interactional spaces, and configurations of actors in the General Chemistry course

Shift focus to exploring the relationship between problem solving practices and affordances of these novel learning environments

Records Added to the Archive for Phase 2a Analysis
- Six weeks of classroom observation in two studio courses (video/audio records include whole class, table group, and lab-partnered group interactional spaces)
- Fieldnotes of class observations and informal conversations with instructor
- Course documentation to include quizzes, exams
- Student work and performance (grades)
- Constructed data: Event map constructed in Phase 2a, observation tables

Records Added to the Archive for Phase 2b Analysis
- Student survey modified from Phase 1 to address the primary course events or activities where students conduct "problem solving"
- Email correspondence
- Constructed data: Event map, observation tables, transcripts, activity flow charts and others

FIGURE 9.1   *(Continued)*

As indicated in Figure 9.1, this axis of development illustrates the processes Kalainoff undertook to address her overarching questions as will be explained in Telling Case 1. This graphic (re)presentation of Kalainoff's axis of development is not intended to be a prescribed plan for how the research will proceed with respect to identifying the phenomena under study and developing particular research questions prior to entering the "field". Rather, at this point in this chapter, we present Kalainoff's axis of development to illustrate the principled actions for conceptualizing and characterizing how an ethnographic archive partners with the ethnographer as the researcher develops cycles of analyses.

Grounding the axis of development is a view of learning and development as ongoing social (Gergen, 2009) and cultural (Lee et al., 2020) processes for both the ethnographer and participants in the studies. From this perspective, in any educational setting or social group (including the research process), actors co-construct social, cultural, linguistic, and academic understandings through interactions across developing times and events. However, ethnographers do not conduct analyses of these interactions in the field. Rather, at the center of the IE analytic process, is an ethnographer interacting with (re)presentations of actions and interactions through archived recordings (i.e., video, fieldnotes, etc.) of the site.

As indicated in Figure 9.1, two strands rotate about a central axis. One strand represents the ethnographer guided by what they presume to know from their preparation for entering the field and their ongoing fieldwork. The ethnographer interacts with the second strand, the actions of people captured on archived records, by entering the archive to identify potential records to construct datasets to address the question under study for a particular cycle of research. If the ethnographer does not find the records, he/she/they can return to the field to collect additional records.

Each full rotation of the strands represents a cycle of analysis bounded within a developing research question and a way of engaging with the developing archive. The continuing interactions between the ethnographer and the archived records form the central axis, which represents the ethnographer's overtime developing understandings of the phenomena of study. The ethnographer's understandings develop as unknowns become known and new questions or *rich points* (Agar, 2006) emerge, leading to further analyses. Intersections of known and unknown arcs in Figure 9.1 indicate the end of one cycle and the beginning of the next. As such, Figure 9.1 illustrates how what was learned from one cycle of analysis and abductively (not linearly) initiates the new cycle of analysis guided by a new research question. Thus, the axis of development is a way of (re)presenting the ethnographer(s)' actions and decisions and the progressive nature of ethnographic research as illustrated in Telling Case 1, Kalainoff's research process.

Telling Case 1: Mapping Kalainoff's Logic of Analyses within an Axis of Development

Figure 9.1 situates the five cycles of analyses over three years constituting three phases of the study across the axis of development; each phase (re)presents various time scales for fieldwork:

1. Pre-fieldwork – June–December 2010;
2. Pilot study – two cycles of analyses, January–December 2011;
3. Dissertation study – two cycles of analyses, January 2012–May 2013.

Using a cycle of analysis or phase as a base in the next sections, I demonstrate how I engaged with the archive as a partner and discuss each principled action from Table 9.1 as each unfolds dynamically overtime.

Phase 0: Pre-fieldwork

Pre-fieldwork comprises actions to prepare an ethnographer prior to entering the field. This phase laid a foundation for IRB approval of my study in January 2011. In this section, I discuss my decision to adopt an IE perspective to guide my research and make visible the roots of my study. The roots included initial conceptualization of the archive in the IRB approval process. In presenting this history, I address a core principle of ethnographic research framed by Smith (1978) and taken up by Green and colleagues (Green et al., 2020), i.e., the *importance of reporting on the origins of the study* being undertaken by the ethnographer (Principled Action).

How I Came to the Study Site

With degrees in chemical engineering and chemistry, I took up education and interactional ethnography as an epistemological lens (Green et al., 2012) for examining educational phenomena that I could use as a base for my next professional context: leadership in undergraduate General Chemistry courses at the university to which I would return after completing my PhD. Grounded in my past work with other scientists and engineers in higher education, I understood the need for a principled approach to decision-making (rather than a personal one) in order to make institutionally- or discipline-grounded interpretations as the basis for decisions. This goal led me to take up ethnography, and IE, in particular, because it requires empirically warranting claims as evidence of the research, much in the same way that claims are warranted in engineering and the sciences.

In the first semester of my PhD program, my advisor recommended a potential site for study in a nearby state university: two physical learning spaces (classrooms) called science studios, one for undergraduate General Chemistry and one for an undergraduate science class for preservice elementary teachers. These were classrooms with a novel *studio* feature of "integrated" lecture and laboratory functions, where students could shift between these functions in the same physical space whereas undergraduate lecture and lab in the sciences are traditionally isolated events occurring in different physical spaces.

In this phase, I conducted an initial visit of the potential research site and informally proposed the scope of my research to an instructor who taught in both learning environments in the same ten-week quarter. These initial interactions were necessary to explore her interest in participating in the research, build a relationship, and gain her support for the ethnographic field-work in her courses.

During the initial site visit, the instructor gave me a tour of both studio classrooms. I created maps of the two studio learning environments and included key features and cultural artifacts that she identified as significant. These maps served as my resource for detailed planning for video recording, such as positioning cameras to record these key features and artifacts of the site. Recognizing phenomena or artifacts of the site that are of social significance to the participants is a way that IE ethnographers learn from and with participants (Principle of Conduct). Recording and archiving these records (e.g., video, fieldnotes, and other) for re-entry at a later time during analyses processes is a Principled Action in Table 9.1.

The instructor also pointed to digital resources, where I located the roots of this program at an institutional level. Collecting and analyzing publicly accessible documents from the campus website enabled me to situate the research site within a larger institutional system. Therefore, based on my history as a chemistry instructor in a different institution in higher education, I understood the need to explore the roots of these studio learning environments within the broader institutional contexts that shaped this innovative process of merging lab and lecture sessions.

Ethnographer-as-Learner of Interactional Ethnography: Preparing the Mind

To prepare to enter to this novel site for research, I considered what actions I needed to take, to position myself from an IE perspective having only discussed these actions theoretically up to that point in time. I found that particular facets of an IE perspective implicated decisions for how I needed to enter the site, engage in the site, and construct the archive.

One facet of an ethnographic perspective is that patterned actions happening in classrooms are cultures-in-the-making (Dixon et al., 1999), meaning that once actors come together in a site, culture does not automatically exist. Rather, actors co-construct patterns and practices that define, and continuously re-define, the culture. Therefore, culture is never static.

I recognized that "culturing," culture as a verb (Street, 2013), would be initiated between the actors in this site before the first day of class, namely, when the instructor provided information to students about what to expect in the course. Therefore, I archived any communications (email) or messages (syllabus, course documents) made available to students prior to the first day of class. Ideally, I would have also collected records of classroom interactions beginning on the first day where, at the onset of a course, instructors and students make their roles, relationships, and expectations explicit. However, I could not enter the classrooms until I had received my study's IRB approval, which occurred on the fourth day of class.

Another facet of an ethnographic perspective that influenced my actions was taking up an *emic* perspective, that is, I needed to position myself to see from the actors' – instructor and collective students' – points of view. Therefore, I planned to conduct interview conversations (see Skukauskaitė & Sullivan, this volume) with the instructor to understand the institutional circumstances that initiated the transition to a studio learning environment and how she came to teach in these spaces.

Ideally in the pre-fieldwork phase, interviewing key actors and reading course documentation, all of which must be archived, the ethnographer prepares their mind to understand what he/she/they might see upon entering a research site. More generally, this prepares an ethnographer to have an initial understanding of the language of that learning environment and/or discipline. Reconstructing these histories is also important so that an ethnographer is attuned to the presuppositions they may be bringing into the site and how these may influence ways of seeing, observing, analyzing, and interpreting. In this way, the actions of doing background history of self as ethnographer, of the site, and of the actors (Principled Action) are a consequence of stepping back from ethnocentrism (Principle of Conduct).

Planning for Records/Data Collection

During the pre-fieldwork phase, I made several decisions informed by my initial inquiries and discussions with the instructor and required for IRB approval so that I could formally initiate the research and *enter the field*. However, a consequence of stepping back from ethnocentrism, a principle of conduct (Heath & Street, 2008), means that I could not predefine salient phenomena of my research sites prior to entering the field (Principled Action). Therefore, my goal was to learn enough about the situated nature of the site in an initial site visit to develop *orienting* research questions and a records/data collection plan for the IRB proposal.

Therefore, for the IRB, I proposed studying a broad topic of "teaching/learning processes in this studio learning environment" as the basis of my yet unspecified research questions. Extending this principle of conduct to the contents of the archive, I could not state *a priori* the full scope of the records that my planned archive would *contain* (Principled Action).

However, in the IRB, I could state the types of records and amounts of records (e.g., x hours of video records in each of two studio classrooms) that I planned to collect. In IE studies (Green et al., 2003) where the observables are interactions, the IE conceptual framework implicates ways of recording and documenting interactions through varied types of records (e.g., classroom video/audio, actor interview video/audio, fieldnotes of classroom observations, transcripts, etc.) which can be made explicit in the IRB proposal. Because of nuances in taking fieldnotes when partnering with video from an IE perspective, I provide a more detailed discussion of this topic.

Taking ethnographic fieldnotes from anthropologic traditions has been discussed more generally elsewhere (Emerson et al., 1995; Hoey, 2014). In partnering with video (Bridges, this volume), I constructed my fieldnotes as a guide to the video records. First, to organize my fieldnotes in one place, I planned to collect fieldnotes in a bounded book using both sides of the pages in parallel. Secondly, I did not write "word-for-word" dialogue because these can be transcribed from the video records where needed during analyses. Rather, I used the fieldnotes to construct a "running record", that is, annotating the time and actions taken by participants in real time during my observations. Identifying and bounding related actions for a range of time is the basis for constructing a "map" of the events so that I could locate particular records in the archive for retrospective analysis after leaving the field.

Prior to entering the field each day, I prepared my fieldnotes for my observational note-taking as shown in Figure 9.2. These key elements were locating the observation in time and space, time of a particular action and actor, and theoretical, methodological, and personal notes (Corsaro, 1985). Details of these elements and examples are annotated within Figure 9.2.

When taking fieldnotes, I also included a detailed map of the site with dimensions, camera positions showing left and right limits of each camera angle, and the rationale for these positions. Thereafter, I recorded when, how, and for what reason the camera position or angle changed. Recording *all* physical perspectives is not possible just as any one person does not have access to all possible perspectives. In conceptualizing video as a partner in the recording and collecting process, identifying the perspectives of the cameras as a fieldnote acknowledges the limitations of what can been seen/heard and, therefore, limitations of what can be analyzed, and potentially limit or shape research questions.

Phase 1a: Records Collection for the Pilot Study (2011)

The pilot study, phase of records collection (Phase 1a, the first full cycle of analysis in Figure 9.1) and subsequent preliminary analysis (Phase 1b, the second full cycle of analysis), is the portion of the study that is typically unseen, not reported in the formal research report. However, the pilot study was necessary for me to learn about the mechanics of archiving as well as ground my new conceptual understandings of IE in a real-world research study.

[Information that will locate the observation in time and space such as Setting identifier/Day of observation/Date/Day of Week:]
GC/Day 1/Jan 3, 2012/Tues

[Theoretical, methodological, and personal notes as discussed by Corsaro (1985)]

Time		Actor and Actions		Notes		
Actual	Recording	Instructor (I) or TA	Student(s) (Ss)	Theoretical	Methodological	Personal
[Time(s) that are most convenient for referencing actions to other records such as video]		*[Annotate as a running record of actions; Identify actor and action(s) taken as verb or gerund; often helpful to separate the actions of actors in this space by separate columns; actions that happen in parallel can then be represented horizontally within this running record. Examples for actions of the instructor (I), teacher assistants (TAs) and students (Ss) in the whole group interactional space follows:]*		*[Example: "What is going on? Is this the start of a new activity?"]*	*[Examples: diagram of classroom, diagram of changes to camera position]*	*[Examples: "Do students select their own lab partners?"]*
0755		opening class door	entering classroom			
0805	0:00				**Video recording begins** *[Allows for syncing of video running time with actual time]*	
0810		**Initiating class with admin introduction to class expectations**	**looking at Instr until told by Instr to view their monitors**			
0845		**"the final is multiple choice I don't want you to forget that"**		**What is the significance of multiple choice?**		
//			//	//		//
0936		**TAs: taking each table of 8 Ss and conducting an experiment/demo**	**noting observations in notebooks**			**When/how are TAs prepped for demonstrations?**

FIGURE 9.2 An Example of Preparing and Taking Ethnographic Fieldnotes When Partnering With Video

Learning in the Field

I formally *entered the field* once the IRB approved the study. I physically entered the General Chemistry class for the first time in the 4th class lesson in January 2011. My primary question in a general sense was "what is happening here?", not knowing what particular elements of the learning environment had the potential to be studied. At the onset of these classroom observations, there were details of collecting video records and fieldnote-taking that I had not considered which prompted me to make two significant methodological decisions.

First, I needed to ground "time" in a common reference because many possible significant "times" existed in this space:

- actual time (determined from my phone),
- scheduled class start time (determined by the institution),
- actual start time (determined by the instructor and student onset of whole group), and
- running time (which could be initiated from scheduled class start time or actual onset of class).

Furthermore, *time* could also be annotated on the video in multiple forms through the camera settings. This may seem like a simple question of standardization, but the methodological implications are more complex (see Adam, 2006, for a theoretical conception of *time*). Each day, I observed and collected video records of the site beginning as early as the first student entering the classroom and until the last student departed. However, setting a time reference as the beginning of the video recording each day would not have been a meaningful reference, especially when analyzing over days. Eventually, I realized that by setting my reference for time at *0:00* as the time that the instructor begins class each day, I could easily identify this moment on the video records and match this time to the running time of the video. Moreover, by putting actual time from my phone in view of the camera at the onset of recording, all *times* then could be referenced to each other.

Thinking about *time* led to the second related decision – how to address the need for constructing a broader referential (cross-referencing) system for *indexing* information (e.g., records types, data types, and information within these records and data types) as an organizing mechanism for archiving information (Principled Action). As I began to construct the archive, I realized that I needed an indexing system so that I could archive the records after leaving the field each day to retrieve information within them for retrospective analysis.

That is, I needed to strategically index information from video digital files in relation to my fieldnotes so that upon reentering the archive for later analyses, I could most effectively cross-reference or map the fieldnotes to particular points in and over time in the video/audio records. Central to cross-referencing fieldnotes to the video records is maintaining a running record of time and corresponding actions with annotations for personal, theoretical, or methodological notes as needed (see Figure 9.2).

This way, I used the fieldnotes as a guide to the video records to construct a first draft of an event map (Kelly & Chen, 1999) (re)presenting the events and sub-events for how time was spent in the research site. Because video was the primary source of records in the study and salient dimensions (e.g., events by time, disciplinary content, and interactional spaces) were annotated in the event map, the event map served as a visual index for the video records in the archive.

Learning From the Preliminary Analysis

Addressing the question of "what's happening here?" was my first layer of analysis because this form of mapping of events from video records produced a higher layer of data that I used in analyses to identify layers of activity. However, in Phase 1a my research advisor made clear that my first attempt at event mapping the four days of activities in each course did not communicate what was happening. I had bounded and labeled events as either "lab" or "lecture". When the advisor asked "how are lecture and lab integrated in this studio?" it was clear that she required further evidence that addressed *what actions constituted lecture and lab in each site*.

This question was a methodological frame clash causing me to step back and reflect on how I was positioning myself in the analyses. Reflecting and taking action to resolve a frame clash where the ethnographer does not understand what is happening, constitutes a rich point in the analytical process. Acting on this rich point shifts the trajectory of the research into a new cycle of analysis to reconcile the new unknown. Despite my efforts to step back from ethnocentrism, this frame clash and rich point made visible to me that I had applied a personal *etic* (ethnocentric) understanding of what constituted "lecture" and "lab" events from my prior experience in chemistry courses when I should have constructed evidence from actions taken by participants.

In addition to learning what actions were required to take an emic perspective, I reframed the new unknown from the rich point in Phase 1a into a new orienting research question "how are lecture and lab integrated?" in Phase 1b. I reframed this new research question with the knowledge that the information in the archived records could address this new question. That is, the new research question was within the *analytic potential* of the archive to address (Principled Action). This shift in research question also informed what records from the archive I needed to construct a dataset for the next analysis.

Phase 1b: Re-conceptualizing and Re-analyzing the Studio Sites

Using the same video records as I used in my preliminary analysis, I re-analyzed with a more nuanced understanding of an emic perspective. Addressing the question, *"How are lecture and lab integrated in this learning environment?"*, required that I show the differences and similarities of actions and interactions among the actors in lecture and lab modes in these learning environments.

To address the research question, I assembled the relevant records from the archive (i.e., event map as the primary record with other supporting records such as the course syllabus) as a dataset. Then I iteratively analyzed the dataset to identify the structuring dimensions through repeated patterns of actors co-constructing disciplinary knowledge through events and activities within and across disciplinary content areas. Assembling datasets from the archived records for analysis to construct warranted claims of the phenomena under study is a Principled Action in Table 9.1.

The layers of analyses and outcomes of Phase 1b made visible how this studio learning environment functioned in terms of the following structuring dimensions of the research space and their interrelationships:

- patterns of activity to include bounded disciplinary content,
- interactional spaces in which these patterns of activity were enacted,
- actors that interacted in these spaces,
- events that constituted the patterns of activity, and
- actions required and expected of different types of actors.

Identifying these dimensions of the learning environment were important because these served as potential pathways for tracing teaching and learning phenomena (i.e., tracing of a particular phenomenon over patterns of activity, interactional spaces, configurations of actors, etc.).

By interacting with the archive to identify dimensions of the sites during analyses in Phase 1b, I also gained a more nuanced understanding of the analytic potential and limitations of the archive I was constructing. I found that I could visually observe the two-student lab groups within the eight-person table group were but there was no separate audio to record verbal discourse *within* these spaces. Also, the recordings of four class meetings, two weeks of the ten-week course, in each of the two sites were not of sufficient length of time to effectively warrant claims of patterns of activity as overtime repeated patterns. Furthermore, because student outcomes (grades) and student interactions within two-student lab groups had not been part of this records collection, there was no means to link "teaching" (what was being proposed to students) at the whole group level to "learning" (student take-up) at the individual student level. These limitations of the archive to address a broader range of potential research questions at multiple layers of analysis led me to conduct a second data collection in these studio learning environments. These limits also informed how I framed a new orienting research question that served as the basis for my dissertation study.

Phase 2: Records Collection and Analyses Processes for Dissertation Study

In this section, I shift from discussing details in unfolding IE analytical processes to focus on particular principled actions for constructing and engaging with an archive that are more effectively addressed in Phase 2. This section focuses on two principled actions:

- modifications to the research design, namely, the scheme for indexing the records into the archive with respect to labeling conventions, and
- how the rich point in this study became an anchor for tracing across research questions.

Modifying Records Collection and Indexing Scheme

Re-entering the field one year after the first records collection required that I step back from my prior experience in the sites except to inform what I *might* see. In other words, I stepped back from my prior experience in that I was open to process and practices for learning disciplinary content developed in *these* spaces through interactions between *these* configurations of actors. I learned what I *might* see from the pilot study the year prior and modified records collection and indexing scheme in response to that knowledge.

I re-entered the site in Winter 2012: same instructor, same two courses, same two physical classroom studio spaces, but with different students and modifications to the range of time for classroom observations and records to be collected. These modifications required approval of an amended IRB with records added to the archive as shown in Phase 2a in Figure 9.1. Consequently, the changes to the records collection plan for Phase 2 added additional dimensions to the indexing scheme with respect to file naming conventions.

Because I collected all records myself and the collection was relatively small, my indexing strategy consisted of file-naming conventions that could be cross-referenced in time with the fieldnotes. File-naming conventions are one way to index the records in the archive for ease in identifying and retrieving interrelated records to construct datasets for analysis. I indexed file-naming conventions for video records first by date, then camera perspective (Instructor "IN" or Table Group "TG"), and then number of the video segment taken on that day. For example, the filename of a video file taken on January 6th of 2015 by the instructor camera in the first 30-minute segment of recording on that day was "150106_IN_1.mp4" for an mp4 file. I used a similar scheme for audio files and added identifiers for documents of individual student work. Other forms of records can also be indexed by time, events, activity, or configurations of actors through file-naming conventions depending on the salient dimensions of the environment.

In effect, using an *a priori* strategically defined indexing and file-naming scheme and adding identifiers as needed across all forms of records, *maps* the contents of a digital archive as it is being constructed. However, the actual process of indexing records into the archive will also depend on the digital tools (i.e., video analysis software) used by the ethnographer.

Anchoring Phenomena and Tracing Across Overtime Layers of Analysis

At the onset of Phase 2a, my two goals were to: (1) construct the archive while developing an understanding of its analytic potential for addressing questions of teaching and learning, and (2) be keenly aware for frame clashes signaling potential dimensions of cultural phenomena within one or both of the sites that I may want to pursue as a rich point. This rich point served as an anchor (e.g., point of entry into the archive) for constructing warranted accounts by tracing the phenomena of interest across layers of analysis in Phase 2b.

Anchoring Phenomena in This Dissertation Study

After the planned records collection and archiving, in an email dated February 15, 2012, the instructor shared that she had anticipated that students would have difficulty with a particular question on the major exam conducted February 10th. The instructor elaborated that students had "horrible time applying concepts to different contexts" signaling that *applying concepts* was a socially and academically significant practice.

The instructor's comments piqued my interest and I asked *what's going on here?* and *why do students have a hard time applying concepts to new contexts?*. Given my understanding of the analytic potential of the archive, I believed it could support pursuing this frame clash as a rich point. In practical terms, this means that at that moment, I envisioned that I could use the disciplinary content in the exam question as a point of entry into the archive to initiate the pathway through the records. I believed that I could use the records to construct evidence to backwards trace how the instructors and students in the General Chemistry course co-constructed this disciplinary content over time through the opportunities for learning this content.

My decision to pursue this particular anchoring phenomenon in the archived records transitioned Phase 2a to a new cycle of analyses, Phase 2b (see

Figure 9.1). The unknowns conceived in the rich point shaped a new orienting research question, *Within this studio environment, how are problem solving practices proposed and taken up by students?* Furthermore, this transition also changed how I engaged with the archive from primarily collecting and archiving in Phase 2a to primarily analyzing functions in Phase 2b.

Tracing the Phenomena of Study Across Research Questions as a Logic-of-Inquiry

At the onset of Phase 2b, my goal was to craft a logic-of-inquiry (see Baker et al., this volume, for an example) that would collectively address the overarching questions. Through IE analytical processes of iterative, recursive and abductive decision-making of re-entering the archive to construct datasets to address potential research questions, I developed five research questions (RQs) concurrently:

- RQ1: How did this undergraduate general chemistry class function in the daily processes and practices within a chemistry studio learning environment within the first exam cycle of activity?
- RQ2: How did participants structure daily practices and processes in the second exam cycle of activity in comparison to the first exam cycle of activity?
- RQ3: In what ways did the instructor frame (or position) problem solving in course documents and introductory comments in the course?
- RQ4: In what ways was select disciplinary content proposed and negotiated by instructor and students in collective activity?
- RQ5: In what ways did students construct opportunities for learning how to use or apply concepts for the select disciplinary content (in RQ4) within lab-partnered group and table interactional spaces?

RQs 1 and 2 analytically explore how the course was structured and functioned. RQs 3–5 address how problem solving practices were proposed and taken up by students within the structuring features that were unfolded in RQs 1 and 2.

The research questions unfold linearly in the dissertation, where one question is posed and addressed and then leads to the next question (see Kalainoff (2013), for the logic-of-inquiry showing the representing data and analyzing events for each RQ). However, this (re)construction of the logic of the study obfuscates IE analytic processes that are more complex and dynamic. With event maps of the data collection period and other supporting documents that were indexed to the records in the archive, I backwards traced from the disciplinary content proposed in the anchoring phenomenon to the initial course documentation provided to students prior to the first day where the instructor proposed problem solving as an important practice required in this course. I developed RQs 3–5, each RQ consisting of multiple interrelated analyses, concurrently as three interrelated perspectives of this tracing process or layers of analysis. Because *tracing the phenomena of study* meant tracing through particular over time events and activity in RQs 3–5, I used these same events as the evidence for RQs 1–2. In other words, I recursively constructed datasets of records for detailed analysis in RQs 1–2 that were related to the particular disciplinary content in the anchoring phenomenon so that I could build on these resources for unfolding the phenomenon (i.e., "applying a concept" as a problem-solving practice) in RQs 3–5. Tracing the phenomena of study across research questions with evidence constructed from the archived records is a principled action shown in Table 9.1.

Summary of Telling Case 1

This telling case focused on presenting a set of principled actions that I took as an IE ethnographer to conceptualize (Principled Action), construct, and engage with an archive of records in an overtime developmental process. I unfolded this process using an axis of development (Principled Action) (re)presentation in Figure 9.1 to show my analytic actions and decisions that led to my dissertation study. To further validate these principled actions and potentially add others, we explore a second telling case of Chian (second author) entering an ongoing research study with an existing archive of records.

Telling Case 2: Axis of Development for an Existing Archive

In this telling case, I (Chian) make transparent my logic-of-inquiry in engaging with an existing archive of an ongoing two-year research project to address a set of overarching research questions (See Table 9.1). I entered as a member of a newly formed external IE team of ethnographers hired to provide support to a team of internal ethnographers to study the development and implementation of a novel project called Long-Term Futures Thinking (LTFT). The research site was a regional university 300 miles away; thus, we were unable to be physically present at the site. Entering the research project at the conclusion of the first year of implementation, I also entered an existing archive collected by the internal research team (Chian, 2016, 2020).

The goal of this funded project was to integrate novel disciplinary constructs such as forecasting and futures thinking, with disciplinary content within established undergraduate courses in an Organizational Communication Bachelor Arts program to meet the institution's mission and vision to foster 21st-century skills among their graduates (Chian, 2016). My role was to lead a team of graduate students to develop ways of conducting empirically grounded analysis to trace the decision-making processes and actions involved in (re)formulating the integration of LTFT concepts and organizational communication theories within the eight courses over two years. My team's responsibility was also to analyze how the integrated courses met both the LTFT project and institutional goals. In the following sections I unfold the axes of development by phase (see Figure 9.3) to make visible the ways I interacted with the archive to address the overarching research questions.

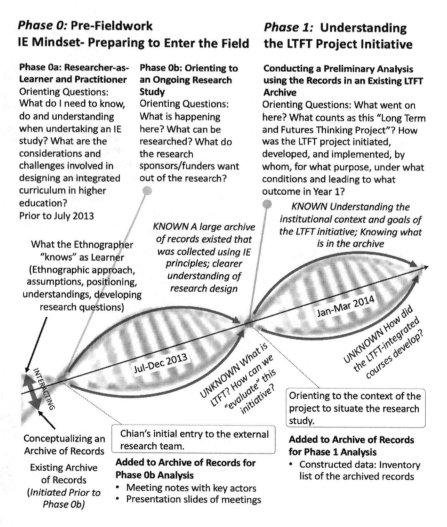

Phase 0: Pre-Fieldwork
IE Mindset- Preparing to Enter the Field

Phase 0a: Researcher-as-Learner and Practitioner
Orienting Questions:
What do I need to know, do and understanding when undertaking an IE study? What are the considerations and challenges involved in designing an integrated curriculum in higher education?
Prior to July 2013

What the Ethnographer "knows" as Learner (Ethnographic approach, assumptions, positioning, understandings, developing research questions)

INTERACTING

Conceptualizing an Archive of Records

Existing Archive of Records
(*Initiated Prior to Phase 0b*)

Phase 0b: Orienting to an Ongoing Research Study
Orienting Questions:
What is happening here? What can be researched? What do the research sponsors/funders want out of the research?

KNOWN A large archive of records existed that was collected using IE principles; clearer understanding of research design

Jul-Dec 2013

UNKNOWN What is LTFT? How can we "evaluate" this initiative?

Chian's initial entry to the external research team.

Added to Archive of Records for Phase 0b Analysis
• Meeting notes with key actors
• Presentation slides of meetings

Phase 1: Understanding the LTFT Project Initiative

Conducting a Preliminary Analysis using the Records in an Existing LTFT Archive
Orienting Questions: What went on here? What counts as this "Long Term and Futures Thinking Project"? How was the LTFT project initiated, developed, and implemented, by whom, for what purpose, under what conditions and leading to what outcome in Year 1?

KNOWN Understanding the institutional context and goals of the LTFT initiative; Knowing what is in the archive

Jan-Mar 2014

UNKNOWN How did the LTFT-integrated courses develop?

Orienting to the context of the project to situate the research study.

Added to Archive of Records for Phase 1 Analysis
• Constructed data: Inventory list of the archived records

FIGURE 9.3 Axis of Development of Chian's Research Process *(Continued)*

Phase 2: **Exploring Program Implementation and Curricular Design for Year 1**

Phase 2a Entering the Field for Preliminary Analysis and Participating in Ethnographic Observations Virtually
Orienting Question: How was the LTFT curriculum developed, evaluated and refined after each quarter?

Phase 2b: Developing the Logic-in-Use for the Study
Overarching Question: How and in what ways did the actors conceptualize the processes of integrating an external disciplinary framework into established courses in higher education?

KNOWN *Critical elements required in (re)formulating integrated curricula; each course had different LTFT-integrated constructs*

Jul 2014 – Jun 2015

Apr-Jun 2014

UNKNOWN *What design elements characterize the 'best course to date'?*

Shift research question(s) to examine the processes of designing the "best (integrated) course to date" through a focused contrastive analysis of four select iterations of the LTFT course.

Orienting to the beginning processes in designing the integrated courses of study.

Added to Archive of Records for Phase 2a Analysis
• Video recorded virtual interviews with the Lead Professor and the Project Consultant
• Notes on LTFT disciplinary key concepts
• Constructed data: Textual analysis of LTFT disciplinary content; analysis of the LTFT project digital resources and institutional descriptions

Added to Archive of Records for Phase 2b Analysis
• Course Artifacts (lesson planning notes, course notes, course texts and resources, student discussion board responses)
• Video interviews with key actors
• Fieldnotes of virtual ethnographic observation of class
• Program documents and reports
• Email threads (approx. 100) between the research teams and the project team
• Fieldnotes of the research meetings
• External IE research team's collaborative work schedule and IE guide
• Biographies of key actors and the authors of course resources

FIGURE 9.3 *(Continued)*

Phase 0: Preparing the Mind and Negotiating Entry Into the Field

Similar to Kalainoff, prior to my entry to the research site, I engaged in developmental processes as a researcher-as-learner and practitioner. Entering the LTFT project and research at the end of the project's first year presented challenges for my team and me at the onset of our entry. Given that we did not participate in developing the initial research design, did not collect ethnographic records, and were never physically present on site, our team faced numerous unknowns. The unknowns included the context of the study, rationale for the research design, the goals of the LTFT projects, content in the archived records, among others.

Hence, it was difficult for us to decide how to begin the research process. Thus, my first principled action was to step back from ethnocentrism (see Table 9.1) and conduct an ethnographic review of the various records from the archive by asking "what's happening here?". To begin to make sense of the LTFT project and the research goals, I reviewed the meeting notes and presentation slides from the project meetings, which I added to the existing archive (see Figure 9.3). Reviewing these documents led me to uncover the multiple actors involved in the initiation and development of the LTFT project and gained initial understanding of the goals of the LTFT project (Chian, 2016).

Knowing that there were multiple actors involved in the project, the challenge for our team was to understand the role of each member and the relationships between them, which led to subsequent analysis later in the research. We also considered multiple actors from the design and internal ethnography team as potential partners and/or collaborators (i.e., cultural guides) to support our analyses by helping us understand the developmental pathways of the LTFT project.

Through further review of the LTFT website and informal conversations with the LTFT research team, we learned that this research was funded externally. Therefore, it was crucial for me, in consultation with the Principal Investigator of the external IE team and the support of the research team members, to conduct an ethnographically informed study of the context of the project (Principled Action). This additional action enabled my team to propose an appropriate epistemological and methodological direction for the study as will be unfolded in the subsequent sections.

Phase 1: Understanding the Development of the LTFT Project in Implementation Year 1

In this phase, the orienting question (see Figure 9.3) guided the cycle of analyses that my team undertook to gain a better understanding of the LTFT project and decide on our approach to evaluating the project, as the Principal

Investigator of the LTFT had requested. Given that we entered the project in its second year, we needed support from the design team and internal ethnographers to reconstruct what happened in the first year. Unlike Kalainoff, who was familiar with the site of her study, my team and I were unfamiliar with the LTFT constructs or Organizational Communication theories, which required additional steps in learning the languaculture (Agar, 2006) of these disciplines. Learning the key constructs of LTFT and theories of Organizational Communication was critical in understanding how these disciplines were being integrated (Principled Action). The research goals of this phase were to understand the institutional context and the goals of the LTFT project and know what was in the archive.

Thus, my next set of principled actions involved taking inventory of the existing records while interrogating how these records were collected, their purposes, and the intended outcomes. This process required interviewing and corresponding with key actors through computer-enhanced communication (i.e., email, Google Hangout). Consequently, the ongoing dialogues enabled us to generate an inventory of the records collected in Year 1, which led us to identify what additional records to collect for the Year 2 implementation. The inventory we (re)constructed was added to the existing archived records. As we began to add records to the archive, we recognized the need to modify the indexing scheme, separating the records collected in Year 1 by the internal research team and records that my team and I constructed or requested from the lead professor.

As my team and I began to understand the events in Year 1 and the goals, components, development, implementation and the unique contexts of the LTFT project, we still had not formulated a research focus or identified from whose point of view we needed to explore in order to address the goals of the research. This unknown led to a new cycle of analysis I undertook in Phase 2.

Phase 2: Conducting the Research Study

Phase 2 involved two cycles of analyses, Phases 2a and 2b, respectively (see Figure 9.3). In Phase 2a we aimed to develop an understanding of the insiders' perspectives on the processes involved in developing, evaluating, and refining the LTFT-integrated curriculum. I also sought to identify a potential rich point and/or frame clashes (Agar, 2006; Tannen, 1993) that would provide a point of entry into the archive and anchor our tracing of the phenomenon under study.

Phase 2a: Preliminary Analyses

To construct datasets to address the orienting question for Phase 2a, I undertook principled actions. First, I continued engaging in virtual dialogues with relevant actors to ask particularities about the set of records to be analyzed to address the orienting question for Phase 2a (see Figure 9.3). My team and I also conducted multiple interviews of the Lead Professor and Project Consultant and later interviewed the PI of the LTFT project. The interview transcripts were added to the archive records.

I also conducted an analysis of the annual report of Year 1 to gain a historical perspective of the courses offered in Year 1. This analysis confirmed the need to understand the language-in-use within the disciplines; therefore, I studied key concepts of organizational communication, futures thinking, and forecasting to uncover the discourse embedded within the archived records. These research activities resulted in collecting new records and record types as well as my constructing other forms of data such as transcripts, all of which were added to the existing archive, as shown in Figure 9.3, Phase 2a.

Conducting a preliminary analysis of interview transcripts led to identifying a rich point, where the lead professor identified the last course of the eight courses offered within the two-year period as the "best course to date". My desire to know why the instructor claimed this course as "the best course" and how it came to "be the best course" became a rich point (Agar, 2006) to anchor the study. This anchor provided the focus of my logic-of-inquiry and transitioned the study into Phase 2b.

Phase 2b: Developing the Logic-in-Use

To focus the analysis on the characteristics of the "best course to date" (i.e., Comm. 4107, Spring 2014), I conducted cycles of analyses of existing records and added another set of records to address this new research question (see Figure 9.3, Phase 2b). One key analysis was uncovering that the "best course to date" was offered three times (i.e., Fall 2012, Fall 2013, Spring 2014), across the span of the two-year project and each course offering had different subtitles (Chian, 2016). The differences in the course subtitles led me to further investigate the rationale for the subtitles and to understand if and how those courses differed.

The multiple reviews of the archived records, preliminary analyses, and prior emails from the LTFT team and our IE research team did not provide an answer to my inquiries. Thus, I initiated an email conversation with the lead professor to understand the rationale for the differences in the subtitles across multiple iterations of Comm. 4107 (Chian, 2016). This email exchange, the over 100 emails between and among members of the research team and the LTFT team that were accumulated over a two-year period, was added to the archive. This exchange also became central to understanding of the curricular design team's logic-in-use in integrating LTFT concepts into the Organizational Communication courses, consequential to the development of the "best course to date."

Summary for Telling Case 2

By using the axes of development, I made transparent the decisions, actions, and considerations involved across my research process. While my context and point of entry were different from Kalainoff's research study, my actions and decisions converged with her more comprehensive cycles of analysis (re) presented in her axes of development. Contrasting our axes of development enabled us to identify common principled actions in engaging and constructing ethnographic archive records as shown in Table 9.1. We attribute these common principled actions to our shared epistemological foundations guided by IE.

Conclusion

The axis of development introduced in this chapter proposes a way of graphically representing cycles of analyses undertaken in IE studies in educational contexts. The axis of development was designed purposefully to address the calls for transparency in reporting on research processes in educational research (Duran et al., 2006; Candela et al., 2004; Kumpulainen et al., 2009). These calls for transparency are grounded in the need for guiding a reader in understanding how a particular outcome of a study was achieved.

The ongoing nature of ethnographic research and its consequential progression of cycles of analyses means that the archive of records will be continuously developing as well. We designed the axis of development for use by ethnographic researchers to (re)present the developing analytic processes undertaken to gain understandings of the lived experiences of participants in educational settings. Therefore, the axis of development is designed to support the researcher in making transparent the phases of entering and reentering an ethnographic site to record the developing cycles of learning in educational contexts as well as the archiving and analyses processes.

The axis of development was also designed to support readers in exploring the levels of analysis undertaken in one ethnographic study to explore how, if, and under what conditions the decisions and actions taken by one researcher can inform their own processes. Thus, the axis of development is a way of making transparent the goals, purposes and ways of analyzing educational sites as cultures-in-the-making.

Suggested Readings

Agar, M. (1996). *The professional stranger: An informal introduction to ethnography.* Emerald.
Ochs, E. (1979). Transcription as theory. In E. Ochs & B. Schieffelin (Eds.), *Developmental pragmatics.* Academic Press.
Spradley, J. (2016). *Participant observation.* Waveland Press, Inc.
Walford, G. (Ed.) (2008). *How to do educational ethnography.* Tufnell Press.

References

Adam, B. (2006). Time. *Theory, Culture & Society, 23*(2–3), 119–126. doi: 10.1177/0263276406063779.

Agar, M. (2006). Culture: Can you take it anywhere? *International Journal of Qualitative Methods, 5*(2), 1–12.

Bloome, D., Carter, S., Christian, B., Otto, S., & Shuart-Faris, N. (2005). *Discourse analysis and the study of classroom language and literacy events: A microethnographic perspective.* Routledge.

Candela, A., Rockwell, E., & Coll, C. (2004). What in the world happens in classrooms? Qualitative classroom research. *European Educational Research Journal, 3*(3). doi: 10.2304/eerj.2004.3.3.10.

Chian, M. M. (2016). A reflexive approach in coming to know: Uncovering the logic-of-inquiry in ethnographic research. (Unpublished doctoral dissertation). University of California, Santa Barbara.

Chian, M. M. (2020). Tracing the development of literacy practices for integrating interdisciplinary curriculum in higher education: Interactional ethnographic study. *Trabalhos em Linguistica Aplicada.* https://doi.org/10.1590/010318135896415912020

Corsaro, W. A. (1985). Entering the child's world: Research strategies for field entry and data collection. In J. Green & C. Wallat (Eds.), *Ethnography and language in educational settings.* Ablex.

Dixon, C. N., Green, J. L., & Frank, C. R. (1999). Classrooms as cultures: Understanding the constructed nature of life in classrooms. *Primary Voices K-6, 7*(3), 1–8.

Duran, R. P., Eisenhart, M. A., Erickson, F. D., Grant, C. A., Green, J. L., Hedges, L. V., & Schneider, B. L. (2006). Standards for reporting on empirical social science research in AERA publications: American Educational Research Association. *Educational Researcher, 35*(6), 33–40.

Emerson, R. M., Fretz, R. I., & Shaw, L. L. (1995). *Writing ethnographic field-notes.* The University of Chicago Press. http://dx.doi.org/10.7208/chicago/9780226206851.001.0001

Gergen, K. J. (2009). *An invitation to social construction* (2nd ed.). Sage.

Green, J. L., Baker, W. D., Chian, M. M., Vanderhoof, C., Hooper, L., Kelly, G. J., Skukauskaitė, A., & Kalainoff, M. Z. (2020). Studying the over-time construction of knowledge in educational settings: A microethnographic discourse analysis approach. *Review of Research in Education, 44*(1), 161–194. https://doi.org/10.3102/0091732X20903121

Green, J. L., Dixon, C., & Zaharlick, A. (2003). Ethnography as a logic of inquiry. In J. Flood, D. Lapp, J. Squire, & J. Jensen (Eds.), *Researching in the teaching of the English language arts* (pp. 201–224). Lawrence Erlbaum.

Green, J., Skukauskaitė, A., & Baker, W.D. (2012). Ethnography as epistemology: An introduction to educational ethnography. In J. Arthur, M. I. Waring, R. Coe, & L. V. Hedges (Eds.), *Research methodologies and methods in education* (pp. 309–321). Sage.

Heath, S. B. (1982). *Ethnography in education: Defining the essentials.* In P. Gilmore & A. Glatthorn (Eds.), *Children in and out of school: Ethnography and education* (pp. 33–55). Washington, DC: Center for Applied Linguistics.

Heath, S. B., & Street, B. V. (2008). *On ethnography: Approaches to language and literacy research.* Teachers College Press.

Hoey, B. A. (2014). A simple introduction to the practice of ethnography and guide to ethnographic fieldnotes. *Marshall Digital Scholar*, June, 2014. https://www.cedar-network.org/wp-content/uploads/2016/06/Wasserfall-Intro-to-ethnography.pdf

Kalainoff, M. Z. (2013). *Making visible the complexities of problem solving: An interactional ethnographic study of a general chemistry course in a studio learning environment.* Unpublished doctoral dissertation. University of California, Santa Barbara.

Kalainoff, M. Z., & Clark, M. G. (2017). Developing a logic-of-inquiry-for-action through a developmental framework for making epistemic cognition visible. In M. Clark & C. Gruber (Eds.), *Leader development deconstructed.* Springer.

Kelly, G. J., & Chen, C. (1999). The sound of music: Constructing science as sociocultural practices through oral and written discourse. *Journal of Research in Science Teaching, 36*(8), 883–915.

Kumpulainen, K., Hmelo-Silver, C., & César, M. (2009). *Investigating classroom interaction: Methodologies in action.* Sense Publishers.

Mitchell, C. J. (1984). Typicality and the case study. In P. F. Ellen (Ed.), *Ethnographic research: A guide to general conduct* (pp. 238–241). Academic.

Lee, C. D., Nasir, N. S., Pea, R., & McKinney De Royston, M. (2020). Introduction: Reconceptualizing learning: A critical task for knowledge-building and teaching. In N. S. Nasir, C. D. Lee, R. Pea, & M. McKinney De Royston (Eds.), *Handbook of the cultural foundations of learning* (pp. xviii–xxxv). Routledge.

Smith, L. M. (1978). An evolving logic of participant observation, educational ethnography and other case studies. *Review of Research in Education, 6*(1), 316–377.

Street, B. V. (2013). Anthropology and education. *Teaching Anthropology, 3*(1), 57–60.

Tannen, D. (Ed.) (1993). *Framing and discourse.* Oxford University Press.

10

MAPPING-TRANSCRIBING PROCESSES WITHIN IE LOGIC-OF-INQUIRY

On Studying a Languaculture-in-the-Making

Maria Lucia Castanheira, Judith L. Green, and Krisanna Machtmes

Our goal in this chapter is to introduce the concept of mapping and transcribing developing cultural discourses, processes and patterns that shape opportunities for learning in classrooms from an Interactional Ethnographic (IE) logic of analyses, an epistemology, not a method. From an IE logic of analysis, a culture of a class (or other social space) is not assumed to be static prior to a group entering. Rather, IE researchers, guided by theories of culture from anthropology, conceptualize "culture as a verb" (Heath & Street, 2008, p. 11).

In this chapter, we introduce how recording, transcribing and mapping developing events of the first morning of a bilingual Fifth-grade class, when analyzed through an IE logic of analysis, supported Castanheira (first author) in constructing warranted accounts (cf., Heap, 1995) of this class as culture-in-the-making, or rather, as a *languaculture-in-the-making* (cf., Agar, 1996; 2006). This conceptual argument is central to the analytic logic we present in three telling case studies (Mitchell, 1984) grounded in Castanheira's (cf., 2000; Castanheira et al., 2007) logic-in-use in studying how Yeager, the teacher and co-ethnographer (2003), engaged students in developing a community of inquirers (her term). Through these telling cases, we unfold the processes of analysis that led Castanheira (and our author team) to make transparent how Yeager was developing a local and situated understanding with students (and the ethnographer) of what to do, know, and understand as a member of this developing languaculture.

An Overview of the Three Telling Case Studies

In Telling Case 1, we (re)construct the analytic decisions and actions that Castanheira, guided by an IE logic of analysis, developed to construct warranted accounts of how Yeager, in and through her discourse and interactions with

DOI: 10.4324/9781003215479-13

students initiated a range of cultural processes and practices that oriented students upon entry to ways of being a member of the Tower Community. Through this process, we make transparent how Castanheira constructed a visual/graphic/textual process for constructing a map of the developing actions and flow of conduct (Giddens, 1984) by partnering with video records and her fieldnotes to create an analytic grammar of the developing social processes of this first event.

In the second telling case, we introduce how Castanheira, added to her logic-in-use an IE-guided approach to discourse analysis (cf., Castanheira et al., 2000; Green & Kelly, 2019) to trace the developing discourse and social interactions of the teacher with students. Our goal in this telling case of her logic-in-use is introduce how and why taking a hearer as well as observer approach supported Castanheira in constructing a warranted account of the ways in which Yeager's discourse and interactions with students supported them in transitioning from the arrival phase to a collective space.

By (re)constructing, how, in and through the verbal and nonverbal discourse and actions of the teacher with students, we make transparent how Castanheira created a graphic/visual mapping discourse-based process for tracing the developing text of the collective event (Green et al., 2008/2013). Through this process we introduce how and why IE researchers assume a hearer's perspective to transcribe the discourse-in-use and flow of interaction among members.

Conceptual Perspective on Language-Culture Relationships Guiding Castanheira's Logic-in-Use

Underlying the first two telling case studies of Castanheira's logic-in-use is the following conceptual argument about of the relationship between language and culture proposed by anthropologist Michael Agar (1994):

> The concept of "culture," like the concept of "language," has to change.

> The two concepts have to change *together*. Language, in all its varieties, in all the ways it appears in everyday life, builds a world of meanings. When you run into different meanings, when you become aware of your own and work to build a bridge to the others, "culture" is what you're up to. Language fills the spaces between us with sound; culture forges the human connection through them. Culture is in language, and language is loaded with culture.

> *(p. 33)*

Additionally, in this telling case, we also make visible how Spradley's (1980/2016) argument that people are *map makers, not map* readers, guided Castanheira analysis of the class as a *languaculture-in-the-making*:

> Culture is not simply a cognitive map that people acquire, in whole or in part, more or less accurately and then learn to read. People are

not just map-readers; they are map-makers. People are cast out into imperfectly charted, continually revised sketch maps. Culture does not provide a cognitive map but rather a set of principles for map making and navigation.

(Frake, 1977, pp. 6–7 cited in Spradley, 1980. p. 9)

In this argument, Castanheira (2000) made visible how she viewed the actors (students, teacher, and others) as they were:

acting in their cultural milieu, for example, a class. This learning process is not a passive one. People are not receivers or passive readers of cultural maps, but rather are makers and contributors in the process of culture construction.

(p. 53)

In the first two telling cases, we provided a sketch map of principles guiding an IE analytic logic for transcribing and (re)presenting ways of mapping the flow of conduct (Giddens, 1984).

In Telling Case 3 of Castanheira, logic of analysis, we move forward in time to the first academic event of this first morning of school, to trace (i.e., create a map of) how Yeager engaged students in a process for solving a mathematical problem, the Watermelon Problem. As part of this telling case, we also present how mapping individual, table group, whole class interactional spaces the teacher engaged students in across cycles of activity, provided a basis for empirically contrasting how students in each phase of this event engaged in subsequent phases with differing configurations of participants.

Guiding the Goals of the Three Telling Cases Studies of an IE Logic of Analysis

Through these three telling case studies of Castanheira's logic of analysis, we illustrate key facets of the IE logic-of-inquiry that guided her in creating a conceptually grounded process of constructing data, not finding data (cf., Ellen, 1984) to develop warranted accounts of this languaculture-in-the-making in order to *write culture, not find culture* (Clifford & Marcus, 1985). That is, we introduced her goals for the initial phases of her year-long ethnography. As (re)presented in the three telling case studies, Castanheira constructed an analytic logic for:

- Mapping developing social and academic terrains of a class (e.g., sites for learning) being discursively and interactionally constructed by participants as they develop norms and expectations, roles and relationships, and rights and obligations guiding ways of being a member of the class.

- Transcribing how participants in a class, in and through moment-by-moment discourse and interactions, construct local and situated ways of knowing, engaging in, and learning what is socially and academically relevant and significant to know, understand, and do to accomplish academic goals set for them.

The following description of ethnographic goals, grounded in a two-year dialogue between anthropologist Amy Zaharlick and educational researcher Judith Green, second author, (Zaharlick & Green, 1991), concludes this conceptual introduction to an IE logic of analysis. In the following excerpt from their article on this process, we make transparent how Green expanded her understanding of the potential of an anthropological perspective to guide IE as a logic-of-inquiry:

> The influence of a cultural perspective can be seen in the comparative nature of this approach. Ethnographers are constantly comparing what they are observing and identifying in one situation with other similar situations within and across groups in order to identify and explain the cultural beliefs and practices of the group under study. Ethnography, therefore, is concerned with the descriptive study of a group's customary ways of life.

While this is an overarching goal of IE research, the fact that the class' customary processes and practices, roles and relationship and norms and expectations did not exist on the first morning, frames the importance of introducing Castanheira logic-of-inquiry of the first morning. By unfolding three telling case studies, therefore, we introduce how she began a process of mapping, transcribing, and (re)presenting these cultural processes as they were being proposed to students in and through a series of developing interactions within and across events (i.e., participation spaces) on this first morning.

Mapping -Transcribing Analyses: Three Analytic Telling Case Studies

For each analytic telling case study presented in the remaining sections of this chapter, we unfold, a series of mapping-transcribing relationships. Through this process, we make transparent how Castanheira's analytic logic-in-use was a developing process, like the cultural processes being studied. That is, we present how each phase of her analysis through an IE-guided logic-in-use was designed to support her in addressing a growing series of questions to understand how Yeager and her students were constructing a developing set of ways of knowing, being, engaging in, and participating with others to initiate this bilingual community of inquirers (see Commentary by Yeager).

Telling Case 1: Mapping-Transcribing Relationships for First Morning

To understand the decision processes that Castanheira (cf., 2000) undertook to construct a map from fieldnotes and video recordings, our author team decided to present the processes in this section (and others) through a first-person narrative to capture Castanheira's logic-in-use. Thus, we shift our descriptive approach (our team's narrative approach) to a first-person narrative genre to make her logic-in-use come alive (cf., Kumpulainen et al., 2009).

Phase 1 Analyses: On Recording and Analyzing Fieldnotes and Video Records

In Table 10.1, I present my initial approach to constructing a map of the event that oriented students as they entered the Tower Community space and engaged with Yeager as well as other members and physical spaces of this class (cf., Castanheira, 2000). By drawing on this map as an anchor for this section, I create a ground for identifying layers of analyses that led to this (re) presentation of events of the first morning. In the following section, I (re) construct the processes and phases of the logic-in-use that I developed to construct this map and to decide what level of transcribing I would use to (re) present the actions among participants in this initiating phase of this Fifth-grade bilingual class.

I entered the classroom on this first morning of school prior to the students' entry.[1] Upon entry, I negotiated with Yeager where to position the camera so I could capture ways she engaged students in entering the class for the first time, and who entered with them (see Baker et al., this volume). Based on my discussions with Yeager, I positioned the camera diagonally facing the door to have a wide-angle on the class space (see Bridges this volume). This decision was also based on discussions with members of the ethnographic research group in the university, who had previously engaged in IE-guided ethnographic work with Yeager in this bilingual class (see Yeager Commentary). In this way, I sought to capture Yeager's interactions with participants to record how she initiated ways of being a member of this developing class, not classroom (a physical space) in which they were entering.

While I was able to record on video ways in which these actors entered the Tower classroom and engaged with Yeager, on my fieldnotes I decided to begin a process of registering (i.e., writing a description of) who entered, i.e., a parent with students or a student alone. From an IE-guided logic of recording, this form of writing is a *running record*, i.e., brief descriptions, not a detailed account, of the developing actions, and thus, does not have the discourse-in-use. That is, I registered (i.e., inscribed) the time when things happened, I put

TABLE 10.1 Analytic Logic for Constructing a Mapping Process of the Developing Phases of the First Event in a Bilingual Class

Time	Speaker	Actions	Language	Interaction Space	Sub-event	Event	Opportunities to explore self, others, and physical environment as texts
8:10	St/P	*arriving* in the classroom		T-I			- observing and 'reading' what others are doing
	St/P	*meeting* teacher		I-TG		ONSET	- re-establishing contact with friends
	T	*greeting* St/P	S/E				- meeting other class members
	St/P	*responding* to T	S/E				- listening to English and Spanish being spoken
	T	*orienting* students to *finding* name card, *choosing* place to sit	S/E			OF	- speaking English or Spanish
	St	*choosing* where to sit		I-I	ENTERING THE TOWER		
	St	*decorating* name square	S/E			COMMUNITY	- meeting other members of the class
	St	*talking* to classmates sitting at table group	S/E				- getting acquainted with others
(45')	T/T	*talking* to Sts at table groups	S/E				- choosing language to interact with others
	St	*talking* to T/T.A. and St. Teacher.	S/E				

(Continued)

TABLE 10.1 Analytic Logic for Constructing a Mapping Process of the Developing Phases of the First Event in a Bilingual Class (*Continued*)

Time	Speaker	Actions	Language	Interaction Space	Sub-event	Event	Opportunities to explore self, others, and physical environment as texts
8:55	T	*introducing* chime as a sign	**S/E**	**WC**			
	T	*welcoming* participants	**S/E**	**St/WC**			- re-situate self within whole group
	T	*celebrating* the languages of the Tower	**S/E**				
(40')	T	community: Spanish and English					- getting support from adults and classmates
	T	*explaining* way of using Spanish and English in the classroom	**S/E** **S/E**				- helping student teacher learn her job
	T	*introducing* adult members to students	**S/E**		WELCOMING TO THE TOWER COMMUNITY	WELCOMING TO TOWER	- becoming an ethnographer; - knowing local community ways of leaving
	T	*introducing* ethnography as community practice	**S/E**				- making decisions about routine aspects of norms being established for the class
	T	*talking* about basic routines: drinking water, signing up for lunch, bathroom, recess, etc.	**S/E**				- becoming a Tower community member
	T	*exploring* students' knowledge about Tower community	**S/E**				- exploring own knowledge and experience in constructing Tower community in 96/97; - defining uses and exploring multiple spaces; - hearing S/E and speaking language of choice
	T	*introducing* Tower as community with traditions					
	T	*presenting* multiple physical spaces of Tower classroom					- exploring physical spaces of Tower as classroom

(*Continued*)

TABLE 10.1 Analytic Logic for Constructing a Mapping Process of the Developing Phases of the First Event in a Bilingual Class (*Continued*)

Time	Speaker	Speak	Actions	Language	Interaction Space	Sub-event	Event	Opportunities to explore self, others, and physical environment as texts
Time	Speaker	Speak	Actions	language	Interaction Space	Sub-event	Event	Opportunities for Exploring Self, Others, and Physical Environment as Texts
9:35	T		*explaining* that students would meet each other	E/S	**WG**			
	T		*explaining* students would help each other	S/E	**TG**			- Establishing contact among classroom participants
(28")	T		*describing* appropriate/ inappropriate actions	S/E	**I-TG**			- Establishing relations between space and actions
	T		*exploring* students' knowledge of adjectives	E/S			N	- Understanding what counts as material resource within the classroom spaces
	T		*presenting* examples of procedures for choosing adjectives and support others	S/E			A / M / E	- Modeling ways of describing self
	T		*opening* the possibility for classroom ethnographer to use Portuguese	S/E		CHOOSING ADJECTIVE		- Using language(s) of choice in order to participate
	T		*emphasizing* expectation that members of tables groups help each other	E/S			G	- Establishing others as resources
	St		*choosing* adjectives in table groups	E/S			A / M / E	- Exploring with others possible ways of
	T, TA/ St T		**helping** students on request	S/E				Naming/describing self and others
	T		*extending* time on request of student	E/S				- Establishing time for learning as flexible

(*Continued*)

TABLE 10.1 Analytic Logic for Constructing a Mapping Process of the Developing Phases of the First Event in a Bilingual Class (*Continued*)

Time	Speaker	Actions	Language	Interaction Space	Sub-event	Event	Opportunities to explore self, others, and physical environment as texts
9:58	T	*discussing* next activity	S/E	**WC**			
	T	*explaining* what 'introducing themselves' in 'Tea Party' would look and sound like	E/S	**I-I**			- Broadening the basis for establishing contact, from individuals in TG, to individuals within the whole Group.
12'	T'	*providing* examples (student in skit)	S/E	**WC**			
	T	*ringing* chime to signal beginning of Tea Party	E/S				- Positioning individuals as members of the larger collective *as* a collective
	All	T/S Teacher/T Assistant/R/Sts *performing* introductions	E/S		TEA PARTY		
	T	*asking* students to reach others they did not know	E/S				- Opening possibilities of including new people
	T	*ringing* chime to end performance of Tea Party	S/E				- Engaging in a collective work *for* the collective (meeting others, reaching out to new people)
	T	*discussing* 'community' in context of Tea Party	E/S				
	T	*exploring* the diversity of the Tower	S/E				- Framing Tower as diverse group

(Continued)

TABLE 10.1 Analytic Logic for Constructing a Mapping Process of the Developing Phases of the First Event in a Bilingual Class (*Continued*)

Time	Speaker	Actions	Language	Interaction Space	Sub-event	Event	Opportunities to explore self, others, and physical environment as texts
10:10	St	*attempting* to name as many names with adjectives as possible (volunteers)	S/E	**WC**			- Taking risk within classroom activity
	T	*clarifying* expectations for playing Name Game	E/S	**St-WC**	NAMING MEMBERS		- Acknowledging others and being acknowledged
		attempting to name as many names with adjectives as possible (volunteers)	S/E				- Picturing classroom as constituted by a large number of members
(8)	T	*re-stating* names and adjectives of all students	S/E				- Using others as texts for learning

Key: **I S**: Interactional Space; **T-I**: Teacher-Individual Student; **I -TG**: Teacher – Table Group; **I-I**: Individual – Individual; **St-WC**: Student – Whole Class down phrases that I heard (e.g., the teacher said, *all eyes on me*), as well as the actions I was observing students take. I also drew a map of the positions of participants; therefore, map making became part of my fieldnote records and served to foreshadow this process throughout my study.

For example, I registered in my fieldnotes how students were being positioned, or positioned themselves (cf., Green, Brock et al., 2020), in particular events and engaged in proposed actions: selecting their name cards, personalizing the name card with crayons provided, and selecting a table to join to talk with friends, or if new in this school and thus to other students, then a place to sit. I also recorded the material resources in the room available in the class (e.g., books, notebooks) that students were engaging with, or could observe. I did not attempt to record the discourse among students at their table groups or of the different actors working with Yeager (the student teacher and the teacher aide) at this point in my study.

In creating this narrative about my actions in making notes about the first event, *Entering the Tower,* I made transparent decisions about how I inscribed in my fieldnotes what I was observing, as an IE-guided researcher. After the class concluded, I drew on my fieldnotes as an anchor for examining the video records of the classroom interactions. My goal in examining these records was based on my understanding that what I was able to inscribe was limited to what I saw, and could write about as developing processes, as well as what I was able to hear and understand in a particular moment and/or across times and actions in the developing events (cf., Birdwhistell, 1977).

This awareness led me to understand that the sketch map I constructed in my fieldnotes, like a political map of the boundaries of states geographically (Woods, 1982), did not represent the detailed processes and practices being proposed to the students. Thus, I reviewed the video records to add to the developing map of the arrival time the information flow as well as the physical shifts in the social structuring of the class, after leaving the field. My goal in taking this chain of actions was to identify dimensions (facets) of the dynamic processes being proposed to and responded to by students as they entered this bilingual class. As the following description of my processes will demonstrate, this action was critical to my being able to learn from their actions and discourse how to understand what members were experiencing on this first morning.

The video analysis process provided a ground for identifying discursive texts through which Yeager supported students (and me as ethnographer) in developing insider knowledge of social, cultural, and academic processes in which they would engage as members of the Tower Community. The video analysis also provided a ground for adding deeper insights of observed activity that enabled me to identify who proposed what or responded to whom, in what ways, when and where, for what purposes, and with what outcome for individual members and the collective (cf., Cazden et al., 1972; Mercer &

Hodgkinson, 2008/2013). Through analysis of the video records, I sought to identify and (re)present:

- How Yeager oriented participants,
- How and in what ways participants (students) attended individually and collectively to the facets of developing events, and
- How Yeager and students responded to each other to jointly construct a set of norms and expectations as well as roles and relationships for the developing Tower Community.

In this way, I was able to step back from what I saw and recorded in my fieldnotes, to develop warrants for my interpretations of ways Yeager proposed actions to students. As part of this process, I also sought to understand how she "read" (made inferences about) the students' responses to what she was proposing in order to (a conditional process) support them in achieving the goals for the events they were interactionally and discursively constructing with her guidance.

Mapping the First Event of the Morning

To identify elements (re)presented in Table 10.1, I now unfold how I constructed this map of the flow of conduct as it was being proposed to and constructed with students. My actions began by moving beyond my fieldnotes to a process in which I (re)viewed the video recording multiple times to add details of the *actions* taken by participants to my running records. This process led me to inscribe what was being signaled to and by participants in the form of present continuous verbs and their objects (see Column 3 in Table 10.1) as well as who proposed what to whom, in what ways leading to what ways of responding (Column 2).

To (re)present what was being interactionally and discursively accomplished by participants, I used a descriptive language (a kind of grammar) for inscribing what Yeager was orienting students to as well as referencing about the expected actions in the developing event. In this phase of my research, the video records provided a ground for identifying nuances of particular facets, and patterns of interaction. that were visible from the angle of the video recording of a particular segment of the room (cf., Castanheira et al., 2000).

As indicated in Table 10.1, I created columns for (re)presenting the following inter-related phenomena:

- Times for the developing actions and events (video recorded time) (Column 1)
- Speakers (who to whom) (Column 2)
- Actions identified (re)presented as present continuous verbs plus objects (ing verbs + actions) (Column 3)
- Languages of choice to participate or order of language of speakers (English, Spanish; Spanish/English; or English/Spanish) (Column 4)

- Interactional spaces created (teacher-individual; teacher to group; individual-individual; student-student interactions; whole class; student-whole class; individual-table group) (Column 5)
- Sub-events and events constructed and bounded discursively by participants (Column 5 and 6, respectively)
- Analytical Interpretations (grounded inferences, i.e., analytic induction) of what was being made present to students (Column 7)

Once these elements were identified, and the table (re)presenting the flow of conduct constructed, I was able to develop a grounded approach to tracing and interpreting the opportunities afforded to, and jointly constructed by, students as they explored self and others in these developing spaces (see Column 6 in Table 10.1).

As indicated in Table 10.1, the elements of this level of map making were grounded in developing times identified for the events from the video records. These time markers created an anchor for analyzing time-space-actor interactions (cf., chronotopes, Bakhtin, 1981, p. 257 cited in Kumpulainen, 2019), as well as speaker-hearer/individual-collective interactions (cf., Bakhtin, 1986; Fairclough, 1992; Gumperz, 1982). By constructing this table as a more detailed and complex level of map making than was possible from the fieldnotes, I demonstrated how tracing and (re)presenting developing discourse and interactional processes from video records extended the power of my analytical lens.

As indicated in the column action, I also constructed a *language of description* that (re)presented actions, in the form of present continuous verbs (words ending in "ing") plus the object of the actions. This language of description, a grammar for analysis, became a language for (re)presenting actions that supported me in tracing referential content of the discourse framing the action as well as identifying to what the actions were oriented.

What this form of transcribing-(re)presenting developing social processes enabled me to foreground was how people developed the actions and what was being referenced (oriented to). Thus, I was able to (re)present the dynamic and complex processes of orienting participants to particular phenomena and actions, rather than creating categories that nominalized the actions. Through these processes, I introduced how this form of map making enabled me to make transparent how I created warranted accounts of people and how they became texts and contexts for each other (Erickson & Shultz, 1981; McDermott et al., 1978).

This conceptual approach, therefore, led me to construct an initial set of roles and relationships possible to engage in with others as well as material cultural processes of this class (Gee & Green, 1998). For example, in Table 10.1 (Column 7), through this form of mapping times, actors, languages-in-use, and actions in and across interactional spaces, I created a foundation for examining how people were constructing *Opportunities for Exploring Self, Others, and Physical Environment as Texts.*

Table 10.1, however, did not make transparent how the transition to the next event was signaled and accomplished by the ringing of a chime at 8:55 am. The chime, as I make visible in the next Telling Case Study, marked the end of the first phase of the morning and thus the end of Telling Case 1. Table 10.1, therefore, (re)presented a meso level of map making of different facets of the developing languacultural spaces of the class (i.e., ethnographic spaces, Agar, 2006). That is, the analytic grammar I created enable me to identify the patterns of action and interaction in this first event (Welcoming to the Tower). Thus, this level of map making provided a *panoramic view* of the norms and expectations for participating that Yeager created with and for students as they entered this bilingual Fifth-grade class for the first time.

Telling Case 2: Mapping and Transcribing the Transition to Collective Activity

In this telling case of my analytic process, I present a different approach to transcribing the discursive construction of the events and mapping the flow of conduct within a class as a languaculture-in-the-making. This level and form of analysis drew on the analytic discourse system that IE researchers have developed to trace how the teacher (or other speaker) in and through her moment-by-moment discourse with students was composing a text (cf., Fairclough, 1992) that students heard, read, and interpreted to participate in the developing event.[2] This system for discourse analysis also provided a basis for mapping moments where students responded in a way that was not thematically tied to the developing text, creating a potential divergence for the group based on the teacher's (speaker's) response (cf., Green & Kelly, 2019; Green & Wallat, 1981; Green, Brock et al., 2020).

In this Telling Case study, therefore, I introduce how this process of discourse analysis supported me in identifying how participants were being oriented to, in what ways, for what purposes, and with what potential consequences for engaging in the developing event as well as in future actions within and across events (cf., Putney et al., 1999). As I show through this telling case of my analytic logic-in-use, I constructed a foundation for making visible ways in which Yeager created a *meta-discourse* that signaled to students, individually and collectively in two languages (Yeager et al., 2009), ways of participating and interacting with each other, to create a "community of inquirers".

Table 10.2 provides a grounding for introducing units of analysis that I drew on to engage in discourse analysis of how Yeager was (re)orienting students to ways of creating a collective space for learning (cf. Bloome et al., 2005; Green & Bridges, 2018; Green & Wallat, 1981).

TABLE 10.2 The Chime: Creating a Collective Orientation and Initiating a Cultural Practice

	Teacher's actions		Students' actions (cf., Bloome & Theodorou, 1988; Lin, 1993)	Choices of discursive and non-verbal cues (cf., Ivanič, 1994)	Consequences for community practice
Tran-script line	Verbal message units/action units	Non-verbal			
168 nv		T rings chimes		Theme: chime as a signal	Initiating a collective signal for creating a whole class interactional space
			Students stop what they are doing and look at the teacher J is reading a book		
169	oh			Congratulates students for their precision and gives	
170	that was great			Students another opportunity	
171	we should try		Students laugh and start	to "practice"	
172	again hablan bastante		Pretending to talk to each other Joseph continues to read his book (30 seconds)	Our translation–talk a lot to each other]	
173nnv					
174nnv	oh	T rings chimes	Students stops talking		
175	that is great		Joseph continues to read		
176					
177	Joseph		Joseph stops reading and looks up at BY	Looks at Joseph and calls on him, given he was not participating in group activity	
178	that would be a signal				Reaffirming the meaning of the signal
179	for you to look up				

(Continued)

TABLE 10.2 The Chime: Creating a Collective Orientation and Initiating a Cultural Practice (Continued)

	Teacher's actions		Students' actions (cf, Bloome & Theodorou, 1988; Lin, 1993)	Choices of discursive and non-verbal cues (cf, Ivanič, 1994)	Consequences for community practice
Tran-script line	Verbal message units/action units	Non-verbal			
180nnv		(pause)			
181	una campana			Our translation: one bell/chime and you have to listen	
182	hay que escuchar			Addressed to all students – you=all	Positions Spanish and English speakers as her Interlocutors
183	it may be that you			Switches to Spanish without pause and creates Interwoven use of Spanish with English	Demonstrates the place for using Spanish and English so that students learn to listen through the two languages
184	you know				
185	you are in the middle				
186	of doing something				
187	o que estan				
188	trabajando en algo				
189	y si escucha esa campana				
190	tienes que mirar arriba				Teacher authorizes use of chime by others in future
191	y escuchar				
192	cualquier persona que esta ablando				

Key: nv: Non-verbal

As indicated in Table 10.2, my transcribing process was not a linear process but rather, like the mapping process in Table 10.1, was a theoretically grounded way of inscribing the interactional flow between Yeager and the students and students and Yeager (Green et al., 1997; Ochs, 1979). In (re)presenting the flow of discourse and actions in different columns, as in Table 10.1, I make visible a core foundation of an IE transcribing process: the mapping of discourse is not a linear process grounded in turn exchanges and sentence grammar as in written texts, or even in some forms of transcribing spoken texts (Markee, 2015).

This discourse analysis process focused me on taking a hearer's perspective (cf., Green & Wallat, 1981); that is, to identify the bits of talk and the developing text, I recorded how they were being proposed and what actions or cues were co-present that helped me understand the message. By taking a hearer's perspective I was able to trace how other hearers (students, the teacher) on the video recording responded to the verbal and non-verbal cues that were co-present to them as they engaged with and contributed to the developing text of particular slices of life (cf., Gumperz, 1982; Hymes, 1972).

In this system, by taking a hearer's perspective, according to Gumperz (1982) the analyst listens and looks for *contextualization cues* such as: *pitch, stress, pause, juncture,* and *eye gaze, intonational contours, kinesics* (body movement), as well as *proxemics* (distances between and among participants), and *gesture.* These contextualization cues provide an empirical approach to interpret meanings for the ways in which the message (bit of talk) was communicated to participants. These cues created a basis for me to interpret not only meaning of what was being proposed in and through lexical and grammatical forms but also how they were being communicated as well as perceived by those hearing the bit of talk.

In Table 10.2, I inscribed not only what was proposed but also the response pattern that I observed and heard being constructed by both the teacher and the students as they (re)oriented from personal spaces to a collective space and a group activity. Thus, by tracing the flow of conduct of the teacher with students and the students' responses to the teacher, I provided a ground for (re) theorizing how to understand both boundaries of events (i.e., when an event starts and ends) as well as how to interpret observed responses of students (or other participants).

By building on the concept of contextualization cues to identify and interpret what was being communicated by particular speakers, Green (Green & Kelly, 2019) created the following units to trace the developing texts of the instructional event that were central to my transcribing process. This approach to mapping developing texts as they are being composed by participants in an event, involves the following logic of analysis that guided me in creating the transcript (re)presented in Table 10.2 of the chime event. Thus, the analysis of units presented in Table 10.2 provided an empirical approach to creating a grounded interpretation of how and in what ways Yeager, in and through her choices of discourse and interactions, signaled to students how to (re)orient to a collective activity space.

By listening to and observing these cues and actions related to them, I, as transcriber, assumed the position of member-as-hearer, as well as observer, of how the teacher was signaling the transition from small group activity to collective activity. In taking this position, I identified the following units of discourse and actions being signaled by Yeager on a bit-by-bit basis, somewhat equivalent to Lego blocks as a metaphor for building a larger structure in and through bits of discourse-in-use.

The units recorded in Table 10.2, Column 2, include: Message units (MUs). For example, Line 169 constitutes an MU I inscribed as I heard Yeager saying the word "oh" in a rising tone with an elongated "o" sound. I also noted that as she said "oh", she also looked around the table groups ($n = 6$) as she observed what students were doing and if they had responded to the chime by looking towards her. By listening to how the word "oh" was said and what contextualization cues were co-present, I identified this message unit as a signal to me and members of the class that Yeager was not finished with the message and was a signal that hearers need to listen further to what she was saying as she held the floor (Goffman, 1981).

Message Units in turn tie to other message units (MU) to create an Action Unit (AU), e.g., Lines 169 and 170 form an action unit to show what the "oh" was signaling. Additionally, MUs registered in Lines 171 and 172, created a new action unit in which Yeager included two languages to communicate a common idea (not a literal translation). In this moment in which Yeager used two languages, I was able to identify a more detailed perspective than was (re)presented in Table 10.1, which only recognized *that two languages were spoken*, not how they were spoken and to what they referred in a particular moment.

Action units can also tie intertextually to construct a Turn Unit (a person's turn at talk) and Turn Units (TU) become building blocks for potential exchanges of turns to construct intertextually another interactional level, an Interaction Unit (IU). Interaction Units, themselves within this form of discourse analysis, tie together to form a Sequence Unit (SU), a sequence of tied messages, actions and interactions through which members construct a particular topic, the actions expected for the collective. This SU is represented by the dotted line on the transcript above Line 173 nv (nonverbal) ringing of the chime, which led to the students stopping their talking (Line 174).

As indicated in Table 10.2, this non-verbal action was followed by Yeager once again saying to students, "Oh" (line 174), followed by "that was great" (line 175), creating a new AU within this developing Sequence Unit. This AU showed once again her process of reading the students' actions and responding to them. In turn, Sequence Units tie to make phases of activity, and Phase

Units tie to make sub-events, within a developing event. Events, therefore, are social constructions not a given that the researcher frames in an *a priori* manner. The boundaries of an event therefore can be identified retrospectively by examining what is said next and retrieving what was said prior to its initiation.

From this perspective the bits of discourse, i.e., languaging processes (Bloome et al., 2005), provided a foundation for inscribing and interpreting what is being proposed to and recognized, or not, by members of a class or interactional space within a class, not at the end of turn, interaction or event, but as each is being proposed to hearers/seers (see Hong & Bloome, this volume). Thus, in Table 10.2, I identified interconnected tied bits of talk as units of different kinds that were available to be heard and seen as they were being proposed and responded to in and through the developing phases of the Chime event.

This form of transcribing languaging processes enabled me to create a multi-faceted map of the discourse for the teacher (Columns 3-4), and for the students (Columns 5–6) to (re)present the developing actions-interactions through which a text of the event was being composed by multiple participants in particular points in time (cf., Fairclough, 1992; Green, Brock et al., 2020). As indicated in Column 7, this way of transcribing-mapping what Yeager was signaling to students supported me in interpreting a set of norms and expectations, and roles and relationships, for interpreting how Yeager and her bilingual students constructed ways of using languages, not one language as registered in Lines 180–192, to accomplish social as well as academic processes of the class.

What was important to note in these lines is that, as in the first switch between English and Spanish, what was communicated was not a literal translation of each language but a developing languaging process that involved all students in listening through both languages to learn what was being proposed to them. Thus, through this process of recording developing units, I was able to construct an understanding of how the developing texts of the class formed intertextual webs of meanings, (inter)actions, and activity (Bloome & Egan-Robertson, 1993). Through transcribing-mapping processes, I made transparent how I identified bounded units of analysis (e.g., events) as well as units through which the events were developing. In Table 10.2, I also included columns to register the choices of discourse and nonverbal cues and (re)presented them as units in columns (re)presenting Yeager's and student(s)' actions.

On Identifying Outliers to Collective Actions

What is visible in Table 10.2 is a local and situated social process for engaging with others in this class as framed by the teacher's actions. That is, the action of ringing the chime was an official beginning of the transitioning from an individual choice event in the morning to a collective event. However, in (re) visiting the video recording of the first event, I located a message that Yeager had given to students that served to foreshadow what the chime would mean. That is, as she went from table group to table group in the first event, she quietly told them to listen for the chime in 10 minutes and when the chime rang, they should stop and "look at her" to begin a process of transitioning to a new event, a collective activity.

However, even though she created two messages to indicate the meaning of the chime, as indicated in Table 10.2, Joseph did not immediately respond to the chime, and thus was an outlier to this developing process (Smith, 1978). Yeager's response to him was telling in that, rather than calling him out for not doing what was proposed to the students earlier (her meta-discourse to the groups), she engaged the students in practicing this transition. As indicated in the Student Column lines 171–172, the group responded with laughter and engaged in her request to talk again, MUs given in English then Spanish. Following this set of exchanges, a Sequence Unit, (SU), Joseph joined the group and Yeager, once again acknowledges their responses in a positive manner.

In this brief discussion of Table 10.2 of my discourse analysis of the developing text of this event, I introduced a logic of transcribing ways in which speech and nonverbal actions as well as contextualization cues were central to a hearer's perspective and how Yeager signaled ways of being a student in this class. In Table 10.2, I made visible two cultural understandings that Yeager was signaling to the students. By switching between languages, English and Spanish, in this event as well as in earlier events (Table 10.1), she signaled to students that to be a member of this class you were expected to listen through the two languages (Yeager et al., 2009), given that literal translations were not the norm. In this way, she engaged monolingual English speakers as well as Spanish speakers in understanding a developing norm for language-in-use in this class.

In this way, she made visible to students how both languages were a resource for all members of this community. In the next telling case, I provide evidence of this process as well as how Yeager engaged bilingual speakers in serving as cultural guides for both English and Spanish speakers as they engaged in common events at their table group as well as in public events in which table group members reported their work to members of the class as a collective.

Telling Case 3: The Watermelon Project as Evidence of a Bilingual Languaging Process

In this section, we present a third telling case of Castanheira's (Castanheira et al., 2000; 2020) analytic logic-in-use. Through this telling case, we foreground how she drew on the analytic grammar she created for Telling Case 1 to construct a graphic (re)presentation of how and in what ways Yeager introduced students to the first academic area of inquiry – exploring ways of asking questions as mathematicians. Given this goal, we will not present the detailed discourse analysis of how Yeager introduced the history and goals for student of this Watermelon Problem in a detailed discussion at the onset of this event, as space (word limits) does not permit.[3]

Our goal in this telling case is to (re)present how Castanheira created a process for tracing developing spaces for learning that Yeager constructed with students, drawing on her analytic grammar presented in Telling Case 1. Figure 10.1 provides a graphic mapping of differing interactional spaces and demonstrates how the analytic grammar of Table 10.1 was held constant in this new set of analyses. In this way, we make visible this analytic logic, like the discourse analysis approach, was a resource for subsequent analyses of developing events in this class.

As indicated in Figure 10.1, Castanheira, guided by this analytic logic, created a way of (re)presenting the developing actions within and across spaces of the Watermelon Problem. For instance, in the first phase of this project, Yeager proposed to the whole class the following actions and their object of focus:

- Establishing interactional spaces
- Constructing a place in learning logs (student notebooks)
- Making a guess
- Establishing procedure
- Defining mathematics
- Defining what it means to be a mathematician
- Establishing types of questions mathematicians ask
- Defining a common question to be investigated by groups: *How much did the teacher pay for your group's watermelon?*
- Defining ways to approach the problem
- Distinguishing between a guess and an estimate (getting to a closer estimate rather than a 'right answer')

The present continuous verb + object analytic grammar, therefore, provided a logic for examining the actions taken by individual members in creating a personal and a collective (table group) estimate of the cost of a watermelon that Yeager provided for each table group, which were the goals of the first phase this event.

As indicated on Figure 10.1, the whole class phase of this developing event led to the individual registering their personal estimate in a notebook (learning log) that Yeager provided for each student.

- **Constructing** a personal estimate
- **Registering** your personal estimate in personal learning log

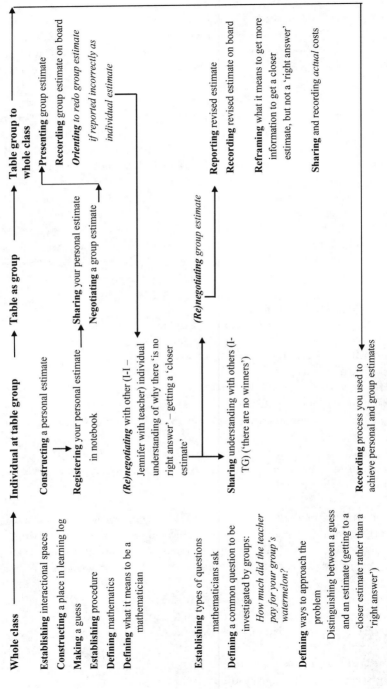

FIGURE 10.1 Tracing Developing Spaces and Cycles of Learning to Estimate as a Mathematician

Analysis of the intertextually tied sub-events (re)presented on Figure 10.1 show that after the full cycle of events, Yeager had the students return to these notebooks, what she framed as a learning log, to register the "Recording process you used to achieve personal and group estimates".

As indicated in Figure 10.1, the table group then negotiated bilingually a collective estimate, which was then presented bilingually to the whole class. In this event, two members of the table group assumed the role of reporter for the group, in one of the languages of this community, Spanish and English, based on student decisions, not on assigned roles by Yeager. Analysis of the actions taken for reporting the estimates showed that Yeager then became a form of scribe by *recording group estimates on the board.*

Analysis of the intertextually tied sub-events (re)presented on Figure 10.1 show that after the full cycle of events, Yeager had the students return to these notebooks, what she framed as a learning log, to register the "Recording process you used to achieve personal and group estimates". As indicated in Figure 10.1, the table group then negotiated bilingually a collective estimate, which was then presented bilingually to the whole class. In this event, two members of the table group assumed the role of reporter for the group, in one of the languages of this community, Spanish and English, based on student decisions, not on assigned roles by Yeager. Analysis of the actions taken for reporting the estimates showed that Yeager then became a form of scribe by *recording group estimates on the board.*

As further indicated in this whole class phase of this event in Figure 10.1, Yeager also assessed whether the students reporting the group estimate selected to report their personal estimate or the group's estimate. As indicated in Figure 10.1, *if* the reporter did not follow the expected protocol that Yeager framed and other students had undertaken, *then* Yeager re-oriented the students who did not follow the expected process to return to their table group and (re)negotiate what would be reported. This led to the following actions:

- **Reporting** revised estimate
- **Recording** revised estimate on board
- **Reframing** what it means to get more information to get a closer estimate, but not a "right answer"
- **Sharing** and recording *actual* costs and weight of the Watermelon by providing the sales slip from the market

In providing the sales slip of Watermelon's cost by weight on the sales slip, Yeager provided students with a basis for actions that they would take on the following day (Day 2 of school). In that phase of this developing cycle of activity, as recorded in my fieldnotes, students would contrast their group estimates with the actual cost by weight of the Watermelon and learn the visual and discursive language of this mathematical process.

A Summary to Phases of the Watermelon Problem from Fieldnotes

By returning to my fieldnotes, and watching the videos of subsequent days, I was able to trace related phases of the Watermelon Problem (Green et al., 2011). While the public sharing on the first morning made visible the individual-small group's decisions and reasoning processes, this contrast was primarily verbal. Tracing this event across days enabled me to identify how the differences in group estimates would be contrasted publicly, i.e., visually/graphically, with the actual cost from the sales slip.

By examining each physical space in this intercontextual (Heras, 1994) cycle of opportunities for learning ways of thinking as a mathematician, I was able to identify processes used and connections or pathways proposed and then taken up from previous events of this first morning of this Fifth-grade class. Also, by using the convention of present continuous verbs + object(s) to map the flow of activity, and the intertextual (Bloome & Egan-Robertson, 1993) ties constructed in and through a series of iterative and recursive processes, I was able to construct the visual/graphic (re)presentation of the texts (i.e., discourse and interactional processes) as they were being proposed to and constructed by students and the teacher. Figure 10.1, therefore, made visible how the patterns of organization created in previous events of the morning were drawn on and thus became a resource for Yeager to introduce students at different table groups to ways of reasoning as a mathematician in this class on this day.

A Closing and an Opening: On Principles of an IE Logic of Analysis

In this chapter, we unfolded a series of telling case studies that (re)presented the logic-in-use that Castanheira undertook to examine the developing *languaculture* of Yeager's bilingual Fifth-grade class. Through (re)presenting the analytic processes and logic of analysis of three events from the first morning of school, we made visible how analysis of each event built on earlier ones. This intertextual web, when presented as maps of the flow of interactions and conduct, led to a principled way of interpreting how and in what ways Yeager engaged students in initiating what was becoming their community of inquirers.

By (re)constructing the phases of Castanheira's logic of analysis across the events of this first morning, we created a foundation for constructing meta-narratives about what the ethnographer learned from these inter-related phases of analysis. That is, we created a warranted account of how Castanheira's reasoning processes and logic of analysis led to the identification of organizational patterns, events, and sub-events in which Yeager engaged students to develop norms and expectations and roles and relationships as well as rights and obligations for being members of this developing social group, a community of inquirers.

Additionally, in each cycle of analysis, we presented an analytic process for constructing ways of mapping and identifying practices were introduced and used by the group to guide collective activities as well as for individuals-within-the-group. Each telling case study presented a form of transcribing, revisiting, and mapping, central to undertaking of particular levels of analysis.

Analysis of these telling cases, therefore, made transparent the logic guiding these ways of transcribing-mapping developing events within a cycle of the morning as well as across cycles as Yeager engaged students in developing local and situated ways of:

- entering the classroom, to
- creating a collective group, to
- engaging in a process of thinking to
- moving from collective to individual recording of work to
- sharing with small group (a table) to then
- sharing the group's interpretation of a task with the collective

By (re)constructing Castanheira's logic-in-use for these telling cases, we introduced how she created a common logic of analysis for transcribing and (re)presenting (mapping) what was being proposed to, interactionally recognized and accomplished by members of this class. Additionally, we demonstrated how the principles guiding each phase of analysis provided a theoretically grounded approach to identifying the distribution of opportunities that recurred across time and where new ones were introduced to the group for particular purposes.

Through (re)presenting Castanheira's analytic grammar and her IE-guided discourse analysis processes, we introduced how and why IE researchers approach the study of educational spaces by entering, when possible, with participants during the initial phases of a class. In this way, we were able to make transparent how analyses across events support the argument that a class is a languaculture-in-the-making.

Although this is a goal of many IE ethnographers, a previous study demonstrated how tracing one student across classes is also possible through the IE logic of analysis presented in this chapter. In a study of five classes for one student in a vocational and higher education context in Australia (Grades 11–12), Castanheira et al. (2000), examined for each class the following set of questions through processes of transcribing and map making of the developing events of each class:

- Who could talk or (inter)act with whom,
- about what,

- when and where,
- under what conditions,
- in what ways, leading to
- what outcomes for both the individual through the interactions with the teacher and tasks presented to them.

Like the analyses presented in this chapter, the common application of analytic processes in this study, formed a basis for constructing warranted accounts of how in each class, the flow of conduct of the instructor with the student and his classmates shaped not only the opportunities for learning afforded to the collective but also the social identities of students in each class.

The analytic logic that Castanheira undertook showed how within IE-guided studies, the analyst is able to construct, i.e., (re)present variability and change that always exists in a class as a languaculture-in-the-making as well between classes for a student. From this perspective, the stability and variability of the discourse and flow of conduct are heuristics for analysis, not preexisting actions or opportunities for learning. Thus, through Castanheira's process of transcribing and mapping this complex and multifaceted set of events of the first morning in Yeager's class, we introduced how mapmaking-transcribing relationships can, and do lead to multiple forms of (re)presenting individual-group-collective processes.

Suggested Readings

Beach, R., & Bloome, D. (Eds.) (2019). *Languaging relations for transforming the literacy and language arts classroom.* Routledge.

Mercer, N., & Hodgkinson, S. (Eds.) (2008/2013). *Exploring talk in school: Inspired by the work of Douglas Barnes.* Sage. https://dx.doi.org/10.4135/9781446279526

Wyatt-Smith, C., Elkins, J., & Gunn, S. (Eds.) (2013), *Multiple perspectives on difficulties in learning literacy and numeracy.* Springer.

Notes

1 IRB approval for studies in Yeager's class was approved for ongoing research ethnographically. This began in 1990–1991 school year as a collaborative research program with permissions from the school administration, faculty, and Yeager and continued for 12 years, with Yeager entering the doctoral program in 2000 and obtaining her PhD in 2003.

2 Markee (2015) provides a comprehensive picture of systems of discourse analysis and classroom interactions that will enable readers to situate the IE approach within the larger community of research in classrooms. Rex et al. (2006) provide a contrastive picture of perspectives and Green and Harker (1988) for contrasts among perspectives and what each makes possible to know.

3 An analysis is available in Mills (1993) as part of a collection of studies in Yeager's class between 1991 and 1993.

References

Agar, M. (2006). Culture: Can you take it anywhere? *International Journal of Qualitative Methods, 5*(2). Retrieved from http://www.ualberta.ca/~iiqm/backissues/5_2/pdf/agar.pdf

Agar, M. (1994). *Language shock: Understanding the culture of conversation.* Quill.

Bakhtin, M. (1981). *Dialogic imagination: Four essays.* University of Texas Press.

Bakhtin, M. M. (1986). *Speech genres and other late essays* (V. W. McGee, trans. University of Texas Press.

Birdwhistell, R. (1977). *About Bateson: Essays on Gregory Bateson.* A Dutton.

Bloome, D., Carter, S. P., Christian, B. M., Otto, S., & Shuart-Faris, N. (2005). *Discourse analysis and the study of classroom language and literacy events: A microethnographic perspective.* Lawrence Erlbaum.

Bloome, D., & Egan-Robertson, A. (1993). The social construction of intertextuality in classroom reading and writing lessons. *Reading Research Quarterly, 28*(4), 305–333. https://doi.org/10.2307/747928

Bloome, D., & Theodorou, E. (1988). Analyzing teacher-student and student-student discourse. In J. L. Green, & J. O. Harker (Eds.), *Multiple perspective analysis of classroom discourse* (pp. 217–248). Ablex

Castanheira, M. L. (2000). *Situating learning within collective possibilities: examining the discursive construction of opportunities for learning in the classroom.* Unpublished dissertation. University of California, Santa Barbara.

Castanheira, M. L., Crawford, T., Dixon, C. N., & Green, J. (2000). Interactional ethnography: An approach to studying the social construction of literate practices. *Linguistics and Education, 11*(4), 353–400. https://doi.org/10.1016/s0898-5898(00)00032-2

Castanheira, M. L., Green, J. L., & Dixon, C. N. (2007). Práticas de letramento em sala de aula: uma análise de ações letradas como construção social. *Revista Portuguesa de Educação, 20*(2), 7–38.

Castanheira, M. L., Yeager, B. V., & Green, J. L. (2020). Tracing opportunities for learning across times, events, and configurations of participants: Interactional ethnography as a logic-of-inquiry. In M. Knobel, J. Kalman, & C. Lankshear (Eds.), *Data analyses, interpretation, and theory in literacy studies research* (pp. 95–122). Meyers Press.

Cazden, C., John, V., & Hymes, D. (Eds.) (1972). *Functions of language in the classroom.* Teachers College.

Clifford, J., & Marcus, G. E. (Eds.) (1985/2010). *Writing culture: The poetics and politics of ethnography.* University of California Press.

Ellen, R. F. (Ed.) (1984). *Ethnographic research: A guide to general conduct.* Academic Press.

Erickson, F., & Shultz, J. (1981). When is context? Some issues and methods in the analysis of social competence. In J. L. Green & C. Wallat (Eds.), *Ethnography and language in educational settings* (Vol. V, pp. 147–150). Ablex.

Fairclough, N. (1992). Intertextuality in critical discourse analysis. *Linguistics and Education, 4,* 269–293.

Frake, c. (1977). Plying frames can be dangerous: some reflections on methodology in cognitive anthropology. *Quarterly Newsletter of the Institute for Comparative Human Development, 3,* (pp. 1–7). Rockefeller University.

Giddens, A. (1984). *The constitution of society.* Polity.

Gee, J., & Green, J. L. (1998). Mapping instructional conversations. *Review of Research in Education, 23*, 119–169.

Goffman, E. (1981). *Forms of talk.* University of Pennsylvania.

Green, J., Brock, C., Baker, W. D., & Harris, P. (2020). Positioning theory for learning in discourse. In N. Nasir, C. Lee, R. Pea, & M. Royston (Eds.), *Reconceptualizing learning in the 21st century: The handbook of the cultural foundations of learning* (pp. 119–140). Routledge.

Green, J., Yeager, E., & Castanheira, M. (2008/2013). Talking texts into being: On the social construction of everyday life and academic knowledge in the classroom. In N. Mercer & S. Hodgkinson (Eds.), *Exploring talk in schools: Inspired by the work of Douglas Barnes* (pp. 115–130). Sage. https://dx.doi.org/10.4135/9781446279526

Green, J. L., & Bridges, S. M. (2018). Interactional ethnography. In F. Fischer, C. E. Hmelo-Silver, S. R. Goldman, & P. Reimann (Eds.), *International handbook of the learning sciences* (pp. 475–488). Routledge.

Green, J. L., Castanheira, M. L., & Yeager, B. V. (2011). Researching the opportunities for learning for students with learning difficulties in classrooms: An ethnographic perspective. In C. Wyatt-Smith et al (Eds.), *Multiple perspectives on difficulties in learning literacy and numeracy* (pp. 49–90). Springer Publishers.

Green, J. L., Franquiz, M., & Dixon, C. (1997). The myth of the objective transcript: Transcribing as a situated act. *TESOL Quarterly, 31*(1), 172–176.

Green, J. L., & Harker, J. O. (1988). *Multiple perspective analysis of classroom discourse.* Ablex.

Green, J. L., & Kelly, G. J. (2019). Appendix a: How we look at discourse: Definitions of sociolinguistic units. In G. J. Kelly & J. L. Green (Eds.), *Theory and methods for sociocultural research in science and engineering education* (pp. 264–270). Routledge.

Green, J. L., & Wallat, C. (1981). *Mapping instructional conversations.* In J. L. Green & C. Wallat (Eds.), *Ethnography and language in educational settings* (pp. 161–208). Ablex.

Gumperz, J. J. (1982). *Discourse strategies.* Cambridge University Press.

Heap, J. L. (1995). The status of claims in "qualitative" educational research. *Curriculum Inquiry, 25*(3), 271–292. doi: 10.1080/03626784.1995.11076182.

Heath, S. B., & Street, B. V. (2008). *On ethnography: Approaches to language and literacy research.* Teachers College Press.

Heras, A. (1994). The construction of understanding in a bilingual sixth-grade class. *Linguistics and Education, 5*, 275–299.

Hymes, D. (1972). Introduction. In Cazden, C., John, V., & Hymes, D. (Eds.), *Functions of language in the classroom.* Teachers College.

Ivanič, R. (1994). I is for interpersonal: Construction of writer identities and the teaching of writing. *Linguistics and Education, 6*, 3–15.

Kumpulainen, K. (2019). Commentary: Constructing transparency in designing and conducting multilayered research in science and engineering education. In G. J. Kelly & J. L. Green (Eds.), *Theory and methods for sociocultural research in science and engineering education* (pp. 256–264). Routledge.

Kumpulainen, K., Hmelo-Silver, C., & Cesar, M., (Eds.) (2009), *Investigating classroom interaction: Methodologies in action.* Sense Publishers.

Lin, L. (1993). Language of and in the classroom: Constructing the patterns of social life. *Linguistics and Education, 5* (3&4), 367–410.

Markee, N. (Ed.) (2015). *Handbook of classroom discourse and interaction.* Wiley.

McDermott, R. P., Gospodinoff, K., & Aron, J. (1978). Criteria for an ethnographically adequate description of concerted activities and their contexts. *Semiotica, 24*, 245–275.

Mills, H. (1993). Becoming a mathematician: Building a situated definition of mathematics. *Linguistics and Education, 5*(3–4), 301–334.

Mitchell, C. J. (1984). Typicality and the case study. In R. F. Ellen (Ed.), *Ethnographic research: A guide to general conduct* (pp. 238–241). Academic Press.

Ochs, E. (1979). Transcription as theory. In E. Ochs & B. Schieffelin (Eds.), *Developmental pragmatics* (pp. 43–72). Academic Press.

Putney, L., Green, J. L., Dixon, C., Durán, R., & Yeager, B. (1999). Consequential progressions: Exploring collective-individual development in a bilingual classroom. In C. Lee & P. Smagorinsky (Eds.), *Constructing meaning through collaborative inquiry: Vygotskian perspectives on literacy research* (pp. 86–126). Cambridge University Press.

Rex, L., Graciano, S. C., & Steadman, M. K. (2006). Researching the complexity of classroom interaction. In J. Green, G. Camilli, & P. Elmore (Eds.), *Handbook of complementary methods in education research* (pp. 727–771). Lawrence Erlbaum Associates.

Smith, L. M. (1978). An evolving logic of participant observation, educational ethnography and other case studies. *Review of Research in Education, 6*, 318–377. https://doi.org/10.2307/1167249

Spradley, J. P. (1980/2016). *Participant observation*. Holt, Rinehart, & Winston.

Woods, D. (1982). *The power of maps*. The Guilford Press.

Yeager, B. (2003). *I am a historian: Examining the discursive construction of local situated academic identities in linguistically diverse settings*. Unpublished dissertation, University of California, Santa Barbara.

Yeager, B., Green, J., & Castanheira, M. (2009). Two languages, One community: On the discursive construction of community in bilingual classrooms. In K. Kumpulainen & M. Cesar (Eds.), *Social interactions in multicultural settings* (pp. 235–268). Sense Publishers.

Zaharlick, A., & Green, J. L. (1991). Ethnographic research. In J. Flood, J. S. Jensen, D. Lapp, & J. Squire (Eds.), *Handbook on research on teaching the English language arts* (pp. 205–226). Macmillan.

11

ANCHORING ANALYSIS IN RICH POINTS

Kim Skinner

This chapter explores how rich points (Agar, 2006) as analytic anchors foreground insiders' understandings and illuminate the cultural patterns and shared meanings of members of a group. Using examples from a study grounded in an interactional ethnographic (IE) logic of inquiry, I demonstrate how to construct systematic analyses (logic-in-use) by identifying and "chasing" a rich point. In the first section of the chapter, I introduce Agar's notions of rich points and languaculture and discuss the role of rich points as anchors of analysis in IE research. In the second section, I present the context for an ethnographic study conducted with participants in a Children as Philosophers club and discuss how I reframed my insider status when an unexpected difference in understanding (rich point) occurred. In the third section, I demonstrate how the nonlinear systematic analyses of a rich point within and across group members' linked sequences of activity make visible how participants individually and collectively engage in processes and practices of knowledge construction. The chapter concludes with recommendations for scholars interested in using rich points as anchors for analysis.

Rich Points and Languaculture

As an analytic anchor in IE research, a rich point, either verbal or nonverbal, is an expression or action by an individual or group within a cultural context (e.g., social space of a group) that is surprising or puzzling to a cultural outsider. Once a rich point appears, the researcher seeks understanding by "chasing" the rich point (backward and forward tracing across time, space, events, and people), to compare and contrast discursive interactions

DOI: 10.4324/9781003215479-14

across people and situations (Agar, 2006). Rich point analyses make transparent patterns (and changes in patterns) of interaction over time and the consequences of those changes, individually and collectively, for members of a group.

Defined by Agar (2006) as *departures from expectations*, rich points show "a difference between what you know and what you need to learn to understand and explain what just happened" (p. 9). Rich points signal a learning opportunity, a point in time and space that indicates a difference between languacultures. Languaculture, Agar (1994, 1996) explained, refers to the prior knowledge and situational information language users draw on; cultural knowledge and meanings intertwine between language and culture, or languaculture.

In any study, the ethnographer and members of a studied group each bring their own languaculture to all encounters, and the languacultural processes and practices become visible when a rich point occurs, signaling a difference between the languacultures. When a rich point is identified in a communicative situation, analyses of the rich point across levels of scale and domains of experience enable the ethnographic researcher to make visible how participants co-construct processes, practices, and relevant contexts of knowledge construction in a learning environment (Skukauskaitė & Girdzijauskienė, 2021).

Drawing on examples from a study with a teacher and students in an after-school philosophy club, in this chapter I demonstrate how knowledge was discursively and interactionally constructed by the teacher and students participating in a philosophy club through rich point analyses framed by IE epistemology's focus on holistic understandings and insider meanings. Before discussing how I identified and chased a rich point in this study, let me first conceptualize and contextualize the study, including my positionality as a researcher.

Contextualizing This Languacultural World

The purpose of the study employed here to illustrate how to construct systematic analyses by identifying and chasing rich points, was to investigate the construction of the situated practices of discussion by members of an after-school children's philosophy club. To examine the discursive interactions of students and their teacher in this setting, I adopted an ethnographic perspective. Through the adoption of IE as an epistemology (Green et al., 2012), a *way of knowing* (Agar, 2006), I viewed the classroom as a culture-in-the-making (Collins & Green, 1992; Putney & Frank, 2008) in which members of a classroom construct social and academic knowledge and develop shared ways of acting, speaking, and interpreting as they affiliate over time; the norms and expectations, roles and relationships, and rights and obligations for successful participation are created by the teacher and students.

The Children as Philosophers Club Context

In this section, I describe the student and teacher participants, the site for the study, the Children as Philosophers club program, and my background and positionality as the researcher.

The Students

Twenty racially and socioeconomically diverse grade four students (9- and 10-year-olds) who attended an elementary school in the mid-southern US participated in the study. Twelve girls and eight boys took part in the weekly sessions of the after-school *Children as Philosophers* club over the span of a school year. Of the 20 students, school records classified four students as "gifted and talented", nine students as "general education" learners, and seven students as academically "at-risk". The children enrolled in the club on a first-come-first-selected basis, determined by the date/time they returned signed consent/assent forms to the school office. Two students had a parent who was an employee of the school (a grade four English Language Arts teacher and a school bus driver), and all student participants' parents arranged for their own transportation home. When pseudonyms were needed for reporting the results of the study, each student chose his or her pseudonym.

The Teacher

With 27 years' experience in public education and a PhD in Curriculum and Instruction from a nearby public university, Dr. N developed and taught the after-school Children as Philosophers club. Employed during the day as the school's gifted and talented teacher, this energetic educator characterized herself as an "iconoclastic teacher and a stubborn individualist" who enjoys teaching children because "every day brings something new". Dr. N stated in her first interview that she valued the teaching experience in the philosophy club due to its freedom from school-related stress, and its potential to develop critical thinking skills in elementary-age children (Dawes et al., 2000).

As the teacher for the club, Dr. N participated with the researcher in planning sessions the day before each scheduled philosophy club session. She wrote lesson plans, read discussion guides, and identified children's literature for group discussions. As the group facilitator, she modeled and explained all instructional content and strategies, assisted the progression of group discussions, and was the contact for all administrative questions that arose about club activities. As a study participant, she inscribed descriptive and reflective notes immediately after each session, answered questions during planned interviews and insight-seeking informal interviews, and member checked transcripts and drafts.

The Elementary School and Classroom

Located in a small-town coastal community in the mid-southern US, a one-story, red brick public elementary school was the site for the study. School enrollment was 466 students, all in grades four and five. The Children as Philosophers club met for one hour most Thursdays in Dr. N's classroom at the end of the main hall immediately after regular classes were dismissed.

Before each philosophy club session, the teacher moved the classroom furniture against the walls to open the center of the room for the children to sit in a circular seating arrangement on the floor rug. The teacher, also a part of the circle, sat in a chair next to the easel during club sessions. Posted on the wall adjacent to the seating area was a chart titled, "Community Rules for Having a Philosophical Conversation." As a reminder of the practices of discussion in the philosophy club, the teacher and students chorally read the Rules chart at the beginning of each session.

Community Rules for Having a Philosophical Conversation
Listen to each other
Think before you speak
Be respectful
Wait for a pause
Let others have a turn
Give reasons for your beliefs
Build on each other's ideas
(I agree with _____ because _____,
I disagree with _____ because _____)
Ask each other questions (I have a question about _____)
There are no "right" answers

In addition to the visibility of the Rules chart, the seating arrangement in the Children as Philosophers club allowed students to direct their questions and responses to any speaker with ease, and the proximity to others in the group enabled listeners/speakers to hear and be heard (Skinner, 2015).

The Children as Philosophers Program

The discussion format introduced by the teacher in the Children as Philosophers club followed Lipman's (2003) guidelines for philosophical inquiry: to listen to one another, build on others' ideas, supply reasons for your beliefs, and draw inferences from the discussion. The teacher's pedagogical goal was that the children *do* philosophy, that they learn to incorporate logical considerations and evaluate their own and others' thinking during discussion (Lipman, 2003; Matthews, 1994).

Dr. N created lesson plans for the Children as Philosophers club drawing from Lipman's (1974) *Philosophy for Children* curriculum focused on children's participation rights, and Matthews' (1994) *Philosophy for Kids* discussion guides using stories as a catalyst for philosophical discussion. Dr. N sought to disrupt the *default* model of classroom discourse, in which the attention and gaze is on the teacher, who controls the patterns of interaction and the predetermined path of the discussion (Cazden, 2001). Each weekly session, the teacher would read a children's book followed by guiding questions as prompts for discussion. The teacher and students explored big ideas framed as questions, such as: What is real? What is truth? What is fair? What makes you you?

Researcher Positioning and Reflexivity

As the researcher for the study, my role in this community shifted between colleague and mentor, ethnographer and community member, field-based researcher and interactive designer, and initiator and analyst. My teaching background experience included 13 years as an elementary school teacher, 2 years as a reading specialist, and 5 years as an educational consultant. My interest and experience with Philosophy for Children stemmed from participation in a summer residential workshop hosted by Montclair State University during which I read curriculum, wrote curriculum, and learned the pedagogical framework for *doing* philosophy with young children. Following the summer workshop, a local grant funded the creation of a Philosophy for Children after-school club that I taught for three consecutive semesters in a suburban school.

Even with considerable prior experience conducting and evaluating philosophical inquiry with children, I was surprised by the rich points revealed through student-teacher and student-student discourse during discussion in this philosophy club. As a member of this community from its inception, I possessed substantial insider knowledge and status in the Children as Philosophers club. Thus, when I first encountered a rich point during Session 7 in this yearlong after-school club, I stepped back, adopting an outsider stance to understand what happened in the moment and over time. Stepping back, I employed backward and forward mapping to understand why the rich point occurred and how it could reveal the cultural meanings and patterns for members of the club.

Thus, as the researcher, I alternately viewed the classroom culture from an emic (insider) and etic (outsider) perspective – terms derived in origin and pronunciation from phonemic and phonetic (Pike, 1954) – as each view is a *way of seeing;* an *orientation,* not a *membership* (Wolcott, 1999). The teacher explained my role to the children at the first session and they seemed almost oblivious to me and my note taking. My regular presence in the sessions allowed the children to view my presence as an ordinary part of this community.

Logic-in-Use

The need to focus on the roots of, and decisions guiding, my logic–in–use was framed over four decades ago by Birdwhistell (1977). He proposed a subtle, and often overlooked, distinction between *logic of inquiry* and *logic-in-use.* Drawing on Bateson's argument that *theory is method* and *method is theory,* Birdwhistell argued that for anthropologists (and by extension other researchers), fieldnotes and other forms of records (e.g., video and audio, documents, photographs) are not the observed phenomena; rather, through the logic-in-use, the analyst constructs particular accounts and warranted claims of what is captured on such records (Baker & Green, 2015).

For this study situated in a Children as Philosophers club, I adopted an IE perspective to explore the cultural knowledge of the group through a recursive, abductive, iterative, and nonlinear logic-in-use (Agar, 2006; Green et al., 2012). Drawing on work in interactional sociolinguistics (Cook-Gumperz, 2006; Gumperz, 1986; Hymes, 1974), literary theory (Bakhtin, 1981), discourse analysis (Bloome et al., 2005; Bloome et al., 2009; Fairclough, 2003; Gee & Green, 1998), and research examining language use in classrooms (e.g., Cazden, 2001; Mercer & Hodgkinson, 2008), I framed this study from the perspective that meaning and significance are located in the social and historical interactions of the teacher and students.

In prior ethnographic studies of classrooms-as-cultures (e.g., Collins & Green, 1992; Green & Dixon, 1993) and the intertextual nature of classroom life (Bloome & Egan-Robertson, 1993), researchers demonstrated the significance of the historical, structural, and intertextual development of an educational setting for understanding participants' interactions. Rich points are spaces for locating cultural knowledge in the interactions. Through systematic analyses (logic-in-use) employed in the study of a Children as Philosophers club, I show how I identified and chased a rich point to make visible how knowledge was constructed by the teacher and students participating in the philosophy club.

Before the Rich Point: Constructing Records

Before identifying and chasing a rich point, the researcher constructs records from observations in the field. As an IE researcher, I constructed extensive records and varied kinds of data. Collected through active participant observation, the data sources included jottings; full fieldnotes; video records of sessions and semi-structured interviews; audio records of informal interviews; transcriptions of sessions, semi-structured interviews, and informal interviews; children's reflection journals; teacher's lesson plans; and classroom artifacts.

Inscribing Jottings and Full Fieldnotes

Fieldnotes are lived experiences reduced to textual form (Emerson et al., 2011). Geertz (1973) explained that by inscribing social discourse, the ethnographer turns observed occurrences into accounts which can be revisited. To chronicle my observations from the philosophy club sessions, I kept a fieldnotes journal divided into three column headings: index (for time stamps and changes in activity), descriptive notes (accounts, dialogue, and descriptions of setting or interactions), and reflective notes (personal thoughts, ideas, and speculation). These initial notes, or *jottings* (Emerson et al., 2011), allowed me to quickly capture as much as possible from the field. On the first day, I sketched the classroom environment and noted how the teacher moved the furniture before each session. For each session, I inscribed notes as soon as the first student arrived in the classroom. During each planning meeting with the teacher, I wrote notes about the teacher's lesson plan decisions and the rationale for her decisions. Each time after leaving the field, I typed up and expanded my initial jottings into full fieldnotes.

Creating Video and Audio Records

As a primary data source, I videotaped each philosophy club session and participant interview. Video recording commenced 5 minutes before each session and ended when the last student left. Through the use of a video camera on a tripod facing the group, I recorded how and when events and group members' interactions began and ended in every session. In addition to club meetings, I recorded all planned interviews with the teacher and students. I audiotaped the shorter, informal interviews using my cell phone.

Transcribing Video and Audio Records

As transcription decisions determine the records available for analyses and the representation of the field, my first level of analysis was the transcription of the video records of philosophy club sessions (Skukauskaitė, 2014). In initial transcription from the video records, line numbers corresponded to participants' turns of talk. The video transcripts were then further converted from simple transcripts that represented turns of talk to transcripts in which the line numbers represented a message unit.

Following Green and Wallat (1981), I considered a message unit as the smallest unit of meaning in conversation. Message units were identified through group members' use of contextualization cues, including pausing and changes in volume. My final analytic transcriptions of sessions included line numbers, speakers, discursive message units, and contextualization cues, including changes in volume, questioning, and pausing. For the interviews, however, the video and audio records were transcribed at sentence level, much like dialogue in a screenplay.

Learning from Interviews

At the beginning, middle, and end of the study, I conducted semi-structured interviews (Brenner, 2006; Kvale & Brinkman, 2009) with the teacher and four students chosen as key participants for their ability to inform the study through insiders' perspectives and member checking. I also conducted informal interviews when further understanding was needed, as member checks, or after a rich point occurred.

Identifying the Rich Point

In spite of my insider status in this cultural context, when conducting ethnographic research there are moments when something unexpected occurs. These points that signal a difference, a surprise, and a departure from expectations are rich points, points where learning and culture become visible (Agar, 2006). As I conducted this study, I was on the lookout for rich points.

Session 7, the Children as Philosophers club session immediately following the winter holidays, began much like the preceding sessions. The students entered the classroom and found a seat along the edges of the floor rug. At 3:45PM, Dr. N conducted the first event, the community meeting, with the students chorally reading the Rules chart. At 3:55PM, Dr. N introduced the book *Tusk Tusk* by McKee (2007).

The book depicts two groups of forest-dwelling elephants (one group of elephants is black and the other group is white) that wage war on each other over their perceived differences. However, each group of elephants has members that are peace-loving, and while the war-loving elephants in each group fight and kill each other, the peace-loving elephants of both colors hide deep in the forest. Years later, when the peace-loving elephants finally emerge from the forest, they are all gray. The story ends with a few of the gray, peace-loving elephants starting to notice there are differences in the size of some elephants' ears.

The theme of prejudice and difference in this narrative proved complex for the children. One student, Monroe (a pseudonym), twice signaled that she was struggling with comprehension of the text and clamored for the conversation to stop as she grappled with the meaning of the characters' actions. Then, her frustration evident, she pressed for a second reading of the book, using "we" as she gazed at her classmates, but switching to "you" as she switched her gaze to the teacher. Below is the Session 7 message unit transcript excerpt of this moment in time.

Speaker	Message unit
Monroe	1 wait
	2 I'm confused
	3 there's no nice
	4 or bad one here
	...
Teacher	5 okay
	6 we will come back
	7 to you
	8 think about it
	9 what was it about
	...
Monroe	10 WHAT
	11 wait wait wait
	12 I don't get that
	13 can we
	14 can you
	15 please just read it
	16 over again?
Teacher	17 okay
	18 well
	19 maybe I DO need
	20 to read the book
	21 again

While Dr. N's lesson plan only indicated a single reading of the book, she acknowledged Monroe's confusion and agreed to reread the story.

Researcher Noted the Difference

Sitting at a table just a few feet behind the circle of philosophy club members, I immediately time stamped 4:12 with a star in my fieldnotes journal and inscribed my surprise at Monroe's request to alter the planned events for today, and also my surprise at the Dr. N's agreement to make the change. Never before had a student suggested altering the events in the philosophy club.

Never before had the teacher added an event not included in her lesson plan. I recorded the incident in my fieldnotes.

Time Stamp 3:55	event-Read-aloud	T read Tusk Tusk by McKee
Time Stamp 4:07	event-Discussions	Qs What is peace? What is hate? What causes war?
Time Stamp 4:12★	event changed by S request!	Now back to teacher read-aloud!

While the students were writing in their reflection journals at the end of class, I noted in the reflexive column of my fieldnotes journal that the students were "so animated today with so many questions." I also inscribed that Monroe accessed her participation rights today, and the teacher allowed Monroe to change the planned activities of the lesson. Even though I was an insider in this club since before its inception, this request and change in events was a such a *departure from expectations*, particularly as the change in events was student initiated. Rich points are those markers of a difference, a surprise, in members of a studied groups' discourse or actions—this was without question a rich point!

But what did it mean? How would it help me understand the culture of this after-school philosophy club? It was time for the chase.

Chasing the Rich Point Through People and Events

As Agar (2006) stipulates, once a rich point occurs, the ethnographer must "chase the rich point" (p. 6). Rich points provide an anchor for multilayered analyses that enable IE researchers to make visible the patterned ways of saying, knowing, being and doing of a group. I wanted to compare the events of Session 7 to the events available to philosophy club members in the previous sessions. So, I went back to my notes and the video transcripts of Sessions 1–6 (backward mapped) and created a structuration map of the type and sequence of events in Sessions 1–7.

Backward Mapping: Tracing Philosophy Club Events

Repeated rereading and examining my notes and the transcripts for Sessions 1–7 made visible the type and sequence of events available to club members within and across each session. Building on studies which investigated how what is constructed in the first day of class is consequential to the future patterns and practices of the group (cf., Castanheira et al., 2000; Lin, 1994), for this level of analysis I constructed a structuration map (Green et al., 2007) to illustrate the structure of the *Children as Philosophers* club across time. I examined the video recordings, video transcripts, and fieldnotes of the seven philosophy club sessions to create a representation of the structure that provided the type and sequence of events constructed across time and sessions by participants in the *Children as Philosophers* club.

To identify what counted as an event, I drew on the work of classroom researchers who located and characterized events as products of interactions, identified by observing how time was utilized, by whom, when, where, under what conditions, for what purposes, and with what outcomes (Castanheira et al., 2000; Green & Meyer, 1991). From this perspective, an event is a set of activities bound together by a common theme or purpose. Through this analysis, I located the study in time and space, giving context to analyses that followed.

Analysis of this representation enabled me to see how the events developed over time as they were formulated and re-formulated throughout the moment-to-moment actions and interactions of the participants (Green et al., 2003). As indicated in Table 11.1, each session began with a community meeting and this event functioned as an opportunity for participants to share personal issues or successes, recap previous sessions, review the Rules chart, and participate in an instructional lesson. A teacher read-aloud (teacher reading of children's literature) typically followed the community meeting, followed by questions and a philosophical conversation about the book read, and written reflection by participants.

The reading of children's literature event in all sessions included a brief introduction of the text and an oral reading of the text, both enacted by the teacher. Every time any text was read in this cultural space, the students sat in a circle on the floor and the teacher sat in a chair that was a part of the group circle. The rereading of children's literature event included the oral reading of the text by the teacher, but unlike the first reading, the teacher did not introduce the text prior to the rereading. As previously mentioned, the rereading of the text was prompted by a student request.

The philosophical conversation event took place after the reading of children's literature event. Subevents included the generation of questions for discussion by the teacher and/or students related to the theme of the book read. The teacher recorded the questions on chart paper, for easy referral during the discussion. The children could freely participate in the discussion without nomination by the teacher.

For the reflection journals event, in each session the students wrote about their interpretation of the text in reflection journals (five-inch by seven-inch composition notebooks). The students were sometimes given the option of sharing what they wrote with the group, but that practice was voluntary and infrequent.

During Session 2 and Session 3, Dr. N directed the students to stop and write before, instead of after, the discussion of literature. The teacher's stated purpose for altering the sequence of the reflection journals event was to give

TABLE 11.1 Type and Sequence of Events in Children as Philosophers Club

Session	Event 1	Event 2	Event 3	Event 4	Event 5	Event 6
1	Community Meeting	Reading of Children's Literature	Philosophical Conversation	Reflection Journals		
2	Community Meeting	Reading of Children's Literature	Reflection Journals	Philosophical Conversation		
3	Community Meeting	Reading of Children's Literature	Reflection Journals	Philosophical Conversation		
4	Community Meeting	Reading of Children's Literature	Philosophical Conversation	Reflection Journals		
5	Community Meeting	Reading of Children's Literature	Philosophical Conversation	Reflection Journals		
6	Community Meeting	Reading of Children's Literature	Philosophical Conversation	Reflection Journals		
7	Community Meeting	Reading of Children's Literature (1)	Philosophical Conversation (1)	Reading of Children's Literature (2)	Philosophical Conversation (2)	Reflection Journals

students the time and space to record their thinking before hearing others' views in the discussion. However, as Table 11.1 shows, the activity of writing in reflection journals before the discussion was discontinued after Session 3. After two sessions of writing before speaking (a practice adopted to "force students to think about their ideas before jumping into the discussion"), Dr. N concluded that writing beforehand "doesn't seem to be leading to a deeper discussion of the topics at all. If anything, I think it is hurting the discussion by taking away valuable minutes and not allowing the children to immediately engage with each other" (researcher's notes from Session 4 planning session).

Changes in type and sequence of activities available within and across sessions reveals the evolving and dynamic nature of the club, and the variance in opportunities made available to the students in any given session. As Table 11.1 shows, only in Session 7 was the book reread by the teacher and a second discussion of the literature accomplished. This variation was not planned in advance and was not duplicated again. The type and sequence of events in Session 7 were unique: unique in structure, content, and purpose.

Backward Mapping: Showing What Pre-empted Change

Building on studies which investigated how what is constructed in the first day of class is consequential to the future patterns and practices of the group (cf. Castanheira et al., 2000; Lin, 1994), for the next level of analysis I constructed a structuration map (Green et al., 2007) from the Session 1 transcript and field-notes to make visible the rights and responsibilities for discussion provided by the teacher on the first day of the Children as Philosophers club (Table 11.2).

In Session 1, the teacher characterized discussion in the Children as Philosophers club as a "NEW kind of discussion" (lines 221–222). The teacher envisioned the philosophy club as a place where questioning by the children would be supported and valued, and the questions themselves would have value, regardless of whether or not they led to answers.

During discussion in this philosophy club community, discussants had the rights to agree, disagree, or question others' views. However, these rights included the responsibility that "we never/make fun/of anyone's ideas" (lines 374–376). The classroom environment was framed as safe, risk-free, and caring; students had the responsibility to maintain that environment through kindness.

Students also had the responsibility to "give reasons for what you're thinking" (lines 559–560). While they had the right to agree or disagree with the responses of others, they could only do so if they gave a reason for their views. Thus, with the rights also came responsibilities, and combined, they provided students with access, power, and the opportunity to think critically about their views and the views of others.

The rights and responsibilities in the philosophy club were also revealed by the teacher's framing of participation in this community. Explicitly stated,

TABLE 11.2 Framing Philosophy Club Members' Rights and Responsibilities for Discussion

Line	Teacher's discourse	Actions signaled through the discourse
219	this is a place	Framing discussion in the philosophy
220	where we are going to learn	club as new and needing to learned
221	to have a NEW	
222	kind of discussion	
(…)		
368	in our community	Identifying right of discussants to
369	we can agree	agree or disagree with other's ideas
370	or disagree	
371	with ideas	
372	we can ask people questions	Identifying right of discussants to
373	about their ideas	question other's
374	but we never	
375	make fun	Framing classroom environment as
376	of anyone's ideas	safe and caring
(…)		
546	we are going to learn about	Framing teaching and learning goals
547	some great thinkers	for philosophy club members
548	some philosophers	
549	and their ideas	
550	I'm going to read you	Identifying teacher as access-provider
551	some interesting books	to thought-provoking books
552	books that will make you think	
(…)		
559	and you'll give reasons	Identifying students' responsibility to
560	for what you're thinking	provide reasons
(…)		
563	my role during our conversations	Locating teacher's responsibility
564	will be to get you started	during discussion
565	but after that	
566	you guys are in control	Framing students' access rights and
567	of who talks in this community	responsibilities during discussion
568	and you're in control	
569	of what you talk about	
(…)		
584	when you want to talk	Locating students' participation rights
585	just join	
586	join the conversation	
587	you don't have to raise your hand	
588	or wait on me to call on you	

the teacher viewed her role as a facilitator of the discussion, sharing authority with the children, as "you guys are in control/of who talks in this community" (lines 566–567) and "and you're in control/of what you talk about" (lines 568–569). The children had the right to act as discussion leaders, with the locus of control intentionally shifting from teacher to students after Dr. N read the book.

The final right articulated by Dr. N in these Session 1 transcript excerpts is the right of the children to self-nominate for turns-of-talk. This opportunity gave the students participation rights that they did not have during the school day, as their teachers determined who had the right to speak in the students' daytime classes.

Backward and Forward Mapping at Moment of Rich Point

The historical context of the Session 7 events pointed to the need for further levels of analysis to understand why, how, and with what consequences the events of this session varied from prior sessions. To understand this rich point, I used a backward and forward mapping approach to return to the points of time in the group members' discourse immediately before and after the rich point, to identify the reasons for the unexpected and unplanned rereading of the text.

Table 11.3 locates the discourse segment in which the student, Monroe, appealed for the change in read aloud practices during the group discussion.

TABLE 11.3 Analysis of Transcript Excerpt of the Rich Point

Line	Discussant	Discourse	Action signaled
076	Monroe	wait	Requesting halt in conversation
077		I'm confused	Signaling confusion
078		there's no nice	
079		or bad one here	
080	Teacher	okay	Controlling turns of talk
081		we will come back	
082		to you	
083		think about it	Signaling need for reflection
084		what was it about?	
(…)			
108	Monroe	WHAT?	Repeating request to halt conversation
109		wait wait wait	
110		I don't get that	Displaying confusion
111		can we	Appealing for repetition of previous
112		can you	event, to reread book
113		please just read it	
114		over again	
115	Teacher	okay	Consenting to student's request for new
116		well	activity, rereading of book
117		maybe I DO need	
118		to read the book	
119		again	
(…)			
123		okay	Locating the purpose for the repeated
124		good discussion so far	reading of book
125		but let's reread	
126		and try to clear up	
127		the misunderstandings	

Less than one minute before the rich point, Monroe signaled she was having difficulty with comprehension of the characters' actions and the meaning of those actions. She then repeated her call for the conversation, followed by a request to the teacher to read the book again. No participants objected to the rereading and all students looked intently at the illustrations and words of the text as the teacher reread the book, *Tusk Tusk*.

As demonstrated in Table 11.3, Monroe's recurring indication of confusion of the meaning of the text was the impetus for her appeal to the group to discontinue the discussion and for the teacher to read the book again. Monroe's petition made visible the power she possessed to influence the teacher's actions and thus the activities available to the group. However, through a closer examination of the video records comparing her discursive actions, I found that while Monroe demanded the group halt the conversation, when she turned toward the teacher, she lowered the volume of her voice. This time her appeal took the form of a question, a request, with "please" inserted midway through the discourse. By asserting power in different ways when addressing the group or the teacher, she made visible her belief that power was not equally distributed in this context and acknowledged that the teacher controlled the access to the text for all participants.

Dr. N resumed her instructor role when she agreed to Monroe's plea for a repeated reading of the text. The teacher evaluated the previous conversation with the comment "good discussion so far" (line 124). As this excerpt from Session 7 shows, Dr. N further positions herself as the content designer by setting a purpose for the second reading of the book: "let's reread/and try to clear up/the misunderstandings" (lines 125–127). Her use of "let's" in the first line indicates Dr. N's desire to remain a part of the group and points to her understanding that the children must first comprehend the text before they can engage in dialogue in which they warrant their claims. Though an individual student initiated this learning opportunity, the outcome of the change provided opportunity for construction of meaning for the collective.

Forward Mapping: Making Visible the Consequences of the Rich Point

Using a forward mapping approach for analysis of the rich point allowed me to see beyond the change, to determine the consequences of the change for the group and individuals. As the analysis makes transparent, the rights and responsibilities of group members in this Philosophy Club were fluid as members of the group negotiated and renegotiated those rights and responsibilities discursively and interactionally. In the transcript segments shown in Table 11.4, several students provide evidence of this process by discursively asserting their authority in the conversation that occurred after the second reading of the book.

TABLE 11.4 Students Enacting Rights and Responsibilities

Line	Student	Eye gaze	Discourse	Students' actions
076	Monroe	Gazing fixedly at teacher	wait	Requesting halt in conversation
(...)				
108 109	Monroe	Gazing at multiple students	WHAT? wait wait wait	Repeating request to halt conversation
(...)				
111 112 113 114	Monroe	Gazing at students, then turning gaze to teacher	can we can you please just read it over again	Appealing to students, then teacher to reread book
(...)				
133 134 135	Monroe	Gazing at two other students	okay don't talk at the same time	Assuming authority, controlling the *floor*
(...)				
156 157 158 159	Lonnie	Gazing around the circle at students	is this like the war between Martin Luther King? you know the whites and the blacks?	Querying students about connection to content learned during school day
(...)				
168 169	Monroe	Gazing at multiple students	how did this turn into about people?	Attempting to redirect topic of discussion
(...)				
182 183 184 185	Marlee	Gazing at student who just spoke	I disagree with that it's good but they're not worried about it	Evaluating previous student's response
(...)				
238	Maddie	Gazing at Monroe	go ahead	Assigning turn-of-talk
(...)				
290 291 292	Monroe	Gazing at multiple students	and guys I think Marlee and Trentin are right	Evaluating correctness of previous students' responses
(...)				
358 359 360	Monroe	Gazing around the circle at students	and we're supposed to be concentrating on what is peace	Admonishing students, redirecting attention to one of the questions on chart
361	Marlee	Gazing at Monroe	what is HATE	Competing for control of discussion topic, citing another question on chart
362	Monroe	Gazing at Marlee	what is PEACE	Disagreeing on discussion topic
363 364	Marlee & Eva	Gazing at Marlee	(in unison) NO WHAT IS HATE	Correcting another student, using volume for control

My examination of these Session 7 transcript segments of student talk and actions during the discussion revealed that various students successfully enacted many of the practices common of a teacher guiding a group discussion, specifically, controlling the floor (lines 133–135), assigning turns of talk (line 238), initiating a group question with connection to prior knowledge (lines 156–159), changing the topic of discussion (168–169), and evaluating students' responses (lines 182–185 and 290–292). The successful accomplishment of the practices of a discussion leader by several individuals demonstrated that the collective recognized the authority of individuals besides the teacher to direct the discussion.

In other instances, however, the students attempted to appropriate the role of discussion leader but the effort was either not acknowledged or was challenged by other students, thus the bid was unsuccessful. When Monroe attempted to redirect the discussion with a knowledge-level question about the characters in the book by posing "how did this turn into/about people?" (lines 168–169), her effort failed, and the students continued their discussion of relationships between black and white people, instead of elephants.

The final time Monroe attempted to redirect the path of the discussion by arguing "we're supposed to be/concentrating on/what is peace" (lines 358–360), she warranted her appeal as a return to the norms and expectations for the discussion topic, as the discussion had moved away from the initial questions formulated. However, one student, soon joined by another, adamantly disagreed, not to the restoration of the initial focus of the discussion, but to what question represented the appropriate focus, and thus theme, of the literature under scrutiny.

In both instances, when the student's attempts at adopting the role of discussion leader failed, the teacher intervened. This analysis makes visible that the students successfully adopted the role of discussion leader in some instances and vied with other students for control of the direction of the discussion in other instances during this situated philosophical conversation event.

The outcome of Dr. N's second reading of the text and subsequent discussion of the literature was the absence of confusion and evidence of comprehension in the students' responses. The allocation of time by the teacher, time originally designated strictly for discussion but interrupted and partially appropriated for a second reading, demonstrates the adaptable structure she maintained for the club and her willingness to adjust her practices based on students' needs. Comprehension of the text by the students was facilitated and enhanced by the student's request and the teacher's support of the request to reread the book. Time in this setting was used by the teacher as a resource, and its purpose in use was to provide opportunities for students to reason together and construct meaning.

Forward Mapping: Students' Awareness Conversation Has Changed

The students participating in the second Session 7 philosophical conversation event were aware this conversation varied from previous conversations. The students' appropriation of turns of talk, access, and control resulted in the students speaking directly to each other about the text and their ideas in a confrontational manner. At the 30:42 time marker, 16 minutes and 32 seconds after the second conversation commenced, Lonnie appealed to the teacher to intervene and direct the conversation, as illustrated in Table 11.5.

In the midst of often-pointed back and forth student-to-student interaction, Lonnie looked directly at the teacher and pleaded with her to resolve the debate. By petitioning the teacher, Lonnie indicated his level of discomfort with the conversation and his desire for the teacher to reassert her power to resolve the conversation. Two other students supported his request, as both began their subsequent turns of talk with "yeah" (lines 268 and 274) and also noted the argumentative nature of the discussion. Lonnie's appeal and the discursive affirmations by two other students for teacher intervention and resolution represent the second time in Session 7 that students requested the teacher intervene in the events of this session. The teacher concluded the discussion by

TABLE 11.5 Noticing Difference in This Conversation

Line	Discussant	Discourse	Action signaled
260	Lonnie	I only have one question	Appealing to teacher
261		to ask Dr. N	to intervene and
262		when are we going	direct the
263		to get to the point?	conversation
264		because all these conversations	Acknowledging
265		are confusing me	discomfort with
266		I just want	conversational style
267		to get to the point	
268	Eva	yeah	Affirming need for
269		this is the longest conversation	teacher intervention
270		we've had	
271		and it's kind of like we're fighting	Characterizing features
272		some are agreeing	of conversation as
273		and some are disagreeing	different
274	Maddie	yeah	Linking conversation
275		it's kinda like the book	to content of text
276	Teacher	I think the point is	Identifying current
277		we're having a philosophical conversation	discussion as
278		and that's what doing philosophy is about	philosophical, thus
279		different points of view	not needing
280		is there a right	resolution
281		or wrong?	

labeling this discussion as a philosophical conversation and ended her response with a rhetorical question: Is there a right or wrong?

The role of the text as an opportunity to learn was also made visible by the discourse of the students in this session. In lines 274–275 of the transcript segment from Session 7, Maddie links the students' adoption of a controversial conversation style to the provocation depicted by the book characters. This link makes visible the role of the text in the interactions of the students and shows how the teacher's choice of an "interesting" text provided the means for student accomplishment of philosophical discussion.

Seeking Insiders' Meanings

For IE researchers, seeking insiders' meanings is critical for understanding. When Session 7 ended, I turned to the teacher to query if she had also noticed a difference or was surprised by the students' discourse and actions during the session. I audio recorded and later transcribed an informal interview with Dr. N. Below is an excerpt of that conversation.

RESEARCHER: Some of the events in this philosophy club session really surprised me. Was there anything different or surprising to you in today's session?

TEACHER: Well, at first the kids were not following the story, which did surprise me because I didn't see that coming. I mean, I thought the theme of the book was pretty obvious. Then Monroe just wouldn't let it go, so I reread it. I hadn't intended to, so that was unexpected, but they seemed to understand better after that.

RESEARCHER: What about how they talked to you and to each other today after you read the book again?

TEACHER: Yes, there certainly was a difference in how they discussed. Did you see how frustrated Lonnie became? He did not like how argumentative it all felt. At all. But maybe they're finally starting to stand up for what they think. They sure didn't hesitate to speak up.

As Dr. N made transparent, the students' lack of understanding and the rereading the book were not expected. She was not upset by the student-initiated change in events though, quite the contrary, reporting that adding the event seemed to benefit students' understanding. Dr. N acknowledged the difference carried over to the discussion as well. She viewed the students' confrontational engagement as a move in the right direction, stating, "maybe they're finally starting to stand up for what they think."

A few minutes before the next session, I conducted an informal group interview with three students. I chose one student due to the power she appropriated, one student who expressed discomfort with the conversation, and one student who had only responded one time during the entire conversation. I audio-taped the brief, informal group interview in the hall. Below is the transcript segment of the brief interaction that transpired.

RESEARCHER: What do you remember about last week's Children as Philosophers club? Does anything stand out to you as surprising or different?

LONNIE: Well, I mainly remember how much kinda like fighting there was about the book.

MONROE: What I remember is how glad I was that Dr. N read the book again where I could really check out the pictures. It's not very fun to talk about something when you have no idea what it's about.

COLT: A lot of stuff was different. We heard the story two times. We talked about it two times. We barely had any time left at the end to write or grab our snack.

RESEARCHER: Okay, just one more question. After seven weeks attending the philosophy club, what would you say are your rights as a member of this club?

MONROE: My rights? Like what do I have the right to do? (notices researcher nodding.) Let's see, I have the right to not raise my hand. I have the right to sit where I want in the circle. Oh, and I have the right to talk, but not talk back.

LONNIE: All I can think of is the right... like the right to tell my own opinion. Like there's no grade or anything.

COLT: I think it's all about choice. Like I can choose to just listen or to talk. Like I can just think about things if I want to. And some people are really smart.

While Monroe acknowledged the right to request a change in events, to freely participate without nomination to speak, and to have choice in seating, Colt considered the right to not talk and to choose to listen as valuable. Lonnie identified the right to express his opinion and the right to participate without evaluation or grades. Monroe also identified one of the responsibilities within the club: to not "talk back", to show respect.

What is available for the class is not always adopted in ways anticipated by the teacher, and jointly constructed opportunities for learning can have differential take-up by students (Baker, 2001; Putney et al., 2000; Tuyay et al., 1995). This study made transparent that students engaged in the same classroom tasks do not always equally access common opportunities to learn.

Discussion

In this chapter, I made visible how I constructed systematic analyses by identifying a rich point in teacher-to-student discourse and chasing the rich point, through repeated forward and backward mapping, to understand how the teacher and students constructed knowledge through participation in the Children as Philosophers club. My analysis was recursive, as I purposively constructed and re-examined data to conduct multiple analyses. My analysis was iterative, as I sought insiders' meanings through instructional conversations with participants. And my analysis was non-linear, as the analyses I conducted were not preselected but rather proceeded backwards and forward across time, people, and events after the identification of a rich point.

To chase a rich point, I had to step back from my insider's perspective to see the philosophy club with fresh eyes, from the perspective as an outsider. Stepping back allowed me to see how the children were adopting and adapting the practices of philosophers through the learning opportunities provided by the teacher, acting as a cultural guide.

Principles of Practice for Rich Points Analyses

The following principles are ones that I recommend to readers new to an IE-guided logic-in-use:

- Make transparent the logic-in-use throughout the analyses
- Collect and construct rich data sources
- Be on the lookout for rich points
- Be able to step back and alternately adopt an insider or outsider stance
- Explore insiders' meanings and be open to how those may change your perspective

Suggested Readings

Agar, M. (1999). How to ask for a study in qualitatish. *Qualitative Health Research, 9*(5), 684–697.
Edwards, D. A., & Mercer, N. (1987). *Common knowledge.* Methuen.
Spradley, J. P. (2016). *Participant observation.* Waveland.

References

Agar, M. (1994). *Language shock: Understanding the culture of conversation.* Quill.
Agar, M. (1996). *The professional stranger: An informal introduction to ethnography* (2nd ed.). Academic.
Agar, M. (2006). Culture: Can you take it anywhere? *International Journal of Qualitative Methods, 5*(2), 1–12.
Baker, W. D. (2001). *Artists in the making: An ethnographic investigation of discourse and literate practices as disciplinary processes in a high school, advanced placement studio art classroom.* Unpublished doctoral dissertation. University of California, Santa Barbara.
Baker, W. D., & Green, J. L. (2015). Transdisciplinary dialogues through interactional ethnographic studies: A commentary on Skinner. *Mind, Culture, and Activity, 22*(4), 364–370.

Bakhtin, M. M. (1981). *The dialogic imagination*. University of Texas Press.

Birdwhistell, R. (1977). Some discussion of ethnography, theory, and method. In J. Brockman (Ed.), *About Bateson: Essays on Gregory Bateson* (pp. 103–144). Dutton.

Bloome, D., & Egan-Robertson, A. (1993). The social construction of intertextuality in classroom reading and writing lessons. *Reading Research Quarterly, 28*(4), 304–334.

Bloome, D., Beierle, M., Grigorenko, M., & Goldman, S. (2009). Learning over time: Uses of intercontextuality, collective memories, and classroom chronotypes in the construction of learning opportunities in a ninth-grade language arts classroom. *Language and Education, 23*(4), 313–334.

Bloome, D., Carter, S. P., Christian, B. M., Otto, S., & Shuart-Faris, N. (2005). *Discourse analysis and the study of classroom language and literacy events: A microethnographic perspective*. Lawrence Erlbaum.

Brenner, M. E. (2006). Interviewing in educational research. In J. L. Green, G. Camilli, & P. B. Elmore (Eds.), *Handbook of complementary methods in education research* (pp. 357–370). Lawrence Erlbaum.

Castanheira, M. L., Crawford, T., Dixon, C., & Green, J. L. (2000). Interactional ethnography: An approach to studying the social construction of literate practices. *Linguistics and Education, 11*(4), 353–400.

Cazden, C. B. (2001). *Classroom discourse* (2nd ed.). Heinemann.

Collins, E., & Green, J. (1992). Learning in a classroom setting: Making or breaking a culture. In H. H. Marshall (Ed.), *Redefining student learning* (pp. 59–86). Ablex.

Cook-Gumperz, J. (2006). *The social construction of literacy* (2nd ed.). Cambridge University Press.

Dawes, L., Mercer, N., & Wegerif, R. (2000). *Thinking together: A programme of activities for developing speaking, listening, and thinking skills for children aged 8–11*. Imaginative Minds.

Emerson, R. M., Fretz, R. I., & Shaw, L. L. (2011). *Writing ethnographic fieldnotes* (2nd ed.). University of Chicago Press.

Fairclough, N. (2003). *Analysing discourse: Textual analysis for social research*. Routledge.

Gee, J. P., & Green, J. (1998). Discourse analysis, learning, and social practice: A methodological study. In P. D. Pearson & A. Iran-nejad (Eds.), *Review of research in education* (vol. 23, pp. 119–169). American Educational Research Association.

Geertz, C. (1973). Thick description: Toward an interpretive theory of culture. In C. Geertz (Ed.), *The interpretation of cultures* (pp. 3–30). Basic.

Green, J. L., & Dixon, C. N. (1993). Talking knowledge into being: Discursive and social practices in classrooms. *Linguistics and Education, 5*, 231–239.

Green, J. L., Dixon, C. N., & Zaharlick, A. (2003). Ethnography as a logic of inquiry. In J. Flood, D. Lapp, J. R. Squire, & J. M. Jensen (Eds.). *Handbook of research on teaching the English language arts* (2nd ed., pp. 201–224). Lawrence Erlbaum.

Green, J. L., & Meyer, L. A. (1991). The embeddedness of reading in classroom life: Reading As a situated process. In C. Baker & A. Luke (Eds.), *Towards a critical sociology of reading pedagogy* (pp. 141–160). John Benjamins.

Green, J. L., Skukauskaitė, A., & Baker, W. D. (2012). Ethnography as epistemology: An introduction to educational ethnography. In J. Arthur, M. J. Waring, R. Coe, & L. V. Hedges (Eds.), *Research methodologies and methods in education* (pp. 309–321). Sage.

Green, J. L., Skukauskaitė, A., Dixon, C., & Cordova, R. (2007). Epistemological issues in the analysis of video records: Interactional ethnography as a logic of inquiry. In R. Goldman, R. Pea, B. Barron, & S. Derry (Eds.), *Video research in the learning sciences* (pp. 115–132). Lawrence Erlbaum.

Green, J. L., & Wallat, C. (1981). Mapping instructional conversations: A sociolinguistic ethnography. In J. L. Green & C. Wallat (Eds.), *Ethnography and language in educational settings* (pp. 161–195). Ablex.

Gumperz, J. J. (1986). Interactive sociolinguistics on the study of schooling. In J. Cook-Gumperz, (Ed.), *The social construction of literacy* (pp. 45–68). Cambridge University Press.

Hymes, D. (1974). *Foundations in sociolinguistics: An ethnographic approach.* University of Pennsylvania Press.

Kvale, S., & Brinkman, S. (2009). *Interviews: Learning the craft of qualitative research interviewing* (2nd ed.). Sage.

Lin, L. (1994). Language of and in the classroom: Constructing the patterns of social life. *Linguistics & Education, 5,* 367–409.

Lipman, M. (1974). *Harry Stottlemeier's Discovery.* International Association of Philosophy for Children.

Lipman, M. (2003). *Thinking in education* (2nd ed.). Cambridge University Press.

Matthews, G. (1994). *The philosophy of childhood.* Harvard University Press.

McKee, D. (2007). *Tusk tusk.* Andersen.

Mercer, N., & Hodgkinson, S. (2008). *Exploring talk in classrooms: Inspired by the work of Douglas Barnes.* Sage.

Pike, K. L. (1954). *Language in relation to a unified theory of the structure of human behavior.* Mouton.

Putney, L., Green, J., Dixon, C., Durán, R., & Yeager, B. (2000). Consequential progressions: Exploring collective-individual development in a bilingual classroom. In P. Smagorinsky & C. Lee (Eds.), *Constructing meaning through collaborative inquiry: Vygotskian perspectives on literacy research* (pp. 86–126). Cambridge University Press.

Putney, L. G., & Frank, C. R. (2008). Looking through ethnographic eyes at classrooms acting as cultures. *Ethnography and Education, 3*(2), 211–228.

Skinner, K. (2015). Acts of thinking: At school but not during school. *Mind, Culture, and Activity, 22*(4), 348–363.

Skukauskaitė, A. (2014). Transcribing as analysis: Logic-in-use in entextualizing interview conversations. In *Sage research methods cases.* Sage. doi:10.4135/9781446 27305014532202.

Skukauskaitė, A., & Girdzijauskienė, R. (2021). Video analysis of contextual layers in teaching-learning interactions. *Learning, Culture and Social Interaction, 29.* https:// doi.org/10.1016/j.lcsi.2021.100499

Tuyay, S., Jennings, L., & Dixon, C. (1995). Classroom discourse and opportunities to learn: An ethnographic study of knowledge construction in a bilingual third grade classroom. *Discourse Practices, 19*(1), 75–110.

Wolcott, H. F. (1999). *Ethnography: A way of seeing.* Altamira.

12

RETHINKING PARTICIPANT OBSERVATION IN TEACHER EDUCATION

Laurie Katz and Melissa Wilson

Our goal in this chapter is to make transparent how we adapted an interactional ethnographic (IE) logic of inquiry to understand challenges that occurred for us as leaders of a program at a university level. The challenge was an unanticipated disconnect between university planned assignments and the implementation of these plans by preservice teachers in their classroom placements. Our concern as leaders and ethnographers was how to collect information that would inform us in taking actions to support preservice teachers in our program so they would obtain their teaching credentials. As ethnographers grounded in an IE logic of inquiry (Katz & Green, 2012; Green et al., 2012), we had to step back and consider the disconnect as a rich point (Agar, 1996; 2006), that is, an anchor for identifying the sources of the disconnect in order to resolve the problem.

In this chapter we (Katz and Wilson) present two telling cases (Mitchell, 1984) of actions and decisions each of us made to engage in an ethnographic exploration of the programmatic disconnect we faced as program leaders. Although we were insiders within the university and had access to actors from whom to collect information, we were not the primary observers in the preservice field placements. Thus, traditional ways of engaging in participant observation (e.g. Spradley, 2016) to gain insider perspectives needed to be reformulated. Also, this set of conditions led us to reconsider the types of records, from whom, in what ways, and through what kinds of contact points would be possible to collect in each of our studies.

Our goal in presenting these two telling cases is to make transparent how we, as insiders, guided by an IE perspective, used direct participant observation in different ways in each of our sites. We demonstrate how the IE perspective enabled us to gain understandings of the sources of the disconnect for

DOI: 10.4324/9781003215479-15

different participants as well as the potential consequences for the preservice teachers and their mentors. As we will show, this also led each of us to reconsider the following processes:

- how to engage with particular members of the community,
- how to record their engagements (e.g., conversations),
- what records to collect,
- when and where to collect them,
- in what ways to collect them,
- what permissions are needed to engage with this process given the official relationship with members.

Underlying these processes is the IE conceptual framework guiding how we engaged in and reformulated participant observation and how we collected records in each of our sites. To understand the experiences our preservice teachers, mentor teachers, and program faculty faced at points of disconnect, we drew on varied sources of data, including fieldnotes, video/audio recordings, digital/print documents, and other artifacts.

The Origins of the Telling Cases Within Teacher Education

Before turning to the telling cases, we elaborate for readers what constitutes the disconnect by conceptualizing the *educational contexts* as purposely defined institutions and bounded spaces. In the two telling cases these educational contexts include the university teacher education program and the field placements (i.e., classroom settings). At the center of these telling case studies is Agar's (2006) concept of languaculture, which we adapted to refer to these bounded contexts. We view the University program and personnel as bounded context or Languaculture 1 (LC1) and field placements for the mentor/classroom teacher and preservice teachers in the field placements as Languaculture 2 (LC2).

Both bounded contexts have specific structures and norms to guide ways of preparing competent teachers according to yet another educational context, state and national mandates and standards. At times, these contexts aren't aligned, thus creating challenges for preservice teachers, field-based teachers as well as university program faculty. For example, a national initiative and central guiding goal of our Early Childhood Teacher Education (ECTE) program has been to address issues of diversity within the teaching profession and prepare preservice teachers to work with students in linguistically and culturally diverse schools (Haddix, 2010).

Our ECTE program was designed to address these diversity goals through resources and teacher practices; for example, assignments in literacy methods courses may require preservice teachers to enact pedagogy that center these philosophies of teaching in their field placements. However, in preservice teachers' field placements, mentor teachers, who have considerable power and influence as they co-plan with, provide guidance for and assess preservice teachers' abilities to teach, often have different expectations for ways of addressing (or not) these diversity goals based on local curriculum and ideology. In other words, when the mentor teacher's ways of implementing these diversity goals conflict with those of the ECTE program, a potential disconnect is created as Wilson's telling case will show.

Contextualizing the Two Telling Case Studies

The first telling case study focuses on Katz's (first author) exploration of cross-institutional dialogues that occur among actors in an innovative program in which two preservice teachers were placed with one mentor/classroom teacher in an inner city 3rd grade classroom. This approach Katz designed contrasts with traditional models of one preservice teacher/one mentor teacher model. Both models have one university supervisor who acts as liaison to the field placement.

During this case, Katz became aware of a disconnect between the two institutions through conversations with the university supervisor of the two preservice teachers in their field placements; the university supervisor was also a researcher who contributed data to this telling case. In that conversation, the university supervisor of the two preservice teachers shared her concern that they were not following university expectations for lesson planning and lead teaching in their field experience (see Katz & Green, 2012; Katz & Isik-Ercan, 2015).

Katz's positionality as an insider who was the ECTE faculty lead and made decisions regarding university coursework and assessment of how preservice teachers met (or not) competency requirements, led her to experience a frame clash (Tannen, 1979). As leader of the program, she became concerned that this disconnect might impact the preservice teachers' opportunity to obtain licensure as a teacher of students from preschool to third grade. It further challenged her own 25 years of experience in teacher education, in which she had not experienced this form of disconnect.

In the first telling case, Katz unfolds how she traced the sources of this disconnect and learned to step back from the expected practices of the university to (re)consider how to collect information to show that the preservice teachers had met the goals of the university program in other ways. Through (re)constructing the archive of informal interviews and email trails between the actors in the two institutions, we demonstrate how Katz identified sources of these disconnects and developed ways of supporting the preservice teachers as well as the supervisor.

The second telling case study focuses on Wilson's reflexive decisions and actions that she, as a literacy instructor, developed in working as part of a research team, including one additional faculty member and four doctoral students as they researched how the instructional practices taught in the university class were implemented (or not) by the preservice teachers in their field-based classrooms. The research team collected videos and engaged in interviews of the preservice teachers' experiences in their field-based sites to explore with the students how they implemented their planned instructional processes.

As the instructor of the literacy methods course, Wilson taught the class and also assumed the role of researcher. In the researcher role, she recorded observations of what was occurring as preservice teachers planned literacy instruction for use with students in their placement classrooms. Wilson's positionality as an insider was grounded in her experiences as an elementary teacher for 30 years and a leader in literacy instruction in the ECTE program for five years prior to this study. Similar to Katz, she had not experienced the disconnect between university planned lessons for diverse learners and the implementation of such plans in the field placement settings.

In the following sections, we present each telling case to make visible how Katz and Wilson implemented participant observation through an IE perspective to understand the sources of the disconnects. To present their telling cases, Katz and Wilson use first person to foreground each of their actions and decisions to address their particular disconnects between the university planned actions and those in the local field placement sites.

Telling Case 1: Tracing Sources of Transformation of Practices in Innovative Student Teaching Katz Experienced as Program Leader

To describe the roles and relationships among the actors with whom I engaged at different points of contact in both bounded contexts (i.e., university ECTE program and field placement in an elementary school), I posed the following research questions grounded by Spradley's (2016) dimensions that constitute every social situation.

- What are the set of activities that the preservice teachers carry out for:
  - the supervisor?
  - the mentor teacher?
  - each other?

- Where are these activities accomplished?
- What act(s) do the preservice teachers perform for the mentor teacher, the supervisor?

As an insider, I considered the most relevant types of participation to generate records for exploring these research questions. During the entry phase of the study, I decided to not directly observe the two preservice teachers in their student teaching placement by entering the classroom, even though I received consent from both the mentor teacher and two preservice teachers.

My reasons to not directly observe included a) the small physical classroom size that contained 28 students and the two preservice teachers and mentor teacher, b) management issues of several students, c) the two preservice teachers and mentor teacher were still figuring out how to work together to address the students' needs, and d) my position as faculty lead that might be intrusive for the two preservice teachers. Given these reasons, I decided that the supervisor (who was also a researcher) would primarily enter the classroom because her position was sanctioned to move between both contexts.

I proceeded to engage in passive participation by observing through a one-way mirror of the classroom (a school structure) and recording observations that occurred in the classroom as a way of complementing the supervisor's fieldnotes based on the research questions listed above. However, observations through the one-way mirror only captured a narrow angle of the classroom and were unhelpful for observing the dynamics of the actors within the classroom. Therefore, I decided to get information through interview conversations and emails with the supervisor about the preservice teachers' experiences in the field placement.

Frame Clash: As a Rich Point

I continued to engage in passive participation until the fifth-week of the preservice teachers' field placements when the supervisor encountered a problem in reviewing the two preservice teachers' lesson planning. During this phase of the ECTE program, preservice teachers are in their field placements twice during a week and taking university courses three times per week. A frame clash occurred because the supervisor found their lesson planning incomprehensible due to the university teacher education program's format for lesson plans and procedures for completing lesson plans that had been shared many times with the preservice teachers.

The supervisor sent emails to both preservice teachers about missing parts in their lesson plans and not following procedures for the timing of the lesson plan to be developed, implemented, and reflected upon between the preservice teachers and the supervisor. The supervisor shared with me the nature of their lesson planning, further explaining that their lesson planning wasn't the same process she taught or other preservice teachers completed.

I realized that it was important to focus on this frame clash for possible negative ramifications for the actors (i.e., not successfully completing competencies). This awareness led me to step back and seek ways of turning this frame clash into a rich point. Thus, I pivoted (a term adapted from Larson, 1995) my form of participation process by shifting my approach from general descriptive observations to focused observations on lesson planning processes. This pivot led me to engage in interviewing the preservice teachers separately in an effort to situate the preservice teachers' work in their field placement.

Spradley (2016) defines this type of participation as moderate when the "ethnographer seeks to maintain a balance between being an insider and an outsider, between participation and observation" (p. 60). Following is an excerpt from my (Katz's) interview with Brad (one of the preservice teachers) that included a question about the lesson planning in the placement. Brad refers to the other preservice teacher, Amy, in this transcript (all but author names are pseudonyms). After I completed the interview with Brad, I stepped back and wrote personal notes (below) as I was reflecting on the interview.

Transcript 1: Lesson Planning Interview

KATZ: So when you were here two days, how did you plan things?

BRAD: Amy and I would meet on Tuesdays in between (university) classes. And we would bring ideas together what we need to discuss with Megan (mentor teacher). And on Thursdays, we would all meet to reflect on the week and then discuss what was going on next week, as far as, I would try a math lesson and Amy would try a social studies lesson or what kinds of assignments we would be working on and who would need to pull out students for assignments.

Personal notes (Katz):

There seems to be a system worked for lesson planning. It doesn't just include the two preservice teachers but the mentor teacher as well. Do we have the power to change what they're doing if the mentor teacher is involved and it benefits the classroom students? But will they be competent in lesson planning through this system? Could it be that what we (the supervisory part of the program) is asking them to do may not be fitting with their placement? Perhaps sharing this information with [the supervisor] will give her another perspective on lesson planning?

Gathering information about the preservice teachers' lesson planning helped triangulate (cf., Green & Chian, 2018) differences in how the ECTE program and field placement was referencing the construction of lesson planning. My interview with Brad highlighted a different lesson planning format in the field placement than the University program's lesson planning format. Furthermore, their field placement lesson planning appeared to be working for the two preservice teachers and the mentor teacher as a "classroom-based team".

Uncovering More Layers: Inviting an External Ethnographer to Our Insider Team

These frame clashes continued, posing questions about the nature of lesson planning by the student teachers as well as other unexpected challenges to the university plan for who would teach each lesson or sequences of lessons. The university expected each of the two preservice teachers in the class to assume the role of a "lead" teacher, who planned and implemented a sequence of lessons to teach over a given period of time.

The plan by the university program was that after the first "lead" the preservice teacher planned and completed, the preservice teachers would exchange positions by shifting their roles from teacher to observer and support the next "lead" teacher. A disconnect occurred when the classroom mentor teacher engaged Amy and Brad in an innovative model in which she co-planned lessons with the two pre-service teachers. Additionally, rather than one lead teacher, she modified the process so that the team supported the person leading a particular lesson in interactive ways. In this way, the university-held procedures of how to accomplish student teaching clashed with the field based team's approach.

To understand this disconnect and its potential impacts, I undertook a process of collecting sources of information from the archive and the interview conversations as well as from email trails between the supervisor and program faculty (Katz & Green, 2017). This set of records enabled me to create a data set for exploring in more depth the roots of the clashes that the supervisor and I had experienced.

At this point, I (Katz) invited Judith Green to serve as a virtual external ethnographer for several reasons. First, Green would be able to ask questions previously unasked by the embedded ethnography team to enable her to identify and trace potential program actors not previously considered. In addition, I realized, as ECTE faculty lead, I needed to step back again from what Heath (1982) calls ethnocentrism in order to create the possibility of identifying program factors that were invisible to me at the time.

Grounded in the questions Green raised for us, the supervisor and I returned to the archive to examine fieldnotes that were part of emails originally collected but not previously analyzed. From this archive, our *insider* (Katz & supervisor) – *outsider* (Green) ethnographic analysis team constructed a data set of emails between February 28th and May 17th that identified points of tension between the field-based team (two preservice teachers/mentor teacher) and the university program's expectations around lesson planning.

For example, we identified the earliest inscription of a frame clash in lesson-planning in a reflective email (February 28) from the supervisor to me. In this email the supervisor referenced a growing awareness about "missing lesson plans for teaching from both candidates". From records of March 4–7, we identified an exchange between the supervisor and one of the preservice teachers

(Brad) about missing assignments and reflective logs. As part of this chain of emails, Brad responded by sending the requested reflections. In a later exchange identified on March 18, Brad, again, failed to submit his lesson plan. This time, however, the omission was not due to a lack of understanding of the required content but to an absence from the field placement due to a job search.

The analysis of the data set of Brad's email exchanges formed a rich point, one that raised questions for Green, the external ethnographer, about the reporting system within the ECTE program and the relationships among actors in the chain of supervision. Green's question led to identification of a chain of interactions between the program manager and the supervisor on April 30/May 1. These email chains reflected the supervisor's concerns about Brad's growing pattern of not submitting lesson plans until requested and how to assess his competence in this area.

On May 12, in an email, Brad "informed" the supervisor that he places the past lesson plans in a folder in the classroom, suggesting there was a norm at the classroom level that was agreed to by the field based team as to what to do with lesson plans and where they should be placed. Brad's message created a new anchor and led to an additional search of the archive to identify any contextual information about the processes of the field placement. The goals of this search and analysis were to identify the reasons that led Brad to keep the plans in the classroom, even though he knew that he was expected to send them to the supervisor prior to her observations.

This search led to an email from the mentor teacher (May 12) inscribing for the supervisor what she would observe during her observation of the lesson(s) being conducted by the two preservice teachers collaboratively, or in different centers in which her students were engaged. She explained in the email that the supervisor would observe her and the two preservice teachers functioning as a team:

> you might see one or two of us in a "helper" position while one teacher… We agreed that the lead teacher would be the one who makes these on your feet decisions based on the needs of the students for that particular part of the lesson.
>
> *(Mentor Teacher Email, May 12)*

The mentor teacher's explanation was in reference to how the preservice teachers would be conducting their "student teaching". This inscription created another clash (a disconnect) between the university supervisor's expectations and the classroom teacher's expectations of how the preservice teachers would conduct their student teaching.

In this example, the emails served as a form of fieldnotes, or rather a "note from the field". Given this view of emails as forms of fieldnotes, we provide grounded evidence of how, as in other ethnographic sites, these notes from the field were grounds for gaining an insider perspective of the roles and relationships occurring in these bounded contexts.

Ethnographer as Learner: The Program Leader's Perspective

In Telling Case 1, we provided a framework for exploring points of contact and disconnect among actors within two bounded contexts related to teacher education. During this exploration Katz traced how points of disconnect led her to shift ways of participating and observing according to her positionality as a faculty lead engaged with other actors, who also faced disconnects, i.e., the supervisor of preservice teachers, as well as the preservice teachers and their mentor teacher.

These shifts involved making decisions regarding how to gather information, i.e., initially being a passive observer, then interviewing preservice teachers and bringing to the research team an external ethnographer. This process led to iterative, recursive and abductive processes of collecting records from the field (observations, email trails, and other documents). The notes and records from the field enabled her to construct data sets for analysis of the sources of particular forms of disconnect between the university and the field placement personnel.

Given her roles of leader and her history with IE research, Katz was able to not only identify relevant data sources but to use those sources to explore how the preservice teachers met the university expectations in unanticipated ways. Through assuming an ethnographic perspective, and engaging with different actors, Katz created ways of showing how the experiences of the preservice teachers in the field, while not matching expected processes, met the standards set for them by her program.

Additionally, her processes of working with others made transparent ways she showed respect to the actors with whom she interacted: the supervisor, mentor teacher, and preservice teachers. In this telling case, Katz, in (re)constructing the actions she and others took when faced with the disconnects, provided ways of identifying and exploring the disconnects by tracing the source of these challenges. Throughout the process and engagement with members in different bounded contexts Katz had assumed the role of ethnographer as learner (see also Baker et al., Guerrero et al., Skukauskaité & Sullivan, and other chapters in this volume).

Telling Case 2: Wilson on Censoring a Read Aloud in a Second Grade Field Placement

In Telling Case 2, we introduce the frame clash in Wilson's study that occurred during a University assignment when a small group of preservice teachers selected a particular book to use for an interactive read aloud in each of their field placement classrooms. One preservice teacher was unable to read the book as planned when her mentor teacher objected to her reading some of the text in the book. This censorship presented a challenge to the University's teaching about introducing and using diverse picturebooks in the classroom. As in Katz's section above, Wilson will present her actions in response to the frame clash in the first person.

On Participant Observation and Participation

As the instructor of the literacy methods course, I both taught the class and recorded observations of what was occurring as preservice teachers planned literacy instruction for use with students in their placement classrooms. I, of European descent, had taught at the elementary school level for 30 years in the city where the University is located. I had also taught for the past five years as part of the ECTE program.

Similar to Katz, there were social, historical and political orientations which constituted certain assumptions I made regarding the relationships between the University classroom (LC1) and the field placement (LC2). Both as a previous classroom teacher who had hosted preservice teachers in my classrooms and a University instructor, I held assumptions about the field placement classroom teacher's (also known as Mentor Educator) role in preparing the preservice teachers to become educators. I was aware of tensions that might occur in the field between the actors, and worked to develop a relationship with the preservice teachers to help them complete the coursework smoothly and with a minimum of friction.

In my role as teacher and participant observer, the following comprised my fieldnotes: the class syllabus, weekly lesson plans, assignment descriptions, the "Read Aloud Lesson Study" assignment, teaching videos and any observational notes I made during and after class. In addition, the "Read Aloud Lesson Study" group's lesson plan and individual teaching videos were also viewed as forms of fieldnotes created by the participants in the teaching methods class. The participants recorded their planning and enactment of that assignment. The final set of research records or fieldnotes came from a debriefing meeting, in which the group met with me to reflect on their collective experience through an interview. Taken together these varied forms of fieldnotes revealed different perspectives between the University classroom and the field placement classroom, making visible a frame clash. My fieldnotes also helped me consider the ways in which social groups construct a languaculture to reflect their practices. The questions I posed included:

- how do preservice teachers use language during literacy instruction; and
- how do preservice teachers reflect on and analyze their literacy instruction?

Frame Clash

The group I focus on in this telling case included three preservice students who self-identified as:

- Paula, an African American woman in her early thirties;
- Nicole, a European American woman in her early twenties; and
- Kristy (Daiyu), an Asian woman in her early twenties.

After planning their interactive read aloud for the book *White Socks Only* (Coleman, 1996), each member of the group completed the teaching/reflecting cycle which included: videotaping the read aloud with their students; discussing the lesson with their group; and revising the lesson as appropriate for the next preservice teacher to teach. When this cycle was completed, the group (Paula, Nicole, and Kristy) met with me in a debriefing session, to reflect on their individual read alouds and the lesson study process as a whole (Stepanik et al., 2007). I facilitated this final debriefing using a set of questions developed and used across all the sections of this course. These questions were:

- How did it go?
- What did you think of this iterative planning process?
- What changes did you make and why?
- What value do you see in this process? (big picture learning)

Notes from my observations of the conversation among the students during the debriefing meeting indicated that the students discussed the fact that, although Paula's teacher wanted her to bypass the racial issues addressed in the book and just focus on respect (as was written in the collaborative lesson plan), the other two students in their classes addressed the racial issues raised by the book more directly. In my fieldnotes I wrote about the differences in the three students' implementation of the lesson.

> 11-28-2017 *White Socks Only* (Kristy, Paula and Nicole) (typed notes by Wilson):

> Nicole didn't have to change the lesson plan too much and just added a few things and some tweaks; Kristy added introduction; tailoring lessons to audience was important learning; Paula's teacher wanted to bypass racial issues and teach respect so made Paula cover parts of book; thought some of the issues might be over students' heads but in Kristy's and Nicole's class the students got the racial issues; they seem to think this was a short sighted decision by CT; didn't have to make our planning more about respect vs. racial inequality —underestimated the children

My typed notes of this conversation of the debriefing meeting indicate that the general consensus by the preservice teachers based on their experiences during the read aloud was that it was a "short-sighted decision by Paula's teacher" (CT) to avoid this discussion as being "over the students' heads". Nicole and Kristy reported students in their classes "got the racial issues". They reflected that their initial planning around the theme of "respect" had underestimated the children's capacities in their two classrooms to take up a discussion of racial inequality as part of the interactive read aloud discussion. This comparative process between the planned read aloud discussion and the actual read aloud discussion led me to identify factors that differed for what both Paula and the students in her classroom were permitted to discuss and learn.

Furthermore, the during the debriefing meeting I learned for the first time how Paula's mentor educator had censored what Paula was to read to the students and how. The mentor had directed Paula to cover up parts of the text on several pages with post-it notes. My personal note (WTF: I REALLY NEED TO TALK TO PAULA!) at the end of the November 28 fieldnotes captures my personal response to this frame clash and my first moments of learning about this challenge.

From Frame Clash to Professional Actions

Grounded in this frame clash, I engaged in an exploration of how planned lessons approved by the university instructor were not always possible for preservice teachers to implement with their students. The frame clash exposed the conflicting goals of a field-based teacher and made visible how those goals led to the change in the preservice teacher's plan for reading the book aloud to her students.

This frame clash also led me to (re)think what I had observed and experienced in the debriefing meeting, leading me to realize my biases about censoring books and what kinds of books were possible to share with early childhood students. Taking note of my frame clash and realizations about my own perspectives as an educator led me to seek an additional time to meet with Paula on December 5th. In preparation for the meeting with Paula, I re-watched the video and re-read the group lesson plan for the read aloud. I traced and reconstructed what had happened during Paula's read aloud, making a video log of the lesson and transcribing parts of the discourse during the lesson (specifically the segments where the reading was censored).

Through this process of (re)viewing the video, I found key dimensions of the video I had not noted in my first watching of the video. In the first viewing of the video, I had observed a light yellow post-it note as well as a dark orange one on one page and assumed (from my past experiences working with preservice teachers) that these were notes about questions Paula was going to ask students when reading that particular page. Once I knew what to look for, however, the post-it notes covering the text on the other pages became visible.

At this point, I became aware of the limits in observing from video without further grounding of what it was a record of. That is, I became aware that observing alone does not necessarily make transparent the story behind the actions captured in a video clip (for similar arguments see Skukauskaitė & Sullivan; Baker et al., this volume). This awareness further highlights how participant observers, when guided by an IE logic-of-analysis, can move from observational notes to analytic notes to examine the frame clash from multiple points of view. This logic of inquiry supported me in reconstructing my interpretation of what the video record enabled me to understand both as a researcher and as the insider (i.e., the leader of the preservice teachers' experiences).

Uncovering the Layers

As is often the case in IE, our data can be used to provide layered analyses of the processes and practices used to co-construct understandings by and about people in moments of their activity and over time (Skukauskaitė & Girdzijauskienė, 2021). This is indicated in the telling case of my responses to the frame clashes I experienced and explored to uncover the sources of the disconnect between university and field-placements. I found myself stepping back from my observations of the students during their planning and their reports of what was possible in the field placement. This process of stepping back (Green & Bridges, 2018) led me to engage further in conversations with Paula, as indicated above. The meeting in which I sought to understand Paula's experiences in the context of her field placement took place on December 5th, seven days after the debriefing on the last day of class. In a 90-minute lunch meeting with Paula, I explored with her how and in what ways literacy practices (such as a read aloud) were taken up, adopted and adapted, or not, in her local context.

As I talked with Paula, I learned that the read aloud instructional activity revealed only the surface of Paula's experience with this assignment. Centering the conversation in the school and classroom where she was a preservice teacher, Paula discussed the ways in which her classroom teacher and other members of the staff treated her, detailing many racial microaggressions. Paula also shared her concern about the ways in which she, as a teacher of color, could support her students of color in this setting and in her own classroom. Her commentary reflected the history of teachers of color within the US public education system – one of "subliminal racism", "racialized relationships", and exclusive curricula (Cheruvu et al., 2015).

My conversation with Paula led me to understand that as a woman of European descent I had limited understanding of what it feels like to experience racism and the sort of racial battle fatigue Paula was describing. It also brought forward the need to: a) rethink how to address the multi-layered experiences of preservice teachers with diverse histories; and b) plan future work in ways that grounded the books they were exploring in order to be better prepared to address the sorts of multiple frame clashes that Paula had experienced.

Encountering the frame clash Paula confronted between the bounded contexts of the local classroom and the University classroom, I shifted in my ways of observing and participating based on my positionality as a University instructor and a White woman. For example, I shifted from gathering information about the assigned classroom activities to interviewing the preservice teacher. These additional notes and records helped me construct data sets to analyze the disconnect between the university classroom goals and the field placement classroom teacher's practice. Further, through the use of the ethnographic perspective I participated with Paula as a "witness" to the ways in which she, as a teacher of color, was experiencing the frame clashes within the local context of her school and field placement classroom.

Concluding Remarks: An Opening for New Dialogues

In this chapter we created two telling cases and shared our converging understandings of the previously invisible challenges we and our students faced as we all, individually and collectively, navigated the two bounded contexts of the university teacher education program and preservice teaching in the field. These telling cases also provide examples of the human connections experienced between the researcher and their actors across the different field sites and different sources of information constituting fieldnotes. Guest and colleagues (2013) argue, "Participant observation connects the researcher to the most basic of human experiences, discovering through immersion & participation the hows and whys of human behavior in a particular context" (p. 75). As we faced the disconnects and explored the frame clashes, we developed deeper connections to our students, ourselves and the phenomena we studied. The IE logic of inquiry which guided our work as researchers and practitioners provided us a way of systematically tracing and responding to the unanticipated human challenges in the lived experiences of members within and across educational systems. Understanding these challenges from insider points of view, in contextually bounded systems, prepares us for making more informed and locally responsive and responsible decisions.

Principles for Practice

1. Pay attention to disconnects. While they may be uncomfortable, explore them so you can learn what is behind them and what they can teach you.
2. Collaborate with colleagues/peers to explore similar telling cases across your practices in teacher education. Collectively, you may develop deeper understandings of patterns in the phenomena studies.

3. Remember the importance of developing relationships in IE. You want to try to leave the field/participants in a better place than when you initially entered the site(s).
4. Think creatively of tools for gaining an insider perspective, such as field-notes (e.g., email chains, video, class assignments, and other artifacts). Reconceptualize your methods and tools for your situated practice so they fit your study.

Suggested Readings

Bloome, D., Power-Carter, S., Baker, W. D., Castanheira, M., Kim, M., & Rowe, L. (2022). *Discourse analysis of languaging and literacy events: A microethnographic perspective*. New York: Routledge.

Frank, C., & Bridges, L. B. (1999). *Ethnographic eyes: A Teacher's guide to classroom observation*. Heinemann.

Haddix, M. M. (2012). Talkin' in the company of my sistas: The counterlanguages and deliberate silences of black female students in teacher education. *Linguistics and Education, 23*(2), 169–181.

References

Agar, M. (1996). *Language shock: Understanding the culture of conversation*. William Morrow.

Agar, M. (2006). Culture: Can you take it anywhere? *International Journal of Qualitative Methods, 5*(2), 1–16.

Cheruvu, R., Souto-Manning, M., & Lencl, T. *et al.* (2015). Race, isolation, and exclusion: What early childhood teacher educators need to know about the experiences of pre-service teachers of color. *Urban Review, 47*, 237–265.

Coleman, E. (1996). *White socks only*. Albert Whitman & Co.

Green, J. L., & Bridges, S. M. (2018). Interactional ethnography. In F. Fischer, C. E. Hmelo-Silver, S. R. Goldman, & P. Reimann (Eds.), *International handbook of the learning sciences* (pp. 475–488). Routledge.

Green, J. L., & Chian, M. M. (2018). Triangulation. In B. Frey (Ed.), *The sage encyclopedia of educational research, measurement, and evaluation* (pp. 1718–1720). Sage.

Green, J. L., Skukauskaitė, A., & Baker, W. D. (2012). Ethnography as epistemology. In J. Arthur, M. Waring, R. Coe, & L. V. Hedges (Eds.), *Research methods and methodologies in education* (pp. 309–321). Sage.

Guest, G., Namey, E. E., & Mitchell, M. L. (2013). *Collecting qualitative data: A field manual for applied research*. Sage.

Haddix, M. (2010). No longer on the margins: Researching the hybrid literate identities of black and Latina preservice teachers. *Research in the Teaching of English, 45*(2), 97–123.

Heath, S. B. (1982). Ethnography in education: Defining the essentials. In P. Gillmore, & A. A. Glathhorn (Eds.), *Children in and out of school: Ethnography and education* (pp. 33–55). Center for Applied Linguistics.

Katz, L., & Green, J. (2012). Exploring continuities and discontinuities for teacher candidates between university and early childhood classrooms. In *(Doing) ethnography in early childhood education and care. Proceedings of an International Colloquium at the University of Luxembourg*.

Katz, L., & Green, J. (2017). Researching the intersection of program supervision and field placements: Interactional ethnographic telling cases of reflexive decision-making process. In M. A. Peters, B. Cowie, & I. Menter (Eds.), *A companion for teacher education research* (pp. 237–251). Springer.

Katz, L., & Isik-Ercan, Z. (2015). Challenging points of contact among supervisor, mentor teacher and teacher candidates: Conflicting institutional expectations. *Pedagogies: An International Journal, 10*(1), 54–69. doi: 10.1080/1554480X.2014.999772.

Larson, J. (1995). Talk matters: The role of pivot in the distribution of literacy knowledge among novice writers. *Linguistics and Education, 7*(4), 277–302.

Mitchell, J. C. (1984). Typicality and the case study. In R. Elen (Ed.), *Ethnographic research: A guide to general conduct* (pp. 238–241). Academic Press.

Skukauskaitė, A., & Girdzijauskienė, R. (2021). Video analysis of contextual layers in teaching-learning interactions. *Learning, Culture and Social Interaction, 29.* https://doi.org/10.1016/j.lcsi.2021.100499

Spradley, J. P. (2016). *Participant observation.* Waveland Press.

Stepanik, J., Appel, G., Leong, M., Mangan, M. T., & Mitchell, M. (2007). *Leading lesson study: A practical guide for teachers and facilitators.* Sage Publications Ltd.

Tannen, D. (1979). What's in a frame? Surface evidence for underlying expectations. In R. Freedle (Ed.), *New directions in discourse processing* (pp. 137–181). Ablex.

PART 4
Commentaries

13

INTERACTIONAL ETHNOGRAPHY AS A RESOURCE FOR LEARNING IN K-12

Building Communities of Inquiry

Beth V. Yeager

> The work of an ethnographer…helps you know what people are doing and talking about… You are observing…We had to observe our community and groups.
>
> *(Juliana, 1997)*

> We are ethnographers so we can learn about what happens every day in our community.
>
> *(Jonathan, 2002)*

Drawing on an Interactional Ethnographic perspective, the developing ethnographers, Juliana and Jonathan, in the above statements, conceptualize ethnography and their work as ethnographers, much as the authors in this book have done. Rereading these two conceptualizations *and* considering that these ethnographers were in 5th and 2nd grades, respectively, when they wrote them, provided me with the inspiration to frame this commentary.

My overarching focus is to discuss the potential of IE principles in educational practice in pre-K-12 settings. The authors in this book have composed a rich set of chapters that present and conceptualize Interactional Ethnography (IE) as epistemology (Green et al., 2012) (i.e., a way of knowing, being and doing) and a logic of inquiry *in* and *for* education (Bloome et al., 2018). They also unfold ethnographic principles and practices as ways of studying and understanding the work and everyday life of people ("what happens every day") in particular social groups (e.g., "our community"), who co-construct through their actions and interactions (e.g., "what people are doing and talking about"), "cultures-in-the-making".

As I thought about how I wanted to focus this commentary, I reflected on my own journey as a practitioner researcher in preschool and elementary

DOI: 10.4324/9781003215479-17

bilingual classrooms, and as both an external and an internal IE researcher of my classroom and in other settings. I also thought about my experiences as a member of communities of inquirers, and, currently, as a thinking partner supporting professional educators and their students in a local school district. I also considered the journeys of my former students, like Juliana and Jonathan, toward developing as and *being* ethnographers, while part of a community of inquirers. Finally, I thought about the journeys over the last few years of teachers and other educators who are working with me and colleagues, drawing on an IE perspective, to develop and enhance their capacity for culturally responsive and socially just inquiry-based instructional design and practice.

Based on these reflections on the compelling chapters in this book and on my own work from an IE perspective, in this commentary I argue for making visible an *invisible* piece that could support what this book is already contributing. This potential piece, focusing on drawing on IE to support learning-in-practice in and for education, serves as a way to both complement and (re) conceptualize ethnographic spaces (Agar, 2006) and possibilities. To support this argument, I present three brief, interrelated parts of an overarching telling case (Mitchell, 1984) of what IE-in-practice, as an example of "ethnographic possibility" and/or "space", might look and sound like (see Skukauskaitė and Green's introduction for ethnographic spaces). In this telling case, I make visible instances of IE as a resource for supporting deeper learning in the context of building culturally responsive communities of inquirers. From an ethnographic perspective, I also consider this process as building a *culture* of inquiry (Yeager et al., 2020) within and across educational settings, and across professional roles (e.g., teachers, counselors, administrators, external researchers, community members), ages/grade levels, and more.

The three parts of this telling case serve as examples of potentials for how IE, as represented in this book, can support deeper, inquiry-based learning. This theoretical/methodological logic, at the nexus of theory and practice, can also support building *cultures* of inquiry within and across classes and/ or schools (communities of inquirers), and new ways of knowing, being and doing in educational spaces.

Telling Cases

Part 1: Teacher-as-Learner to Teacher-as-Ethnographer and Ethnographer-as-Teacher

I argue here that informing practice and learning in pre-K-12 educational sites comprises an important ethnographic space as possibility for an IE perspective. I begin by first considering why, when, how, under what conditions, a pre-K-12 educator might elect to take up such a perspective. I introduce this potential by unfolding my own experience as learner entering the world of IE.

I initially took up an ethnographic perspective because it made sense to me, in the context of my experience, my history, what I knew as a teacher, and what more I wanted to understand about my students, our classroom, and my practice. This is critical to understanding how new ways of looking and understanding – in this case, Interactional Ethnographic principles, practices and perspectives – can potentially inform practice: understanding how they can make sense to teachers and other educators who are seeking new ways of looking.

I had been a bilingual teacher for 21 years in 1991, when I was asked to become part of a school/university research partnership. This partnership, composed of university faculty, graduate students, K-12 teachers, and administrators, became a *community of inquirers* that would be called the Santa Barbara Classroom Discourse Group (SBCDG). The invitation grew out of my participation as a Fellow of the South Coast Writing Project (National Writing Project). The model for this SBCDG partnership was one of interacting communities, with distributed expertise and mutual respect, engaged in classroom research from an ethnographic perspective (e.g., Yeager, 1999). In addition to my Writing Project experience, I brought my previous involvement in teacher research along with a background in social sciences as well as literacy, a disposition to engage in inquiry-based instruction, and an orientation toward understanding theory/practice relationships.

As I've written elsewhere, teachers know that everyday life in classrooms is complex. It is not something that can be seen and understood in the moment. They understand that especially when visitors make snap judgments about what is happening or not happening after only brief observations (Yeager, 2006). Like other teachers, I also knew that, even when teachers plan similar activities or instructional approaches collaboratively, one classroom will not look or sound exactly like the classroom next door (Yeager, 2006, p. 7). In addition, I knew, as most teachers do, that not only do we as teachers bring a history and ways of doing to the classroom, but that each student also brings their own history from multiple school, family, cultural, and community experiences. No year or group is ever "exactly the same". What I, and other teachers, need(ed) was a way to "construct a theoretical framework for making sense of, and an evidence-based language for talking about, what I had come to understand as a classroom teacher [and wanted to understand better] and for using what I learned to make informed instructional decisions" (Yeager, 2006, pp. 8–9). Drawing on this previous understanding and what I needed, an ethnographic perspective and the elements, principles, practices, and foundational IE theoretical frameworks, made sense to me.

In particular, a central concept underlying IE of classrooms as cultures, or as cultures-in-the-making (Collins & Green, 1992), was compatible with what I had observed about different school years or different classrooms doing the same activities. I had also brought a focus on the role of language to the partnership that made sense in the context of the discourse-base complementing the ethnographic perspective. The overtime nature of an ethnographic approach made sense. It also made sense that we were co-constructing a collective history and community in my classrooms over time. Most of all, an ethnographic perspective, grounded in theory at the nexus of practice, was compatible with inquiry-based instruction, which was foundational to my teaching.

In order to understand what was being accomplished in my classroom, the basic IE underlying questions made sense: who can do or say what, when, where, how, for what purposes, under what conditions, with what potential consequences and outcomes (Santa Barbara Classroom Discourse Group, 1992b). Asking these questions, observing, and then stepping back from the moment (Heath, 1982; Heath & Street, 2008), provided a means of identifying how the people in our classroom community accomplished everyday life, as 2nd grader, Jonathan, theorized in the opening to this commentary. Using my developing *ethnographic eyes* (Frank, 1999), I saw how my students and I negotiated what *counted* as knowledge, action, task, and membership through the patterns of interaction among members. Through these interactions, we constructed a common language *of* the classroom (Floriani, 1993; Lin, 1993; Yeager et al., 1998) and what Agar has identified as languaculture (Agar, 1994; 1996). Exploring these theoretical constructs, practices, and ways of looking at what was happening in my classroom led to how and why I took up an ethnographic perspective to inform my instructional practice in the contexts of learning. They also supported me in understanding *how* we were co-constructing a culture-in-the-making that was becoming a community of inquirers (Yeager, 1999).

Initially, asking ethnographic questions and using an ethnographic perspective over time in my classroom, enabled me to do systematically what already made sense to me as a teacher. In the first year of participating in SBCDG, I was able to articulate the invisible premises underlying everyday life in my classroom, but which, until that time, had become invisible to me (i.e., taken for granted). In other words, I engaged in a process of making the invisible visible. I drew on what I learned from that first year through a reflexive/responsive process to inform my teaching in the contexts of learning. For example, I became more explicit in what I said and did with students to make visible the connections among different contexts and to reveal explicitly what resources they would need in each new context. I began to draw on an ethnographic perspective to look at student work (e.g., patterns, thematic references), in the context of what was available to be learned (Yeager, 1999; 2003; 2006).

Over a 12-year period, with ethnographer partners in the classroom and later on my own, I continued as a teacher-as-ethnographer, as described in the following excerpt:

> What I could not do as a teacher in the moment was record field notes, find enough time to stand back and observe what was happening,

or watch hours of videotape in order to analyze it. While teachers understand what it means to look over time at what is being accomplished in the classroom, what we observe is often in the form of "head notes. We cannot necessarily stop in the moment to record our observations as "field notes". What teachers can see over time, however, is essential to making visible what is being accomplished in the everyday life of the classroom. What I found, in taking up an ethnographic perspective, was a way of looking and later reconstructing my "head notes" as a form of written data that helped me when I was outside of the moment. Taking up an ethnographic perspective on life in our classroom brought a heightened sense of *paying attention* for me, ... that was different from the ways in which I had paid attention before.

(Yeager, 2006, p. 11)

Guided by an IE perspective, as I transitioned from teacher-as-ethnographer to ethnographer-as-teacher and moved between school settings and university settings in my roles as internal and external ethnographer, I was able to shift angles of visioning (points of viewing) to construct data from new contexts. Thus, I engaged in a reflexive process to rely on certain instances of insider knowledge gained as a teacher-ethnographer. Building on this prior knowledge, I could shift my angle of visioning to step back from that knowledge to interrogate data in the new context. This process enabled me to ground my questions in data, not in prior assumptions, and to encounter surprises, or *rich points* (Agar, 1994), through which I developed new understandings.

However, I did not do this work in isolation. As described before, I was a member of a *community* of inquirers (SBCDG) in which we relied heavily on an overtime dialogic model of interaction. This enabled members to bring diverse angles of visioning to what we were doing, while relying on a common, underlying theoretical/methodological logic of inquiry, IE, complemented by critical discourse analysis. In the case of teacher members, we took up opportunities for looking and seeing in different ways while maintaining a common thread/a logic linking us as a community, because we saw the potential of our diverse work in K-12 schools as ethnographic spaces of possibility for supporting learning. This perspective became evident when K-12 teacher and administrator members of our community created a themed issue for a journal of *Primary Voices* (1999), a National Council of Teachers of English (NCTE) journal. Each wrote in a different way about different issues, but drew on the same common IE foundation and a view of classrooms as cultures. For example, while I wrote on constructing a community of inquirers in my classroom, Steve Flores, from a principal's perspective, wrote:

As my understanding of ethnography grows, my perspective on classrooms as cultures continues to evolve. This evolution has forced me to reflect upon my observational style as a school administrator and has challenged me to implement a shift in focus when visiting classrooms at the school site.

(1999, p. 54)

What occurred for us as a community of inquirers is reflective of how IE foregrounds the uncommon, local and situated (Heap, 1991) nature of groups and members of the group, their individual classrooms, research sites, and so on. In this way, much as the authors of the chapters in this book are, we were also guided by a common underlying theoretical/methodological foundation.

In the next section, I turn to the potential of IE principles and practices for taking up an ethnographic perspective in support of deeper *student* learning. Guided by an IE perspective myself, I was able to see, from the outset of our SBCDG research partnership, potentials for involving students as active partners in research processes, with implications for co-constructing communities of inquirers within a culture of inquiry.

Telling Case, Part 2: Students as Ethnographers

In the excerpts from essays on their classroom communities that began this commentary, Juliana and Jonathan theorize the *work* of ethnographers. They do so in the language of action, using verbs ("doing", "talking", "observing") to make visible how they, *as* ethnographers ("we are ethnographers") learn about "what happens every day in [their] community" (i.e., their class). Being an ethnographer, and using an ethnographic perspective, is seen by both these young scholars as a resource for learning ("helps you know", "so we can learn about what happens every day in our community").

This notion of the *work of people* is integral to an IE perspective. What people do and say, when, where, to whom, how, why, under what conditions, with what potential outcomes and consequences helps the ethnographer to understand what *counts as* x or y (Spradley, 1980), and what an *insider* needs to know to be a member of a particular group or class. Just as these notions of insider knowledge and of the situated nature of what *counts* made sense to me as an inquiry-based instructor, it also came to make sense to my students as researchers, whether in 5th, 6th, or even 2nd grade. Students constantly have to read their worlds (Freire, 1970/2000 edition) – e.g., is this a place where I can talk freely (or not)? is this a place where I can make choices (or not)? and so on.

Having a principled way of looking and talking about what they see, and learn from what they see, provides students with a repertoire of actions they can take based on what they learn, and supports them in reading their worlds – and often changing or contributing to changes in what is available to be read. As fifth grader, John, says in his end-of-year essay on his class community: "... members must have insider knowledge of their own culture or class, which is very useful in our classroom" (1998).

As a teacher/ethnographer, who valued an inquiry approach, I wanted my scholars to have ways of looking, being, doing, and knowing that would serve them as resource both in and out of the classroom. I hoped that taking up such a perspective grounded in IE, would support them in coming to understand the work of people in at least two ways. First, I wanted them to be ethnographers of their own class community in order to understand their work within that community. Second, I wanted them to act as ethnographers of the work of people as members of disciplines and to understand how their own work looked and sounded within and across those disciplines.

Therefore, from the first day of each school year, students were invited to become ethnographers of their classroom community. We began to think about community as an evolving culture, with norms or "customs", as one student called them, or co-constructed ways of being, knowing and acting that we shared in common in a particular year. In other words, we began to think about the notion of insider knowledge, about our own work as people within a community of inquiry grounded in particular inquiry-based practices, all compatible with an ethnographic perspective (Yeager et al., 1998). The work of examining what it meant to be a member of our class community meant that students engaged in larger reflexive/responsive processes (Yeager et al., 2020) of looking at the group across the year. This further enabled them to begin to look at themselves, their own lived experience and work within the collective – learning what it meant to be a student in *this* class community, this year.

This process continues to be relevant now, particularly as educators explore what it means to increasingly afford students opportunities to drive and evaluate their own learning with teacher as facilitator. For example, taking up a practice-based ethnographic perspective, affords students opportunities for understanding the nuanced differences between looking and seeing when one observes. It also shapes how to record ways that reflect conceptual differences between observing and interpreting using the tools of an ethnographer (e.g., taking fieldnotes – notetaking/note making (Yeager & Córdova, 2009). Thus, an IE perspective enhances students' capacity and repertoires for actions

The process of doing the work of an ethnographer in a class as a culture of inquiry is captured in an excerpt from 5th grade bilingual student, Erika's, end-of-year community essay (excerpted). In this excerpt, Erika explains what a new member would need to know about how students engaged in using a key ethnographic process in her classroom – creating fieldnotes for particular purposes:

> I'm an ethnographer…An ethnographer means that you have a folder where it says Notetaking/Notemaking. In notetaking, you write what the class is doing … Then, on the right side, the notemaking side, you

> write what you think your notes might mean. That is how you are an ethnographer in the [class]. You might be an ethnographer to know how everybody's doing their work. Ethnography helps me to know about the class. That is how I know how the class works (1997).

As the year progressed, students as ethnographers continued inquiring into their everyday life and lived experience in my class community. This culminated in writing essays on their community based on what they had learned about it across the year. They used what they had learned about the community as a collective as resource for thinking about their own work within and across disciplines in relation to what was *available* to be learned. Thus, students and teacher, as ethnographers of the community, co-constructed an ethnographic perspective as academic resource for students to question what counted as disciplinary knowledge and being a member of a discipline, in the context of this class community.

My goal in engaging students in ethnographic processes within and across disciplines and disciplinary knowledge was for them to understand the outcomes of the work of people in a discipline in ways that were comparable to their own work. I wanted them to understand the practices and processes in which members of disciplines engaged, and to understand them as situated, both locally and culturally, as well as in what we each brought to the work as mathematicians, historians, artists, writers, scientists, anthropologists, and other members of disciplines. I wanted them to *envision* themselves as members within and across disciplines, *engage in the practices* of disciplines, and *understand* how those comparable inquiry-based practices (e.g., observing, interpreting, analyzing, asking questions) looked and sounded in different contexts for different purposes. This goal is captured in second grader, Joskua's, end-of-year essay as she conceptualizes what counts as being a "scholar" in her particular "community of scholars": "A scholar is someone who works hard being a mathematician, a scientist, a historian, a writer, a reader and a student (2002)". Joskua, therefore, inscribes what *counts* as being a scholar in this class, based on her ethnographic work across the year.

Fifth grader, Keith, also inscribes what it meant in his class community to engage in particular inquiry-based practices to do a disciplinary or transdisciplinary investigation. He draws on two critical ethnographic processes as resources – the practices of gathering data and supporting with evidence in order to engage in investigation/research – and, on a central IE analytical construct, point of view (angle of viewing):

> As a member of our community, you would also have to know about investigations. That's when you go out into the field to gather data (you send someone out to get information). In an investigation you don't just get information, you get evidence.

Evidence is proof of something you say. In an investigation, you also have to look at point of view. That's looking at something through other people's eyes and thinking about how they would think about it (1997).

This section, and the student voices shared, makes visible examples of the potential of IE as an ethnographic space for supporting deeper student learning of both disciplinary knowledge and practice. By engaging students in an IE perspective, we afford them opportunities for using ethnographic inquiry-based practices in disciplinary contexts as well as developing academic identities as members of those disciplines (Yeager, 2003). As students inquire into their own classroom community and their own work as members of a community of inquirers, in reflexive/responsive ways, I have learned that they enhance their capacity for evaluating their own work and taking action on what they have learned. In this way, IE perspective has the potential to become part of students' repertoires for action as learners.

Telling Case, Part 3: Building a Professional Community of Inquirers

In this section, I present ways in which colleagues and I in a school district have addressed the following question: *If* an IE perspective makes sense to many teachers in the context of their own learning, practice, and also of student learning, *then* how do we draw on that to inform change and growth over time in a district, or within and across school sites? In this section, I describe two interrelated models where colleagues, the Superintendent and I are drawing on an IE perspective in a school district. The models I present were designed to inform work with teachers, counselors, other educators and students to make visible the potential of an ethnographic perspective for supporting and informing deeper learning and the building of communities (a culture) of inquiry. The first is a professional inquiry group model, a community of inquirers, who draw on a common theoretical foundation guided by IE to explore inquiry-based instructional design and take an inquiry stance to practice. The second model involves ongoing, long-term one-on-one dialogic thinking partner relationships (myself or a colleague and a teacher), a description of which is beyond the scope of this commentary.

The first model is an inquiry group founded by teachers in the Rio School District that they named as Inquiry-Based Instructional Designers (IBID), created in 2013 by six teachers across grades 1–6. These teachers had been involved in a brief District-sponsored institute on inquiry-based instruction I facilitated with a colleague, the late Dr. Faviana Hirsch-Dubin, and the Rio District Superintendent, Dr. Puglisi. These teachers asked Dr. Faviana and myself to co-facilitate the inquiry group they were forming. By the summer of 2014, we held an IBID Summer Institute with approximately 22 teachers participating. We modeled the institute to some extent on National Writing Project summer institutes (Lieberman & Wood, 2002). The district supported the work and the Superintendent paid teachers for their participation.

IBID is not a training program, does not focus on one "program" or way to do inquiry-based instruction. It has grown through word of mouth and is fluid in its membership. The model is one of collaboration, community, building leadership capacity, and teachers teaching teachers. What is unique to IBID is that it is always intergenerational and interprofessional since IBID members can attend Institutes every year and, at the same time, new participants can join the community of inquiry. IBID crosses all school sites and grade levels and is always voluntary. Figure 13.1 shows ways in which members of IBID move fluidly within and across layers of "expertise". The model is a

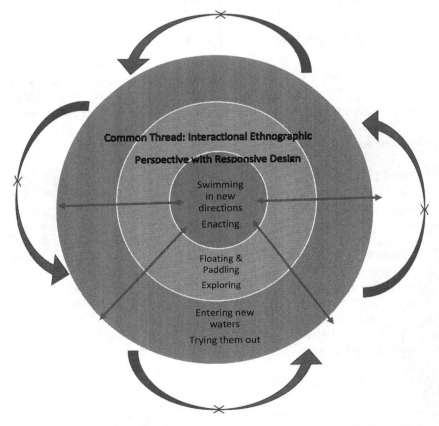

FIGURE 13.1 IBID's Intergenerational Overtime Inquiry Process: Different Pathways and Entry Points, Guided by Common IE Perspective

situated one. Like students in the previous section, each member takes different paths at a different pace.

As indicated in Figure 13.1, what is held constant is a common underlying theoretical framework grounded in an IE perspective and fluid layers for entering and exploring ways of looking at teaching and learning. Thus, IBID's ways of looking at practice and teaching in the contexts of learning have their roots in IE, inquiry practices, and an amalgam of IE and other theoretical constructs, e.g., Responsive Design (Córdova et al., 2017).

A central question guiding the work of IBID is "whose knowledge counts and how?" In other words, IBID members are concerned with issues of student, teacher, family and community and indigenous knowledges as resources. They are interested in making visible hidden histories, voices, and practices; and in adding resources often missing in school curriculum.

Underlying IBID's work is a view of learning as abductive, iterative and recursive, as informed by IE and ethnographic processes (Agar, 2006). Through their work with Córdova, a co-facilitator, and others, members have begun to see learning as spiraling overtime, with movement across interconnected layers in iterative and recursive ways. As one teacher said, "I can see the spiral learning. Everything connects". That understanding impacts the kinds of instructional design decisions she makes. Arriving at the understanding occurred in dialogue within a larger community of inquirers and thus shows the value of an inquiry group such as IBID.

The common underlying perspectives and guiding principles, coupled with a dialogic approach, intergenerational participation, with differentiated pathways, and the overtime approach have resulted in changes and growth over time. Evidence of this process is captured by Jackie, a teacher in a Dual Language Academy, following her 2nd year in IBID:

> The IBID inquiry group is a group of teachers, principals, counselors, and researchers working together to obtain and exchange inquiry-based ideas to be implemented in the classroom. IBID group learns that inquiry is a process, a process that begins, but there is not a precise recipe for this beginning. This group develops the confidence to try new things, to expose students to the inquiry process, the wonders and connections of life. It is a process that we learn by doing, by exposing, and learning from it. It is a process that is not linear, it is a process that spirals and moves back and continues forward (2019).

In this section, I introduced how building a community of inquirers drawing on a common IE theoretical frame, processes and practices, has enabled educators to collaborate, share expertise, and engage in iterative, recursive, and nonlinear pathways to enhanced learning and instructional decision-making. The IE perspective has allowed IBID members to find a common thread that informs their learning and has led to change and growth overtime in the context of opportunities they are now affording their students. The IBID work in one school district illuminates the potential of IE to inform collective learning opportunities for K–12 educators within a larger setting and community of inquirers (cf., Puglisi & Yeager, 2019).

Potentials and Possibilities: Possible Directions

In presenting this reflexive commentary, I have tried to make visible ways in which the principles, processes, and practices of IE can contribute to and inform K–12 education in practice. The chapters in this book bring forward these underlying foundational theoretical principles as well as key elements comprising ethnography in practice, but they do so across different educational contexts. In doing so, they make visible what Agar (2006) calls ethnographic spaces or spaces of possibility for ethnographic work. What I have presented in this commentary is how IE can inform and support deeper learning for K–12 teachers, counselors, students, and other educators, particularly in the context of communities of inquirers, thus creating another set of ethnographic possibilities.

Like the chapters in this book, diverse in direction and focus, but linked by a common theoretical/methodological thread – IE – the teachers as learners and ethnographers, the students as ethnographers in a community of inquirers, and those who become part of a larger community of inquiry across sites, all grow and change at different paces, have differentiated levels of take up of an ethnographic perspective, and bring diverse perspectives. These ethnographers reflect the situated nature of this kind of work. At the same time, those informed by an ethnographic perspective in practice in K–12 are also linked by this common thread as a foundation, which enables them to come together as a community of inquirers, to build a culture of inquiry guided by IE.

References

Agar, M. (1994). *Language shock: Understanding the culture of conversation.* William Morrow and Company, Inc.

Agar, M. (1996). *The professional stranger: An informal introduction to ethnography* (2nd ed.). Academic Press.

Agar, M. (2006). An ethnography by any other name… *Forum Qualitative Sozialforschung/ Forum: Qualitative Social Research,* 7(4). Retrieved from http://www.qualitative-research.net/fqs

Bloome, D., Beauchemin, F., Brady, J., Buescher, E., Kim, M.-Y., & Schey, R. (2018). Anthropology of education, anthropology in education, and anthropology for education. In H. Callan (Ed.), *The international encyclopedia of anthropology* (pp. 1–10). John Wiley & Sons, Ltd.

Collins, E., & Green, J. (1992). Learning in classroom settings: Making or breaking a culture. In H. Marshall (Ed.), *Redefining learning: Roots of educational restructuring* (pp. 59–86). Ablex.

Córdova, R. A., Taylor, A., Balcerzak, P., Whitacre, M. P., & Hudson, J. (2017). Responsive design: Scaling out to transform educational systems, structures, and cultures. In S. Goldman & Z. Kabayadondo (Eds.), *Taking design thinking to school: How the technology of design can transform teachers, learners, and classrooms* (pp. 112–125). Routledge.

Flores, S. (1999). Classrooms as cultures from a principal's perspective. *Primary Voices*, 7(3), 54–55.

Floriani, A. (1993). Negotiating what counts: Roles and relationships, texts and contexts, content and meaning. *Linguistics and Education*, 5(3–4), 241–274.

Frank, C. (1999). *Ethnographic eyes*. Heinemann.

Freire, P. (1970/2000). *Pedagogy of the oppressed: 30th anniversary edition*. Bloomsbury.

Green, J., Skukauskaitė, A., & Baker, W.D. (2012). Ethnography as epistemology: An introduction to educational ethnography. In J. Arthur, M. I. Waring, R. Coe, & L. V. Hedges (Eds.), *Research methodologies and methods in education* (pp. 309–321). Sage, Ltd.

Heap, J.L. (1991). A situated perspective on what counts as reading. In C. Baker & A. Luke, *Towards a critical sociology of reading pedagogy* (pp. 103–139). John Benjamins.

Heath, S. B. (1982). Ethnography in education: Defining the essentials. In P. Gillmore & A. A. Glatthorn (Eds.), *Children in and out of school: Ethnography and education* (pp. 33–35). Center for Applied Linguistics.

Heath, S. B., & Street, B. V. (2008). *On ethnography: Approaches to language and literacy research*. Teachers College Press.

Lieberman, A., & Wood., D. (2002). *Inside the national writing project: Connecting network learning and classroom teaching*. Teachers College Press.

Lin, L. (1993). Language of and in the classroom: Constructing the patterns of social life. *Linguistics and Education*, 5(3–4), 367–409.

Mitchell, C. J. (1984). Typicality and the case study. In R. F. Ellen (Ed.), *Ethnographic research: A guide to general conduct* (pp. 238–241). Academic Press.

Puglisi, J., & Yeager, B. V. (2019). Putting the STEAM in the river: Potential transformative roles of science, technology, engineering, arts, and technology in school district culture, organization, systems, and learning environments. In A. Stewart, M. P. Mueller, & D. J. Tippins (Eds.), *Converting STEM into STEAM programs: Methods and examples from and for education* (pp. 185–202). Springer Nature.

Santa Barbara Classroom Discourse Group (1992b). Do you see what we see? The referential and intertextual nature of classroom life. *Journal of Classroom Interaction*, 27(2), 29–36.

Spradley, J. (1980). *Participant observation*. Harcourt Brace.

Yeager, B. (1999). Constructing a community of inquirers. *Primary Voices*, 7(3), 37–52.

Yeager, B. (2003). *"I am a historian": Examining the discursive construction of locally situated academic identities in linguistically diverse settings*. Unpublished Ph.D. dissertation. University of California, Santa Barbara.

Yeager, B. V., Castanheira, M. L., & Green, J. (2020). Extending students' communicative repertoires: A culture of inquiry perspective for reflexive learning. In E. Manolo (Ed.), *Deeper learning, dialogic learning, and critical thinking: Research-based strategies for the classroom* (pp. 84–104). Routledge.

Yeager, B., Floriani, A., & Green, J. (1998). Learning to see learning in the classroom: Developing an ethnographic perspective. In D. Bloome & A. Egan-Robertson (Eds.), *Students as inquirers of language and culture in their classrooms* (pp. 115–139). Hampton Press.

Yeager, B. (2006). Teacher as researcher/researcher as teacher: Multiple angles of vision for studying learning in the context of teaching. *Language Arts Journal of Michigan* (Summer), pp. 26–33.

Yeager, E., & Córdova, R. A. (2009). How knowledge counts: Talking family knowledge and lived experience into being as resource for academic action. In M. L. Dantas & P. Manyak (Eds.), *Home-school connections in a multicultural society: Learning from and with culturally and linguistically diverse families* (pp. 218–236). Taylor and Francis.

14

INTERACTIONAL ETHNOGRAPHY ACROSS SPACE AND TIME

Kristiina Kumpulainen

Year 1994 marked a special year for me. Not only did I give birth to my beautiful daughter Elmiina and finished my doctoral thesis, but earlier that year in April I attended my first American Educational Research Association (AERA) conference in New Orleans. The theme of the conference was *"Learning Across Contexts: Work, School, and Play"*. This conference was a rich turning point for my research scholarship and personal life. It was in this conference where I came across and learned about Interactional Ethnography (IE) and met with several insightful and intriguing researchers from the Santa Barbara Discourse Group – a collaborative community of teacher ethnographers, student ethnographers and university-based ethnographers – who were developing and using IE as their logic of inquiry to make sense of discourse, knowledge and social practice in educational settings (see, e.g., Santa Barbara Classroom Discourse Group, 1992, 1995). Research questions asked by this collaborative include; How do children gain access to school knowledge?; What counts as literacy and learning in school settings?; How is disciplinary knowledge socially constructed?; What opportunities for learning are constructed in classrooms, and who has access to these opportunities?; and How does the theory you select shape your research questions, the methods you use, and the claims that you can make about a phenomenon?

At the 1994 AERA conference, I participated in several sessions that addressed IE and its use in research on classroom interaction research, followed by extended discussions through emails and researcher visits across the continents, between Finland and California. Through these exchanges, I learned how IE's logic of inquiry moved beyond studying the forms and functions of language, and instead directed its attention toward the situated interactional processes of classroom interaction, highlighting the purposes, outcomes, and

DOI: 10.4324/9781003215479-18

consequences of classroom interaction for learning and educational opportunity across space and time. Importantly, I learned about IE's nuanced and sophisticated ways to shed light on the everyday interactional routines and practices of the classroom, and how these situated, relationally and iteratively constructed interactions develop into more stable classroom cultures with consequences for learning and education. As a researcher interested in interactional processes in education that open up and create opportunities for students' engagement, learning, and identity building, I began to see and harness the expressive potential (Strike, 1974) of IE to address and explain classroom interaction, learning, education, and social justice in socioculturally nuanced ways, taking account of part-whole relationships and micro-macro level, over-time analyses of educational processes (Green & Castanheira, 2012).

I am happy to see IE addressed in this volume from an international perspective including scholars from Lithuania. In a global world that is very much about experimental research and big data, it is important that consideration is given to the explanatory power of qualitative, ethnographic research in diverse sociocultural contexts, thus moving beyond predefined and de-contextualized understandings of learning and education. It is clear that this volume contributes to such research knowledge, and demonstrates how IE as a logic of inquiry conceptualizes "the objects worthy of investigation, the research questions that may be asked, the units of analysis that are relevant, the analyses that may be conducted, the claims that may be made about the objects of investigation, and the forms of explanation that may be invoked" (Kamberelis & Dimitriadis, 2005, p. 24).

Dominant educational research typically aims towards the production of the so-called "stabilization knowledge" through which we can register and deal with an educational challenge or phenomenon (Engeström, 2007). Although such research is at times needed, the categories and knowledge produced unfortunately often turn into narrow, one-sided, and simplified labels for phenomena, including human beings, social practices, and learning. IE as a logic of inquiry offers an alternative approach to educational research. It thrives toward "possibility knowledge" through its interest in educational phenomena for their situated meanings as part of everyday interaction, movement, and transformation in situ and over time. The generation and use of possibility knowledge through IE has the power to destabilize knowledge and put it in a movement which can again open new possibilities for discourse, knowledge, and social practice (Kumpulainen, 2019). Many of the chapters in this volume demonstrate how IE has many characteristics that offer potential instrumentality to educational research toward the generation of possibility knowledge. The chapters illustrate how the research knowledge generated by IE not only offers complementary methods to study and make sense of learning and education but creates an expressive and reflexive language of possibility, justice, and hope.

The chapters in this volume communicate rich, contextual insights about the uses and possibilities of IE to advance our language, knowledge, and understanding of educational interactions and cultures and how these create opportunities for engagement, learning, and identity building. Rather than treating culture as a container, as an independent variable that "influences" engagement and learning, many of the chapters treat culture as historically, culturally, and socially constructed and entangled and developing during situated interactions and meaning-making processes. The chapters in this volume also demonstrate how IE understands culture as a situated resource that participants in interaction can draw upon to make sense of their social and material worlds and to participate in it.

By underscoring the relationality, the "in-betweenness" of learning and education, the chapters move away from individualistic and trait-like explanations of success and failure, to consider cultural continuities and discontinuities in situ, across space and time. By emphasizing both processes of acculturation and transformation, many of the chapters in this volume are also positing an agentic learner whose capacities are afforded and constrained by the discourses, knowledge, cultural practices, and tools they can access within their social setting. In doing so, the volume points out how education is always a normative and ethical endeavor, affording or constraining access to value-laden discourses, practices, and resources that affect the level and kinds of participation that individuals might achieve (Kumpulainen & Renshaw, 2007; Renshaw, 2013).

Importantly, the chapters evoke a humane and socioculturally nuanced approach to the investigation of educational processes and learning opportunities as constructed into being in situated interactions. The humanness of IE is also reflected in the ways in which it challenges more traditional power relationships and hierarchies between the researcher, research participants and the research context. The chapters make visible how IE strives for and affords a delicate and culturally sensitive approach to constructing an emic perspective toward the research context(s) and the research phenomenon in question while developing more co-participatory research relationships and arrangements *with* the research participants. Here, the actual research process turns into a relational endeavor, inviting the researcher to become reflective of one's position, role, and perspective in data generation and interpretation.

One prime audience of this volume is educational researchers interested in the study of discourse, knowledge, and social practice in diverse classrooms and among diverse students and teachers, and the possibilities and consequences of these studies to advance educational theory and practice. This volume illuminates what it entails to conduct educational research based on IE, and the expressive potential (Strike, 1974) of its language, concepts, and social practices for educational research, educational opportunity, and educational change. These chapters also make it clear how IE is not a fixed methodology but a "living logic of inquiry" that develops and transforms itself together with researchers, research participants and the cultural contexts, motivations, and questions of the inquiry. The volume also speaks to teachers, curriculum developers, and policymakers. As such, the volume creates powerful narratives for professional development and educational change. The chapters also make clear that there is a history to each of these chapters, reflecting personal and professional journeys of the authors in their production, thus making educational research human and situational.

I started my commentary by describing how I came across and learned about IE more than 27 years ago, and how its logic of inquiry has informed my thinking and research in education. Our lives, societies, and worlds have changed in many significant ways over these years due to major social, cultural, technological, and environmental changes, presenting many complex "hairy" problems and challenges to education and educational research. In trying to respond to some of these societal, technological, and ecological changes and challenges, my more recent research has focused on 'learning across contexts' as part of the Nordic research network (Erstad et al., 2016; Kumpulainen & Erstad, 2017) with attention to theoretical and methodological approaches that can best inform such research.

Although the theme of my first AERA conference in 1994 already addressed *"Learning Across Contexts: Work, School, and Play"*, it is clear that this important topic has turned even more complex and acute in our precarious times, not the least because of the pandemic. There is now a need to recognize the dynamic processes of learning and education that are increasingly situated across space and time, online and offline. Digitalization and expanded practices of teaching and learning that stretch across space and time and across formal and informal contexts are resulting in significant changes in children's and young people's interactions, learning practices and ecologies with consequences to their education and learning (Kumpulainen & Erstad, 2017). Here, formal education is losing much of its control over information and knowledge available to learners (Hillman & Säljö, 2016). The consequences of such changes to the practices and outcomes of learning, including the development of values, skills, and identities, clearly deserve closer examination and explanation. Not only is this a pragmatic challenge, that is, how to trace learners across physical contexts but also very much a conceptual and methodological one. How IE as a logic of inquiry can inform educational research on "learning across contexts" clearly requires more consideration.

Another important line of research for today's education is to address the environmental crises. In my more recent research in Finland and Canada, my inquiry has extended from investigating classroom interaction and social justice to investigating human/nature relations and socio-ecological justice. In this research, I have become more familiar with posthuman theorizing (e.g., Barad, 2003, 2007; Bennett, 2010; Haraway, 2008, 2016;

Lenz Taguchi, 2010, 2011) that challenges human-centered research and agency, and instead attends to the co-agency of humans and nonhumans including trees, plants, animals, and insects through which meanings and actions emerge. As a result, instead of focusing on language and discourse, posthuman theorizing attends to "material-discursive" forces of education and learning, sustainability, and equity. Similarly, posthuman theorizing underscores the unity of relations between human and nonhumans and approaches these relations as a subject-subject relation. In doing so, it moves beyond an anthropocentric view that regards humans' relations with the nonhuman world as a subject-object relation (Kumpulainen et al., 2020, 2021).

Importantly, the posthuman approach recognizes the need for multimodal inquiry that can address the non-representational, multisensory-experiential qualities of agential encounters that emerge across the human and nonhuman worlds embedded in the materiality, fluidity, and messiness of entangled bodies and things. I am confident that IE as a living and continuously evolving logic of inquiry holds potential to continue to address such educational topics and challenges connected to our current times and futures. I conclude this commentary with the following question I raise for IE authors, and other researchers to frame potential future dialogues: How can IE respond to environmental challenges and explain human relationality with the other than the human world, and how it can complement and even challenge posthuman theorizing in its ontology, epistemology, and logic of inquiry?

Acknowledgments

I am grateful to Drs. Judith Green, Audra Skukauskaitė, Carol Dixon, LeAnn Putney, Lesley Rex, Maria Lucia Castanheira, Ralph Cordóva, Gregory Kelly, and many other members of the Santa Barbara Discourse Group for helping me learn and grow as a scholar and person with and through Interactional Ethnography.

References

Barad, K. (2003). Posthumanist performativity: Toward an understanding of how matter comes to matter. *Signs*, *40*, 801–831.

Barad, K. (2007). *Meeting the universe halfway: Quantum physics and the entanglement of matter and meaning*. Duke University Press.

Bennett, J. (2010). *Vibrant matter: A political ecology of things*. Duke University Press.

Engeström, Y. (2007). From stabilization knowledge to possibility knowledge in organizational learning. *Management Learning*, *38*(3), 271–275.

Erstad, O., Kumpulainen, K., Mäkitalo, A., Schrøder, K. C., Pruulmann-Vengerfeldt, P., & Jóhannsdóttir, T. (2016). Tracing learning experiences within and across contexts. In O. Erstad, K. Kumpulainen, A. Mäkitalo, K. C. Schrøder, P. Pruulmann-Vengerfeldt, & T. Jóhannsdóttir (Eds.), *Learning across contexts in the knowledge society* (pp. 1–13). SensePublishers.

Green, J., & Castanheira, M. L. (2012). Exploring classroom life and student learning: An interactional ethnographic approach. In B. Kaur (Ed.), *Understanding teaching and learning: Classroom research revisited* (pp. 53–65). Sense Publishers.

Haraway, D. (2008). *When species meet.* University of Minnesota Press.

Haraway, D. (2016). *Staying with the trouble: Making kin in the Chthulucene.* Duke University Press. https://doi.org/10.1215/9780822373780

Hillman, T., & Säljö, R. (2016). Learning, knowing and opportunities for participation: Technologies and communicative practices. *Learning, Media and Technology, 41*(2), 306–309. http://dx.doi.org/10.1080/17439884.2016.1167080.

Kamberelis, G., & Dimitriadis, G. (2005). *Qualitative inquiry: Approaches to language and literacy research.* Teachers College Press.

Kumpulainen, K. (2019). Commentary: Research methods for the advancement of possibility knowledge and practice in science and engineering education. In G. J. Kelly & J. L. Green (Eds.), *Theory and methods for sociocultural research in science and engineering education* (pp. 256–263). Routledge.

Kumpulainen, K. & Erstad, O. (2017). (Re)Searching learning across contexts: Conceptual, methodological and empirical explorations. *International Journal of Educational Research, 84,* 55–57.

Kumpulainen, K., & Renshaw, P. (2007). Cultures of learning. *International Journal of Educational Research, 46,* 109–115.

Kumpulainen, K., Byman, J., Renlund, J., & Wong, C. C. (2020). Children's augmented storying in, with and for nature. *Education Sciences, 10*(6), https://doi.org/10.3390/educsci10060149

Kumpulainen, K., Renlund, J. A., Byman, J. S., & Wong, C. C. (2021). Empathetic encounters of children's augmented storying across the human and more-than-human worlds. *International Studies in Sociology of Education.* https://doi.org/10.1080/09620214.2021.1916400.

Lenz Taguchi, H. (2010). *Going beyond the theory/practice divide in early childhood education: Introducing an intra-active pedagogy.* Routledge.

Lenz Taguchi, H. (2011). Investigating learning, participation and becoming in early childhood practices with a relational materialist approach. *Global Studies of Childhood, 1*(1), 36–50. https://doi.org/10.2304/gsch.2011.1.1.36.

Renshaw, P. (2013). Classroom chronotopes privileged by contemporary educational policy: Teaching and learning in testing times. In S. Phillipson, K. Y. L. Ku, & S. N. Phillipson (Eds.), *Constructing educational achievement: A sociocultural perspective* (pp. 57–69). Routledge.

Santa Barbara Classroom Discourse Group. (1992). Constructing literacy in classrooms: Literate action as social accomplishment. In Marshall, H. H. (Ed.), *Redefining student learning* (pp. 119–150). Ablex.

Santa Barbara Classroom Discourse Group. (1995). Two languages, one community: An examination of educational opportunities. In R. Macias & R. Garcia (Eds.), *Changing schools for changing students: An anthology of research on language minorities* (pp. 63–106). Linguistic Minority Research Institute.

Strike, K. (1974). On the expressive potential of behaviorist language. *American Educational Research Journal, 11*(2), 103–120.

AUTHOR INDEX

SUBJECT INDEX